George S. Nares

Narrative of a Voyage to the Polar Sea During 1875-76 in H.M. Ships 'Alert' and 'Discovery'

Vol. 2

George S. Nares

Narrative of a Voyage to the Polar Sea During 1875-76 in H.M. Ships 'Alert' and 'Discovery'
Vol. 2

ISBN/EAN: 9783337322557

Printed in Europe, USA, Canada, Australia, Japan

Cover: Foto ©Andreas Hilbeck / pixelio.de

More available books at **www.hansebooks.com**

NARRATIVE

OF

A VOYAGE TO THE POLAR SEA

DURING 1875–6

IN

H.M. SHIPS 'ALERT' AND 'DISCOVERY'

BY

CAPT. (SIR) G. S. NARES, R.N., K.C.B., F.R.S.

COMMANDER OF THE EXPEDITION

WITH NOTES on the NATURAL HISTORY

EDITED BY

H. W. FEILDEN, F.G.S., C.M.Z.S., F.R.G.S.

NATURALIST TO THE EXPEDITION

IN TWO VOLUMES

VOL. II.

LONDON

SAMPSON LOW, MARSTON, SEARLE, & RIVINGTON

CROWN BUILDINGS, 188 FLEET STREET

1878

CONTENTS

OF

THE SECOND VOLUME.

—•◦•—

CHAPTER I.

CHAPTER II.

CHAPTER III.

CHAPTER IV.

CHAPTER V.

CHAPTER VI.

APPENDIX.

LIST OF ILLUSTRATIONS

IN

THE SECOND VOLUME.

———•◦•———

PHOTOGRAPHS.

FULL-PAGE ILLUSTRATIONS.

WOODCUTS.

MAP.

NARRATIVE

OF

A VOYAGE TO THE POLAR SEA

DURING 1875-76.

CHAPTER I.

THE crippled state of Commander Markham's men raised serious apprehensions regarding the health of the western division of travellers. They were due at the Joseph Henry depôt on the 13th, but as Aldrich's last accounts informed me that the provisions he had saved would enable him to prolong his journey six or seven days, and not expecting that his men would be called upon to undergo much more severe labour than former Arctic travellers had successfully combated, I was not greatly alarmed about him. Nevertheless frequent and anxious visits were made to the look-out hill, from whence the black pile of provisions forming his depôt could be indistinctly seen, though thirty miles distant, whenever the atmosphere was clear.

I continue to quote from my journal :—

' 14*th*.—After seeing Markham's men made comfortable, and distributing Sherard Osborn's champagne to those among them whom the doctor permitted to receive it, I ascended to the look-out cairn. The depôt appeared smaller than when last seen, so I conclude that Aldrich has visited it. If so he will be at Knot Harbour to-morrow, and will signal from thence.

' 15*th*.—The invalids are already showing signs of improvement, and are in excellent spirits. Misty weather prevents our seeing the depôt, but there was no flag hoisted at Cape Richardson.

' Although the ice is apparently free to rise and fall with the tide, it does not do so to the full extent, the water rising and falling from four to eight inches in each crack in the floe. As the ship is firmly sealed to the ice any tidal observation dependent on the register being secured to the ship would require a correction.

' 17*th*.—The depôt was distinctly in sight to-day ; it has certainly not been disturbed. If Aldrich does not arrive there to-morrow a relief party must start to meet him ; however, he is so judicious an officer that I have every confidence in his actions whatever may overtake him. Arctic sledging is necessarily precarious work ; although with specially equipped expeditions it has hitherto been attended with success yet there have been many hair-breadth escapes.

' In favoured localities the purple saxifrage is in full flower. A bright piece adorned the dinner-table to-day.

' 18*th.*—Last night the temperature, which has been up to freezing point for two days, fell to 20°. This is highly favourable for the travellers. The colder the weather the better road will they find across Feilden Peninsula. The snow on the floe is now wet and heavy in places, but the thaw cannot be said to have set in. In the immediate vicinity of the ship it is more in advance than elsewhere; the dirt and smoke from the funnels collected on the floebergs in the neighbourhood help to absorb the heat-rays from the sun and to quicken the natural decay. Owing to the pool of water which surrounds the ship it has been necessary to construct a long gangway with two spare topsail yards to bridge over the space.

' All the powder has been brought on board, but I am waiting for warmer weather to dry the magazine before stowing it away.

' The depôt being still untouched, Lieutenant May, with well-rested dogs and three strong men, Malley, Self, and Thornback, started this evening to meet Aldrich and his party, with orders to continue their journey if necessary to the depôt at Cape Colan, where Aldrich was due twelve days ago.

' 19*th.*—The country in our neighbourhood is so covered with snow that it would be useless for shooting parties to leave the ship. But as the hills near Cape Richardson present a more promising appearance Parr and Feilden, drawing a small sledge, have started for Knot Harbour in the hope of obtaining some fresh game ready for Aldrich's men.

' Nelly, Markham's dog, and both the cats, are suffering in health, and are supposed to have scorbutic

symptoms.   Bruin, an old dog that refuses to work
with the sledge team, has for some time been performing very valuable service in dragging fresh-water ice
from the quarry to the ship.   The men merely load
the sledge and start him on his journey, when he
runs home by himself.   To-day I observed one of the
men riding on the empty sledge for a short distance
where the road was hard : the dog was therefore
dragging about two hundred pounds' weight.   The
poor thing looked over its shoulder occasionally, begging
for compassion and a little more consideration.

'20th.—At 3 A.M. I could see the depôt plainly ;
at nine it was not so distinct, probably on account of
mirage.   A small tern (*Sterna macrura*) with a black
head and light slaty-blue wings was shot while hovering
above one of the water-pools formed on the surface of
the ice.

'A few brent geese have passed us flying from
Robeson Channel towards the north-west, but two of
them were observed to return south again.

'All the ice hummocks which have projecting
upper surfaces, and the mushroom-shaped floebergs,
denoting age, are now enveloped in a drapery of
gigantic icicles, and the entrances to the few caves
are completely blocked up by them.   The sharp edges
are rounding off much quicker than we anticipated.
Consequently the formation of the glassy ice-knolls
on the surface of the aged floes, out of a range of
lofty hummocks of pressed up angular blocks of ice,
may not occupy a very great number of years.   While
the ice above water is thus melting rapidly from the
influence of the sun, that exposed to the warm surface

water, now at a constant temperature of 30°, is decaying even quicker. By eating out a notch at the water-
line a new mushroom-shaped top is being produced
with a projecting spur below water. At a depth
below six feet, and down to the bottom in twenty-
seven feet, the temperature is 29°·2, a rise of more
than half a degree since the winter. Unless the ice,
when in course of formation or subsequently, posesssed
the power to cast out a very considerable proportion
of its salt, this temperature would be sufficient to
melt it rapidly; but owing to the comparative purity
of the salt-water ice it is decaying very slowly, and
has undergone very little change during·the last three
weeks.

'21st.—To-day Markham and I, after an hour's
stay on the hill-top, with the atmosphere fairly clear,
could see no signs of the depôt. Our not seeing it
may, however, be due to the rapid melting of the snow
background from behind the black stack of provisions,
leaving it no longer in relief.

'A small pool of water was met with for the first
time on shore under a cliff with a southern aspect.

'Now that the ration of salt meat is reduced, the
rough salt obtainable from the salt meat brine is not
sufficient for our consumption. It is a curious fact
that such a simple but necessary article was the only
thing forgotten in our ample outfit.

'22nd.—A westerly gale which set in yesterday
has continued all day, with a temperature up to 35°.
This will materially hasten the thaw.

'The temperature of the land eighteen inches below
the surface is only 6°. As the temperature of the air

has been higher for the last forty days, the conducting power of the frozen ground must be very small.

'A light mist prevented our seeing the depôt, so we remain in an anxious uncertainty about Aldrich's party.

'A flock of a dozen king-ducks arrived from the southward, the first that we have seen. They apparently have not paired yet. They remained near us for two or three hours, but were too wild to allow the sportsmen to approach near enough for a shot. Dr. Moss has fixed a wooden decoy-duck in one of the water-pools near the ship; but the passing birds are not readily attracted.

'When we compare the fairly-cleared black hills of the United States Range with our snow-covered ground we cannot wonder at the absence of game in our neighbourhood. No bird or beast would remain where there is scarcely a bare stone on which to rest itself when it sights the prospect of well-vegetated pastures near Cape Richardson.'

The ducks appeared to follow immediately on the setting-in of the thaw. At Floeberg Beach they arrived on the 22nd of June, the day after the first pool of water was observed on the land. At Discovery Bay they were seen on the 12th; but there the thaw was also earlier, the ravines commencing to run on the 11th. At Polaris Bay in 1872 a few streamlets of water were observed by Captain Buddington as early as the 3rd of June; three days afterwards the ducks arrived.

'23rd.—To-day, with the temperature risen to 37°, the snow has become so soft that, except in the deepest snow-drifts, our feet sink through it to the ice

below. The gravel and cinders strewed over the floe
near the ship, to hasten its decay, have at last commenced to eat their way down through the ice. This
is more than a month later in the season than the
same event occurred at Melville Island in latitude
75° 0′ in 1853.

'It would appear that the sun, unassisted by other
causes, is, after a cold winter, not sufficiently powerful
to produce a thaw on a snow-clad ground until it
attains an altitude of about thirty degrees; if this is
the case, then at the North Pole it is doubtful whether
the snow ever becomes melted. At the South Pole,
where the climate is little affected by warm ocean
currents, no thaw can ever take place.'

The 21st proved to be the warmest day of the
year at Floeberg Beach. The sun having then an
altitude of 31°, the same that it has at London on the
12th of March and the 2nd of October, the black bulb
thermometer exposed to the sun's rays registered a
temperature of 128 degrees. In the sheltered position
of Discovery Bay and with a southerly aspect, a similar
thermometer registered the same temperature on the
6th of June when the sun was the same height above
the horizon. In May when the sun attained an altitude
of twenty-three and-a-half degrees, the height it reaches
at the Pole at midsummer, the greatest amount of
heat registered by the black bulb thermometer was
95 degrees. The thaw, however, is as much dependent
on warm southerly winds as on the direct heat of the
sun at the place.

'25th.—The gale died out this morning, leaving
the temperature at 39°. Several ducks were observed

returning south, evidently dissatisfied with our late
season.

'As the atmosphere cleared, a large party visited
the look-out hill, Markham, Giffard, and Egerton using
snow-shoes.   On our arrival at the summit, to my
intense relief we observed a tent pitched on the ice in
Dumbell Bay, which, as May would not be returning
without having news of Aldrich, indicated the near
approach of both parties.

'At the same time we were again treated with the
glorious iridescent colouring in the clouds surrounding
the sun ; surely conveying some message of reassuring
love and protection from the Divine Maker and Pre-
server of us all.'

The usual time of the commencement of the thaw
—between the 14th and 20th of June—having passed,
May's journey was a most uncertain one ; for once the
delayed melting of the snow set in, the dogs would
be powerless until after the waters had drained off.
His early return, proving that he had not been called
upon to perform a 'forlorn hope' journey beyond the
snow-filled valleys of Cape Joseph Henry, was naturally a very great relief to me, and the deep anxiety
which I had experienced during the past week for
the safety of each party gave place to a feeling of
thankfulness to God for the protection He had extended
to them.

On the morning of this same day Lieutenant Rawson met Beaumont on the Greenland shore, struggling
homeward to Polaris Bay with his crippled crew—the
very last march they could possibly have performed
but for the relief afforded them.

Timing our departure in order not to disturb Aldrich and his crew while taking their daily rest, a large party started in the evening and met them when about five miles distant from the ship.

As in the case of Markham's men, scurvy had made sad havoc in their ranks. Out of the eight members composing the party Lieut. Aldrich and Adam Ayles were alone able to work. James Doidge and David Mitchell were gallantly struggling along, each with the assistance of a staff. The four others, after holding out as long as human nature permitted, had to be carried on the sledges.

Although the disease had actually commenced during the outward journey, it was not known to be scurvy until they were half-way on their return to the ship. Then the desolating scourge decidedly proclaimed itself, and most nobly was it combated with by officer and men, the distressed invalids struggling painfully and slowly along until they reached to within half-a-mile of the depôt at Cape Joseph Henry. At the very moment when four out of the eight were completely prostrated, and it was physically impossible for the party to have advanced farther, and Aldrich had arranged for Ayles to proceed by himself to the ship for succour, as Lieutenant Parr had done only a few days previously, to their great and mutual joy May with his relief party most providentially met them. But so close a race were they running with the season that the day after they crossed Black Cliff Bay the thaw set in; and Parr and Feilden, when returning only twenty-four hours afterwards, were so frequently imbedded up to their middles in the wet snow and cold water, which covered the surface of the sodden floe, that they could scarcely recover themselves. They reported it quite impassable for any men not in full health and strength, and totally impassable for heavy sledges.

The following is a summary of Lieutenant Aldrich's journey, with extracts from his official report:—

After parting company with Commander Markham on the 11th of April, Aldrich and Giffard, with their two sledges, crossed Feilden Peninsula—the watershed of which was estimated to be 500 feet above the sea-level. They arrived at the shore of James Ross Bay on the 15th, having been obliged to resort to double-manning the sledges for the greater part of the distance. Four hares had been shot, and traces of ptarmigan seen. Expecting to obtain future supplies the game was cooked at once; it was fated to be the only fresh meat meal that they obtained.

On the 16th they were travelling across the bay for several hours, uncertain whether they were on ice or not, so much did it resemble the snow-covered land. In crossing, no sign of any rupture or crack in the ice was met with except close to the shore, where there was a slightly raised ice-hinge, evidently due to tidal motion, and proving that although the ice in James Ross Bay does not clear out during the summer, it was not frozen solid to the bottom of the sea.

Sheltered as the bay is from the prevailing westerly winds, the snow lay in a very soft state, and caused severe labour in advancing the sledges. On the 17th Crosier Island was visited. The line of ice-hummocks, which denote the boundary line between the stationary ice and that in motion during the summer, was observed to leave the coast at a point about three miles west of Cape Joseph Henry, and to pass a mile outside of the island, and apparently a short distance outside of Cape Hecla. On the 19th the Parry Peninsula, two and-a-half miles in breadth, was crossed, and the shore of Clements Markham inlet reached. From a height of 700 feet above the sea the line of ice-hummocks was observed extending to the westward in a line crossing the mouth of the inlet towards Cape Colan with a level ice-floe to the south-ward, which, like that in James Ross Bay, never clears out. Aldrich remarks in his official journal:—'I question if the ice ever breaks up altogether; the land south of Cape Colan is steep, and would seem to indicate deep water.' With clear weather it was apparent that no land extended to the northward of Cape Columbia, and the travellers' hopes of attaining a high northern latitude were greatly lessened. Towards the south-west a misty atmosphere prevented the land at the bottom of Markham inlet being distinguished.

On the 22nd Cape Colan, the west point of the inlet, was reached, and a depôt of provisions left for the return journey. The shore-hummocks extended in a line parallel to the general direction of the land, but at a distance of about three miles from the apparent coast-line, leaving a fairly level sledge road along shore, which, had it not been for the extremely soft snow, would have permitted as rapid an advance as arctic sledges farther south had usually made. The snow continued soft as long as the coast-line was pro-tected from the prevailing wind; to the westward of

Cape Columbia it was hard, and afforded fair travelling.

It was often difficult to decide whether they were travelling over land or ice. From the formation which we observed taking place later in the season, when the early thaw changed the upper crust of the snow into ice, above which the summer torrents afterwards deposited soil and gravel, it is probable that the whole coast-line between the shore-hummocks and the high land is a combination of the two and formed in a similar manner.

On the 22nd, when near Cape Colan, Aldrich remarks:—

'While camping I dug down, and found the snow to vary from one to four and-a-half feet in thickness. At the latter depth I came to what I at first thought was land, but which turned out afterwards to be a thin layer or covering of soil or mud lying on top of the hard ice. This may possibly have been washed down from the hills. We are about half a mile from the shore, which slopes very gradually up from the ice. From the great changes in the depth of the snow, the floe would appear to be of a round, hummocky nature, similar to a " blue top," and from the absence of hummocks or floebergs probably never breaks up.

' I have called the coast-line " apparent," as it is difficult to determine where the land begins and the ice ends.

' We now and again come across a crack, generally about a foot or eighteen inches wide ; these, as a rule, extend in a north and south direction. We sounded the depth of one and found it to be fourteen feet.

We could trace snow ten to eleven feet down, a great deal of which was probably drift.'

On the 25th Giffard and his crew, after completing the other sledge to forty-four days' provisions, parted company, to return to the 'Alert.' On the last day of their advance Aldrich writes :—

'No improvement in the travelling, and the sledge came to a dead stop over and over again in the deep soft snow, and this notwithstanding the desire of all to get as far as possible, before parting company. Had anyone been in the neighbourhood, and unacquainted with the method of progression in this detestable travelling, they would very probably have been astonished at the constant shouts of "One, two, three, haul!" varied by "Main topsail, haul!" etc., to relieve the monotony of the same "old yarn." However, we had the whole country to ourselves, and were at perfect liberty to expend as much of our breath in shouting as we could spare, without fear of awakening or frightening anybody. Halted for luncheon at noon, up to which time we had been steering inshore to find a place to leave the depôt. The whole of the land was covered in snow, without the slightest sign of a brow or other convenient spot, and we therefore altered our course parallel to the coast.

'After lunch we proceeded till 4.30 P.M., and then left the "Poppie's" cook behind to make tea ready for his sledgemates by their return. Halted a little after 5 P.M., when, after an exchange of hearty cheers and good wishes, Lieutenant Giffard and his party took their departure, and left us to our solitary journey.'

For the next seven days, when Cape Columbia

was reached, Aldrich's sledge being fully laden, the daily advance was very slow, as usual in similar journeys, and the soft snow entailed very severe labour on the crew.   Two days afterwards when passing Cape James Good, named after the petty officer, captain of the sledge, Aldrich remarks :—

'The men are all very much done up, the fact being that, light loads or heavy loads, this thick snow takes it out of one tremendously, and the constant standing pulls shake one to pieces.

'The double journeys are most discouraging to the men, and their looks of disappointment when, after nine hours' labour, they find themselves only two and a-half to three miles from where they started, show how much more they would do if they could.   The air is very cold, and the sun very warm.   The thermometer hanging on my chest registered minus 12°; when on my back, minus 30°.

'Half our daily journey is necessarily done with the sun in our faces, causing a few slight cases of snow-blindness.'

The 29th was the last day on the outward journey that they were obliged to advance with half-loads at a time ; they were then a few miles east of Cape Columbia.

Aldrich observes :—

'A great deal of mirage to the north-west ; its effects in some places led us to think there were very extensive pools of water out on the heavy floes.   It required careful watching for some minutes to dispel the illusion.   The line of hummocks is visible three and-a-half to four miles distant.   I dug down through the snow, which I found to be exactly four feet deep, getting much harder and more compact below the surface than before. Between it and the ice was a space of over two inches. The latter gave me the impression of being young, and not of the blue-topped description. Lines of sastrugi north-west and south-east, which is about parallel to the line of hummocks.

'The temperature of the air while travelling was minus 15°. When encamped at mid-day it rose to 40° on the sunny side of the tent inside. Positive luxury!

' 30*th*.—The north-west wind died away in the night. Started at 6.50 A.M. with the whole load. The sledge does not appear to get much lighter; I suspect the increase in weight of robes and bags, &c. (small as it is compared with autumn travelling), fully compensates for the provisions consumed to the present, and that it is as heavy, if not heavier, than when we left the ship. However, we all pulled with a will, and were encouraged by the travelling improving at almost every step. Camped at 3.30 P.M. Made good three and a-half miles.

'This was a short march, partly on account of shifting our travelling hours still farther into night travelling, and partly on account of its being Sunday. My men are all in capital spirits; the improved travelling, the warmer weather, and prospects of getting on, all tending to a rapid rise in the "social barometer," which, in our small community, is as desirable as welcome. I read the Evening Service after supper.

'The Sergeant-Major has just shown me a very ugly-looking red patch or blotch just above the ankle; the limb is slightly swollen.

' *May* 1*st*.—The questionable pleasure of having a

man dancing on you when brushing down the condensation collected on the inside of the tent was dispensed with this morning, there being none to brush down. Under weigh at 3.20 A.M., got abreast Cape Aldrich at 4 A.M., and then steered for a bare patch on the brow of the low spit which runs off the cape, and nearly due north of it, and reached the foot of the ascent at 5.20 A.M.

'Found some difficulty in securing the depôt, as there was not a stone to be had; the ground was very hard, and composed of soil and very small shingle, with here and there a thin covering of ice, probably caused by the snow melting in the sun and freezing again before it could sink into the hard frozen ground. On this mixture the pickaxe made but very little impression, and it took four of us, working in spells, two and a-half hours to get a hole ten inches in depth and large enough to place the bottom of the gutta-percha case in, wrapped up in an extra coverlet. "Treboggined" down the hill on the empty sledge, packed sledge, lunched, and started at 9.15, being lighter by about 300 lbs. We were not at all sorry to get under weigh again; securing the depôt was too cool to be pleasant. Temperature minus 15°. Wind, force 6, from the N.W., and a cutting drift. We now had a very heavy drag up the low spit, which extends from Cape Aldrich for one or two miles towards the north, and curves to the eastward. We reached the top at 11 A.M., and were disappointed to find we could only see land five miles ahead, bearing about W. by N., and terminating in a bold high cape, since named

"Cape Columbia," and which proved to be the most
northern point attained.

'Travelling across hard sastrugi, which ran more in
line with the land, and patches of level snow, as hard
and nearly as slippery as ice. Over this we flew along,
and our spirits rose as rapidly as ever they did on a
good lead opening up north for the ship, on her way
up Smith Sound.

'As we drew near Cape Columbia we opened out
a conical hill, having the appearance of an island,
distant about thirty miles, and immediately afterwards
a succession of capes or bluffs. The former was in
transit with Cape Columbia N. 16° E. by compass, the
extreme of the latter N. 15° E., and about twenty
miles off; so that the coast-line runs as nearly due west
as possible. The hummocks continue to the N.W.,
and get farther from the land.

'Off Cape Columbia, at a distance of about 100
yards from the shore, the ice is of the older type, but
has been merely pressed up against the fringe of loose
stone and rubble which surrounds the cape, without
being broken into hummocks, but leaving large cracks
and fractures. Inside the fringe above mentioned, is a
sheet of hard and perfectly smooth ice, but extending
only for a very short distance. We reached the cape
at 3 P.M., and camped on the old floe, just outside of the
cracks.

'From observation to-day I place the cape in latitude 83·7 N., longitude 70·10 W.

'At about two and-a-half miles to the eastward of
Cape Columbia, and about 200 feet above the ice level,
the snow appears to have fallen or slipped, leaving a

perpendicular wall some hundreds of yards in length, and of considerable height. I at first thought it was a tremendous snow-drift; originally, perhaps, it may have been, but now it is either compressed snow or bluish ice, and resembles the face of a glacier.

'As the weather gives every promise of being fine, I intend remaining off Cape Columbia to-morrow, and to ascend Cooper Key Peak, from which we shall get a splendid view. The whole crew are so anxious to come, I told them to draw lots for one to remain with the tent; poor Doidge is much down on his luck, having been " elected" to stay behind. The Sergeant-Major's leg still gives him no pain, but the angry red colour has spread considerably; I do not like the look of it at all. I have given him turpentine liniment to rub in, which he uses with a will.

'2nd.—During breakfast a fog-bank appeared on the N.W. horizon, and it clouded over; the wind freshened, and shortly afterwards the increasing mist rendered any attempt to go up the peak useless. We were all very disappointed, but we could not afford time to wait for the weather to clear. Under weigh at 3.20 A.M. Temperature minus 10°.

'After travelling a short distance over the old ice, which was covered with level but spongy-looking snow, we got on to excellent ice some forty or fifty yards broad, over which the sledge followed me at a rate of about three miles an hour. This, however, only lasted for half-a-mile, when we came to moderately hard sastrugi, running parallel to the land, with a little soft snow on top. By this time the fog had come down and rendered all things and everything of no colour.

I was about two miles ahead of the sledge, but could see nothing and do nothing, so turned back and sought refuge in the drag-belt and the company of my sledge crew. Steered by sastrugi, which I had observed ran directly *from* the point for which we wanted to shape a course. With a very little care this plan answered admirably, and enabled us to go on knowing we were losing no ground.'

On the 7th the camp was pitched a mile east of Cape Alexandra. Aldrich writes :—' We crossed a fox track and a few lemming tracks to-day. These are the only signs of life we have come across for a long time. The land is entirely covered in snow, except a few bare places on the face of the cliffs.

'The health of the crew is very good, except stiff legs, which are pretty general, and only to be expected. The two worst are the Sergeant-Major and Jas. Doidge.'

After passing Cape Albert Edward, Aldrich refers to the extremely low and level character of the shore, and describes a remarkable formation of what he designates ' ice-waves.'

'Several low ridges from thirty to forty feet high, and varying from a few hundred yards to about a mile in length, show up in front of the cliffs. Their general direction is S.E. and N.W., hence on the east coast of the bay they extend at, or nearly at, right angles from the land, while to the south-westward they are nearly parallel with it. I imagine these ridges are composed of hard ice under the snow, though I had no means of penetrating it to a sufficient depth to find whether or no land lay underneath.

'In passing between Ward Hunt Island and the

main land, we crossed a ridge about thirty feet high, and half-a-mile in width, which extends for a mile from about the middle of the south shore of the island. Thinking it was land, I dug down through three feet of snow, and came to ice. Similar looking ridges extend to the eastward and westward.

'8th.—A perfect morning. Temperature minus 15°. Under weigh at 3.20. Crossed another ice-wave; dug down, and came to ice under three feet of hard and compact snow. Travelling very good, though not very slippery. I cannot make out where the land ends and ice begins; a second time to-day I sounded with our shovel, to find ice on a slope not fifty yards from where bare stones were visible. There is no crack, but the shelving land appears to blend with the ice, which rises in the form of a roller, with a second roller behind it, exactly as water rolls on a beach after a breeze of wind. The line of hummocks is between five and six miles off, and does not seem to differ from those farther east. Floes exceedingly small, and the fringes between them very close and numerous.

'After lunch we crossed two cracks, which extend northward, and look fresh. Got on to rising ground in an hour. In walking ahead I came to what appeared like a ravine in our path. Altered course down an incline to clear it, then began a gradual ascent up low land, which extends two to three miles from the hills, and in the form of rollers like the ice-waves before mentioned. We dragged up hill till 2 P.M., when we camped. I walked on about two miles after camping; the ascent being so gradual, I got scarcely any better view for so doing. The hummocks appear

to be closing in towards the land, and promise to be
very near the next cape or point.

'The ground round the depôt is beautiful-looking
soil, with small shingle, last year's saxifrage and
poppy, and this year's moss, which latter was of
such a brilliant green we all thoroughly enjoyed
looking at it. It did our eyes good. A solitary
lemming track was the only sign of animal life. The
country gives no promise of game whatever, although
I had a good look all about while the depôt was being
secured.

'9th.—Under weigh at 3.25. Continued our ascent
parallel to, and about one and-a-half miles from the
hills, until nearly lunch-time, when we got a good
view of the distant land. Afterwards we proceeded
along level and very fair travelling, over moderately
hard snow, until at 10.30 A.M. we came to a steep
descent of a good 200 feet, the result of all our
uphill work, which we had hoped would have sloped
down gradually instead. It was necessary to back
the sledge down ; the men sitting on the snow, hauling
back on the drag-ropes. When two-thirds of the
way down, the men became a little too confident,
and the whole apparatus took charge. Fortunately,
nothing caught the runners, and no harm resulted, but
the astonishment which its capers caused the crew will
probably induce them to be more careful on similar
occasions.

'We now crossed over a series of undulating rollers
of lowland, which were parallel to one another, and
extended to the northward about two miles from the
hills. The travelling during the latter part of the day

has not been so good, the sastrugi which extends east
and west being very deep and rugged.

'Although tired, everyone was loth to go into the
tent, the sun being warm enough to admit of a comfortable pipe outside.

'The ground over which we have lately travelled,
rising as it does gradually from the eastward, and
terminating in a steep descent to the westward,
may be worthy of observation, as also the existence
of the numerous ridges and rollers of land and ice,
which abound hereabouts. The snow-drifts about
Cape Stephenson are very heavy, and of considerable
depth. The cape is about 300 feet high, and the hills
close to the eastward of it range from 400 to 600
feet.'

Although an outbreak of scurvy was not then anticipated, the unsatisfactory condition of the men was
causing Aldrich much anxiety. On the 10th he
writes :—

'The men are nearly all suffering a great deal with
their unfortunate legs, which appear to get worse
every day. This we all feel to be very disappointing,
as it affects the journey, and although stiff limbs were
expected, everyone thought the stiffness would wear off
in time. It seems, however, inclined to hang on, and
sets at defiance all the limited medical skill we possess
among us, and to scorn succumbing to turpentine liniment, bandages, good " elbow grease," etc. The legs
get a little more comfortable after being a short time
under weigh; but, somehow, the men do not appear
up to the mark. Ayles and I are the only two who
eat all the pemmican we can get. I should like the

men to have a rest, but too much time was lost in the outset to admit of it.

'Day by day we look forward to the land either going north or south; but hitherto we have been travelling nothing but west, or very little southerly of it. Camped at 2 P.M. about two miles from Cape Richards.

'The line of hummocks appears to be nearing the land, so we are looking out for some decided alteration in the trend of the coast-line. When we first left the ship our hopes pointed to a north-running coast; now, as our outward journey approaches an end, we shall rejoice to see it go either way, except east and west.

'11th.—The travelling is excellent, smooth, level, and with the soft snow only two to three inches deep.

'At noon reached the old floe, which is pressed up against the land, broken in several places by cracks, and has forced up small ridges and heaps of stones and shingle, but without forming a single hummock.

'A short distance outside us are a few isolated hummocks or floebergs, with heavy snow-drifts around them; but the actual line of hummocky ice is still about two miles from the shore. We found the travelling very fair, and skirted along the edge of the shelving land.

'12th.—Temperature plus 12°. Strong wind from the south-west. A continuance of yesterday's disagreeable weather. Thick, and a stinging drift in our faces. Our travelling was none the better from the entire absence of light and shadow. Proceeding a short

distance along the floe of yesterday, we began to round
the low land in the direction of the cape, which we
saw now and then.   We soon arrived on some deeply-
scored and hard sastrugi, on which we found it impossible to make certain of our footing, and the way we
all fell and tumbled about would have been ludicrous
had it not been so tiresome.   This work was not at all
good for the " game legs," as the men call them ; the
Sergeant, Good, and Doidge suffered especially.   We
reached Cape Fanshawe Martin about four hours after
starting.

   ' A perpendicular wall of ice, between fifteen and
twenty feet high, and some seventy yards in length,
occupies the dip between the land rising to the cape
and the shelving land round which we had travelled.
This looks like the face of a miniature glacier, and
is situated about thirty or forty yards from the floe.
Fog prevented our seeing anything but the wall
itself.

   ' After rounding Cape Fanshawe Martin we crossed
the tail of a low spit, which extends about a mile to
the northward, and followed the trend of the coast,
which from here was about south-west (true).   Halted
for lunch at 8.20 A.M., and pitched the tent.

   ' I picked up the leaf of a willow to-day, which
shows there must be bare places somewhere ; but the
snow-drifts in this neighbourhood are tremendous.

   ' Though the line of hummocks is somewhat closer
in, there appears to be a great similarity in the condition and quality of the ice here and off Cape Columbia.
Between the two capes is a distance of nearly eighty
miles, and about midway between the two lies Ward

Hunt Island. The coast-line is broken by three bays, two of which are of considerable extent; and off the points, and now and again for a few continuous miles, are projecting low spits and ice ridges. The hummocks do not come in close to Ward Hunt Island, its northern face being protected apparently by one of the usual fenders.

'13th.—Temperature 6°. The same persistent head wind, and a fog which would rival the densest specimen ever experienced in London on a November day. The crew are less lively in spirits than usual; I fancy the miserable weather, their stiff legs, and extra wear and tear due to so much fog, all combine to subdue them a little. I should like to give them a rest, but they are as anxious as I am to get on. Under weigh at 3.30 A.M. Weather cleared a little. Steered to cross the usual incline, which runs from Cape Bicknor, the extreme point now in sight. I remained behind to get a sketch of the land, &c., and on overtaking the sledge found it making but slow progress. The Sergeant and Doidge struggle manfully on; but they are not up to much, and there are a few more not much better. The actual weight on the sledge is nothing comparatively, but it is the inability to walk rather than drag well which impedes the party. We in time came to a piece of down-hill, on our descent to another bay or inlet, a portion of which easy travelling I reserved for to-morrow, to ease the stiff legs at starting. Shall make a short march to-morrow, in the hopes it may do the men good. It will be their first spell since leaving the ship.

'14th.—Roused cook at 3 A.M., having given all

hands an extra two hours and a-half's sleep. Wind gone, but the dull leaden weather remains. A Sunday morning, with a desultory conversation going on while waiting for pemmican, now of England, now of fresh food and vegetables—a pretty constant topic—and an occasional lamentation as to the wretched state of the legs, with an expectation that they may be the only cases, and the fear that in consequence their work will not bear comparison with that performed by the other sledges and former Arctic travellers. About 6 A.M. the mist cleared off gradually, and the sun burst forth after an absence of several days.

'Under weigh at 6.15 A.M., and the sledge went merrily down the hill ; but I repented my decision of last night to keep easy work for a start, for the sledge was too lively for the unfortunate cripples, some of whom were in positive agony. After proceeding about a mile we reached the level floe of a bay seven to eight miles deep, with steep cliffy shores and hills rising from 400 to 1,000 feet in height. These hills, like all those we have met with, do not run in ranges, but are scattered irregularly about, and separated and cut up by ravines in all directions. The south-west point is low and shelving, and just open of it, about twenty miles distant, shows out another cape, which I have pointed out to the men as the spot from which I shall be perfectly satisfied to turn back.

'The bay we are crossing is Milne Bay of the chart. The travelling would be very good were it not for frequent soft patches of snow, into which we sometimes sink above our knees. A snow-bunting flew within twenty yards of the sledge, and is the first

living creature we have set eyes on since leaving the
" Poppies."

' 15th.—Temperature minus 6°. Bright sunshine
and calm. Everything hoisted up to dry. Travelling
a little better than yesterday. Misty about the horizon
iceward.

' On camping in Yelverton Bay, a very fair journey,
the pickaxe was found to have been left behind at the
last encampment, where it had been used for securing
the tent guy to. I prepared for a walk back, but the
crew all wanted to go instead, so I ultimately arranged
to take Ayles with me to-morrow, while the sledge
goes on ; we should pick them up by camping-time.
The men have, I think, been all the better for their
rest yesterday. No snow-blindness except my own—
my eyes being extremely painful.

' 16th.—Gave Good orders to take the sledge on,
with six hands, for the extreme point ; proceed the
usual eleven hours, or, in the event of fog, camp.

' Ayles and I started off for the pickaxe with our
luncheons. Arrived at previous encampment after
four and-a-half hours' walking ; from the travelling
and pace we had come I put it at ten statute miles.
Just as we got the pickaxe a puff of wind came from
the north-east, and a fog bank to iceward made us
hurry on our way back. The wind soon increased to
a moderate gale, with a very high drift, which
threatened to destroy our friend the sledge tracks.
About an hour afterwards we lost sight of the extreme
of land, so I concluded Good would camp.

' Reached our morning starting-point in nine hours,
where we halted, standing with our backs to the wind,

for five minutes to eat some pemmican, biscuit, &c.
Two hours afterwards we passed their luncheon-place,
and then found they had gone on under sail, before a
wind which was now blowing a fresh gale, with tremendous drift.   My companion began to show signs of
fatigue (which with Ayles means a great deal), but we
tramped on before the gale at a rattling pace.

'We followed the meandering sledge track for
nearly another two hours, with comparative ease, after
which we lost it very frequently from its being entirely
obliterated for yards at a time.   Our plan now was
for Ayles to stand still, while I walked round in a
circle until we found the track again.   We had almost
prepared ourselves for an uncomfortable lodging in
the snow, by the aid of our friendly pickaxe, when
the tent came in sight, about fifty yards distant.   Just
as we saw it a gun was fired, and the boatswain's
mate's pipe sounded above and among an unearthly
yelling, and the row of the wind—a continuation of
the programme they had been assiduously carrying out
in case we might be passing.

'We arrived after an absence of fourteen hours;
and never were men more rejoiced, I believe, than
they were when they saw us.   Although they had
been camped for some three hours, there they were,
seated anyhow, without having shifted or eaten anything, and as anxious as they could be.   The cook
bustled out into the drift and gale, only too glad to
have the chance of giving us all our supper; and hot
tea and pemmican soon. put all to-rights.   After a
short yarn as to the day's proceedings, we rolled ourselves up and slumbered peacefully, and fully appre-

ciating the comforts of our Arctic tent. The sail had driven the sledge very fast—in fact, too fast for some of them. They proceeded till the regular time was up, having made good (to judge by our walking) ten miles.

'17th.—Temperature 12°. Blowing a whole north-east gale all night; so although Ayles and I were late returning yesterday, we have lost no time. The porch was completely filled with drift, which formed a wall quite three feet thick, through which the cook and I burrowed out with a shovel. The drift was still blowing some fifteen to twenty feet above the floe, hiding everything a few yards distant, though a bright sun was trying to penetrate through, and there appeared plenty of blue sky overhead. The sledge was all but buried.

'After half a pipe in the tent, digging out sledge, &c., made sail, but the gale broke half an hour after, as suddenly as it began, and the men were not sorry to resume their drag belts. The drift has made the travelling soft and heavy in places, but in others it is as hard as ever. It is worth observing that in no case did bare ice show out, which leads me to think the floes in the bays are not round-topped, or being so, the hillocks are small and the snow very deep on them. Another thing is the entire absence of even isolated hummocks, which would seem to indicate either that the water is too shallow to admit of their being drifted in, or that the ice in the bays is of great thickness, and the influence of tide so little felt that it does not break up from year to year.

'18th.—Taking into consideration the state of the

crew, and the quantity of provisions remaining, I think it advisable to turn back for the ship to-day. The biscuit remaining is five days' full allowance, which with a healthy crew would be ample, but looking, as I must, to marches not much better than we have been performing lately, it will have to last ten days.

' With this in view, I left the tent pitched, and Mann (who is not fit to march, but better than last night), to look after the gear, while with the sledge, cooking gear, luncheons, pickaxe, &c., the rest of us went on for a half-journey to try and reach a place for building a cairn, and to get a little more extended view of the coast-line. A very clear and beautiful day. After seeing Mann comfortable, and leaving him means of cooking his tea, I soon overtook Doidge and the Sergeant limping along several hundred yards in rear of the sledge. I told them they had better go back, but this they begged off, and continued their painful journey. Overtaking the sledge I walked ahead up a steady incline, which began about two miles from the camp. After walking some four miles I came to the conclusion there was no cape at all, but that the coast-line trended round more to the southward after clearing Yelverton Bay. The land was covered deeply in snow, and there was no place within reach of the party at all suitable for building a cairn.

' I was now 200 feet above the sea or ice-level, and had a very good and careful look all round. No land was visible, except the coast along which we were travelling, my view of which extended about seven miles farther than our position, the trend being gradually southward and westward.

'The line of hummocks was about four miles off,
and appeared to incline slightly to the southward in
the distance. The land itself is not high, and there
being no cliffs, not a speck bare of snow was visible.
The hills sloped gradually from the ice, and the
ridge on which we were at the extreme of our journey
was a portion of undulating low land, attached to the
coast, and continuing south-west with it.

'I turned back and met the sledge. Halted for
grog and biscuit. Hoisted the Union Jack, and drank
Her Majesty's health.

'After lunch we sounded, and came to solid ice,

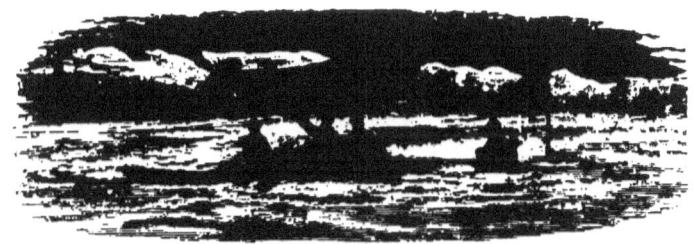

SOUNDING FOR LAND.

under five feet of snow, but from the height and extent
of the ridges, I should imagine land lay underneath.

'Looking back on to the bay, I observed a series of
ice rollers, two of which we crossed over yesterday.

'The remaining two or three marching hours I gave
up to the men, who used them in patching up foot
gear, and other little things which had become necessary.

'Our foot gear all became thoroughly wet to-day,
one may say for the first time. Temperature in the
shade 14°.

Latitude of extreme point   .   .   82° 16′ 0″ N.
Longitude of extreme point .   .   85° 33′ 0″ W.
Latitude of farthest land seen   .   82° 10′ 0″ N.
Longitude of farthest land seen   .   86° 30′ 0″ W.'

On the homeward journey the attack of scurvy gradually became more pronounced, and the fast increasing weakness of the men rendered the daily distance accomplished so short that the provisions placed in depôt on the passage out were insufficient to last them, on full allowance, while travelling from one depôt to another. Doubtless the necessarily reduced ration helped to accelerate the advance of the dreadful malady.

On the 30th Ward Hunt Island was reached, and Aldrich's journal thus continues :—

'Had a hard clamber up a steep slope on the south side of the island, which was covered with deep snow, and reached the top of a ridge about 600 feet above the ice, and which runs to the west in the direction of the cone. I found this nearly bare of snow, and composed of small stones and earth, similar to Crozier Island, in James Ross Bay. Vegetation was fairly represented as regards quantity, in the poppy, saxifrage, and small tufts of grass. I saw no actual tracks of animals, but hares had evidently visited the locality, though not recently. One or two snow-buntings were flying about.

'The island, as far as I have seen, appears to be formed of small rubble, &c. There is no sign of a cliff, except at the north-west end, the rest being very rounded. Like Crozier Island, and the low projections off the capes, it is steeper to the westward, and low and shelving to the eastward ; and to whatever their formation may be due, they resemble one another in so many ways that their existence may very probably arise from the same cause.

'Camped at 7.30 P.M. Temperature 14°. Travelling rather better, but the journey is not a very long one. The men are regularly done.

'Our whiskers, moustaches, and beards are very much lighter than their natural hues, and their delicate " golden tint " imparts an air of cleanliness to our features, which much require something of the kind to do away with the sooty and begrimed appearance of our stearine-smoked countenances.'

On the 5th of June they passed Cape Columbia on their return ; and on the 7th the dreaded word ' scurvy ' was used for the first time.

Aldrich's journal continues :—'Temperature 23°. A very splendid day can see to within thirty miles of the ship, a fact I have impressed on the men, with good effect. Observed a large bird some distance off, it flew something like a gull. Snow-bunting are numerous on the land.

'Camped about one mile W.S.W. of Point Stubbs. A curious afternoon; sudden and very thick fogs, breaking occasionally to give us an hour or so of magnificently clear weather.

'We are all very agreeably surprised at the state of the travelling, which has vastly improved in our absence. The snow is fine-grained, and eight to ten inches deep.

'I have heard many mild complaints of late as to

the effects of the pemmican ; latterly everyone, except Ayles and I, suffer more or less. I attribute it to weakness. Had we had the good fortune to procure game, I daresay this would not have been experienced; but where game is not to be got, I believe an occasional change to preserved meat might be beneficial. Another symptom which has become apparent yesterday and to-day with four of the crew, is tender gums, which I hope may be due to the increased allowance of biscuit. Hitherto, while rather short of it, we always soaked it in tea or pemmican to make it go farther, now we eat it, or some of it, without softening it. I hope it is not scurvy, though Jas. Doidge asked me the question to-day, " Is scurvy ever got while sledging, sir ? "

' I answered in perfect truth in one sense, though not in another, " No," and attributed everything to the hard biscuit. All hands have been in the drag-ropes to-day.

' 8th.—The temperature is 3 degrees above freezing point, and the wet snow forms a bad road ; it appears to change marvellously quickly with the temperature.

' Could not get on at all ; halted, unpacked, and loaded to 300 lbs. This was nearly as bad. Took everything off the sledge except the cooking gear, and a few small things.

' At 10 Stubbs came to me very ill, and I was obliged to excuse him from the drag-ropes. Shortly after, the Sergeant became out of breath, and too weak to get on, so I sent him back ready for the second load. After taking a spell, finding Ayles and I could get on quicker by ourselves, I sent them all back,

while he and I dragged the sledge and tramped down
a road. Halted, unpacked, and back for the remainder
of the gear, which came up slowly but surely. After
lunch, started with whole load, snow a little crisper.
Got along tolerably for half an hour, then came to a
dead stop. Canted sledge on to the medical box, and
scraped the runners, which in some places had as much
as three inches' thickness of ice on them underneath,
which assisted in enlarging the tremendous cakes of
snow the sledge forced before it. A second time we
did this, and at the end of an hour we had advanced
just ten yards. However, we got on much better afterwards.

'9th.—I ought to put Stubbs on the sledge, the
Sergeant ought to be put there too, but there is not
strength enough left to drag them. Came across
numerous deep places, which cost us much trouble to
get through. I found it a good thing dragging the
sledge over the shovel occasionally. Pitched tent for
lunch. Stubbs is perfectly easy, so he says, though I
daresay he does not feel as well as he wishes to make
out, as he puts a very good face on things in general.
After lunch, the Sergeant and Mann both gave in,
leaving five of us on the drag-ropes, Ayles and I
becoming permanent leading men. Did a very good
afternoon's work, considering all things. Temperature
down to plus 27°. We had the tent pitched by the
time the sick came up. Gums very tender, which
prevents the allowance of biscuit being eaten. It
will be observed, that it is the bluejackets who hang
out—the marine, shipwright, and blacksmith being
disabled.

' 10th.—Under weigh at 9.55, three invalids following. Poor Stubbs requires all his courage and endurance.
Several times as we went on, Ayles and I sank nearly
up to our hips, but occasionally we came to long
stretches of good hard travelling, and we camped
abreast Point Moss at 9.30.

' 11th.—We are looking forward to news from the
ship as we draw near our depôt,—something to give
us a change to the conversation, which tumbles into
the same groove pretty well every night. Read the
Morning Service.

' After lunch, the travelling became much harder
and better, which enabled us to make a good journey,
and brought us abreast the Cape Colan depôt at 11.30,
all very fagged. I walked up to it while the tent
was being pitched, with the intention of getting the
letters, &c., but I found Lieutenant Giffard had erected
such a magnificent structure, that I could make but
little impression on it, and contented myself with his
note, which I found attached to the staff.

' There were several hare tracks round the cairn.
Good is thoroughly knocked up again, and can eat
nothing. Made good five miles.

' 12th.—Temperature of the air 25°, in the tent 51°.
Left invalids in the tent. Remainder of us up to the
depôt, which was all right except the lime-juice jar
broken in the neck. Fortunately none of the contents
were spilt. Packed sledge, read news to the crew.
All hands glad to hear " Discovery " was all right, and
communication established. Their success with the
musk-oxen caused our mouths to water. We feel the
increased load very much, the sledge is heavier by 400

lbs., which, with the constants, brings up the total to 1,000 lbs., or a load of 200 lbs. per man.

'13th.—Breakfasted off 6 lbs. of preserved meat which had been forwarded with the depôt. Everyone relished the change, and ate well.

' A heavy fall of snow, and a dense fog puts an end to my only chance of getting down the inlet. We have not been fortunate in our weather as far as fog is concerned. Took the collapsible boat off the sledge, fitted her with drag-ropes, and with a light load gave her in charge of the three worst invalids, who managed to keep together and get along slowly, but causing us to lose much time by waiting for them. Got on very fairly till eight o'clock, when Good nearly fainted. There appears to be utter inability to get breath, no pain, and no difficulty to speak of in breathing when at rest. The least exertion brings it on. I am half afraid we shall not get on board without assistance, for which either Ayles or myself will have to walk in. An entirely lost day, one way and another. Made good a mile and-a-half.

' Notwithstanding the sickness, the consumption of food to-day has been very large.

' 14th.—Order of travelling the same as yesterday. Snow hard and good, seldom letting one in above the ankle. Pitched tent for lunch and to wait for invalids.

' Made good way again after lunch, until within a mile of Sail Harbour, when we came into the most villainous snow, which caused nothing but standing hauls. In this our comfort greatly depended on keeping way on the sledge, and our struggles to do so would have been ludicrous to anyone not engaged in

them. Ayles and I leading, often got in nearly up to
our middles, we could not afford to stop hauling, which
we continued on hands and knees, until we got on to
a firmer footing, or came to a helpless standstill. For
us it was bad enough, but when the other three went
in, separately or altogether, they had barely time to
throw themselves clear of the runners. Made good
four and-a-half to five miles.

‘Adam Ayles has not been very well to-day, the
effects of being trodden on by an invalid in getting out
of the tent last night. I could ill afford to lose his
services.

‘15th.—Temperature inside the tent 67°. Mann
and Stubbs better. After reaching Sail Harbour we got
on with but little trouble, being delayed only by the sick
lagging behind. Waiting as we had to in a dense fog,
and with a cold east wind, was not comfortable after
the violent perspiration brought about by our exertions.
Halted at six for two hours. Under weigh at eight to
cross Parry Peninsula, but found the hill too steep for
the small amount of strength we could command. The
strongest of us carried the gear up, and in one hour
had advanced our whole baggage about a quarter of a
mile.

‘16th.—Under weigh at 2.55 A.M., actually of the
17th, and proceeded downhill with standing pulls
through deep soft snow. At last we reached the ice
in the small indentation on the east side of Parry
Peninsula, with very good travelling; thence up
another small rise which we got up a few yards at a
time, by constantly waiting for some one or other to
recover breath. However, all things come to an end,

and on reaching the top of the hill I was glad to turn the invalids off to their boat again.

'A lovely evening. Made good five to six miles.

'17th.—Started off the invalids ahead, while we struck tent and packed sledge. The travelling in splendid order. Temperature 21°.

'Overtook the invalids toiling drearily along by the time we had cleared James Ross Bay and begun the overland route immediately south of Observation Peak. We are singularly fortunate in the weather; there is a dense fog everywhere except in the valley for which we are steering, some curious eddying of the light air keeps it from settling there.

'Joseph Good and Doidge are at the drag-ropes, but not pulling an ounce; they are very plucky, but utterly unable to do anything.

'With our small power we had a very heavy pull up the incline, the snow on which was, however, in beautiful condition, hard and slippery enough to cause Ayles and myself often to lose our footing. Had it not been so I really do not know what we could have done.

'Halted at 8.40 for lunch and invalids. Despatched invalids ahead—it is dreary work, such constant waiting. Not being able to leave the sledge, I cannot go on to see the road. I hope we shall come out all right, but to me the route is new, and whether Giffard tried it or not I do not know. Under weigh at 10.30, and proceeded as in forenoon, stopping and waiting continually. Camped at two, and I walked on to see the route, which cost me three hours' heavy walking. I was well repaid by finding it all clear, and much

preferable to the longer and more tortuous journey by
Guide Hill. Sighted Conical Hill, and having ascertained my whereabouts, returned to the tent at five,
very tired and with a splitting headache, the effects of
a very powerful sun. Invalids arrived five minutes
after me, having occupied six hours and-a-half in
walking a distance we hauled the sledge slowly in two
hours and-a-quarter.

‘Had we but one invalid, or perhaps two, we could
put them on the sledge. As it is, they must walk, or
give in altogether, in which case I must send Ayles on
from View Point Depôt, trusting in his intelligence,
strength, and endurance to reach the ship and ask for
assistance. When I spoke to him on the subject, he
expressed his readiness to start, and I have every confidence in the man; he has been with me both in the
autumn and spring, and I cannot speak too highly of
him. Having the blessing of health, his assistance to
me throughout has been and is invaluable; and the
anything but cheering circumstances in which we are
placed enables me fully to appreciate it. I keep an
anxious look-out on the weather, dreading the thaw
which must shortly set in, and which will soon render
the route between View Point and the ship very bad,
if not impassable.

‘*Sunday*, 18*th*.—Read the Morning Service. Rejoicing in a cold morning, but it is thick and inclined
to snow. It is fortunate I walked ahead last night, as
we followed my tracks. James Doidge collapsed soon
after starting, and having brought him to with a strong
dose of sal volatile, left him to come on with the others,
while Good, Mitchell, Ayles, and I marched on with

the sledge, poor Good complaining bitterly we were
going too fast, and Mitchell scarcely able to put
one foot before the other. Halted for lunch and
invalids, and under weigh at 11.20 again. The
crew showed such evident signs of giving way to
their ever-increasing sickness, and that before we could
reach View Point, I took Good on one side, and told
them they must all try their hand at dragging again.
I explained the actual necessity there was for reaching
our next depôt, and that, failing to meet anyone there,
I should communicate with the ship. To further impress this on the men, I loaded the collapsible boat to
130 lbs., and absented myself with it from the party
for over an hour, leaving them to follow. I was able
to do this without getting far away, as the fog was
very dense.

'Having hit off the ravine just north of View Point,
I returned to the sledge, and found them hauling five
or six yards at a time, and then halting a few seconds
to recover breath. The poor fellows were all struggling, and fully alive to the effort they had to make.
Nothing could exceed the patience and endurance
they showed; and I fell in with them, and we reached
the boat and camped at 2.30 P.M.—the whole of them,
except Ayles, thoroughly done up. Under these circumstances pitching and cooking comes heavy. We
divided those duties, keeping to the usual turns for
cooking as often as it was possible for the proper man
to take it; but our cuisine suffered.

'Made good three miles (overland).

'19th and 20th.—A great deal clearer than yesterday, and the wind gone down.

'Travelling most excellent, fortunately, and the ravine taking us down, so as to admit of the sledge following with the least possible strain on the drag-belts. As the Sergeant was exceedingly ill, and I did not like the look of him at all, we put him on the sledge, and I walked on with the boat well loaded. Mitchell, Good, Doidge, and Ayles came with the sledge. On coming to a little bit of level travelling, which required more strain on the drag-ropes, I got the Sergeant down, and supported him along while I dragged the boat at the same time. There was nothing for it but to go on very slowly, waiting as they required, and urging on for the depôt and ship news; but the fact of getting the latter does not raise their spirits, although the actual fact of getting it has been more or less talked about all the homeward journey. At seven came to View Point. Observed a staff placed in the snow by Dr. Moss, which gave us the intelligence that the Commander's party had passed, but no particulars, the latter being left farther on at the depôt. We were glad to hear of their safe return, but sorry they were before us, as we had half hoped to have met with some assistance from them. As events have become subsequently known, we should not have benefited one another by meeting.

'Little by little we crept on, but every moment made our inability to go on for the ship without assistance the more apparent.

' "There's a silver lining to every cloud," and never did one appear so welcome as that which came in the form of a shout from the hill above View Point and the discharge of a gun. It turned out to be

Malley, and what he thought of my proceedings I don't know, for with a yell of " Challenger " I disappeared back among the hummocks, and returned to the sledge where it was waiting for me to shackle on again. My news was received with a shout, and thinking it might be a shooting party, I promised them hare for supper. I then left them to pitch their tent, and walked in towards the shore. As I neared it, among the hummocks, I met Lieutenant May and Malley.

'On learning that they had been despatched to our assistance by Captain Nares, on his seeing the condition of the Northern Party when they returned, the relief to my mind I cannot describe. All difficulties seemed to vanish ; and the very sight of the fine healthy and " clean " appearance of our visitors led me to look for a much more rapid and comfortable return on board than I have thought about for some weeks. I accompanied May to his tent at the depôt, while Malley went out to the men to lend them a hand in pitching their tent and cooking, &c. As soon as possible we sent off Thornback with medical comforts for their supper ; and I cautioned both him and Malley about saying anything of the deaths which had occurred during our absence, fearing the effect it might have on the men.

'I was truly distressed to hear of the death of my poor servant, George Porter, and Petersen ; and I congratulated myself, and felt deeply grateful, that we had arrived with all hands alive, if not well.

'Having arranged with May to send two hands to help us along in the morning, and that the depôt should be demolished, as a preconcerted signal to the Captain, I returned to my tent, and found the " social barometer" had risen several inches; but I heard afterwards that Malley was received with tears.

'21st.—Under weigh at 9.45.

'The dog-sledge brought on the invalids by relays, two at a time. This plan we continued until we reached the ships; the dogs and their blue-jacket driver doing their hard work splendidly. As I feared the inaction for the sick, I constantly made them do some walking. The only exception I made to this rule was in the case of the Sergeant, whom we kept permanently on the "Challenger." It was now that we observed with satisfaction the way in which my men sought to relieve the dogs by walking themselves. Mitchell did not get on the sledge at all, but trudged on with great pluck and perseverance. Camped at 9.30 P.M. Reaction has set in, and the excitement of yesterday has given way to greater weakness and lowness of spirits. Regaled the crew with two pots of oysters, apple jelly, and egg flips, much to their satisfaction.

'Made good and travelled eight miles.

'22nd.—As I did not want my men to hear of poor Porter's death, and his grave was a short distance ahead on the floe, I sent Self on with the ostensible object of carrying the five-man tent and baggage ahead first, but really to remove the cross which marked the spot. This he did, and returned to go on with the same work as yesterday, advancing the sick two at a time. Directed Self to replace the cross over the grave, which was accordingly done.

'Travelling very good, except latter part of the

day, when the snow became soft and the sledge very dead in her movements. It is thawing fast in the sun, but we did not pass through much sludge.

'Ayles has shown his first sign of weakness of limb to-day; strength of will remains as before. His knee is rather swollen and stiff; he says he hit it against a hummock, but it is the increased pace at which we come. I know it taxes me to the utmost to haul with the men we now have. Made good nine miles.

'23rd.—Arrived at Cape Richardson, and were welcomed by Lieutenant Parr and Captain Feilden to their tent; they cooked for us, and gave us what we had not tasted for many long days—hare and geese. We all ate heartily of this fare, which, with the port wine, made the invalids different men. .

'The travelling has been heavy, "One, two, three haul!" pretty constantly, and snow soft and sludgy, above the knee in places. Temperature 35°. Made good seven miles.

'24th.—Lunched off north end of Simmonds' Island at eight. After lunch marched for the boats, which we reached after four hours' very hard travelling, through sludge and pools in places. The dogs and Self had a very hard day, and the last of the invalids did not reach the tent till two hours after us. No fainting to-day, but the Sergeant is very, very weak indeed, and there is no visible improvement in the others. Ayles is better, but evidently touched with the malady. The travelling is beginning to get very bad, as we come to many places where the snow looks sound enough, but in which we sink down till we come to water underneath. Temperature 35°. Made good six miles.

'*Sunday, June 25th.*—Lunched in Ravine Bay, and reached the tents on Mushroom Point about 3 P.M. As we were now only six miles from the ships, and we had reason to expect good travelling, we rested for three hours in the tents already pitched, and I served out the remainder of the medical comforts, which was sufficient to give all the sick a very fair meal; then, after a short nap, we hauled the sledges over the land. On reaching the next bay we found to our dismay that the travelling was extremely bad, deep soft snow, water in places, and sludge, through which we had great difficulty with both sledges, the dogs being afraid of water and useless in the deep snow. A fair fresh breeze sprang up, to which we made sail, but it was becoming apparent we would have to camp out another night, when we sighted a sledge in the distance. This turned out to be a volunteer party of officers and men, with Captain Nares and Commander Markham, who soon hurried us on, and we reached the ship just after midnight, amid the cheers and congratulations of our shipmates. Adam Ayles and David Mitchell in the drag-ropes, the latter allowed to totter alongside in his belt, in consideration of his own request.'

Lieutenant Aldrich having discovered that the continuous border of the heavy Polar pack extends for a distance of two hundred miles towards the westward from Floeberg Beach, and that at the farthest point reached it was trending towards the south-west, demonstrates that no land exists for a considerable distance to the northward or westward, or within the reach of a sledge expedition, however lightly equipped.

He also discovered that the entrances to all the bays and harbours to the westward of Cape Joseph Henry were so barred by the Polar ice-wall that the ice on the inshore side of it is unable to escape to seaward during the summer. Consequently, should the pack move away from the shore-ice with a southerly wind, which we must suppose to happen occasionally, and a vessel succeed in passing to the westward of the Cape, the only protection that can be hoped for will be that afforded by an accidental break in the continuity of the ice-wall—she must not expect to find any harbour open.

Lieutenant Beaumont, whose journey along the North Greenland shore is described in a succeeding chapter, likewise found that there the heavy barrier of ice which leaves the land near Cape Bryant, and trends in the direction of Cape Britannia, prevents the ice in the bays and fiords from clearing out; a ship, therefore, cannot hope to find any protection on either of these ice-bound shores.

The description of the level plateau of uncertain formation which borders the northern shore of Grinnell Land; whether of ice or soil, but probably alternate layers of the two, formed by the *débris* brought down by summer torrents being spread out above the unmelted ice, bears a remarkable resemblance to that described by Sir Leopold M'Clintock and Mecham in 1853, as existing on the western shore of Prince Patrick Island; I therefore conclude that both coasts are equally exposed to and affected by the heavy ice. On the other hand, as only light ice was met with on the northern shores of the Parry Islands by Sir George Richards, Sherard Osborn, and Sir Edward Belcher, I conclude that Grinnell Land does not turn to the southward at Aldrich's Farthest, but rather extends more or less continuously for the whole distance to Ireland's Eye, protecting the Parry Islands from the Polar ice ; whether its north-western coast-line bordering the Polar Sea runs nearly direct or not can only be conjectured.

Our knowledge regarding Jones Sound is not great ; but we know that the flow of warm water from the southward up Baffin's Bay is to be met with close outside its entrance, and that the tidal currents inside are strong. Further, Sir Edward Inglefield met with Polar ice when navigating inside the sound in 1852. It is therefore probable that Jones Sound affords the most direct route leading from Baffin's Bay in a north-westerly direction to the Polar Sea, and that it separates Aldrich's Farthest from the land which protects the Parry Islands.

The results of the two sledge journeys of Markham and Aldrich, one towards the north over the heavy pack, and the other following the coast-line towards the westward, considered with the fact that the birds do not migrate farther towards the north than the neighbourhood of Cape Joseph Henry, lead me to conclude that no land exists for a distance of at least two hundred miles to the northward.

The following lines were composed by Mr. Pullen after the return of the travellers :—

WELCOME home to the wished-for rest,
Traveller to North, and traveller to West!
Welcome back from bristling floe,
Frowning cliff, and quaking snow!
Nobly, bravely, the work was done;
Inch by inch was the hard fight won :
Now the toilsome march is o'er—
Welcome home to our tranquil shore!

Rough and rude is the feast we bring ;
Rougher and ruder the verse we sing.
Not rough, not rude, are the thoughts that rise
To choke our voices and dim our eyes,
As we call to mind that joyous sight
On an April morning cold and bright,
When a chosen band stepped boldly forth
To the unknown West and the unknown North ;
And we from our haven could only pray—
' God send them strength for each weary day!'

He heard our prayer—He made them strong—
He bore their stalwart limbs along ;
Planted their sturdy footsteps sure ;
Gave them courage to endure.
Taught them, too, for His dear sake,
Many a sacrifice to make :
By many a tender woman's deed
To aid a brother in his need.

And safe for ever shall He keep
In His gentle hand the two who sleep.
His love shall quench the tears that flow
For the buried dear ones under the snow.
And we, who live and are strong to do—
His love shall keep us safely, too :
Shall tend our sick, and soothe their pain,
And bring them back to health again.
And the breath of His wind shall set us free,
Through the opening ice to the soft green sea.

CHAPTER II.

DECIDE TO RETURN SOUTH—SETTING-IN OF THE THAW—MUSK-OXEN
SHOT—INCREASE AND DECREASE OF POLAR FLOES—FORMATION
OF PEN-KNIFE ICE—DISRUPTION OF FLOES—CHARR—GREENLAND
ICE-CAP—DRIFT-WOOD — ARCTIC FLOWERING PLANTS — 'ALERT'
STARTS FOR DISCOVERY BAY.

THE return of the travellers to the 'Alert' so completely broken down in health naturally caused me
much anxiety. Out of fifty-three men on board,
twenty-seven were under treatment for decided scurvy,
four others were slightly affected, and eight had only
lately recovered; five men were in a doubtful state of
health from the same or other causes, leaving only
nine who in addition to the officers could be depended
on for hard work.

Our great desire was to endeavour to obtain fresh
meat for the invalids, and the officers diligently scoured
the neighbourhood in hopes of procuring game. A
small supply of mutton which had remained frozen
in the rigging during the winter had fortunately been
saved; this, with the birds obtained from time to time,
enabled Dr. Colan to give the scurvy-stricken patients
a fair change of diet, on which their health rapidly
improved.

Although I confidently looked forward to the invalids being speedily restored to health, yet when I con-

sidered the magnitude of the outbreak, I felt that it was my first duty to guard against its repetition. Accordingly I determined to give up all further exploration, and to proceed to the southward with both ships as soon as the ice should break up and release us.

I was confirmed in this resolution when I considered the results of the spring exploration. Owing to the absence of land to the northward, and the impenetrable character of the Polar pack, it was evident that the ship could not be taken any appreciable distance farther in that direction than the latitude which we had already gained; and also that it was quite impossible to reach the Pole by sledging from any position thus attainable by the ship.

The sole result that we could possibly expect to gain by remaining on the shores of the Polar Sea would be an extension of our explorations a few miles farther in an east and west direction. But I could not reasonably hope to advance the travelling parties more than about fifty miles beyond the extreme points already reached, even should the men be fit for extended journeys in the following year. The primary object of the Expedition—reaching the North Pole— being thus unattainable, I considered that I was not justified in risking a second winter, which in all human probability would entail loss of life.

At this time I had but slight anxiety concerning the health of the men who were exploring the northern coast of Greenland, fully expecting that Lieutenant Beaumont would be able to obtain enough game to insure his party from an attack of scurvy. The number of musk-oxen procured by the crew of the

'Polaris' in Hall Land was sufficient to justify this expectation.

'26th.—A south-westerly gale having raised the temperature to 40°, the thaw is making rapid progress on both the ice and the land, and the icicles, which only two days ago so gracefully draped each floeberg and hid the original ice-block from view, have disappeared as if by magic. A few ducks and geese are flying about evidently wishing to settle in the neighbourhood; the sportsmen have decided not to molest them for a few days, in the hope of their nesting near us.

'The tidal-crack near Cape Rawson has opened ten feet; this is the first sign that we have seen of a movement in the pack.

'After the long silence on the lower-deck it is pleasant to hear Aldrich playing the piano again in his usual cheerful manner.

'29th.—With the exception of a few deep snow-drifts which still remain among the hummocks, the snow has now all melted from above the one season's ice, and the water has run off through the tidal-cracks. On shore the brows of the hills have become bare, but the snow on the high flat lands and that on the aged Polar floes remains apparently little affected. In the "Gap of Dunloe" a stream of water fifty feet across is running. At high-water it overflows the ice-floe in the neighbourhood where the stream discharges into the sea.

'July 1st.—All the ravines are now running freely, but they are still fordable. The pleasing noise of running water, with the occasional call of a bird, which has now taken the place of the winter silence, is most agreeable, and we linger in the neighbourhood of the ravines purposely to listen to the welcome sound. To-day Parr shot two ducks and a brent-goose—a very acceptable supply, as the last piece of the fresh meat was issued this morning.

'The invalids may be said to live on the upper-deck; all those who cannot walk are carried up every morning. They are recovering very rapidly.

'3rd.—I walked over the hills towards Black Cliff with Giffard and Conybeare. We fully expected to see a few seal on the ice in Robeson Channel, but nothing living was in sight. The temperature ranges between 35° and 40° in the shade, but we find it very warm in the sun both day and night.

'Our dress now consists only of a vest, a flannel shirt and worsted sleeve waistcoat; flannel drawers, cricket-ing trousers and knee-boots, with a light flannel cap. When once the shore is reached ankle-boots and gaiters are preferable to the knee-boots. The snow, although deep and soft enough to reach nearly to the knees, is not very wet.

'4th.—Adam Ayles is out of the sick list to-day. Yesterday another of Markham's men returned to duty.

'We notice, like in the autumn, a pulsation in the tidal-wave as shown in any hole in the ice, the water rising and falling continually with irregular intervals lasting about two minutes. Dr. Moss has discovered a bed of sea-weed which was evidently thrown up on the shore last season. Having been frozen ever since, it now appears quite fresh; mixed with it are numerous crustacea, chiefly *Arcturus* and *Nymphon*, with shells of

Trochus and *Cylichna*. This sea-weed has been torn from the bottom by the grounding floebergs, and floated on to the shore. If we had an opportunity of letting down a dredge in a depth of a hundred fathoms, or where it has not been disturbed by grounding ice, doubtless we should find the sea-bottom abounding with animal and vegetable life, though confined to a few species.

' 5th.—Great rejoicings this morning—Parr having shot three musk-oxen with two bullets and three wire cartridges out of a smooth-bore fowling-piece. Sighting the animals when about two miles distant from the ship, he sent a man on board with the news. A large party started off immediately to surround them; but before we arrived, Parr had crept close up and killed one with the first shot; the others standing by their comrade, as musk-oxen always do, were then easily despatched without assistance being required. Within an hour they were skinned, cleaned, and quartered. They were small animals, a young bull and two cows. The three carcases weighed 350 lbs. Each had a white mane of long soft wool, the remains of their winter coat; it readily came away when pulled, the long black hair remaining firm.

' The animals appear to have come from the south-west, and we most earnestly hope that they are the forerunners of a larger herd.

' 6th.—This morning a solitary bull musk-ox was seen near the ship and shot by Dr. Moss, giving us 212 lbs. more fresh meat. The flesh appears excellent, but is very lean and not equal to that of the fat oxen killed last autumn. This animal came north along the

brow of the coast-hills, and probably belonged to the ·
same herd as those shot yesterday by Parr.

'Poor Bruin, the dog that has performed such good
work in dragging fresh-water ice to the ship from the
quarry, was to day found drowned, having probably
fallen into the water in a fit.

'The water-pools on the surface of the old Polar
floes are not increasing in size to the same extent as
those on the younger ice.   On ice formed from water
newly frozen over during the previous season the
surface is so level that when the thaw first commences
the water from the melted snow collects in one vast
sheet many acres in extent, until at last it runs off
through holes or cracks in the ice.   The snow on the
surface of an old floe, affected only superficially by the
heat rays of the sun, and not appreciably so by the
temperature of the water below, does not melt nearly
so quickly, and owing to the very uneven surface
the snow-water collects only in the hollows, and ·
presents a totally different appearance from that of the
large seas of water which are met with early in the
season on smooth ice.

'Since the first melting of the snow we observe that
several of the floebergs near the mouths of the large
ravines are covered in parts by pebbles and *débris*
carried down by the rapid streams.

'The fresh-water at a temperature slightly above
32° readily melts all the sea-water ice with which it
comes in contact, and smooths off the upper surfaces of
the floebergs, leaving a level icy floor, above which the
stream spreads itself out and deposits a thick horizontal
layer of rounded pebbles which it has transported from

the higher lands. We had previously supposed that the mounds of pebbles met with formed part of the actual shore, but the tidal movement has lately tilted some of the pieces of ice and so displayed the lower stratum below the gravel.

'Lightened as such floebergs are by the melting away of the original upper surface, since they were forced high up on shore, many of them must be floated off to sea when the ice breaks up, carrying with them their cargo of rounded pebbles.

'The marks which were placed in the floe to ascertain how much the ice would decay during the winter by superficial evaporation, and which proved to be *nil*, indicate to-day that ten inches of the upper surface has melted or evaporated during the last fourteen days. Many lost articles which have remained buried during the winter are therefore now again appearing in sight.

'Similar marks fixed in a floeberg show that seven inches of ice has decayed from the upper surface and nearly as much from its southern face. The rounding off of the sharp edges is therefore very considerable. Had we known of this during the autumn, we could readily have ascertained which floebergs had been recently stranded and which had been subject to a previous summer's thaw.

'Although the decay of the ice near us far exceeds our expectations, the large expanse of surface in the Polar pack would not be affected to so great an extent; nevertheless, the evidence is in favour of the superficial decay of the North Polar ice being at least equal to, if not greater than, any possible increase

which may take place on its surface by the change of
the snow into ice or otherwise.

' If the ice increases superficially it is difficult to
account for the absence of annual lines of stratification, or a thick stratum of pure fresh-water ice on
the upper surface of the floes. In no case have we
found the layer of fresh-water ice to be more than
about two feet in thickness. It is only to be found
in the hollows on the surface of a floe; the ice at
the highest parts, above where the water produced
by the melting of the snow would naturally collect, is
invariably more or less brackish.

' Wherever a piece of a floe has been turned on its
side, and when in that position become re-frozen into
the pack, that part of its former upper surface which
was composed of fresh-water ice changes its character
and becomes brackish ice and appears as a vertical
vein running through the newly formed floe; such
veins never present the decided blue tint which is so
frequently to be seen in an iceberg where a crack in
the parent glacier has become filled with frozen water.

' There is, however, evidence that the layer of snow
on the surface of the ice does become changed into ice
under certain circumstances. On one of the large
floebergs in the pack near the ship a quantity of *débris*
ice had become piled up to a height of eighteen feet
above the snow layer of a previous season, which was
about two feet in thickness. In March the snow
immediately under the piled up hummocks had become
changed into ice while that left uncovered remained
unchanged. Although no measurement was obtained
the thickness of the layer which had changed its for-

mation was apparently the same as that of the original snow layer.   Unfortunately a sample was not obtained, and I cannot say whether the ice was brackish or not, but I think that it was so and that the change had taken place by the percolating downwards of the salt brine from the ice above, as noticed in other floebergs.

'On the whole I conclude that the Polar ice increases in thickness below and not superficially, and by the natural freezing of the water at its lower surface during the winter.   As before mentioned, a Polar floe only one year old is composed, not of ordinary ice frozen on the surface of a space of water, but of a quantity of conglomerate ice pressed together by the general movement of the pack and then frozen into a floe ten or twelve feet and upwards in thickness ; and to whatever thickness such a formation is continued the freezing and consolidation of the whole into a compact mass of ice takes place at all depths, for it is remarkable that only once have we found a cavity denoting where a hollow, left when the pieces composing the floe were first pressed together, has not become filled up.   In more southern latitudes, where such cold water is not found at the same depth, similar cavities remain unchanged.

'In the middle of each of the large shore lakes we find very thick ancient ice ; whether it is frozen to the bottom or not we have no means of ascertaining ; but it is apparently immovable by the wind.   Near the shore the inpour of heated water during the summer is sufficient to prevent its growth at a less depth than eight feet.   During the winter the ice newly formed near the border of the lake by the natural freezing of the water only attains a thickness of about seven feet. Last winter the mean temperature of the atmosphere for two months was as low as minus 39°, more than seventy degrees colder than the quiescent water left unfrozen below the ice.

'To what extent the seven feet of ice and its covering, two feet in depth, of such a slow conductor as snow, prevents the escape of warmth from the water below, which must take place before the ice can form, is an interesting question. During the winter a thermometer buried eighteen inches in the frozen ground registered a minimum temperature of minus 12°. For fifty-three consecutive days the mean temperature of the air was minus 44°; which gives the large difference of 32° as being due to eighteen inches of frozen soil and ice.'

Doctor Moss, a very careful observer, after a close study of the Polar floes, differs from me regarding their formation. As the subject is highly interesting I append the following remarks which express his conclusions :—

'The névé-like stratification, the imbedded atmospheric dust, and the chemical characters of our Polar floes indicate, in my opinion, that they are the accumulated snow-fall of ages rendered brackish by infiltration and efflorescence.

'Until Sir George Nares showed me the part of his MS. treating of the growth of the Polar floes, I had no idea that the universality of their stratification would be at all called in question. My notes were, therefore, not made to prove this point, and yet I find amongst them nine sketches made from nature of floebergs in the neighbourhood of H.M.S. "Alert's" winter-quarters, and four sketched on sledge journeys, all showing stratification. The lower part of the floes did not exhibit stratification, and consequently a few apparent exceptions occurred in overturned or much tilted floe-bergs. Some authorities, such as Wrangell ("Wrangell," edited by Sabine, appendix) and Belcher ("Last of the Arctic Voyages," p. 101) have attributed the thickness and the stratification of ice seen by them to the sliding up of one floe over another; but in our ice, the extent and evenness of the stratification, and the invariable progressive reduction in the depth of the strata from above downward to their final disappearance below precisely as in glacier névé, cannot be thus accounted for.

'The saltness of the Polar floes, notwithstanding the (I think) irresistible evidence of their growth by annual snow-fall, is to be accounted for by infiltration and freezing of sea water as the spongy snow-ice sinks season by season, and to a very large extent by the rapid diffusion of briny efflorescence from frozen sea-water crushed up in cracks. We often had uncomfortable evidence of this diffusion in our sledging tea.

'In April and May the passage of snow into ice was experimentally determined to take place through the growth of the deeper, and therefore colder, crystals at the expense of the superficial. Later on an inverse process helps the wind to harden the surface snow into a layer which remains distinct from succeeding snowfalls.

'The birthplace and nursery of Polar floes is not, in my opinion, near land, because in our experience waste exceeds growth near shores. The great " domed " floes tell of gradual decay, because whenever we got a section of them the horizontal strata were cut by the outline of the domes, and the ice of the top of the dome was invariably salt.

'Occasionally deposits of atmospheric dust were to be met with throughout the stratified ice, sometimes scattered in very minute points which, when examined, proved to be air-cells coated with the impalpable dust sometimes occurring in comparatively conspicuous quantities in lines cutting the stratification and marking what had once been the bottom of a "superglacial lake." (Parry, Fourth Voyage.)

'Similar dust was to be found on the present surface of the floes occasionally greatly magnified in appearance by the growth amongst it of an Alga, identified by Professor Dickie as *Nostoc aureum.* The dust often occurred in little granules, so that in mass it formed an oölite. Opposite the Humboldt Glacier I obtained similar oölitic dust, but totally devoid of Alga, from the melted ice of a large iceberg stratified with innumerable perfectly parallel strata only four inches in depth. All the specimens of ice-dust obtained by me from the floebergs are undoubtedly the air-carried *débris* of crystalline rock not traceable to the neighbouring shore.'

During one of Dr. Moss's journeys he met with a very large floeberg, which had been forced up by pressure on a shallow bank close to William's Island ; he thus describes it :—

'It deserves special mention as a type of its class. It stood, a huge rectangular mass, forty feet high above the floe. Its lower fifteen feet were of un-stratified blue ice, enclosing yellow patches of surface salt-water diatomaceæ between spaces of ice with their lines of air-cells differently inclined. The remaining twenty-five feet was banded with eighteen of the usual white and blue horizontal layers—white where the ice is spongy with air-cells, blue in the denser layers above and below. The height was too great to detect " dust-bands." Above all, and covered only by the surface-snow, were sections in olive-tinted ice of what had once been surface-pools.'

It is a question with me whether this may not have been a piece of ice formed in an enclosed sea like Clements Markham Inlet, where the floes do probably increase superficially.

In Captain Markham's journey over the Polar pack during the spring, he and Lieutenant Parr were directed to endeavour to obtain information concerning the creation and yearly change of the aged floes, and to ascertain, if possible, whether the surface-snow became transformed into ice or not either by pressure or otherwise. On their return Captain Markham reported as follows :—

'The opportunities for observations in the transformation of snow into ice on the surface of the floes were rare, and only occurred when a floe appeared to have been recently broken up, and without having had hummocks and snow-drifts piled round its edges. In these cases, the section of the snow was as sharp as that of the ice, and followed all its irregularities.

'Lieutenant Parr was most assiduous in his researches into this interesting subject, and I am much indebted to him for placing at my disposal the information he acquired on this matter.

'The general depth of the snow was from two and-a-half to three feet, the upper portion, underneath the surface crust, consisting of loose grains of about the size of rifle fine-grain powder, and without the least coherency; these gradually increased in size, till about two-thirds of the way down they were as large as rifle large-grain powder, but still separate. Below this, however, the grains began to unite and to form very porous ice, till, at the actual point of junction with the floe, it was very difficult to draw the line of demarcation. In all cases the ice on the surface of the floes had evidently been formed in the same manner, for it was full of air holes, though not nearly to so great an extent as that which was in process of formation.

'The conversion of snow into ice was not confined to the surface of the heavy floes, for in making our roads through the hummocks, we frequently came across pieces of snow-ice which had been formed round some of them, and used it for cooking purposes.

'Digging down into the snow gave the same results, for we could always get the porous ice, and found it very convenient for cooking. On one occasion the surface of a small floe on which we were encamped was composed of separate pieces of ice, about the size of a penknife, placed end up, and covered with snow, but without apparently being joined together in the slightest degree.

'In one case, also, we found a section of a drift seven feet thick at the highest point, which was divided into three equal parts by two layers of ice half an inch thick ; the lower portion being nearly converted into ice, the middle not to such an extent, while the upper had only just commenced. On some of the floes large isolated pieces of ice would be protruding, and in these cases, when tried for cooking purposes, were found perfectly fresh ; though they must evidently have originally been salt, and had no appearance of having had snow drifted up round them, which must either have been the case, or else the briny matter must have melted out of them during previous summers and left that which was fresh. How far the thaw affected the snow on the floes we could not tell, for though the hummocks had got soft before we were clear of them, the snow seemed to be very little affected.'

'7th.—As the land becomes bare of snow, pieces of drift-wood are exposed to view, and tracks of musk-oxen are common ; but as a footstep once formed in the mud would take many years before it became obliterated, they do not lead us to hope that we shall be visited by much game.

'This afternoon we have experienced our first shower of rain this season. The carpenters are employed caulking the upper-deck ; the seams above those parts of the lower-deck which remained dry during the winter are very open.

'9th.—The temperature of the sea-surface was observed to be 32°·4 ; at a depth of six and nine feet, 31°·8 ; between twelve feet and the bottom in twelve fathoms it was 29°·0. The very marked change of nearly two degrees between the water at a depth of nine and that at twelve feet is evidently due to the meeting of the fresh-water running off the melting ice and the sea-water.

' In all the open cracks a feathery efflorescence is observed clinging to the ice below the surface of the water. As the warm snow-water at a slight depth becomes cooled through meeting with the cold sea-water below it, fine ice crystals are formed, which continually rise to the surface in sufficient quantities to form a thin superficial layer of ice, which must be constantly melting and being replenished with ice rising from below.

' 10th.—On this day Dr. Hayes broke out of winter-quarters at Port Foulke, the earliest day that any ship has ever cleared the ice.

' The pack-ice has now become completely detached from the grounded ice, and only waits for the general break-up. An open or close season depends entirely on the strength of the prevailing winds at this period : every southerly gale will bring the navigable water nearer to us. In 1853 no water was visible from the winter-quarters of the " Resolute " at Melville Island until the 17th of August; but this is the latest date that any vessel has been ice-locked unless the pack remained fast the whole season.

' 11th.—We are watering the ship by pumping from a shore stream. A large shooting-party left for the neighbourhood of Dumbell Lakes ; they experienced great trouble in crossing the Cape Sheridan Ravine, the stream being two feet deep and eighty feet in breadth, and running with great velocity. At its mouth the sea-wall is so solid that the water cannot escape directly to the sea, but is deflected towards the south for about a quarter of a mile before it can force a passage for itself. The *débris* brought down by the torrent is being deposited on the land side of the ice wall as a raised beach, and it apparently accumulates as readily above ice as above gravel. Wherever it does so to more than about a foot in thickness—the limited depth of the summer thaw—there the ice must remain and become a component part of the raised beach.'

Dr. Ninnis, at Discovery Bay, on the 23rd of June succeeded in sinking a shaft, five feet deep, at a position twenty feet above the sea-level, and about fifty yards inshore, in order to lay an earth thermometer. After cutting his way through four feet of fragments of rock and pebbles, he came to a layer of solid fresh-water ice, into which a hole was picked for a depth of one foot without reaching the bottom of the stratum of ice.

' While the formation of a raised beach inside of the ice-formed compact sea-wall stretching along the shore is very evident, it is difficult to explain why, with a gradual and continuous rise of the land, such ancient formations are afterwards met with as a series of steps ; but as the height of each step increases, and the number decrease with the increasing steepness of the shore, probably the beaches now exposed are only that part of the original accumulation not carried down to a lower level or worn away by the weather.

' In addition to the boulders and *débris* which fall from the cliffs during the thaw, and those washed down by the summer torrents, which by collecting inside of the ice-wall form a raised terrace with a steep drop to

seaward, each heavy piece of the passing ice planes off
the sea floor immediately outside of the wall, and thus
assists in the first formation of the step.

'The thaw in the neighbourhood of the United
States Range is considerably in advance of that in this
neighbourhood. Here the purple saxifrage is now in
blossom, and the sloping grounds are fairly carpeted
with its bright patches. The Arctic plants that have
been sheltered during the winter by the snow have
their seed-pods left on them; seeds are therefore
readily obtainable. A few patches of dwarf sorrel are
commencing to sprout, and grasses are appearing in
very favoured places.

'Mr. White has shot a snowy owl, and brought on
board its six young ones and one egg from the nest.'

At Discovery Bay seven owlets were obtained on
the 29th of June. These birds were kept alive and
thrived well, being fed on preserved meat and a few
boatswain birds which happened to be obtainable at
the time, until the damp weather was met with on the
passage home, when they all died.

'12th.—A crack in the ice half a mile in length,
extending to the north-east from Cape Rawson, was
observed by Dr. Moss.

'Our complexions are now very different from their
blanched appearance during the winter. Owing to the
constant sunlight and intense glare, we are as brown as
if we had been exposed to a tropical sun. It is remarkable how considerably the constant sunlight had
bleached the hair on the travellers' faces during the
recent journeys.

'15th.—Owing to the danger of being carried off

our feet by the stream when attempting to ford the Cape Sheridan Ravine, I have caused a boat to be moored with lines to either shore for the help of any-one crossing.

'Mr. Egerton left with a strong party of men to bring back the two boats advanced last autumn, but which have not been used. He will make easy journeys, as several of the men are convalescents and have been sent in the hope of their obtaining fresh meat.

'To-day there was a very slight motion towards the east in the outer pack.'

On the 8th of July Captain Stephenson observed pools of water in Hall's Basin and Lady Franklin Sound. On the 15th Lieutenant Fulford crossed Hall's Basin from Polaris to Discovery Bay, and found the ice stationary until he arrived within two miles of the west shore; there he came to broken-up ice in motion, across which he had a difficulty in reaching the shore with his sledge crew.

On the 18th St. Patrick's Bay was nearly clear of ice, and on the 20th pools of water were seen extending across Kennedy Channel from Joe Island to Cape Lieber.

'16th.—The water which last week was observed to have collected in pools on the aged Polar floes has now drained off. In the hollows there is left a columnar structure like the "penknife ice" of Sir Edward Parry, and that described by Sir John Richardson as formed on the surface of fresh-water ice by the summer thaw. The columns are from one to six inches in height, but as large collections of snow are still left unmelted, and the ice has not ceased draining, this measurement will probably be increased. Sir Edward Parry, in 1827, met with some fourteen inches in length on the 12th of July, and eighteen inches in length on the 16th of July.

'While the formation of "penknife ice" is thus very apparent, a somewhat similar formation is taking place as the snow decays by reflected heat.

'Early in the spring, wherever the stratification of the snow covering a floe had become exposed at a newly formed crack, the lower portion of the snow was observed to have granulated, the grains collecting together perpendicularly, the lower ones being the largest and leaving intermediate air-spaces; the whole structure giving promise that during the summer it would assume the columnar appearance like the so-called "penknife ice," which the surface of many of the Polar floes showed had been formed during a previous season.'

While the surface of the floes usually consisted of slightly brackish compact ice, in many cases we found it composed of vertical columns of brackish ice half an inch in diameter and about twelve inches in height, rising from a foundation of solid ice, and having light snow intermixed with them; these were supported at the top by a thin horizontal network of ice, and the whole covered with the usual layer of snow, varying in thickness according to the locality.

'In a few cases we observed a double set of such inverted icicle-like columns, one above the other, divided by a horizontal layer of clear ice about four inches in thickness, and containing air-drops. In the compact ice the dust-line was in all cases below the lowest line of columns. All the ice of this and a similar nature in the neighbourhood of Floeberg Beach melted quickly immediately the thaw had removed the upper stratum of snow. But in the Polar pack where the snow does not all melt during the summer, the same formation, if protected, may outlast the season.

'17th.—From the summit of Cape Rawson we can observe three cracks in the ice extending from the shore to a distance of about four miles towards the north-east, where they are lost to sight. This indicates a decided movement in the ice, and we are wondering whether the final break-up will come from the southward up Robeson Channel or from the eastward round the north of Greenland.

'There is very little snow left unmelted on the hillsides facing Robeson Channel, and the ravines are running much slower. Charr have been discovered in the lake at Cape Sheridan. They are feeding on black midges which are lying on the surface of the water in such large numbers that the fish will not rise to any other bait. Feilden and Parr returned from a shooting excursion to the north-west. The former has made a rich collection, but has not succeeded in finding the wished-for nest of the knot. A considerable quantity of drift-wood has been met with on the beaches of each bay open towards the north-west, as we expected would be the case.

'18th.—Our invalids are improving fast; there are now only twenty-two under Dr. Colan's care, eight of whom are confined to bed. A large party of convalescents hauled the seine in the Cape Sheridan Lake, and succeeded in catching forty-three charr, weighing in all about seven pounds—a very good haul; like every other dainty they were given to the sick.

'19th.—The pack is very slightly in motion; a crack has formed parallel with the shore at a distance of half a mile. The temperature of the water at the surface was 32°·5 ; between a depth of nine feet and the bottom in forty-six fathoms it was 29°.

'Dr. Moss shot a hare and two geese, a very welcome addition to the fresh provisions. During the last few days the convalescents have been able to gather a small daily ration of dwarf sorrel sufficient for their sick comrades.

'20th.—I started for Cape Union to look at the state of the ice in Robeson Channel; Parr and Giffard, with Frederick and the dogs, accompanied me.

'Although we travelled when it was low-water in order to obtain as dry a road as possible inside the ice-barrier, we had hard work to get the very light sledge along, having to travel for nearly half the journey over either wet snow or the gravel itself.

'As we opened Robeson Channel we found that although the pack in the offing was stationary, between it and the land the ice for a breadth of nearly a mile was broken up and moving slowly with the tide, nipping against the shore-hummocks and the outer pack. Parr shot two dovekies in a pool of water about a mile south of Cape Rawson. With the exception of a single example seen by Feilden in lat. 82° 30′ N. these are the only ones we have observed in the neighbourhood of winter-quarters. Seven geese and a hare were shot

near Black Cape ; three young geese newly hatched
were seen near the nests.

'After being detained by a fog for a few hours,
Giffard and I ascended Cape Union, and from the
summit, 1,600 feet above the sea, obtained a magnificent and extended view. The atmosphere being
unusually clear—the precursor of a coming storm—
Cape Cracroft and Cape Bryant, the two cliffy portals of
Kennedy Channel, sixty and seventy-five miles distant,
were distinctly visible. The ice in Hall's Basin and
Robeson Channel had evidently only just commenced
to break up, for in mid-channel it still remained
compact ; but on either side, between the pack and
the land, was a border of broken-up floes about two
miles in breadth. Water-pools were to be seen off
Cape Brevoort, Cape Lupton, and all the prominent
points towards the south, and a strong water-sky over
Kennedy Channel.

'There were also a few disconnected water-pools
near the land in the neighbourhood of Cape Stanton
and in the northern pack ; these would denote that the
disruption in the ice had come both from the north-
east and the southward at about the same time.

'A decided ice-cap was observed above the land
at the bottom of Newman Bay ; also one inshore of
Cape Britannia, far away towards the north-east.

'In the evening the wind freshened from the westward and forced the ice away from the west coast,
leaving a water-channel, about half a mile in breadth,
extending from Cape Rawson southward to an unknown distance. In the neighbourhood of the ship

the ice outside the barrier of floebergs moved off for about fifty yards.

'As each floeberg must have been considerably lightened by the summer's thaw, they are now liable to be forced in nearer towards the land by the first decided pressure. I am consequently rather anxious about the ship; however, the ice between her and the land is so much decayed that I doubt its being able to damage her much; but if forced up on shore we shall have heavy work with our few able-bodied men.

'23rd.—The invalids are continuing their recovery, but slowly: there are yet twenty men under the doctor's care, ten of whom are more or less confined to their beds—one wholly so. While returning to the ship yesterday, the rough gravel road over which we were obliged to journey, between the ice-foot and the cliffs, after first wearing out the steel runners, completely destroyed the sledge by the time we had arrived within a quarter of a mile of the ship.

'A south-west gale is blowing, and has driven the pack off shore for a distance of about a mile—the water-channel reaching to Cape Sheridan, whence a crack extends two or three miles in the direction of Cape Joseph Henry. There the ice is only now breaking up, a day or two later than that to the eastward.

'Mr. Egerton returned this evening with the two boats from Cape Belknap. He brings back 282 pounds of beef, the remains of two musk-oxen shot by the officers at Dumbell Lakes, and seventeen geese—a very acceptable supply, our former stock of fresh meat having been all consumed.

'Many pieces of drift-wood have been met with, particularly in the bays open towards the north-west; but only in one such favoured locality, where the drift would naturally collect after getting into the eddy current to the eastward of Cape Joseph Henry, was there sufficient for Egerton to have supplied his sledge with firewood.

'It is somewhat remarkable that the wood is only found near the margin of the sea and in the lake-beds: it would appear that if left exposed it rots away, but when buried below the frozen muddy soil it remains undecayed for ages.

'Naturally where the wood has collected in the largest quantities ice-borne rocky boulders are also found on the shore.

'In Hilgard Bay, open to the north-west, Mr. Egerton reports:—

'"On the eastern shore of the inner part of this bay there were great quantities of drift-wood, pieces of all sizes, varying from fifteen feet in length to a foot, but apparently all of the same description. Most of the pieces were lying on the surface, but some were slightly covered with soil. I found pieces forty feet above the level of the water. One tree, lying close above the water's edge, was about fifteen feet long and twelve inches in diameter at its thickest part. The shore was generally covered with shells to a height of twenty feet above the level of the water, but in places considerably higher. All the shells were of one or two kinds. On the north-east point of the bay, I came upon a pile of rocks which looked like an old ruin about forty feet above the level of the sea. Upon

examination I found these rocks full of fossils, specimens of which I brought on board. These rocks must
have been transported there by ice, as they are of a totally
different nature from that of the surrounding strata."

' In considering former reports of the finding of
fossil wood, and trees said to be *in situ*, it is noticeable
that the positions where such petrifactions and stumps
of trees have been found, not excepting the case reported by Sir Edward Belcher ('Last Arctic Voyage,'
vol. i. p. 380), are all in the near neighbourhood of
where the water-currents are now collecting drift-
timber, and whither we would expect them to have
borne it when the land was at a lower level than it is
at present, which all the data in our possession proves
to have been the case in very recent geological times.

' With calm weather the pack has closed in again.
There is a very slow movement in it towards the eastward during the flood-tide—none towards the west
with the ebb; but although it is quiet here, with a
sluggish current, the ice to the southward of the
narrow funnel-shaped Robeson Channel must be drifting quickly towards Kane's Sea.

' Parr has commenced to clear away a passage
through our floeberg barrier. I am afraid to open the
channel completely, lest heavier ice should drift into the
vacancy left.

' The gravel and cinders spread out over the ice
have now eaten their way through: this is a week later
in the season than when the same thing occurred at
Melville Island in 1853.

' 26*th*.—Yesterday, in consequence of a slight
movement in the ice, the ship became upright once

more; but she is still borne up about two feet above her ordinary draught of water.

'The last of the stores have been embarked from the shore, and we are now ready to start south at a few hours' notice. Mr. Wootton is naturally anxious to try the engines after their having been dismantled during the winter; but owing to our reduced stock of coal I cannot spare him any for the purpose, and trust that everything will be correct when the order is given to start.

'Great trouble has been experienced in fixing the screw; like in the autumn, when lowered to its right position, the shaft could not be entered to within three inches of the end: we have now discovered this to be caused by an accumulation of ice in the boss of the screw. The nearly fresh-water at the sea surface at a temperature slightly above 32°, carried down inside the screw-hole to the colder and salter stratum below at a temperature of 29°, became quickly frozen and plugged the screw before the shaft could be entered. By removing the plate at the after end, and lowering the screw down slowly, after it had been thoroughly warmed in the air at a temperature of 40°, and thus permitting the salt-water to take the place of the fresh more readily, the difficulty was overcome.

'A notice paper has been placed inside the cairn on the summit of the look-out hill. It contains full information of our doings, with the names of all the officers and ships' companys of the two vessels. The notice is written in indian ink and placed inside a glass tube closed at each end over a spirit lamp—it should last for ages.

' 27*th*.—To-day Parr exploded a forty-three pound jar of powder under a heavy piece of ice closing our door of exit through the barrier. The effect was very great, and proves that we can make our escape at pleasure when the outer ice eases off; always provided that no new floebergs become stranded.'

As gunpowder only explodes upwards, gun-cotton is a far more effective auxiliary in ice navigation. It is now stated that there is no danger in carrying it to cold climates or in permitting it to become frozen.

' The generality of the crew are far more knowing concerning the removal of ice than they were last year, and when clearing away a quantity of rubble do not expend their strength by pushing at the crown of an arch, as they used to do; but many of them still imagine that force alone is required.

' Through careless work in digging it out, the earth thermometer was broken. The earth was frozen at a depth of one foot: the temperature registering 30° previous to the accident. The depth of one foot may therefore be accepted as the greatest thickness of the unfrozen soil during the summer.

' 29*th*.—A beautifully calm day without a cloud in the light blue sky.

' From the summit of Cape Rawson I observed that the large " crossing floe " which was abreast of Black Cape during the winter has drifted three or four miles towards the north, proving that the pre-vailing westerly winds are sufficiently powerful to act in a contrary direction to the southerly running current, and so prevent the heavy ice from drifting through Robeson Channel as readily as it otherwise would do.

In Kennedy Channel so large and heavy a floe as the one the " Polaris " people fortunately happened to light upon is rare.

'The temperature of the air in the shade remains at about 40°.   Although there is only three or four degrees difference between the temperature at noon and midnight, it is yet sensibly hotter in the middle of the day, and the run of water in the ravines is considerably increased.   They are now readily fordable, and it evidently freezes nightly in the higher lands.   In a fortnight's time the warm season will be over and everything on shore will be permanently frozen again.

' The purple carpet of saxifrage profusely spread over the ground early in the week, in consequence of exposure to constant sunlight day and night, has lasted only for about ten days ; it has now given place to the bright yellow ranunculus and *draba*, with a rich sprinkling of the more delicate tinted poppy and mountain avens, and a small yellow saxifrage.   In the richest clumps of vegetation the most homely flower of all, the pretty white *Cerastium alpinum*, is pleasantly interspersed amongst the grass and mosses.

' Since the removal of the snow we have found a considerable quantity of dwarf willow spreading out its branches along the ground in the water-ways.   It would appear that it requires greater protection from the cold than the hardier saxifrage, which can exist without a snow covering.

' There is much vegetation still covered by snow. I cannot think it dead, as even at this late season as soon as a patch is bared by the thaw it gives signs of life. Such being the case, I am inclined to suspect that plants in these Arctic climes do not always become developed on the recurrence of each warm season; but that when screened from the life-giving rays of the sun they can remain dormant for a time, and that those that burst into life too late to become fully developed before the frost sets in again, being covered and protected by the snow, have their growth arrested throughout the winter and remain ready to reawaken, as it were, to a further term of development the next favourable season.

' On the slopes of the coast hills, protected from the prevailing winter winds, where the drifted snow collects in the greatest abundance, a considerable portion will certainly remain unmelted at the end of the season. A quantity will also be left on the level uplands. Decaying as the snow does underneath, near the earth, by reflected heat, as well as by direct heat at the top, the formation of the snow layer must be constantly changing. The oldest snow of a previous season at the bottom of the layer, after granulating into ice, melts or evaporates in the air-space, one or two inches in thickness, between the snow and the land, and gives place to a more recent deposit above it, which in its turn settles down nearer the earth.

' When walking above an extensive surface of snow it readily gives way, and sinks beneath us with a muffled noise, not only immediately under our feet, but a large area of it acting in combination—how large we cannot say, as no crack is visible in the neighbourhood.

' It is only at the foot of the snow slopes that we

find any changed into actual ice. There, in digging down through a drift, we first meet with wet snow, and then ice of a gradually increasing solidity until near the earth it is quite solid.

‘When the thaw first commenced, the water was observed to run down each snow-filled ravine through an ice conduit which it had formed for itself near the surface of the snow. As the thaw advanced, the floor of the channel became naturally lowered, leaving ice cliffs on either side ; but these were only two or three feet in breadth, and the part most distant from the channel was the least compact ; the rest of the snow on each side filling up the ravine had been little affected by the water. How thick the lower part of the ice-pipe was when first formed is uncertain, but I doubt if it extended down to the ground below it.

‘Our gateway through the floeberg barrier has been enlarged to the widest dimension advisable, and several large charges of powder are ready for a final discharge as soon as the pack gives us an opportunity to start.

‘It is quite certain that we can only escape when a strong south-west wind blows the ice away from the shore. As that will be a foul wind for us in Robeson Channel, the ship has been made snug aloft, ready for steaming head to wind. No sailing ship could ever get to the southward from this position.

‘30th.—To-day three young knots were caught on the border of the lake near the ship. It is very strange that we have been unable to find the nests, which could not have been very far away, as the young birds are unable to fly. The old birds are very wild: they

collect in flocks from twelve to twenty in number.
The barometer is down to 29·4 inches, with an overcast sky gradually lowering and heavy cumulus clouds
over Robeson Channel, denoting a south-west wind
before long.

' There are now only eighteen scurvy patients left
under the doctor's care, and of these six are nearly con-
valescent.

' 31*st.*—Snow was falling all last night with calm
misty weather. At 4 A.M. wind set in suddenly from
the south-west. Expecting it to continue, steam was
got up, and after five hours of hard work with the ice
the ship was pushed through a narrow opening, and
was again under steam after an eleven months' rest.'

CHAPTER III.

GREENLAND PARTY ATTACKED WITH SCURVY—DEATHS OF TWO MEN—
CAPTAIN STEPHENSON PROCEEDS TO POLARIS BAY—BEAUMONT RE-
TURNS TO DISCOVERY BAY—ACCOUNT OF HIS PROCEEDINGS.

ALTHOUGH the proceedings of the Greenland travellers were unknown to us on board the 'Alert' until
the 6th of August, by which time we had succeeded
in advancing to within twenty miles of Discovery
Harbour, it will be more convenient if I relate them
previously to describing our return voyage through
Robeson Channel.

On the 15th of July, Lieutenant Fulford, with two
men and a dog-sledge, arrived at Discovery Bay from
Hall's Rest. He informed Captain Stephenson that,
after a most arduous journey, Lieutenant Beaumont
had arrived at Polaris Bay on the 1st with the whole
of his crew attacked by scurvy. Two deaths had
occurred—that of James Hand on the 3rd of June and
of Charles Paul on the 29th, both of whom, carried on
sledges, had lingered just long enough once more to
sight their Arctic home before their spirits were called
away. Seven out of the eleven men composing the
party were still ailing; but through the assiduous
and skilful treatment of Dr. Coppinger, and the invaluable exertions of Hans Hendrich in obtaining fresh

seal meat, the sick men were regaining strength and health in a most surprising manner. Although still weak and powerless there was every reason to hope that all would be sufficiently recovered to cross the strait by the beginning of August.

But for the valuable depôt of provisions which had been established at Hall's Rest by the Polaris expedition, Beaumont would have found the greatest difficulty in obtaining supplies.

Captain Stephenson immediately decided to start with a sledge party for Polaris Bay, conveying medical comforts, etc.

As the ice was then breaking up in Hall's Basin, a small boat was taken; but even with its assistance the crossing occupied them three days, Hall's Rest being reached on the 19th.

After a stay of ten days, during which time the invalids rapidly improved, Captain Stephenson escorted half the men across the channel to Discovery Bay, leaving Beaumont and Dr. Coppinger to follow with the remainder after another week's rest. So broken-up was the ice in Hall's Basin that the ship was not reached until the sixth day, after a very wet journey.

A severe gale detained Beaumont at Polaris Bay until the 8th of August, when a start was made for Discovery Bay. To cross a broad channel at this season of the year was a most hazardous enterprise, the floes being broken up and drifting rapidly to the southward. On the third journey, to save themselves from being driven into Kennedy Channel, a forced march had to be made; and after thirty-five hours of incessant labour they succeeded in reaching the shore

of Daly Peninsula.   On the next march, when crossing
Lady Franklin Sound, after working continuously for
twenty-two hours they were forced through exhaustion
to encamp on the ice about two miles from Bellot
Island.   Fortunately it remained stationary; and the
party reached Discovery Bay on the following day, the
15th of August, where the 'Alert' had arrived a few
days previously.

The following is an account of Lieutenant Beaumont's sledge journey, with extracts from his official
reports.

Accompanied by Dr. Coppinger and sixteen men,
dragging two sledges, he started from the 'Discovery'
on the 6th of April for Floeberg Beach, intending to
make the 'Alert' his base for the exploration of the
North Greenland coast.   Lieutenant Beaumont re-
lates :—

'Although this journey does not form part of our
exploring campaign, it requires some brief notice in
consequence of its being our first experience in
sledging.

'The party set out in good health and in excellent
spirits ; but the extreme cold—minus 40° to minus 30°
Fahr.—making it difficult to sleep at night, together
with the unaccustomed food and hard work, soon told
upon some of the less trained men, and for the two
following days our progress was slow, considering the
nature of the roads.   George Leggatt, ship's cook, was
the worst, and for half-a-day had to walk by the side
of the sledge ; but as there was nothing more serious
than over-exertion they soon began to recover their
strength.   Leggatt's indisposition was chiefly due to

his dislike of pemmican, and he, like many others, would not eat it until hunger compelled him to do so.

'The road, with a few exceptions, was a very rough one, as there seemed to be no choice but to follow the line of the high and very steep cliffs along the ice. Once we tried the land-foot, but after passing some inclines so steep that we had to cut a groove for the hill-side runner, we were forced to lower both sledges and crews down an ice-wall twenty-five feet high, which caused such a delay that for the future we preferred working through the hummocks. Floes were rare, and of no great size, consequently our progress was only moderate. We passed Lincoln Bay on the 11th, and arrived at Black Cape on the 14th, where we were detained one day by a gale of wind, reaching H.M.S. "Alert" on Sunday, the 16th of April.

'This trial trip was of great use to us, for the sledges not being heavy enabled the men to get into the work without undue effort, and gave them time to get accustomed to the food and novelty of the life, so that we reached the "Alert" in excellent condition, and ready to begin work in earnest.'

On the 20th of April, Lieutenant Beaumont, accompanied by Lieutenant Rawson, Dr. Coppinger, and twenty-one men, dragging four sledges weighted to 218 lbs. per man, started for Greenland, the officers themselves, as usual, always dragging whenever not employed in selecting a road through the rough ice.

With the exception of Rawson and two of the men, who had only rested for two days, the whole of the Greenland party under Beaumont enjoyed the great advantage of a thorough rest of four days, after a preliminary ten days' journey, and started in apparently most excellent health.

Had the Committee appointed to enquire into the outbreak of scurvy considered this fact, they would doubtless not have introduced the following paragraph in their report.

'How far, with due regard to the length of the travelling season, these evils could have been mitigated by a recourse to short journeys, utilized for laying out depôts of provisions, and other preparatory purposes, prior to those of a more extended character undertaken to effect the main objects of the Expedition, we are not prepared to say, but it is obvious that the adoption of such a system would have afforded an amount and description of that previous training so essential to the success of sledging, far more efficacious than the exercise obtained during the winter, but limited by its severity.'

The following are extracts from my orders to Lieutenant Beaumont :—

'Equipped and provisioned for an absence of fifty-six days, you will cross Robeson Channel and explore the coast of Greenland towards the north and eastward.

'Your party, although not as strong (numerous) as I would wish, admits of two sledges being advanced for the time mentioned, under the command of yourself and Lieutenant Wyatt Rawson, an officer in whom I have the fullest trust, and of the two others placing a depôt of provisions for your use when returning.

'Dr. Coppinger, in addition to his medical duties, will take executive command of the two sledges thus employed ; George W. Emmerson, chief boatswain's mate, taking charge of the sledge "Alert" under his orders.

' During your advance you are to endeavour to keep one of your sledges on the northern shores. Your best guide for doing so will be to follow the line of heavy stranded floebergs which border the coast, in whatever direction they may lead you.

' Should you experience smoother or lighter ice than that in our neighbourhood, you may reasonably conclude that some protecting land exists to the northward. In such a case you should divide your party—one sledge endeavouring to reach the northern land, and the other continuing the exploration of the Greenland coast. But as you are not provided with a boat, anyone detached should return to the mainland before the 1st of June.

' Should you discover any deep inlet, which in your opinion might prove to be a channel affording an easier journey to the eastward than the coast-line of the Polar Sea, it is desirable that it should be explored this year.

' Your party on returning to the " Discovery " must necessarily cross Robeson Channel after the ice has broken up. This part of the work before you will require more than usual skill and judgment; but I know of no officer in whose hands I would more willingly leave its accomplishment, having the utmost confidence that, with your great ability and forethought, your interesting journey will be successfully accomplished.'

Lieutenant Beaumont's report continues as follows:

' Having completed the two advance sledges " Sir Edward Parry " and " Discovery " to fifty-six days' provisions, and the two supporting sledges " Stephen-

son " and " Alert " in proportion, from the Cape
Rawson Depôt, we started early on the morning of the
22nd of April for Repulse Harbour, on the Greenland
coast.

'Thanks to the road made by Captain Nares'
direction, the passage of the fringe of shore hummocks
at Black Cape was made in safety by the heavy sledges ;
one five-man sledge, however, broke down, and had to
be sent back to the " Alert " and exchanged.

'The line between Black Cape and Repulse Harbour
led us in a south-easterly direction, and was crossed
by many bands of heavy hummocks, necessitating a
good deal of road-making for the heavy sledges, and
great care in the management of the five-man sledges,
which are hardly calculated to stand such rough work.

'As we approached the Greenland coast we passed
several floes of last year's ice ; they were not large,
but were remarkable because they showed no sign of
pressure round the edges ; it seemed to indicate that
from the commencement of their formation, the large
and heavy old floes which surrounded them had been
motionless. The old floes were high, and covered
with deep soft snow, while the young floes lay low,
and had much less snow on them ; in fact, not only
from my observations on that occasion, but later on
when returning, I remarked large extents of level and
unbroken ice, from which I infer that there is less
current or tide-action on this coast than on the other.
The entrance to Repulse Harbour is, however, very
different, being a mass of hummock ridges with small
floes between them, to within 200 yards of the shore,
when you come to a solid barrier of immense floebergs

over which we had to find a way. This took half a
day of road-cutting and bridge-making, for such large
masses have wide gaps between them; our only con-
solation for the delay was the thought that it would be
a lasting work, and might prove useful to others. The
men by this time were becoming skilful road-makers,
and the officers practised engineers.

'The tents being pitched, the provisions were re-
distributed amongst the three remaining sledges, a
cairn built, and a site selected for the depôt to be left
for our return journey. Having written a letter to
Captain Nares of our proceedings up to that date, I
despatched George W. Emmerson on his way back to
the "Alert."

'On the 27th April we started northward, having
secured in the depôt a few things of which we were
not in want, to lighten as much as possible the now
very heavy sledges.

'Our way led us round the harbour, which is about
two and-a-half miles broad, and at present only half
a mile deep; but if this is the Repulse Harbour of the
Americans, it is no wonder that from a distance it
appeared to them a desirable place of refuge; the
background of hills gives it the appearance of a large
bay, nearly three miles deep, with two islands in it,
the remainder of the land between the hills and the sea
being so flat and low as scarcely to be distinguished
from the floe. No doubt it is an old harbour, and
even now, for some considerable distance in, the land
is covered with ice. A wide and deep valley on the same
level runs from the north-east corner of this dry bay.

'On the 28th we passed the farthest point reached

by Lieutenant Rawson in his flying visit a few days
before. He certainly was justified, so far as he saw,
in making a favourable report of the travelling, but
another six miles would have told a different tale, for
it was not until the second day that our difficulties
commenced.   Early in the journey we came to a point
covered so deeply with drift snow that it almost rose
to the level of the huge hummock mass forced on the
end of the point.   This drift, like all accumulations
of snow which the wind makes on meeting with an
obstacle, left a deep and precipitous gap between it
and the hummock, and our only way past was to climb
the snow-hill.   It was so steep and slippery that the
eight-man sledge had to be partly unloaded, and then
each sledge hauled over separately by all hands.   This
point we named Drift Point.

'The coast beyond this trended to the north-east-
ward, and was one continuous, steep, slippery, snow-
slope.   Sometimes, where the shore hummocks were
high, there was a ledge at the bottom covered with
deep soft snow, but more generally the slope ended in
a straight drop of from five to fifteen feet on to the ice.

'The next point was very much the same as Drift
Point, and the slopes continued for some distance
beyond.   We had to double-man the sledges to get on
at all, and even then our progress was very slow.   To
prevent losing ground, and to clear what we took to
calling the " drift-pits," which existed in a greater or
less degree round every hummock, we had to keep
dragging up-hill as well as forward, and thus, making
a great deal of lee-way, the sledges were hauled along
by degrees.

'Next journey we started on a more level road, and hoped to make a better march, but we soon came to another point worse than either of the other two. The slope, which continued for over two miles, was so steep that it was impossible to stand on it, while towards the end it became almost perpendicular. At the foot of this slope was a tortuous and intricate passage along and inside the hummocks, full of deep holes and covered with thick soft snow. The work of getting through this promised to be endless, and it was impossible to say what was beyond, so I sent Lieutenant Rawson, accompanied by Dr. Coppinger, to report on the road; in the meantime we commenced to cut through all obstacles. They returned in about two hours to say that, after two miles of a road that got worse and worse, they came to a cliff that went sheer down into the tidal-crack and which it would be impossible to pass without going out on to the ice.

'I have gone into these particulars to show how important I considered it to keep to the land' on the outward journey, though at the same time I felt it was greatly retarding our advance. It had been impressed upon me that the object of keeping to the land on the outward journey was to prevent leaving an impassable barrier in the rear, which, supposing the ice to break up before our return, would effectually cut off the retreat of the party. But here was a case in which it was necessary to depart from the rule. The cliffs extended, as far as could be judged, for about four miles, and must be passed by the ice or not at all. It was too late to depend on boats being sent to meet us, so we trusted that the ice would remain and befriend us.

'As we had to take to the ice we took advantage of the good floes that lay in our direction, and struck the land again some distance beyond the cliffs, which in consequence of a remarkable black rock like a horn projecting from one part, we called the Black Horn Cliffs.

'The next three journeys were spent in crawling along the sides of the never-ending snow-slopes, sometimes halting for hours, while as many as could be employed were cutting a road in the hard, slippery snow, wide enough for the whole breadth of the sledge. The angle of these slopes—carefully taken with a clinometer by Dr. Coppinger—showed that they varied from 20° to 24°. If the snow was hard it was impossible to stand on this latter incline, and here broad roads had to be cut. So direct and heavy was the pressure from outside on some parts of these slopes, that the floebergs were forced right up on to them, and left us nothing but the steep talus of the cliff by which to pass.

'On the 4th of May we arrived at a place which seemed so suitable for a depôt that we determined on leaving our three water-tight metal cases there, containing 120 rations, or ten days for twelve men, instead of the regular depôt farther on, thus reserving four days for possible delays in repassing the Black Horn Cliffs. Dr. Coppinger, who was to leave us on the 5th, could gain nothing by waiting until that time, as we were then halted in order to cut a long extent of road ; so, giving us such provisions as he could spare, he set out on his return, having himself the day before walked on to Cape Stanton.

'Not only was the slope travelling very slow, but both men and sledges suffered from it. The work was unusually hard, and the strain on the ankles caused them to swell and become stiff; the heavily-loaded sledges, from continually resting on one runner, bent it inwards, and in the case of the five-man sledge, not only exhausted the supply of spare uprights, but eventually proved the ruin of the entire runner. However, the end was near at hand, and on the morning of the 5th we encamped at Cape Stanton, which would have been in sight the whole time had not the weather been densely thick.

'Our next start was made in high spirits, the slopes were passed, the sun shone once more, and a wide bay lay before us, but though it was infinitely better than what we had had, still deep soft snow made our distances travelled very short. It was at the end of this journey, May 6th, that J. J. Hand, one of my sledge crew, told me in answer to my inquiry as to why he was walking lame, that his legs were becoming *very* stiff; he had spoken to Dr. Coppinger about them, but attributing the stiffness and soreness then to several falls that he had had, he did not think much of it, before that officer's departure ; now, however, there was pain as well as stiffness, and both were increasing.

'In our next journey we passed another fine bay, whose level and unbroken surface appeared not to have been disturbed for many years. During lunch-time we dug through two and-a-half feet of snow, and came to ice which was perfectly fresh for three inches down; this was almost at the entrance of the bay. I

observed here also that from Cape Stanton the shore
had been lined with floebergs of great size, particularly
at this bay, which I called Frankfield Bay, while from
Drift Point to Cape Stanton the floebergs were much
broken up, the shore hummocks consisting of accumulated blocks, sometimes attaining a great height.

'To seaward there appeared to be large tracts of
good travelling ice, though the hummock ridges were
undoubtedly heavy. Up to Cape Stanton high land
and rocky cliffs, reaching to the very sea, was the
character of the country, but that seemed to end with
that enormous mass which I named Rockhill. Beyond
was a low foreshore, with point after point projecting
out, the land gradually rising into low rounded hills,
with only a distant background of mountains. This
aspect of the country promised better travelling, and I
was anxious to push on; but as usual, " more hurry,
less speed," for after crossing Frankfield Bay, and
dragging the sledges over a hill 150 feet high—the
only practicable route—both Lieutenant Rawson and
myself came reluctantly to the conclusion that the men
were very much done, and required a day's rest; as
we had been dragging ourselves all the time we were
better able to judge of their feelings. Hand, who had
thought himself better at starting, was now quite lame;
so we camped, determined to wait for a day, in the
hope that rest would restore both the lame and tired.

'I will now explain how it was that I had to send
Lieutenant Rawson back. On coming into camp I
examined Hand's legs, and from his description of the
stiffness and pain I suspected scurvy. I had no reason
to expect it, indeed I had never thought of it, but the

striking resemblance of the symptoms to the ones
described in the voyage of the "Fox," as being those
of Lieutenant Hobson, who suffered severely from
scurvy, suggested it to my mind, and my suspicions
were confirmed by Gray, the captain of my sledge, an
ice quartermaster, who, in his whaling experience, has
seen much of it. He, however, led me to believe, at
the same time, that it would probably wear off. Thus,
from the 7th until the 10th I waited, hoping that his
words might prove true.

'I was very reluctant to order Lieutenant Rawson
to return; it was like sending back half the party; it
would be, I felt, a great disappointment to him to turn
back then, and the loss of his advice and assistance would
be considerable; but the indications of the disease
and their aggravated nature became too plain to be
misunderstood—sore and inflamed gums, loss of
appetite, etc., all pointed too clearly to scurvy; so on
the 10th of May it was arranged that Lieutenant
Rawson, with his party, should take Hand back,
deciding, on his arrival at Repulse Harbour, whether
to cross over to the "Alert" or go on to Polaris Bay.
I at the same time called upon the remainder of my
men to say honestly if they suspected themselves to be
suffering from the same disease, or could detect any of
its symptoms, as in that case it would be better for the
party to advance reduced in numbers than to be
charged with the care of sick men. I did this because
two of them had complained of stiff legs after the hard
work on the snow-slopes; but they all declared themselves to be now perfectly well, and most anxious to go
on.

'I did not take one of Lieutenant Rawson's men to fill up my crew, for I feared that the time might come when he would have to carry Hand, and I suspected that George Bryant, the captain of the sledge, was already affected with the same disease. Thus it was that early on the morning of the 11th of May Lieutenant Rawson left me, much to my regret, he making the best of his way back, whilst I continued to advance with six men.'

It will be most convenient here to follow Lieutenant Rawson in his journey to Polaris Bay.

Owing to two more of his crew breaking down, leaving only himself and one man, E. Rayner, strong enough to drag the sledge, they only succeeded in reaching Polaris Bay on the 3rd of June, after a most arduous journey on reduced rations, and during several days of which Rawson was himself so badly affected with snow-blindness that he had to pull the sledge while blindfold.

James Hand expired a few hours after their arrival at Polaris Bay. George Bryant and Michael Regan were both attacked—the former very severely—but knowing that his extra weight on the sledge would endanger the lives of all, he manfully refused to the last to be carried. It was entirely due to Lieutenant Rawson's genial and inspiriting conduct and to his firm command, that the crippled band succeeded in reaching the depôt.

Four days subsequent to their arrival, Lieutenant Fulford and Dr. Coppinger, with Hans and the dog-sledge, arrived opportunely from examining Petermann Fiord, and the invalids obtained the benefit of professional advice.

Although Rawson's early return had left Beaumont sufficient provisions to last until the 28th, the little party at Polaris Bay were naturally anxious concerning the health of his men. Accordingly Rawson with Hans and eight dogs, accompanied by Dr. Coppinger—whose patients had recovered sufficiently for them to be left to the care of Lieutenant Fulford—started on the 22nd of June, and most providentially met Beaumont in Newman Bay on the 25th, on the very last march the party could possibly have performed without help.

Beaumont, with Alexander Gray, captain of the sledge, and Frank Jones, were dragging forward their four helpless comrades, lashed on top of the sledge and made as comfortable as the circumstances permitted, two at a time, thankful if they advanced only half a mile a-day.

I will now continue the relation of Lieutenant Beaumont's journey.

On the 10th of May he ascended Mount Wyatt, 2,050 feet, called so after Lieutenant Wyatt Rawson.

' I had noticed that morning as we came along the coast that all our big floebergs had disappeared, and now I saw the reason why—for starting from the shore close under our position, and stretching away for ten or twelve miles in the direction of Mount Hooker, was a distinct line of demarcation : it then turned to the northward, and ran straight for the west end of the distant land. All to the eastward of this boundary was smooth and level, while to the westward lay the Polar pack, with its floes and chains of hummocks.

' On the 11th we arrived at the end of the un-

broken coast-line along which we had hitherto travelled
in a north-easterly direction, and, as the general direction of the land beyond was more easterly, this must
have been our highest northern point reached. Unfortunately, though we twice halted here, each time it
snowed heavily, and I was unable to get a meridian
altitude. With a crew reduced to six and a probability of my not being able to drag, which I had done
hitherto, I came to the conclusion that to do good
work in the wide field of operations opening before us
we must lighten the sledge at all cost; so here, at this
point, which I called Cape Bryant, we left a depôt, and
thus lightened started for Cape Fulford, which is the
north extremity of the line of cliffs on the west side of
St. George's Fiord.

'In obedience to my orders it was necessary that I
should examine what appeared to be a deep inlet; but
now that I was alone I felt that the utmost that I
could hope to do, and which seemed to me would be
of the most service, was to follow and ascertain the
direction of the mainland as far as I could, at the
same time taking every opportunity of ascending high
mountains to obtain the fullest information relative to
the off-lying islands, if such existed. Thus it was that,
after looking into St. George's Fiord, I pushed on
towards Dragon Point. The road across the mouth
of the Fiord, which was exposed to the north wind,
was very good (the only good bit we ever had), being
hard and nearly level, and we did the nine miles with
ease and comparative pleasure.

'Arrived at Dragon Point, we opened out another
wide reach of bays and fiords, and while debating in

my own mind which to follow I felt how powerless I was, single-handed, to follow out such numerous and extensive lines of exploration. I was most anxious to reach Mount Hooker, as I considered that from its summit I should not only see the islands to the north, but get the best idea of the trend of the mainland ; at the same time I felt I could not leave these wide and deep fiords behind me, any one of which might be a through passage ; so, holding to my original plan, we started for Cape Cleveland.

'On our way we passed some most remarkable ice-hills, which from a distance we had taken for islands. Some stood singly, huge masses of solid blue ice rising gently, with rounded outlines, from thirty to forty feet above the floe ; others, grouped together, looked like a mountainous country in miniature, and formed far too formidable a barrier for us to overcome.

'Up to the 16th of May the travelling since leaving Cape Fulford had been pretty good and the progress fair, but that same evening when we started again it was through soft snow about eighteen inches deep ; this was very disappointing, for the floe looked most promising ; in fact, the whole of this vast tract as far as we could see, from Mount May to Cape Buttress, was one level plain, over which we expected to travel easily and rapidly. We pushed on, hoping for better things, and at camping time had reached, not the island we had started for—that we had missed in a dense fog—but another smaller one, about one and-a-half miles west of it. The travelling had become worse and worse, the snow varied from two and-a-half to four and-a-half feet in thickness, and was no longer crisp and

dry, but of the consistency of moist sugar; walking
was most exhausting, one literally had to climb out of
the holes made by each foot in succession, the hard
crust on the top, which would only just *not* bear you,
as well as the depth of the snow preventing you from
pushing forward through it, each leg sank to about
three inches above the knee, and the effort of lifting
them so high to extricate them from their tight-fitting
holes, soon began to tell upon the men. William
Jenkins, Peter Craig, and Charles Paul complained of
stiffness in the hamstrings, and all of us were very tired.
The morning was most beautiful, but the island close
to us was inaccessible on account of a reef, which
caused the tides to break up the ice at its margin, and
to maintain a barrier of water round it. I could find
no way past this, and to have gone round to the other
side, or to the other island, would have been four hours'
hard work through that snow, so I gave it up.

'Our next march was made under a hot sun,
through snow never less than three feet thick; we
were parched with thirst, and obliged to halt every
fifty yards to recover breath.

'The shore for which we were making did not
seem more than two miles off, so I went ahead to see
if the travelling was better under the cliffs. I got
about a mile-and-a-half ahead of the sledge in three
hours, and then gave it up. I was nearly done; so I
hailed them to go to lunch, but would rather have
missed three meals than gone back all that distance, so
I had a good rest and made a sketch instead; and
then seeing that the sledge would never reach me that
day I started back for them, walking in my tracks.

In the meantime the men had been struggling on as best they could, sometimes dragging the sledge on their hands and knees to relieve their aching legs, or hauling her ahead with a long rope and standing pulls. When we encamped we had hardly done two miles, and Jones was added to the list of stiff-legged ones.

'The next march, May 19th, they could hardly bend their legs. We tried every kind of expedient. We made a road for the men to walk in, and tracked the sledge. Then we tried a broader one for both sledge and men, but all to no purpose; and at last went back to the usual way, and tugged and gasped on, resting at every ten or twelve yards. In my journal I find this entry for the day: "Nobody will ever believe what hard work this becomes on the fourth day; but this may give them some idea of it. When halted for lunch, two of the men crawled for 200 yards on their hands and knees, rather than walk unnecessarily through this awful snow; but although tired, stiff, and sore, there is not a word of complaint; they are cheerful, hopeful, and determined. Since twelve o'clock it has been my birthday; but I can safely say I never spent one so before, and I don't want to be wished any happy returns of it." That march we did not make much over a mile. Everyone was very tired with the unusual exertions of the last few days, and the work was pain and grief to those with stiff legs. Matters did not look promising at all. I had started across the channel first to see down past Cape Buttress, and after reaching Reef Island the northern shore looked so near that I came to the conclusion that we had better push on, reach the land, and coast along to

Mount Hooker. So we went on for two days, until going back seemed as hard work as going on. Our provisions would compel us to start homeward on the 23rd. We could not do two miles a-day, and the men were falling sick. I did not encourage inspection of legs, and tried to make them think as little of the stiffness as possible, for I knew the unpleasant truth would soon enough be forced upon us.

'We started again on the evening of the 19th, and worked away as before; but our progress was ridiculously small, and something had to be done: so leaving the sledge we started in two ranks, four a-breast, to make a road to the shore, for the actual dragging was nothing compared to the exertion of making the road. The shore still looked about one mile off: it had looked the same for two days past, and, to our astonishment and dismay, we walked for five hours without reaching it. It was evidently impossible, on a floe so level that there was nothing in sight the size of a brick, to estimate the distance of the high and precipitous cliffs in front of us. I altered my plans and sent them back to lunch and rest, while Gray and I went on. It took us two hours more to reach the cliffs, and when we did, it was to find the same deep snow reach their very foot; for a hundred yards from the shore the ice was seamed with wide cracks covered by snow, into which the sledge itself might have disappeared. These had water in them, the surface of which was quite fresh, probably due to the glacier which we knew to be close by, though now everything was hidden by a thick fog.

'I now saw to my great disappointment that we

could not reach Mount Hooker, and I came to the conclusion it would be useless to advance any farther with the sledge, as turn which way we would, there was the same smooth, treacherous expanse of snow, and only two days' provisions, which would not have enabled us to reach any part of the shore ; so I went back to the tent after nine and-a-half hours' hard march, and found two men, J. Craig and Wm. Jenkins, unmistakably scurvy-stricken.

'I therefore decided to wait where we were, if necessary, for two days, in hopes of being able to ascend a high peak just over the glacier, and from that elevation decide the question of the channel past Cape Buttress, as well as obtain a view of the distant islands. It seemed too cruel to have to turn back after such hard work, without reaching the land or seeing anything, and I was pleased and encouraged by the anxiety the men showed to make the end of our expedition more successful. But it was not to be. May 21st—it snowed hard all day ; May 22nd—the same ; and a strict survey of the provisions warned us that we must start homewards.

'We left on the evening of the 22nd, a mournful and disappointed party (for the feeling was shared by all), with two men walking by the drag ropes, and none of the others, Alexander Gray and myself excepted, any the better for their long rest. We found, much to our relief, that keeping to our old tracks enabled us to do three times the distance, as we had not to break the road nor lift our legs. I halted at Reef Island, and left a record in a cairn on its north end, according to my instructions, but reserved the skeleton chart for a place more likely to be visited. We then pushed on through the thickly falling snow, which had not stopped for an instant ; though two of the men were bad, the others soon warmed up to the work again, and the improved travelling enabled us to get on faster in spite of the general thaw, so that we reached the neighbourhood of our camp of the 13th on the 24th, returning in two days what had taken us six to advance.

'Just before camping on the 24th a north wind rose, and, as if by magic, the sky cleared, and it became a beautiful morning : there lay Mount Hooker once more in sight, distance about sixteen miles, from which, as I believed, we should see everything ; it was too tempting, so the men agreeing eagerly, the plan was arranged. Craig and Jenkins were to remain with the tent, provisions, and gear, whilst the remainder, with one robe, bags, and five days' provisions, were to make a dash for the mountain ; the provisions were neatly packed in day's rations, and everything being ready we turned in for a good rest.

'When we awoke it was snowing hard, as if it would never stop, so not a word was said, but we packed up and started homewards more disappointed than I can say. By the time we had reached Dragon Point it had cleared again ; this was the place where I had settled to build a cairn, and leave the chart and record. One of the highest mountains in the neighbourhood was only six miles off, so I determined on one more effort. The cairn was built, the record and chart deposited, and Alexander Gray and I set off for the mountain ; it took us six hours to reach the top ;

the view was magnificent, elevation 3,700 feet, but I did not see what I wanted. The Mount Hooker Land hid the islands, and the Cape Buttress Channel was shut in. Mount Albert I could see was a separate island. Cape Britannia, as far as could be seen, had very high land far back. Stephenson Land was quite hidden behind Mount Hooker Land, which latter towards Cape Buttress extended very far back to the eastward. Cape Buttress overlapped it, but inside and above the cape could be seen either a hummocky floe, or a *mer de glace*, it looked like a floe, but its sky-line had a perceptible curve in it—a haze hung over this part. By the look of the land and shore a passage seemed to connect St. George's Fiord with St. Andrew's Bay. St. George's Fiord could be traced continuing to the south after making a slight bend to the west. The view inland in that direction stretched away without a break as far as the eye could reach, all much about the same elevation. Mount Punch stood out from most of the other mountains, and Grant's Land was distinctly visible, the United States' Range being very conspicuous. The view was so immense that to sketch it would have been the work of a day. I tried after having taken a round of angles, but the cold was intense, and my fingers soon became stiff; rising clouds warned us to descend, and by the time that we reached the tent, twelve hours after starting, it was blowing fresh with thick snow and fog. After a short rest we once more started, making for Cape Fulford; the gloomy and unfavourable weather had a depressing influence on the men's spirits, who, poor fellows, were already rather desponding, for out of seven only Gray and myself were perfectly free from scorbutic symptoms, while the two first attacked kept up with great difficulty.

'In due course of time we arrived at Cape Bryant, and camped below the depôt.

'Quite a foot of snow had fallen since we had passed, and it was rotting the old crust beneath, which gave way under the weight of sledge and men, and made the sledge seem a ton in weight.

'During the very bad weather, which continued about this time for many days, I pitched the tent over the sledge when halted for lunch, thus keeping the men under shelter and the gear dry, and providing a comfortable seat for the sick; by putting the sledge quite on one side of the tent there was room enough for all the rest to sit alongside it on the sail on the other side.

'This comfortable rest of two hours! with an extra half-pint of tea, was thought more of, and seemed to do them more good, than anything else we could devise, and so was adhered to for the remainder of the time.

'On the 28th of May, finding that we could not go on dragging the full load (with four men) through the heavy snow, we made up a depôt consisting of pemmican, a coverlet, all the knapsacks and gear, spirits of wine, part of the tent, &c., in all about 200 lb., and got on much better afterwards. We gradually retraced our steps until the morning of the 3rd of June. Up to this time the weather had been one continuous snow-fall with thick fogs; the sun once or twice came out for an hour or so and then snow fell again. The sick were getting worse steadily; for the last two days neither Paul nor Jenkins could keep up with the sledge, but crawled along after it, and often kept us waiting, for I would not let them get too far behind. Craig was very bad, but still hobbled along with us. Dobing and Jones were getting stiffer and stiffer, but still pulled their best. Gray and myself were the only sound ones left. The sick scarcely ate anything; they could not sleep nor lie still.

'Having left a record at the cairn, and taken forty out of the eighty complete rations, we started again in the evening, and had not gone ten yards before Paul fell down quite powerless, and from that time until the end he was like one paralysed, his legs were so completely useless to him. Jenkins still crawled along, but his time was drawing near, and on the 7th he took his place alongside Paul on the sledge. We now had to make two journeys a day, taking the provisions and baggage on for half the time and then coming back for the tent and the sick. With great labour we got round Snow Point, but Drift Point was impassable to us, and so we had to go out on the ice.

'On the 10th of June we reached Repulse Harbour depôt, the weather having once more relapsed into a steady snow-fall. Feeling the urgent necessity of getting the sick under medical care, for both Paul and Jenkins were alarmingly weak and short of breath, I read the records carefully, and having considered the matter in all its bearings to the very best of my ability, I determined to cross over to the "Alert." Everything was to be sacrificed to getting over quickly; so we again made up a depôt and left everything we could possibly spare, including the tent, gun, and my sextant and knife, the only two things I had left. We started on the evening of the 11th, and had not got a mile from the shore hummocks before we came to water. It was a large black-looking pool, surrounded for some distance by ice, so rotten that sledge, sick, and all would have gone in at the first step off the thicker floe.

' This obstacle at the very outset, where I so little expected it, made me stop short, knowing the strong tides and currents that existed on the other shore. I felt that with a sick and enfeebled crew the risk was too great, so we turned back and landed again. We had completed from the depôt to eight days' provisions ; that would have been ample to cross with. Now we had to make the best of our way to Polaris Bay, forty miles off. The question was how much more to take ; we ate so little, that eight days would last us twelve I knew, and if we went on as we had done that would be enough ; so taking the tent and gun from the depôt we started along the coast. Next march Dobing broke down altogether, and Jones felt so bad he did not think he could walk much longer. Poor fellows ! Disappointment at the change of routes had much to do with it.

' This was our darkest day. We were forty miles off Polaris Bay at the very least, and only Gray and myself to drag the sledge and the sick—the thing did not seem possible. However, it was clear that we must take all the provisions, and then push on as long and as far as we could ; so we went back to the depôt, Gray, Jones, and I, and brought the remainder, ten days, making us up to eighteen days; then on we went.

'Craig now could barely walk, but his courage did not fail. Dobing became rapidly worse, but fortunately Jones revived, and there were still three on the drag-ropes. We toiled painfully through M'Cormick Pass, a very hard road, all rocks and water, but very little snow. The work towards the end became excessively severe on account of the narrowness and steepness of the passes. The sledge had to be unloaded and the sick lowered down separately in the sail. At last we got into Newman Bay, and found the travelling on the floe quite a rest; but the work had told on the men who were left, and though Jones still dragged with difficulty, it was evident that soon both he and Gray would be too ill to pull at all. I felt stiff and sore about the body from constant overexertion, but I did not exhibit any of the well-known scurvy symptoms as yet. We were travelling very slowly now, for Craig, who had held out so long, could scarcely stand, and he and Dobing had to be waited for constantly.

'On the 21st of June we camped about ten miles from the bottom of the bay, close to the west or south shore. It soon after came on to blow a gale, and the squalls were so violent and changeable in their direction that all our efforts to keep the tent standing were unavailing, and we had to put the sick on the sledge and cover them over with the sail; but the drifting snow which whirled around us penetrated everywhere, and soon wet them through, and they caught colds, which made Paul much worse afterwards.

'In the afternoon of same day the wind lulled, and by using the guys, sledge-lashings, and drag-ropes, we managed to pitch the tent after an hour's hard work. We put the sick in, and tried to make them comfortable; but the tent was badly pitched, and the squalls from the cliffs, more like whirlwinds, sometimes made the two sides meet in the middle. We were all huddled up in a heap, wet through, and nobody could sleep.

'This went on until noon of the 22nd, when the wind having gone down we repitched the tent and had a few hours' rest, which we so much needed. At 9.30 we started; but the wet and cold had stiffened our limbs, and for the first time I felt the scurvy pains in my legs. Craig and Dobing almost dragged themselves along, their breath failing entirely at every ten yards—this appears to be the most marked feature of the advanced stage of the disease; all four now, but especially Paul and Jenkins, gasped for breath on the slightest exertion—it was painful to watch them. We were a long way from Polaris Bay still, and I did not see how we were to reach it under the circumstances.

'On the 23rd of June it became necessary to carry both Dobing and Craig, to enable us to advance at all; and although this in our weakened state made three trips each day necessary, and limited our advance to a mile, yet we were still moving on.

'On the evening of the 24th we started for our last journey with the sledge, as I thought; for finding that Jones and Gray were scarcely able to pull, I had determined to reach the shore at the plain, pitch the tent, and walk over by myself to Polaris Bay to see if there was anyone there to help us ; if not, come back, and sending Jones and Gray, who could still walk, to the depôt, remain with the sick and get them on as best I could. But I thank God it did not come to this, for as we were plodding along the now water-sodden floe towards the shore, I saw what turned out to be a dog-sledge and three men, and soon after had the pleasure of shaking hands with Lieutenant Rawson and Dr. Coppinger. Words cannot express the pleasure, relief, and gratitude we all felt at this timely meeting ; it did the sick men all the good in the world.

' Lieutenant Rawson had, in my opinion, acted with great judgment in planning his relief expedition, for had he come sooner he not only might have missed us altogether, but the small force at his disposal would not have been of so much service. As it was, he came in time, with sufficient provisions, and by one great effort got us all into safe quarters, as I shall explain.

' We met early on the morning of the 25th of June, and with the help of his party reached the New-man Bay depôt the next day, Dr. Coppinger watching the four now utterly prostrate sick with unremitting attention. Half a day was spent here in an attempt to obtain a seal, but without success, and so next morning we started for the depôt at Polaris Bay, the dogs, with the assistance of the three officers, dragging both sledges. It is mainly due to Hans' clever management of the dogs, and his skill as a driver, that we were enabled to advance so rapidly with such a heavy load. That evening, when we camped, we were only twelve or thirteen miles from the depôt. Both Paul and

Jenkins were now in a critical condition, but Paul more so than Jenkins.

'I felt the importance of getting them both to a state of complete rest as quickly as possible, an opinion in which Dr. Coppinger concurred; so on the morning of the 28th Dr. Coppinger and Hans, with the two men on the eight-man sledge drawn by the dogs, started for the Polaris Bay depôt. Soon after, Lieutenant Rawson and myself, having placed Craig and Dobing on the five-man sledge, as well as the tent and all the gear, but only two days' provisions, also started for the same destination. Jones and Gray, who could still walk, though slowly, came on behind. Fortunately for us two, the wind helped us for some time; but later on, the travelling becoming very heavy, we were obliged to camp, having accomplished a little over three miles.

'Next day, as we supposed the sledge on its way back to us, and I was anxious to move the sick men as little as possible, I determined to await its arrival. This did not occur until 3 A.M. of the 30th of June; and the whole party were so done, dogs and men, that they had supper and turned in. They brought me a letter from Dr. Coppinger saying that he had had a very arduous journey, and had not reached the depôt until midnight. The extremely rapid thaw of the snow on the plain obliged them to cross broad strips of bare shingle, while the floe was so seamed with cracks that they must have travelled double the distance in looking for a road. The sick had borne the journey well, and eaten with good appetite on their arrival; but from noon of the 29th, Paul had gradually grown

weaker and weaker until he died at 5.15 P.M. Jenkins
was no worse. I was very much grieved at Paul's
death. I had watched him and cared for him so long,
and had hoped so that we might not be too late, that
I felt his death very much. However, we were not far
from the end of this arduous journey now ; the thing
was to get the remainder in as soon as possible ; so at
seven o'clock we once more started, Lieutenant Rawson
and his party taking the sick on the eight-man sledge
round by the sledge route, while I took Gray and
Jones round by the foot of the hills. We three
reached the depôt at 7 A.M., and were warmly welcomed and cared for by Lieutenant Fulford, Dr. Coppinger, and the two men in camp. Lieutenant Rawson,
with his party, arrived at 11 A.M., after a very heavy
journey, having travelled nearly all the way on bare
shingle. So at last we were all safely in, in good
hands and comfortable quarters.

'The next day being Sunday, I read the Morning
Service, all of us joining most heartily and fervently in
rendering thanks to Almighty God for His gracious
mercy and protection towards us.'

CHAPTER IV.

THE gale which was experienced at Floeberg Beach on the 31st of July, and which released the 'Alert' from her exposed position on the shore of the Polar Sea, was merely felt at the sheltered position of Discovery Bay as a light air from the southward. It is worthy of note that at the same time, near the head of Baffin's Bay, Sir Allen Young in the 'Pandora' experienced a very severe storm from the southward, evidently part of the same disturbance as that which reached Floeberg Beach.

As the 'Alert' cleared the barrier of grounded ice, which had proved so excellent a protection to her during the past eleven months, the Polar pack was found to have drifted to a distance of a quarter of a mile from the land, leaving a broad water-passage which continued until Robeson Channel was entered. From that point the water-way gradually narrowed, until, at a position about four miles north of Cape Union, the pack pressed tightly against the shore, and formed an effectual barrier to our farther progress.

ICE-FOOT NEAR CAPE UNION.

(FROM A PHOTOGRAPH.)

There being no good protection attainable unless we retraced our steps to Floeberg Beach, twelve miles distant, I secured the ship in a small indentation of the ice-foot or ice-wall. Our position was close to the southward of a number of floebergs which had grounded in a line with the shore outside of the ice-wall. These I hoped would afford us some slight protection from the northward; but in the direction of Cape Union, the shore being steeper, there was nothing to keep the Polar pack away from the perpendicular face of the ice-wall, which was polished and horizontally striated by the grinding of floating ice during prior seasons.

As we steamed along the coast I noticed that only those points of land which were exposed towards the north bore traces of recent pressure; and generally speaking, there were few signs of the pack having nipped against the shore—that is, with the enormous force necessary to cast up huge masses of ice and deposit them on the top of the ice-wall, which varied in height to between thirty and forty feet; the depth of water alongside was from five to seven fathoms, and permitted the ship to run alongside it without any fear of touching the ground.

During the afternoon the pack drifted with the flood-tide slowly towards the south, always nipping against the ice-wall close to the southward of us, but leaving a narrow water-space near the ship.

The ice in the offing consisted of one large compact floe—that near the shore, alone, being broken up and loose, but in no way navigable.

About 8 P.M., with the commencement of the ebb-tide, a small pool of water formed on the southern side of a large floe which prevented our advance. Expecting an opportunity would occur to glide past the obstruction, I got under weigh, but was disappointed, the pack closing in tighter than ever ; before I could return to our small haven it had become filled with ice. There was, therefore, nothing for it but to retrace our steps towards the north, looking for some other indentation in the ice-wall ; but none was to be found. The main body of the pack having moreover closed in near Black Cape to the northward and cut off our retreat in that direction, I was obliged to secure the ship between two of the stranded floebergs, but as they scarcely projected farther from the land ice than the breadth of the ship, they could hardly be expected to afford us much protection.

In the evening, dark clouds collecting above Cape Lupton on the east shore of the channel, with a falling barometer, foretold a recurrence of the southerly wind.

During the height of the ebb-tide the main pack drifted fast towards the north, but fortunately left, in our immediate neighbourhood, a clear water-space about two hundred yards broad.

On the 1st the large ' crossing floe,' which afforded so good a sledge road during the spring, after being driven completely out of Robeson Channel towards the north during the southerly wind of the previous day, had returned and occupied a position close abreast of the ship. At 2 A.M., the commencement of the flood-tide, the nip towards the south eased a little, and I could have advanced a mile ; but there being no protection available I decided to remain where we were. At three the officer of the watch informed me that the pack was closing in fast. Although the current had changed in the offing, where the ice was drifting towards the south, that inshore was still moving fast to the north, the two movements quickly collecting the ice near us. The heavy floe which had previously stopped our progress was drifting with the eddy current towards the north, scraping its way along the ice-wall in rather an alarming manner as it advanced towards us. Steam being fortunately ready, we cast off, and succeeded in passing between it and the shore through an extremely narrow channel, most opportunely opened for us, as it was pivoting round against the enormous ' crossing-floe.' A few moments after we had passed, it closed in against the ice-wall at the position we had so lately vacated.

The difference between an ordinary floe and Polar ice was here well exemplified. The former, composed of ice about six feet in thickness, on meeting with an obstruction is torn in pieces as it presses past it; the latter, some eighty or a hundred feet thick, forces its way past any impediment which may be in its course, without damage to itself. Such was the case on this occasion: the Polar floe, which we only escaped by a few yards, on nipping against the heavy breastwork of isolated floebergs lining the coast, some of them forty feet high and many thousand tons in weight, tilted them over one after another and forced them higher up the shore, without receiving the slightest harm itself, not a piece breaking away.

Steering onwards through a water-channel, so narrow that the boats suspended at the davits touched the cliff of the shore ice-wall on several occasions, we arrived within two miles of Cape Union, but there we were again stopped at 5 A.M.

Fortunately, about fifty yards of the ice-wall had been removed by a summer torrent, which had melted a passage for itself through the icy barrier, leaving just sufficient space in which to secure the ship, with her side resting against the steep beach, and water on her off side too shallow for any deep floating ice to harm us much.

The wind was blowing in squalls from the southward, and, in consequence, the ice continued to drift towards the north with the flood-tide when it should have been moving the other way.

About nine o'clock a momentary opening occurred at the time of high-water, and I was induced to push off; but within an hour we were obliged to return, and I considered myself exceedingly fortunate when we succeeded in regaining our small haven—the only indentation in the ice-wall for a distance of two miles either way—just as the water-space was closed and we could not have moved a ship's length in any direction. Raising the screw and rudder, and removing the boats from the off-shore side, where they would be endangered by the ice should it close in, we were as fully prepared for a nip as we could be.

The following passage is from my journal :—

' The ice between us and the " crossing floe " is of a decidedly lighter character than we have lately been accustomed to; but floating in shallower water it is really more dangerous to us at present than the heaviest Polar ice would be.

' It is astonishing with what coolness we have each

packed up the very few private articles we could possibly carry with us if the ship were broken up by the
ice. When constantly facing danger such events are
taken as a matter of course.'

At low-water during the afternoon, the wind
having lulled considerably, the pack commenced to
set to the southward, but except within a distance of
about fifty yards ahead and astern of the ship no water
was to be seen anywhere. The pack nipping against
the ice-wall marked its course by deep horizontal
scratches, and although it scraped its way past the
ship, owing to the protection afforded by the small
haven, she was in no way damaged.

Tidal observations obtained during the evening
gave the time of high-water at 9.55 P.M. We had
therefore already caught up the Robeson Channel tide,
which is an hour and a quarter later than that at
Floeberg Beach. With the ebb-tide the pack drifted
towards the north.

Soon after low-water on the morning of the 2nd
the in-shore ice commenced moving towards the south,
while the outer pack continued its course to the north-
east with a westerly wind, from which the in-shore ice
was protected by the high cliffs. At 6.30 A.M a
decided off-shore movement occurring in the ice, steam
was raised, but owing to an eddy current carrying the
rudder under the bottom of the ship, we experienced
so much trouble and delay in shipping it that we were
unable to start for a space of two hours. We then
steamed to abreast of Cape Union, but by that time it
was high-water, and with the change in the tidal
current the channel commenced to close. I then ran

back a distance of half a mile to a very slight indentation in the ice-wall, so small indeed that only one
end of the ship could be in the least protected; the
stern being the most vulnerable part was secured in
the notch. As on the previous day, no sooner were we
secured than the pack closed in with the ebb-tide and
there was scarcely any water to be seen.

With our weakened crew we found the constant
work with hawsers very laborious, and the services of
the capstan or windlass were constantly called into
requisition.

Being close under the lee of Cape Union, the most
prominent point on the coast, the run of the ice as it
drifted to the northward retained its former course and
left a water-pool about two hundred yards broad in
the immediate neighbourhood of the ship; there was
therefore no anxiety for her safety so long as the tide
lasted, but with the south running current there would
be no protection whatever. Accordingly, just before
low-water I was obliged to move the ship, and while
the ice remained stationary we succeeded in forcing
our way into the pack for a distance of a quarter of a
mile from the shore; there the ship was secured among
some fairly sized floes of light ice.

It was naturally with much anxiety on my part
that I thus committed the ship to be drifted helplessly
with the pack, in the hope and belief that it would
convey us past Cape Union, and towards Lincoln Bay,
where we might expect the navigation to become less
difficult; but very little choice was left me.

Although hitherto we had been favoured by finding notches in the ice-wall in which to secure the ship,

I knew that for the next five or six miles we should meet with an unbroken line of ice-cliffs. Independently of the chances of our being carried by the wind or current towards the north-east out of Robeson Channel, there was, I considered, less danger to be apprehended in the pack than if we continued to navigate near the shore.

Shortly after the ship was secured the whole pack commenced drifting towards the south, the ice near the land nipping against the ice-wall and showing how fortunate it was that we had moved the ship out of the way. The weather was calm, with a clear atmosphere and only a few misty clouds flying above the hill-tops from the westward. The land on either side of Robeson Channel was distinctly visible, and the change of scenery as we drifted quickly along, close enough to the western shore to distinguish every detail, afforded contemplation for the minds of all during our forced inactivity. As each man was now sufficiently experienced to know the great danger we were running, this was perhaps a fortunate circumstance.

Observations obtained showed that while the temperature of the water at the surface was 30°, at a depth of five fathoms it was 29°·5, and at the bottom in forty fathoms 29°·0. An undercurrent was running towards the south with the first part of the flood-tide faster than the surface water was moving.

As we were swept past Cape Union, and the land in the neighbourhood of Lincoln Bay came into sight, I observed a large water-pool near the shore at a distance of about six miles from us.

At 10.30 P.M., by which time we had been carried

three miles to the southward of the dreaded cape, the ice inshore ceased drifting to the southward, but the floe to which we were secured continued its course. Taking advantage of the momentary opening in the ice thus occasioned, I steamed towards the land in the vain hope of finding a friendly notch in the ice-wall in which to secure the ship. The water continuing to favour us we reached the shore, and I found to my intense relief that by keeping very close to the ice-wall we should be enabled to force a passage through the lighter pieces of ice bordering the main pack, which by this time was being carried to the northward by the tidal current at the rate of at least two miles an hour.

Such favourable circumstances could not be expected to last for long, so we proceeded at full speed ; but this again was a source of danger, and the very frequent changes of the helm as we made a tortuous course through the narrow water-channel, frequently grazing the ice-wall, caused much excitement.

At 2 A.M. on the 3rd all uncertainty of our reaching the water off Lincoln Bay was at an end, and, the water-way gradually increasing in width, we bade good-bye to the pack off Cape Union with no greater damage than two boats having been badly stove against the cliff of the ice-wall. Pieces of ice often fell into them, and that they escaped being torn away from the davits was a subject of wonder and congratulation.

By this time the fine weather had given place to a very heavy snow-storm from the south-west, with a strong wind, which forced the ice off shore and enabled us to pass Lincoln Bay and Cape Frederick VII. in perfectly clear water. This was so complete a change of circumstances that amid our rejoicing few cared to think of what would have been our fate had we not fortunately escaped from the Polar pack before it commenced to drift to the northward with the change of tide and increasing fair wind.

At 6 A.M. we had passed Wrangel Bay, but found the ice blocking a passage towards Cape Beechey; accordingly the ship was secured to a floe to give time for a channel to open. After a delay of two hours we again proceeded, and with little trouble succeeded in reaching to within half a mile of Cape Beechey just before high-water.

As at Cape Union, the north-running current pressed the ice against the land south of the cape, but immediately to the northward a small pool of water remained clear; in this pool, without any other protection, the ship was secured.

In the afternoon, a sudden squall off the land enabled us to round the cape and to reach a cluster of floebergs lying aground on the shallow beach to the southward of it. These afforded a fair amount of protection, and the ship was secured amongst them close to the shore in three fathoms water.

At Cape Beechey the cliff-like ice-wall rising from deep water, which is found throughout Robeson Channel, comes to an end. South of this cape the land slopes gently down to the sea, and is fronted by a breast-work of floebergs similar to, but somewhat smaller than, those which line the shallow parts of the coast of the Polar Sea.

During the 4th the weather was overcast with snow squalls from the south-west, with a low barometer but very little wind.

As the ice had closed in and locked the ship up completely, the sportsmen visited the lakes where three musk-oxen had been shot the previous summer during our passage north.

A number of brent geese were found; the old birds having moulted their pinion feathers, and the goslings not having learnt the use of their wings, were taken at a disadvantage, and fifty-seven were shot, which proved a very important and opportune supply of fresh food for the invalids, of whom we had still eleven remaining. Although unable to fly, these geese were very difficult to secure, as they kept out of range on the water; indeed, few, if any, would have been shot had not Frederick's kayak been carried up to the lake and launched; by this means the birds were driven within range of the guns.

A large floe, apparently unattached to the bottom, occupied about three-quarters of the surface of the lake; its surface was about twelve inches above the water.

The convalescents enjoyed a run over the hills, and succeeded in picking a considerable supply of dwarf sorrel, but at this late season it had lost much of its flavour.

In my journal of this date I wrote:—' A remarkable opening in the land of Polaris Peninsula, five miles to the southward of Cape Sumner, on the opposite shore of the channel, looks so like an indentation in the coast that I very strongly suspect it to be the Repulse Harbour of the "Polaris" expedition. After a careful study of the narrative of that voyage, and considering the almost constant pressure of the pack against the land north of Newman Bay, I cannot think that any vessel has ever, or will ever, reach that shore, always supposing that she is not carried there against her will by the pack. It is therefore my duty to future navigators to record this belief in order to prevent any being blamed if they fail to get to the northward of Cape Brevoort.

' It is astonishing how different the ice is at different parts of Robeson Channel. As we came south we met lighter ice, but here we again meet with heavy Polar floes. Coupled with the observations of Dr. Bessels and others, who state that the heavy ice drifts up Lady Franklin Sound, that opening would appear to act as a pocket. After being cleared by a south-west wind driving the pack towards the north, it is sufficiently large to receive almost all the ice driven from the Polar Sea through Robeson Channel with the change of wind from the north.'

It is only during seasons when northerly winds prevail considerably over the westerly ones that the heavy Polar ice is carried south in large quantities down Kennedy Channel into Kane's Sea.

The speed of the slowly-moving tidal currents in the Polar Sea becomes gradually accelerated as they pass through the narrow Robeson and Kennedy Channels. At Floeberg Beach the rise and fall of the tide is only from one and-a-half to three feet; at Cape Frazer, at the south end of Kennedy Channel, it is fourteen feet. Consequently, the ice in its passage

southward through the northern portion of that channel is borne onward with ever-increasing speed, and
leaves behind the more sluggish moving pack jammed
together in the funnel-shaped Robeson Channel.

During our detention near Cape Beechey, the ice
in Robeson Channel, which is only thirteen miles wide
at that part, drifted up and down the strait with the
tide, the wind having the effect of increasing the speed
of the current and the duration of its flow both towards
the north and the south.

As Captain Stephenson, by his last orders, conveyed
to him *viâ* Polaris Bay in May, supposed that the two
ships would probably pass a second winter in the
neighbourhood of Discovery Bay, it was necessary to
send him instructions to prepare the 'Discovery' for
sea, and to inform him of my intention to proceed to
England.

On the 5th Mr. Egerton with a seaman started
with the necessary orders. They arrived at Discovery
Bay the following morning, after a march of nineteen
hours. Having missed their way, they had crossed a
mountain range two thousand feet high, and after
having walked at least thirty miles over rough and
boggy ground, arrived on board the ship with their
boots completely worn out.

On the 6th the wind increased considerably from
the north until it blew a gale. During the height of
the flood, or south-going tide, a succession of heavy
floe pieces passed us drifting down the strait, toying
with our barrier of outlying floebergs, and turning one
large one completely topsy-turvy. It was firmly
aground in twelve fathoms water on an off-lying shoal

some two hundred yards from the main line of the floebergs, and had been of great service in keeping the line of the drifting pack at a safe distance from us; but on this occasion the point of a large floe which was drifting south close inshore brought the weight of the whole pack on this particular mass. As it received the pressure, the floeberg was reared up in the air to its full height of at least sixty feet above water, and turning a complete somersault fell over with a tremendous splash, breaking into a number of pieces with a great commotion, and raising a wave sufficient to roll the ship considerably.

Our protecting floeberg having been carried away, the pack closed in, forcing the lighter floebergs one after the other, as they became exposed, farther inshore, and at last nipped the ship slightly.

In the evening Lieutenant Rawson and two seamen arrived from the 'Discovery,' and brought me the distressing news concerning the Greenland division of sledgers which has been related in the previous chapter. He further informed me that Lieutenant Beaumont and a party were still at Polaris Bay, but that they had intended starting on the 5th for Discovery Bay.

Although I had the fullest confidence in Lieutenant Beaumont, I was naturally most anxious concerning his crossing the strait when the ice was so much broken-up and the spring-tides at their greatest height. Consequently, in addition to our incessant watch for an opening in the ice by which we might advance, many an anxious look was directed towards Polaris Bay, and our thoughts were chiefly engrossed on the perilous position of our comrades there.

On the morning of the 7th, the wind still blowing strong from the north-east, but slightly off the land on our side of the channel, the ice eased off shore and cleared the nip round the ship, but did not allow us to move to a more sheltered position.

In the afternoon, a temporary opening occurring, steam was raised and the rudder shipped, but owing to some of the ropes fouling, the latter was not ready before the ice closed in and imprisoned us again.

From the summit of Cape Beechey, Polaris Bay, being a weather shore, was observed to be quite clear of ice, with water extending to a distance of five or six miles from the land. Hall's Basin was full of ice drifting quickly to the southward with the wind and tide.

While the ship was detained at Cape Beechey, Captain Feilden obtained some Eskimo relics. The spot where he found them is evidently the northern limit of the migration of these people on the west side of the channel. From thence they have crossed to Polaris Bay, where their traces are again met with. In the same neighbourhood several rings of stones marking the sites of summer tents were found; and in one locality numerous flakes of rock crystal which had been broken off in the process of making arrow or harpoon heads.

On the morning of the 8th the wind was blowing very strongly down the channel, and completely prevented any ice drifting to the northward with the ebb-tide. With the flood, the pack was carried past us at the rate of two miles an hour.

Owing to several heavy pieces of ice grounding out-

side our barrier line, the inner edge of the pack was guided more towards our position, and at last two floebergs wedged themselves against the ship, and after forcing her very close to the shore, nipped her to such an extent that she was raised bodily three feet. She stood the great strain remarkably well, the cabin doors opening and shutting almost as easily as usual. A heavy piece of ice having grounded outside of the ship, prevented our moving until we had lightened it. Accordingly the fires were put out, the boilers run down, and all hands employed cutting down the stranded floeberg.

Rawson and his two men returned to the 'Discovery.' Feilden and Parr, walking to the southward, found another large flock of geese, but they were unable to shoot any for want of a boat.

In the afternoon there was less wind. Polaris Bay was observed to be free of ice, and a few cracks had opened in the otherwise close pack.

The northerly gale experienced in Robeson Channel between the 6th and the 8th was also felt by Sir Allen Young at Cape Isabella, where, after so zealously keeping his position under very trying circumstances, surrounded by ice on a lee snore, it finally forced him to proceed to Hartstene Bay.

On the 9th the weather was fine. In the middle of Hall's Basin the pack had opened slightly, but was in no way navigable for a ship, even had the ice in our neighbourhood permitted our moving.

A shooting party, with the dingy and Frederick's kayak, went to the southward to look for the brent geese seen the day previously. They returned with

twenty-nine geese and forty-one goslings. At the
same time Dr. Moss and Mr. White brought on board
three hares and four geese from another direction—
a very good day's sport; the neighbourhood was
named Brenta Bay in consequence.

Towards midnight, as the sun hid itself from the
ship behind the northern hills, the temperature immediately fell from 34° to 30°.

On the 10th, after three days' work, the floeberg
aground outside of us having been sufficiently reduced,
floated at the top of high-water, and the ship was once
more free. At the same time a water-channel opened
along shore and we advanced a distance of five miles
without much trouble.

Seals had now become more plentiful; they and
a few dovekies seen in the water-pools gave employ-
ment to those with time to spare.

Early on the 11th, with the last of the flood-tide
the ice again opened slightly and enabled us to
reach some large floebergs lying aground a little to
the north of St. Patrick's Bay, but by being five
minutes too late we were unable to enter the bay
before the ice closed in with the change of tide.
Observing nine hares feeding on shore, Parr and Moss
started in pursuit, and succeeded in shooting four out
of a family party of seven.

On the 12th, soon after high-water the ice commenced setting off shore. Accordingly we at once
pushed on to the southward, the water-channel between
the pack and the land obliging me to enter St. Patrick's
Bay. After several hours' delay in passing Distant
Point, we opened Discovery Bay; finding it full of

LIGHTENING A STRANDED FLOEBERG OFF CAPE BEECHEY.

(FROM A PHOTOGRAPH.)

ice we were obliged to secure the ship near Bellot Island until the evening, when with considerable trouble, and after many narrow escapes of being nipped, we at last joined company with the 'Discovery,' after a separation of eleven months and-a-half.

As there were no tidings of Lieutenant Beaumont and his party, preparations were immediately made for the 'Alert' to cross the channel to Polaris Bay; all the invalids with the official papers and natural history collections being sent to the 'Discovery.'

The ice not permitting us to start, I visited the look-out station with Captain Stephenson, and from an elevation of 1,540 feet, on a clear and calm morning, obtained a magnificent view, but, to our great regret and increasing anxiety, nothing was to be seen of the travellers. A white object was plainly visible at Hall's Rest, but whether it was Beaumont's tent or the second boat, which he would be obliged to abandon and leave there, it was impossible to say; with such fine weather it was most probable that he would have started.

We observed a large pool of water in Polaris Bay, and that the ice between Cape Beechey and Cape Lupton was fairly navigable, but near Discovery Bay and elsewhere in Robeson Channel it was closely packed. On the east side of Hall's Basin and at the north end of Kennedy Channel, there was a great quantity of water near the shore, with large floes drifting with the tidal current in mid-channel.

The look-out man reported that during the last northerly gale the heavy floes which streamed down Robeson Channel struck against the projecting point of

Daly Peninsula, packing heavily; the main portion being then carried into Lady Franklin Sound, and only a small quantity drifting into Kennedy Channel.

The south end of the United States Range was clearly visible to the westward. With the upper part of each valley filled with a glacier, the mountains presented a totally different appearance from those at the north-eastern end of the range, the difference being probably due to the southern hills depriving the warm winds of a great part of their moisture.

On the 12th Mr. Egerton returned on board with part of a musk-ox killed by Lieut. Rawson a few days previously when journeying from the 'Alert' at Cape Beechey to Discovery Bay. Owing to the length of the march Rawson and his two companions were as lightly accoutred as possible. Near St. Patrick's Bay two musk-oxen were sighted, a cow and a bull calf. Although there was no gun with the party, Rawson decided upon attacking the animals with his knife. The following is his narrative of the encounter:—

'Not having any fire-arms with us, and knowing how much fresh meat was required, we determined to try and drive them down towards the ship; for which purpose we made a circuit and got inland of them, hoping to drive them towards a small ravine. On sighting us they immediately prepared to defend themselves, standing back to back; whereupon we attacked them with stones, gradually closing in. At first they took little heed of our volleys, but as we got nearer and made better throwing they commenced snorting, bellowing, and tearing up the ground with their fore-paws. On our endeavouring to get on their flanks they turned their front, pivoting round on their hind legs and always keeping back to back with their heads towards two out of the three of us.

'As my hunting-knife and one of the men's alpen-stocks were our only weapons, there appeared to be little chance of my getting near enough to use the knife so long as they kept in this position.

'By the time we had approached to about five or six yards we discovered that they were extremely sen-sitive in the nose ; and after a few well-directed stones the cow broke through our line and made for the hills. We then closed on the young bull. Charging me he also succeeded in escaping, and would have tripped me up had I not jumped out of his way, much to the amusement of the men.

'We then again surrounded them on the side of the hill, flinging stones all the time ; when nearly close enough for striking with the knife the cow charged and three times forced me to retreat up the hill. Finding that I could get out of the way pretty easily, I felt more courageous, and at last, after a well-directed shot with a stone, I managed to plunge the knife into her side. She was round at once, but I managed to keep above her on the hill-side, and following her up struck her three more blows.

'Although bleeding profusely I could not reach her heart, so at the suggestion of one of the men we lashed the knife on to the alpenstock. I felt con-siderably more at ease with the lengthened weapon, and after three more stabs had the satisfaction of seeing the animal stagger, fall, and then roll down the hill for about a hundred yards, dead.

'The young bull, who had been making himself rather annoying all this time by every now'and then getting behind us, now stood watching the carcase. Thinking this was an opportunity not to be lost, I succeeded in stabbing him, but in the confusion he managed to break through our line and escape over the hills at such speed as to render it useless our following.'

On the morning of the 13th the 'Alert' crossed Discovery Harbour and reached some ice aground near the breakwater at the entrance; there she was secured, ready to start for Polaris Bay immediately an opportunity occurred. The water-pools on the breakwater, each fringed by a bright green border of moss, which afforded the skaters exercise on the 26th of August last year, were at this period being used as a rendezvous by the ducks and wading birds flocking together preparatory for their migration south. They were very shy, and although much patience was displayed by the sportsmen only three or four were shot. Only female ducks were seen, the male birds having apparently started south by themselves, leaving the care of the young birds to the female parents.

At this season the ground was evidently hardening for the winter. During the spring, long before the temperature of the air was above freezing point, the earth became pulverized to the depth of two or three inches, all the moisture which had rendered it hard throughout the winter having evaporated. During the latter part of the summer, the moisture again collects as dew and the earth hardens completely.

The tops of the hills were now covered with newly fallen snow which remained unmelted. The water in the small ravines had stopped running, and the large ones could be easily crossed on stepping-stones without wetting our feet.

Although ice did not form on the largest water-spaces in the pack, the floes were already being cemented together during calm weather, and all the water-pools on the surface of the floes were covered with ice almost strong enough to bear a man's weight.

On the 14th our anxiety concerning Beaumont's party was put an end to by our seeing his encampment only two miles distant from us on the ice. A relief party was immediately despatched to his assistance, and after a few hours I had the satisfaction of seeing the members of the Expedition collected together again. This satisfaction was, however, considerably marred by the thought that four of our original number had sacrificed their lives in the performance of their duties.

Beaumont gave the following account of his perilous journey across Hall's Basin, during which, notwith-standing the indomitable perseverance of the leader and his companions, but for a providential south-east wind setting in, they would have been driven into Kennedy Channel, and in all human probability have sacrificed their lives.

' *August 8th.* Polaris Bay.—A bright beautiful day, but still blowing.

' Everything is packed up and ready, and we are only waiting for the wind to go down. A thick mist lying in the channel indicates open water, but prevents us seeing what the ice is doing.

'Noon. The wind is going down, and the clouds clearing away off Cape Lupton; a sure sign of fine weather.

'Went up the hill, as the mist cleared away, to inspect the ice. A great change has taken place; the old ice of the basin has gone south apparently, and is replaced by large and heavy floes from the north; they are still travelling at a great rate in consequence of the wind.

'It is evident that we shall have a large amount of boat work. I wish we could take the twenty-foot ice-boat, but she is too heavy. We must wait until it is quite calm, as the fifteen-foot ice-boat when loaded is only three inches out of the water.

'9 P.M. It is now quite calm as far as we can see. Closed the house; secured everything, and started at 10 P.M. in the fifteen-foot ice-boat, with the sledge towing astern. We are so deep and the sledge so heavy, that we are going very slow; pulled nearly to Cape Lupton, and then took the ice, shaping course for St. Patrick's Bay. After two hours' work entered a large space of water; it was a time of great anxiety to me, as we could barely keep the water out of the boat—it was three miles broad. Disembarked on the opposite side, placed the boat on the sledge, and started across the floe. During the rest of the march we proceeded in a similar manner; each time we embarked or disembarked it was necessary to un-load the boat, either to launch her or haul her up.

'Though we seem to have been drifted south, we have made very good progress, and when we camped

at 2.20 P.M. we had been sixteen hours at work and
had done ten miles. The convalescents. are standing
the work well.

'I am sorry to find that the ice we are on is in
motion, drifting south. ·

'9th and 10th.—I have been up several times
watching the ice, and now that a little breeze has
sprung up we are drifting faster ; so I called the men,
and we prepared for a start.

'Started at 9.50 P.M. We must have been swept
back a long way during our halt to the south and east.
Worked hard until lunch to make it up, amongst high
but small floes, surrounded by rubble. It would take
much too long, and would be difficult to describe the
variety of obstacles and delays which we met with,
and we have made so little way, that I don't think we
have even kept our ground against the southerly drift.
Now the ice appears to be stationary, and we are
stopped for lunch.

'Started again in an hour and struck straight in
towards Bellot Island, to get out of the influence of
the drift.

'Camped at 11.30 A.M., having been fourteen hours
at work ; Dr. Coppinger is watching the convalescents,
as it won't do to overwork them.

'We are much farther south than we were yesterday, and not so far across.

'10th, 11th, and 12th.—We have been drifted
south several miles during the halt, and matters are
looking serious. We are now abreast of Cape Lieber,
and if this goes on we shall be swept into Kennedy
Channel, and unable to regain the ship.

'Coppinger and myself are quite of opinion that an

effort must be made, for even with the very hard work that we are doing now, we are losing ground every hour—even on the march we seem hardly to recover it.

'Started at 11 P.M., with the intention of going in straight for Cape Baird, and reaching it before we stopped.

'We worked steadily on to lunch, then from lunch on to camping time.

'At that time a breeze sprang up from the west and set the ice in motion, clearing it away from Cape Lieber.

'The water was making fast on the west side of Kennedy Channel; everywhere the ice was on the move, and we were obliged to go on.

'We had been slowly going south all day, and now Cape Baird was in a line with Bellot Island, and we could not see the south shore of Petermann Fiord. There was no time to take angles or bearings, or even to keep a record of events. The change from sledging to boating, and *vice versâ*, became so frequent and hurried, that we had not time to unload, but did everything at full speed, to the imminent risk of both sledge and boat.

'At about 10.15 P.M. the wind changed to the south-east, and began to blow the ice back again, and from that time we made real progress; eventually reaching the land by boat between Cape Lieber and Cape Baird at 7 A.M., 12th of August, after having been under weigh thirty-five hours.

'The men, and especially the convalescents, are dead beat.

'*13th and 14th.*—As there was no danger of being

drifted, I let them sleep on, while Coppinger and myself walked to Cape Baird to examine the ice in Lady Franklin's Strait.

'It was getting very misty, but we were in time. All the ice that was out yesterday is back again close to the shore; it seems quite fast between Bellot Island and ourselves.

'Saw two ships lying in Discovery Bay. The "Alert" being down made me think that they might be waiting for us; so we built a cairn and went back; had lunch and started by boat through dense rubble for a short distance.

'Worked steadily from 7 A.M. until 5 A.M. (14th), with two halts for food.

'I was very anxious to get over in one march, but it coming on thick, and Doctor Coppinger representing it as advisable for the sake of the men not to go on, we camped.

'We could see the "Alert" quite plainly when the fog lifted.

'We have been at work twenty-two hours; no boating; all dragging.

'14th.—While we were having breakfast, preparatory to a start, we heard a cheer, and running out met Commander Markham and his party, who had left the "Alert" to come to our assistance. They brought us a supply of most tempting provisions, fearing that we might be in want.

'Soon afterwards we started in their company, and reached the "Alert" without further accident.

'Probable distance travelled from Polaris Bay to Bellot Island, sixty miles.'

CHAPTER V.

AFTER the return of Lieutenant Beaumont and his men
from Polaris Bay, all the shooting parties were recalled
to their vessels, and the two ships prepared for their
voyage southward; but no movement occurring in
the ice outside of Discovery Bay, we were unable to
start for several days.

On the southern slopes of Bellot Island, which
were sheltered from the north winds and received the
full force of the mid-day sun, the vegetation was
remarkably rich. Six species of saxifrage were common, and the beautiful *Hesperis*, with its lilac blossoms,
attained a height of eight or ten inches; considerable
patches were also covered with *Androsace septentrionalis*, and a single species of fern grew abundantly
under the shelter of boulder rocks. Many other
plants, which I have not enumerated, were collected

on the same spot, and it would thus appear that a
favourable combination of soil, shelter from winds, and
full exposure to the sun have more to do with the
development of flowering plants in the Polar regions
than parallels of latitude.

Two ermines, a male and female, were shot by
Lieutenant Giffard on Bellot Island. We had previously obtained a specimen in a fox's earth north of
Floeberg Beach, and Beaumont shot one on the shores
of North Greenland. Although a great number of
hares had been shot by the sportsmen from the ' Discovery,' there still remained a large number ; many
of these were secured, and provided a daily meal of
fresh meat for our sick men while we remained in the
neighbourhood.

During our enforced detention in Discovery Bay
the dredge and trawl were several times called into
requisition.

On the 16th, the weather still remaining distress-
ingly fine and calm, an excursion was made to the
coal-beds near Cape Murchison. This deposit of coal,
or, more correctly, lignite, is exposed in a ravine near
Watercourse Bay, for a distance of over two hundred
yards. At its greatest exposure the thickness of the
seam is twenty-five feet, but we had no means of
ascertaining how much deeper it descended below the
level of the stream. Above the coal are beds of shale
and sandstones. In these shales were found a considerable number of leaf impressions, similar to those
found in the Miocene coal-bearing strata of Disco
Island and the Nursoak Peninsula, as also in Spitsbergen, leaving no doubt as to the geological age of

this Grinnell Land lignite. The coal was pronounced after trial by our engineers to be equal to the best Welsh. The seam where exposed is at an elevation of about two hundred feet above the sea-level, and at a distance of about a mile from the shore of Watercourse Bay, in Robeson Channel. Unfortunately very little shelter is obtainable for a large vessel among the small floebergs stranded in this indentation. The distance between the coal-seam and Discovery Bay is about four miles, and the track leads over the brow of a hill about 800 feet high.

A short distance above the quarry, in a narrow part of the ravine where a large quantity of snow, collected in a shaded part, remains unmelted during the summer, the mountain torrent has melted away a watercourse for itself through the snow bank. In winter this ice grotto, with a trifling expense of labour, could be readily formed into a convenient Arctic residence.

On the 17th we again visited the coal seam, obtaining a considerable collection of fossils. With a temperature of 35° we found geologising very cold work. The stream in the ravine was still running, but ice was forming in the water.

In my journal I find the following remarks :—

'Now that the temperature at night falls to 28°, it is difficult to account for water running from uplands over the frozen lowlands unless we suppose it to come from some sheltered valley with a southern aspect.

'A lake five hundred feet above the sea thus favourably situated gives no sign of freezing, but we can obtain no water anywhere on the lowlands. The pools of water on the surface of the ice are now frozen over thick enough to bear our weights in most places During an excursion to-day we caught several butter-flies and caterpillars, also some bluebottle flies.'

About one hundred yards from the shore of Dis-covery Bay Dr. Moss picked up part of a human femur. This was the only portion of a human skeleton found northward of Port Foulke.

While swinging the 'Alert' to ascertain the error

POST OFFICE CAIRN.

of the compasses, her stern took the ground with the falling of the tide. She floated again without damage as the tide rose.

On the 18th Captain Stephenson deposited an account of our proceedings in a cairn which had been

constructed out of the empty preserved meat-tins,
refilled with gravel. A post-office box was placed in
the centre of the pile.

The 'Discovery' then crossed the bay and anchored
near Bellot Island. A heavy floe drifting past forced
her on shore with the falling tide; but after a few
hours' discomfort, caused by the ship heeling fifteen
degrees, the rising tide floated her again, without the
ship having suffered any damage.

From the summit of Bellot Island I observed that
the ice in Lady Franklin Sound was commencing to
move, and that water-pools were forming along the
eastern edge of a very large floe which extended half-
way across the mouth of the sound. On the south-east
shore a broad water-channel extended along the foot
of the cliffs of Daly Peninsula, and although it was
nearly calm at Bellot Island the waves raised in the
water showed that a strong southerly wind was blowing on the opposite coast.

As there was apparently a better prospect of our
being able to escape by the passage on the western
side of the island, the two ships proceeded to that
entrance, and after an unsuccessful attempt to push
out into the ice, in which the 'Alert' damaged her
rudder, were secured amongst some heavy pieces of
ice stranded on a ten-fathom bank which extends
across the entrance and connects Bellot Island under
water with the peninsula to the westward of it.

On the 19th the officer of the watch kept his look-
out from the high land of Bellot Island. During the
ebb-tide the ice gave promise of opening, and we
tried to force our way along the edge of the large floe,

THE 'DISCOVERY' ON SHORE

(FROM A PHOTOGRAPH.)

but after an hour's expenditure of coal were compelled to give up the attempt.

The south-west wind was still blowing strongly on the opposite side of the sound, but for some reason it did not extend across the ice to our shore. It was, however, gradually enlarging the water-space near Daly Peninsula, and kept us on the *qui vive*. A channel had formed across the sound from Keppel Head, but the ice remained close to the shore between it and the ships. At Cape Baird the water remained open with both tides, which proved that there was not much ice in the neighbourhood.

During the night the large floe already referred to was driven against Bellot Island ; being then unable to move readily with the ebb-tide, the water-pools on its western edge closed up, while those on its north-east side showed signs of opening. Accordingly, on the morning of the 20th, while I went to the top of the island, Captain Stephenson took the ships back into Discovery Bay. From the summit of the hills I observed that there was only one narrow nip left unopened, and that was close to Bellot Island. At low-water an eddy current opened a channel just wide enough for us to pass through, and with a little trouble we succeeded in reaching the water on the southern shore of the sound.

We left Discovery Harbour in a perfect calm, but on nearing the edge of the pack met with a strong south-westerly wind blowing up Lady Franklin Sound and Kennedy Channel. It is remarkable that for the three previous days this wind had been blowing on the southern shore without penetrating across the bay. In consequence, the ice in Hall's Basin was not driven to the northward but remained closely packed. The water-channel east of Cape Lieber was six miles in breadth, the pack having collected on the eastern side of Kennedy Channel.

Passing Carl Ritter Bay, it was seen to be filled with ice ; but with that exception we met none on the western shore until we were abreast of Franklin Island. From thence to the southward it gradually became thicker and thicker, until at 4 A.M. of the 21st, when abreast of Rawling's Bay, and in the same latitude as the ' Polaris ' was, when beset in the pack in 1872, we were also in danger of being cut off from the land. I accordingly turned back, and succeeded in gaining the shore shortly before low-water.

Cape Lawrence, which forms the northern entrance to the deepest bay on the coast, is by far the most magnificent of the many remarkable headlands that so profusely adorn Kennedy Channel. A grand castellated cliff rises precipitously from the sea to a height of about 2,000 feet. From its top the land slopes upwards for a distance of three miles and attains an altitude of at least 3,000 feet.

On reaching the shore I steamed, as I had lately been in the habit of doing, towards the 'ice-wall,' thinking to make the ships fast to it while waiting for the flood-tide to carry away the ice to the southward. But I found that there was not sufficient depth of water alongside for the ships. In fact, we had bidden adieu to the lofty ice-fringe bordering the shore, which is formed by the pressure of the heavy Polar pack continually casting up new pieces of ice until a solid wall is produced, rising out of water sufficiently deep to float the ships in, and standing thirty feet high; and had returned to the region where the shore is merely bordered by an 'ice-foot,' the upper surface of which is level with the top of high-water, and the bottom of its ice-cliff is at the low-water level.

In Kane's Sea, off the exposed capes which receive great pressure, the ice becomes piled up on the 'ice-foot' until a solid cliff is formed something like that to the northward, but the water at the edge of the cliff is never more than about a fathom deep at low-tide.

With the flood-tide the ice left the northern shore, but packed against Cape Joseph Good. As the weather looked threatening, with a very rapidly rising barometer, we ran up the bay, hoping to find shelter for the ships. Entering a land-locked basin, named Radmore Harbour (after one of Commander Markham's sledge companions), I found several pieces of icebergs grounded on the shore, and secured the 'Alert' to one of them; the 'Discovery' going farther in and making fast to some last winter's ice which had not yet broken up.

At the head of the bay we observed a discharging glacier, which was evidently the parent of the numerous small icebergs studding the harbour. This was to us a very unusual sight, as we had not seen any since leaving Bessel's Bay in August the previous year. The glacier was named Jolliffe, after another of Markham's men.

It being spring-tides, the current ran with great strength into the bay, bringing with it a large quantity of ice, which gradually filled up the harbour;

but in such a sheltered position I never expected
danger to be near.

At the top of high-water a passing floe pushed the
bow of the 'Alert' on shore, but so lightly that, had
it given us room, we could have readily hauled her
off again. Before we had sufficient time to do so the
water had fallen so much that we were hard and fast
aground. As the water fell the ship heeled over to-

'ALERT' ON SHORE.

wards the sea twenty-two degrees. The forefoot being
exposed as far aft as the foremast, I was rather anxious
lest she should fall over altogether.

As the tide rose we used suitable pieces of ice as
rafts to carry out one of the bower anchors and chain
cable, hauling them astern to the desired positions by
a hawser; the raft was then destroyed by gunpowder,
and the anchor fell to the bottom.

At high-water the ship having been lightened of all the stores readily movable was hauled off. The rise and fall of the tide was between thirteen and fourteen feet.

While hunting along the shores of the bay Feilden and Parr found traces of a large Eskimo settlement, and from the grass-covered mounds, which marked the sites of ancient dwellings, several articles made in bone and ivory were obtained.

We noticed that the water in the bay had a very decided green tint, a colour which we had not met with farther north.

On the morning of the 22nd the ice was observed to be leaving the coast. Accordingly, we proceeded to the southward, keeping inshore of the pack. At 9.30 we passed Cape Joseph Good (named after Lieutenant Aldrich's sledge captain), with a strong wind blowing from the south-west up the main channel, but the upper clouds flying from the westward, with thick weather and snow falling.

Passing Richardson Bay a very large floe, a collection of smaller ones frozen solidly together during the last few days, obliged me to steam two or three miles offshore, but a water-channel led us in again near Cape Collinson.

At two o'clock, about the time of high-water, there were many eddy-currents, rendering it difficult to choose the best leads through the ice. On one occasion, when the 'Alert' was obliged to retreat from a channel closing unexpectedly, we ran foul of the 'Discovery,' carrying away one of her boat's davits, but by smart and skilful management the boat was saved.

On our nearing Cape M'Clintock the ice closed in with the north-going tide ; and as the wind was blowing strong, with very thick weather, I ran for shelter behind some stranded icebergs about one mile north of the cape.

With the flood-tide the ice again moved from the shore, but the thick weather prevented our ascertaining whether or no it drifted to the south against the strong wind.

Passing Scoresby Bay, which was observed to be about twenty miles deep and perfectly clear of ice, the wind shifted, blowing down the bay, and enabled us to use the fore and aft sails for the first time since the 1st September the previous year. Owing to the large size of the bay a considerable sea had risen, causing motion in the ships.

On nearing Cape Norton Shaw the wind again came from the south-west and blew with such force that occasionally, with the fires of both boilers alight, we could scarcely make head-way ; however, I pushed on, knowing that with such a wind we should meet with no ice until arriving off Cape Frazer, the turning point of the coast.

While passing Cape John Barrow the squalls off the land were so severe that a large book of drawings belonging to one of the officers of the 'Discovery,' and containing a collection of sketches made during the voyage, which had been inadvertently left on deck, was carried overboard by the wind.

At 3 A.M. of the 23rd the storm had increased so much that the 'Alert' had scarcely steerage way ; I accordingly anchored in Maury Bay to wait for the gale to subside and to save coal. We could not, however, have advanced more than a mile farther south as the pack was nipping heavily against Cape Frazer, while it drifted fast to the northward before the wind. During the gale the temperature rose to 42° ; the frozen pools of water on the surface of the ice were consequently melted.

We remarked at the time that in all probability the gale extended over a large area. On our return to England we learnt that it was on this day that several vessels of the whaling fleet at Behring's Straits, 1,300 miles to the south-westward of our position, were so greatly damaged by the ice as to oblige them to be abandoned, causing a considerable loss of life.

As the strong November gales of the previous year are known to have extended for an equal distance, from near Cape Desolation in South Greenland to Floeberg Beach, and as each disturbance in the atmosphere at the Bay of Mercy in Banks Island in 1853 was felt at Rensselaer Bay, 800 miles distant to the eastward, I see no reason to doubt that this gale extended throughout the whole region between Behring's Straits and Smith Sound.

At 8 A.M., the gale having subsided, and the wind, by coming more off the land, giving promise of the ice opening off Cape Frazer, we weighed and proceeded south, and secured the ships to a large floe near the cape, about a mile from the shore, ready to take advantage of any change in the ice. With the exception of the navigable channel, about a mile in breadth, between the pack and the Grinnell shore north of Cape

Frazer, no water was in sight in any direction; the ice was everywhere closely packed.

A temperature sounding showed the surface-water to be 29°·0; at a depth of thirty fathoms it was 29°·2; from thence to the bottom it gradually increased in warmth until at a depth of forty-five and seventy fathoms it was 30°·0. The specific gravity of the surface water at a temperature of 60° as determined by Dr. Moss was 1·02430; and that at a depth of seventy fathoms 1·02547.

Coincident with the increase of warmth in the bottom water, and the change in colour due to diatomaceæ, walrus, large seal and little auks were seen for the first time on our way south. A dredge which came up much torn showed that the bottom was extremely rich in Echinoderms.

In endeavouring to obtain some water from a depth of a hundred fathoms the brass water-bottle was accidentally sent down with both valves closed. As the air could not escape, on recovery, the bottle was found to have been completely flattened by the pressure of the water.

A common black bottle carefully stoppered with a champagne cork withstood the pressure of one hundred-weight to the square inch at a depth of fifty fathoms. At a depth of eighty-five fathoms, with a pressure of nearly two hundred pounds to the square inch, the water oozed through the cork until the bottle was half-full of water, without apparently affecting the cork.

During the ebb-tide in the afternoon, although the

ICE-FOOT NEAR CAPE FRAZER.

(FROM A PHOTOGRAPH.)

ice near the shore drifted towards the south, the floe to which we were secured moved with the pack towards the north, and not wishing to be carried past Maury Bay I cast off and again anchored inshore at 9 P.M.

Captain Feilden, Mr. Hart, and I then landed, and walked to the raised beach at the extreme of Cape Frazer. It is situated 250 feet above the present sea-level, and being the only one in the neighbourhood renders the Cape conspicuous.

After erecting a cairn and depositing a record of our proceedings we returned to the ship with a rich but extremely heavy burden of limestone fossils.

Cape Frazer being subject to great pressure from the pack in Kane's Sea, the ice-foot is of much the same character as the ice-wall in the Polar Sea, but the depth of water alongside it at low-water is only a few feet; the accompanying illustration from an excellent photograph obtained by Mr. Mitchell when the water had yet to rise two feet, shows the cliffy nature of the sea-face.

On the 24th we experienced calm weather, with a temperature ranging between 35° and 39°. The ice in the offing was much less closely packed, although to the southward of Cape Frazer it remained, as before, tightly pressed against the land.

Expecting that the ebb-tide would carry the inshore ice to the southward, as it did the previous day, I started at one P.M. hoping to arrive at the cape before high-water, ready to take advantage of any change; but none occurred, and we were again obliged to

secure the ships to a large floe that was slowly drifting
to the northward in the water-channel which remained
open on our side of the cape.

At 9 P.M., low-water, the ice drifting quickly to
the northward suddenly opened, and by leaving a
channel close to the shore enabled us to enter Gould
Bay, and to approach within half a mile of Point
Hayes. There a floe about three miles in diameter
remained nipped against the land and prevented our
farther advance. The ships were accordingly secured
inside of three icebergs, lying aground close to the
shore, off the mouth of a large ravine.

The ice-foot in the neighbourhood had been melted
away in parts by the summer torrent, leaving exposed
a very steep beach, which was evidently the abrupt
termination of the flat deposit of gravel collected at
the mouth of the river inside of the ice barrier, and
which with the gradual rise of the land will ultimately
become a raised beach.

Wishing to see what prospect we had of reaching
Dobbin Bay, I landed at 3 A.M. of the 25th to walk
round Cape Hayes.

By this time we had become so experienced in
localizing the positions where the Eskimo were likely
to have selected spots for encampments that we seldom
failed to find ancient remains at the points designated
by us beforehand. Observing a very favourable
locality situated on a smooth raised beach, about
thirty feet above the sea-level, formed there when the
course of the river was different from what it is at
present, Captain Feilden accompanied me on shore.
As we expected, the usual rings of stones used for

holding down the tents and several interesting relics were met with.

Since the formation of the encampment, part of the bank had been worn or washed away, and with it half the stones of one house had been carried off leaving the remaining segment at the edge of the bank.

Among the débris of limestone rock at the foot of the hills we obtained numerous fossils, one of them being a trilobite. A pair of falcons flying around had evidently nested in the same cliffs where we noticed them in the previous year.

Although the large floe which prevented our advancing westward remained immovable close to the shore, I observed that the ice in the offing was opening, and that beyond the cape there was fairly navigable water reaching almost to Cape Louis Napoleon. Accordingly I signalled to the ships to advance and hurried back to the boat. Starting at 6 A.M., during the ebb-tide, the ice was observed to be drifting to the northward, probably influenced by the light southerly wind which was blowing at the time.

By passing on the outside of the large floe we succeeded in reaching a group of icebergs lying aground about two miles east of Cape Napoleon—probably the same that protected us on the 19th of August the previous year.

It was now sufficiently dark at midnight to render it necessary to burn candles on the lower-deck.

In consequence of the rise in temperature to 35° during the previous four days all the streams in the ravines were running again. In the afternoon a fog set in and prevented our seeing what the ice was doing

While on shore I noticed a dovekie fly down from the top of the cliffs, which rose about 800 feet above the sea ; they evidently nest at that altitude.   Captain Feilden had long attributed a peculiar whizzing sound, which we occasionally heard overhead when passing under the shore cliffs, to the dovekies flying down to the water ; but though they descended with extreme rapidity, it was difficult to connect the loud rushing sound of wind with the flight of such a small bird. After passing Maury Bay we noticed dovekies in considerable numbers in the pools of water near the ice-foot, where they found apparently an ample supply of food.

On the 26th the weather remained very foggy. Taking advantage of our forced delay a rich haul was made with the trawl in fifty fathoms, giving us several fishes, echinoderms, sponges, and mollusca.

At 8 P.M. the ice permitted us to proceed one and-a-half miles.   Arriving at the end of the water-channel the two ships were secured to a small iceberg with a piece of ice lashed between them to keep them from fouling each other.

In my Journal I remark :—

'Although there is no opening in the ice towards the south-west, to the eastward, where we have lately been able to advance only a mile or two at a time, there is an open channel one or two miles broad.   How far it extends beyond Cape Hayes it is of course impossible for us to determine.

'During this calm weather I can make little or nothing out of the movements of the ice at certain times of tide.   It appears to follow no fixed laws here, but if it begins to move at the commencement of the tide, it is pretty sure to continue to drift in the same direction as long as the tide lasts.

'Since leaving Discovery Bay we have not once observed the decided southerly drift which we noticed last year; had we not known of the undoubted existence of the current we should not have discovered it by the ice motion lately.'

The 27th was calm with foggy weather and snow falling, with the temperature at 32°. On the same day the 'Pandora' at Cape Alexander experienced a south-west gale which did not reach our position.

In the afternoon the ice opened with the flood-tide and enabled us, after much trouble and by passing closer to the ice-foot than was altogether prudent, to enter Dobbin Bay ; but there, after securing the ships to a floe, we were quickly surrounded by the pack.

During the night and the following day we were drifted helplessly about the bay with the tidal current. Early on the morning of the 29th, as the ice set out with the ebb-tide, the 'Discovery' was carried to within a hundred yards of Cape Hilgard, and by the rotatory motion of the floe left without any ice between her and the shore ; for a time her ex-posed condition caused me much anxiety.

During the last of the flood-tide another move-ment of the ice enabled us to escape and to reach a place of comparative safety alongside a floe hemmed in between Prince Imperial Island and the mainland ; everyone exceedingly glad to get out of the pack and away from the numerous straggling icebergs.

The water-bottle having been repaired, Dr. Moss

obtained some samples from different depths. The following results of his observations denote that' with the increase in temperature of the water below thirty fathoms the density also increases to above that of the Polar water, which numerous observations made during the winter showed to be 1·02245. Hence we may conclude that the bottom water is derived from the Atlantic Ocean.

Depth	Temperature	Specific gravity at 60° Fahr. Standard water at 39°2 = unity
1½ fathoms	30°·2	1·02178
20 ,,	29°·3	1·02462
40 ,,	29°·8	1·02507
56 ,,	30°·0	1·02506
115 ,,	30°·8	1·02567

Shortly after we reached Prince Imperial Island, a northerly wind cleared away the mist from the hills and lowered the temperature to 30°.

The recent snow-fall, which measured about five inches, had changed the whole aspect of the land and re-clothed the richly tinted stratified mountains with their winter's garb, from which they had only been free for a short seven weeks.

After this date the snow only melted slightly in the low-lying valleys, and the young ice formed continually on any quiet water.

The sportsmen shot six hares, a dozen ptarmigan, and a raven.

The 30th was a beautifully clear day with a temperature of 30°, falling in the evening to 20°. During the forenoon Commander Markham and I landed on

Prince Imperial Island, and afterwards on the mainland to observe the ice.

Towards the end of the flood-tide a large water-pool formed near Cape Hawks, and a fairly navigable passage appeared to exist amongst the intermediate ice. Making a signal to the ships to get up steam we hastened on board.

The young ice at this time was so thick and tough that we had great difficulty in breaking a passage-way through it in the dingy ; and after starting in the ships it was found necessary to use both boilers and to put the engines on full speed before we could force them through what would otherwise have been considered fairly open ice.

Whenever we met with a quantity of small ice collected between large floes, so long as the pack was not closing, we had long ceased to wait for the formation of a decided water-channel, as with full steam-power we could usually force a passage for the ships.

But now with the young ice forming and the snow tending to toughen it, we found that when one piece of old ice was struck, although it was itself forced out of our way, it failed to propel the pieces behind it. Consequently, after struggling along for about three miles at a very large expenditure of coal, I was obliged to secure the ships to a large floe amongst a quantity of débris ice which had become cemented together with the frost.

This was our first experience during the season of young ice forming thick enough to be troublesome ; the previous summer it was almost as thick a fortnight earlier in the season. After this date it was always necessary to guard against the ships becoming thus frozen in and unable to move should the ice open.

The floe to which we were secured, during this and the following day, was situated in the main channel between the head of Dobbin Bay and Washington Irving Island, and drifted with the pack to the north or south according to the tide; no water-channel ever opening near us, although there were a few disconnected pools in sight in the offing.

On the 1st of September towards the end of the flood-tide, during calm weather, we were again able to advance, and succeeded in reaching some grounded icebergs near Cape Hawks—probably the same which were there the previous year.

I fully expected that with the ebb-tide the ice would be carried out of the channel between Washington Irving Island and the main, but it did not move sufficiently to enable us to proceed; indeed, we had great difficulty in communicating with the shore, only a quarter of a mile distant, by means of a boat, in consequence of the closeness of the ice. Whenever able to do so we gradually embarked the depôt of provisions left there last year; but a boat and some biscuit still remain. If visited during the summer these will be found on the northern shore of a small bay a mile and-a-half distant from Cape Hawks and about a quarter of a mile from the east point of the bay. During the winter when covered by snow it would be very difficult for a stranger to find the locality—unless, indeed, the pole marking it remains up.

The mean height of the tabular iceberg alongside which the ships were secured was between twenty-four and twenty-six feet, lying aground in 190 feet water ; it had probably been raised a foot or two when forced on shore, and would therefore have about one-ninth of its mass exposed when afloat.

During the afternoon the temperature rose to 35°, and misty weather with light rain set in.

On the 2nd a channel opened with the ebb-tide and enabled us to reach to within half a mile of Cape Hawks, but there a newly-formed floe, of débris ice frozen together, prevented our attaining the shelter formed by three icebergs lying aground a mile distant outside of the cape.   Captain Stephenson, in the 'Discovery,' having steam up in both boilers, with much trouble and by rolling the ship, broke his way through for a distance of about a hundred yards into the ice, and probably could have cut completely through the floe ; but the ice to the westward giving no promise of opening, and a thick snow-storm having set in, we returned to our place of shelter off the depôt, having expended much coal to little purpose.

As we now had only a few tons of steaming coal left, and after it was gone would have to use the coal necessary for warming the ship during the coming winter, its expenditure had become a very serious matter.   I need scarcely add that no ashes were ever thrown overboard.

Again early on the morning of the 3rd the movements in the ice induced me to advance, but again were we obliged to retreat.

During the forenoon I landed on Washington Irving Island, and the weather being very clear, obtained a fine view.

On visiting the cairn erected the previous year our papers were found to have been untouched : so re-dating them, and adding a further notice of our movements, the cylinders were replaced.

I again examined the two ancient lichen-covered cairns, but could find no record of who had built them : they were probably erected by some enterprising and successful navigator who, if he ever returned home, has not published an account of his discoveries.

The snow had collected on the ground to a depth of nine inches, but the fall had evidently been local, for near Prince Imperial Island, on the opposite shore of the bay, the lowlands were bare.

Although I could see the horizon near Cape Albert, thirty miles distant, no cleared water was visible anywhere towards the south : but in the direction of Cape Hayes the water-channel, through which we had advanced with so much trouble, had opened and now presented a clear passage more than a mile wide and extending to within three or four miles of our position.

I remained at the summit of the island watching the ice until noon, when with the commencement of the ebb-tide, I had the satisfaction of seeing the pack to the westward of Cape Hawks in motion.   The ships were immediately got under weigh.   Arriving off the cape we found that the newly-formed floe, which had stopped us twice before, had become fixed between the grounded icebergs and the land, and cut us off from a navigable water-channel beyond.   After an hour's ramming at the young ice with full steam up and by rolling the ships, we succeeded in forcing a passage through it, and in rounding Cape Hawks, much to the rejoicing of all; for the nearer we approached Hayes Sound the better would the ships be placed for exploring that unknown neighbourhood, should we have failed in escaping out of Smith Sound.

After passing the cape we found the ice near the land fairly navigable; it obliged us, however, to make a very tortuous course and to frequently pass within fifty yards of the icefoot; fortunately we always found deep water, and we succeeded in reaching the east side of Allman Bay before the ebb-tide was finished. The ice in the offing, consisting of very heavy floes, always remained closely packed.

ALLMAN BAY.

The ice in Allman Bay consisted of perfectly smooth floes, formed during the previous winter, recently cemented together with newly frozen ice from one to three inches thick, through which we found great difficulty in forcing a passage, having to continually roll the ship for the purpose. The headmost vessel having once formed a channel, the other followed through the cleanly cut canal with very little expenditure of coal.

As we entered the bay the temperature of the surface water rose to 32°. This being very unusual, a sample of it was tested and found to be almost fresh enough to drink, and this again accounted for the unusual thickness of the newly frozen ice.

Dr. Moss on analyzing the water obtained the following result. That at fifty-six fathoms was obtained a few days afterwards in Princess Marie Bay :—

Depth	Temperature	Specific Gravity at 60° Fahr. Standard Water at 39°·2 = unity
Surface	31°·8	1·00217
2 fathoms .	30°·0	1·01743
3 ,, . .	29°·7	1·02388
10 ,, . .	29°·2	not obtained
26 ,, .	29°·2	,,
56 ,, . .	30°·0	1·02506

The fresh water at the surface in Allman Bay was evidently derived from the large John Evans Glacier at its head, named after the President of the Geological Society.

The glacier, running in a south-east direction, ends

at a distance of about three miles from the sea, its front being at least five miles across. It is there joined by a smaller glacier running down a parallel valley.

The melting of all the inferior glaciers north of Smith Sound before they reach the sea is very remarkable, and must be due to the vast power of the ever present sun during the summer being in excess of the small amount of precipitation during the winter.

Were they to reach the sea, meeting there with water which is never, even during the summer, sufficiently warm to melt fresh-water ice, they would force their way onward along the ground until their sea-face or front attained its least elevation, and icebergs were broken off by rising through excess of buoyancy. This may account for the extreme lowness of the face of the Petermann Glacier, which attains a mean height of only twenty-five feet above the water-level, and also for the great number of crevasses near its front, as described by Lieutenant Fulford and Dr. Coppinger.[1]

Dr. Kane, although he estimates the height of the surface of the Humboldt Glacier as ' about three hundred feet,' remarks : ' So far from falling into the sea, broken by its weight from the parent glacier, it (the iceberg) rises from the sea.' But as the icebergs in Smith Sound are never more than about 150 feet in height above water when afloat, this estimate of the height of the sea-face of the glacier is probably that of its south side near the shore where Dr. Kane and others visited it, and not of the sea-face itself at a distance from the side.

---

[1] See Appendix.

In more temperate latitudes, south of Cape Sabine, where the temperature of the water is higher and during the summer is above the melting point of fresh-water ice, the foot of the glacier becomes readily melted, leaving an unsupported mass of ice, from which pieces break off, falling down into the sea as icebergs and floating at a considerably less altitude than the top of the parent glacier. We observed that such was the case with the glaciers on the shores of Ellesmere Land in the neighbourhood of Cape Isabella, and with those on the Greenland shores to the north of Cape York.

The question whether the icebergs in Melville Bay and other protected positions to the southward, where the flow of the warm current is not felt to so great an extent, fall or rise when they become detached from the glaciers, will depend on the temperature of the sea-water in the neighbourhood being above or below 32°.

On the 4th the upper clouds were coming fast from the southward with misty weather and a temperature at 35°.

Deeming it desirable to gain as weatherly a position as possible, in order to take advantage of any opening which might occur with the expected westerly wind, we forced our way across Allman Bay, the 'Discovery' leading and cutting a clear channel through the blackest and thinnest part of the young ice, which was from one to three inches in thickness. On securing the ships to a floe about one mile east of Cape D'Urville, as there appeared no sign of any change in the weather, the steaming fires were put out.

The following is an extract from my journal of the 5th :—

' Another wet misty day, with light variable airs; upper clouds from the southward, with a temperature of 35°.

' All our invalids are now so far recovered that they are doing duty on deck, merely being excused from going aloft or working in the boats ; but as I must expect a recurrence of the disease to manifest itself during the coming winter, the quickly-advancing season makes me rather anxious lest we fail to escape from the ice.

' Now that we have attained a position from whence Hayes Sound can be explored, and the interesting question regarding its being a channel leading to a western sea set at rest, a large number of officers and men would be glad if our retreat to the south were cut off, and there are very few who, so long as the two ships passed the winter near each other, would not accept the inevitable with complacency. However, I cannot think that the winds can be much longer delayed ; and if they don't bring with them too low a temperature we shall free ourselves somehow or other.

' The ice in the bay drifts in and out with the tide, moving a distance of about a quarter of a mile.

' It is instructive to observe how useless our sails have been to us, while navigating to the north of Smith Sound, both last year and this. On our passage south the square sails have never once been set ; we have always had to force our way along through narrow openings in the pack caused by calms or contrary winds.'

On the morning of the 6th the weather cleared up with light airs from the north, which, combined with the release of the pressure from the southward, made a decided difference in the ice, and gave us every prospect of being able to advance shortly. During the flood-tide I landed with Markham and Feilden, and walked about three miles alongshore to the westward until we could see Norman Lockyer Island, then about four miles distant from us. Capes Victoria and Albert, seen for the first time sharply defined against the clear sky, and only twenty miles distant from us, created in everyone a feeling of being within easy and certain reach of home, whatever might occur.

All the coast cliffs west of Cape Hawks are magnificent rampart-like headlands from 900 to 1,000 feet high, presenting nearly a straight line facing the sea—the continuity of the front being broken only by the large ravines and the glacier-cut bays. They are composed of a yellowish-pink conglomerate of water-worn pebbles, and are perfectly inaccessible except by ascending the valleys far inland.

Three or four broods of eider-ducks, still unable to fly, were swimming in a pool near the ice-foot. Owing to the warmer temperature during the few previous days there was a free run of water in the ravines.

At this season, which may be considered to have been the end of the summer thaw, it was noticeable that—while the surface of the ice-foot bordering the shore was, as before stated, level with the top of high-water—at its inner edge nearest the land a deep and broad gutterway had, partly by reflected heat from the hillside and partly by the run of the freshwater off the land, become formed alongshore. When it was nearly high-water, this gutterway becoming filled by the tide, cut off the ice-foot from the land.

The absence of ice piled up above the ice-foot to the westward of Cape Hayes was very remarkable. Nowhere did we find it forced up by recent pressure higher than three or four feet. This was totally different from our experience of the preceding season, when, at all the prominent points, we met with ice piled up to a height of at least twenty feet. Its absence would either denote a remarkably calm season, without any winds blowing towards the shore, or indicate that the pack consisted of heavy floes, which would become stranded before they could reach the ice-foot.

At 2 P.M. of the 6th the ice commenced setting out of Allman Bay with the ebb-tide ; a channel near the land also opening at the same time. Steam was accordingly raised, and after a little trouble in getting clear of the young ice, which was now rather alarmingly thick, we reached Cape Prescott; but there we were compelled to make fast, while the flood-tide was running, to some bergs lying aground in twenty-nine fathoms, a mile and-a-half from the shore.

During the night and on the 7th the pack near Norman Lockyer Island continued to open during both the flood and the ebb tides ; but some young ice lying between the ships and the Island, which would have obliged us to use much coal in forcing our way through it, induced me to wait until a decided water-channel presented itself. By noon the ice had all cleared away near the land, and we reached the neighbourhood of Walrus Shoal, and from thence discovered navigable water extending halfway across Princess Marie Bay.

This position received its name from being the most northern locality where walrus were fallen in with.

As soon as the ships were secured, Captain Stephenson and I, accompanied by Commander Markham, ascended Norman Lockyer Island to inspect the ice.

The weather was remarkably clear, and besides finding navigable water extending four or five miles from the island, we had the cheering prospect of seeing a large expanse of water about fifteen miles distant towards the south-east in about the same position as where we met with the southern edge of the pack on our way north the previous year, and having every appearance of being connected with the water at the entrance of Smith Sound. The prospect was so favourable that I could not hesitate about advancing. Nevertheless, at so late a period of the season, when the young ice was steadily increasing in thickness day and night, we knew that if deceived in the weather, or if one false step were made, we should be beset in the drifting pack during the coming winter, without sufficient coal for warming the ships and none for steaming purposes the following year.

After leaving a notice of our movements on the summit of the island, we bade good-bye to the Grinnell shores, and with the exception of one nip, about two hundred yards in length, where two floes had become cemented together by the frost, and which occupied the whole of both crews, assisted by the 'Discovery' ramming, an hour before it was cleared, we advanced to within four miles of Cape Victoria. There three large Polar floes, which had become locked in by a chain of icebergs aground near the cape, stopped us. The open water was now in sight from the mast-head, but the temperature had fallen to 23°.

During the night and the following day the pack drifted to the eastward and westward with the tides, moving with great regularity.

It was most fortunate for us that we had reached the large floes, as with each movement water-pools formed at their edges and permitted us to move the ships ahead a few yards or more at a time, always on the watch not to be nipped when passing round a point, and not to become frozen-in by the quickly-forming young ice when secured in an indentation in the floes. By taking every advantage that offered, we reached to within a mile of the icebergs locking in the heavy floes on the evening of the 8th. The temperature was 20°; but the frost rather assisted us than otherwise by cementing all the débris ice together; consequently, whenever a movement occurred, instead of the débris dispersing itself in the free water-space with the release of pressure, it was held in bondage, and left us a clear water-channel.

The following is extracted from my journal :—

‘ When I consider the large quantity of ice we find in the opening between Bache Island and Grinnell Land, and the slow-running tidal currents, I cannot think it to be anything but a bay.

‘ Copes Bay is a very deep fiord extending to the north-west. Six or seven miles farther west is a broad opening having three bays running north-west, west, and south-west; but it is impossible to say that Capes Stevens and Baker are not islands.'

At 2 A.M. of the 9th the pack commenced setting out of the bay with the ebb-tide. Observing that the point of the large floe to which we were attached would shortly be carried against the icebergs, and that then a channel would be opened for a short time, steam was kept ready; and as the drift of the floe was checked on its coming into collision with the bergs, the outer ice, borne onward by the current, opened for a moment a clear channel, and permitted us to escape from the pack.

After this there was only one serious obstacle to our advance. Owing to the low temperature and calm weather the newly-frozen ice was never less than two inches in thickness, and obliged us to use full steam. In the thickest places the ships were frequently stopped altogether, and frequently had to back out through the channel they had formed and circle round the obstruction. After passing Cape Albert the pieces of old floes became fewer, and we gradually lost sight of the pack to the eastward, although large fields of young ice were met with until we neared Cape Sabine, but there we bade farewell to the ice for good.

As an instance of the great changes that take place in the pack, and how uncertain its navigation is, it is noticeable that on the 28th of August Sir Allen Young found the ice completely blocking up Smith's Sound, and extending from shore to shore eight miles south of Cape Isabella. Ten days afterwards we entered a navigable sea extending to latitude 79° 10'. Thus a breadth of sixty miles of ice had drifted away in the intermediate time.

Considering the very small quantity of coal there was now left on board either ship, it was with a great feeling of relief that I found myself in blue water once more ; and I trust that I was not unthankful to God for His merciful care of us and for the great success that had attended us in the truly perilous navigation north of Smith Sound.

At the head of Buchanan Strait, in the neighbourhood of the Weyprecht Islands, there was a large quantity of' ice, but we passed at too great a distance from it to determine whether it were navigable or not. Payer Harbour was perfectly clear, one large iceberg excepted.

LEFFERTS GLACIER.

Having left a notice of our proceedings at Norman Lockyer Island, and wishing to take full advantage of the calm weather, to ensure visiting the more important station on Cape Isabella, I passed Brevoort Island without stopping, consequently the provisions left there have not been touched.

As we passed the Lefferts, Alfred Newton, and Wyville Thomson Glaciers, all of which discharge icebergs, the broken-off pieces were observed to be floating at less than half the height of the glacier cliff above the water.

At 10 P.M. we arrived at Cape Isabella, and on Commander Markham climbing up to the depôt he found the package of letters and newspapers left there by Sir Allen Young a few weeks previously; we gathered from them that a duplicate packet had been carried on to Cape Sabine.

It was now a consideration whether I should return to Cape Sabine or not; but as it was quite certain that the 'Pandora' had not advanced north of Hayes Sound, and was not herself in want of assistance, I decided to be content with the letters which we had received, and to push on for Disco while the weather remained favourable.

Owing to the thick coating of snow on the ground, we failed to find the notice Sir Allen Young had buried twenty feet magnetic north of our cairn, which would have informed me that he had considerately landed the principal mail at Littleton Island. To this oversight on our part the loss of the principal mail was due.

Had it not been so late in the season, with so much

young ice formed, or had we had coal to spare, I
would certainly have visited Littleton Island and
Port Foulke.

The officers and men of the 'Alert' and 'Discovery' can scarcely feel sufficiently grateful to Sir
Allen Young and his companions for their determined
and persevering efforts to open communication with
them during two seasons. Sacrificing so great a part
of the short navigable season of 1875 and paying
two visits to the Cary Islands on our account alone,
when Sir Allen's purpose was to explore in a totally
different direction, was stretching a friendly action to
the utmost. Such consideration can only be fully
appreciated by persons situated as we were.

It was past ten in the evening when Markham and
Feilden returned from the shore of Cape Isabella.
When the boat came alongside, and we learnt that
they had found a mail, the feelings of all on board
are not to be easily described. A year and more without hearing from home or friends, or the outer
world, is a long gap in our short lives. What changes
may have occurred in that interval! All of us
seemed to be impressed with this thought, and after
the first exclamations of pleasure and surprise not a
word was spoken until the mail-bags were sorted and
the lucky ones received their budgets of news; along
with the mail was a large number of newspapers
which to some extent consoled those who were not the
fortunate recipients of letters.

After our long sojourn within the Polar ice it was
a strange transition to feel the ship rise and fall once
more on the 'north water' of Baffin's Bay, and to look

astern and see Cape Isabella, one of the massive portals to Smith Sound, fading away in an obscurity of snow and midnight darkness; whilst an ice-blink stretching across the northern horizon reminded us forcibly of the perils, dangers, and anxieties that we had contended against for so many months.

In comparing the voyage of the 'Polaris,' and that of the 'Alert' and 'Discovery,' it is evident that the navigation of the ice which is to be met with every year in Kane Sea is entirely dependent on the westerly winds. Both in 1875 and 1876 we met navigable water off Cape Victoria in latitude 79° 12′, with only a narrow pack fifteen miles in breadth between it and Grinnell Land, which a westerly wind of a few hours' duration would certainly have driven to the eastward. The same wind would have opened a channel along the shore, and any vessel waiting her opportunity at Payer Harbour could under those circumstances have passed up the channel with as little difficulty as the 'Polaris' experienced in 1871.

The quantity of one season's ice met with in the bays on the south-east coast of Grinnell Land in 1876, proves that on the final setting in of the frost, after we passed north in 1875, the pack had been driven from the shore, leaving a navigable channel along the land. Nevertheless I do not recommend future navigators who wish to attain a high northern latitude by this route to wait for such a favourable occurrence. Certainly no one could have made a passage through the ice in 1876 before the 10th September by doing so. At that date the season had advanced so far that the attainment of sheltered winter-quarters would have been extremely problematical.

CHAPTER VI.

LEAVING Cape Isabella during the night of the 9th,
we steamed towards the Cary Islands, passing occasionally through thin streams of loose ice, with a few
icebergs and pieces of floebergs intermixed, but seldom
meeting with floes of any size. Those met with did
not float more than three feet above water, and showed
marks of being much decayed, having long tongue-pieces
extending below the surface of the water.

A southerly wind springing up, we made sail,
standing to the south-west. As we made westing, the
pieces of ice met with increased in size and quantity,
and expecting to find the pack near the coast of
Ellesmere Land, I tacked and stood to the south-east
under steam and fore-and-aft sails.

The weather turning misty and threatening, with
snow, and the wind preventing our making much
progress without the consumption of a large amount of
coal, I decided to make the ships fast to an iceberg;
accordingly, with one ship at either end of a long

hawser, its middle was dropped round the weather side
of a large berg; the ships hanging one on each side
balanced each other, and they rode thus very quietly.

While in this position a sounding was obtained in
220 fathoms, the bottom being mud.

On the 11th, with a temporary lull in the wind, we
proceeded under steam, but on closing the Greenland
shore about Whale Sound, the southerly wind freshened
and obliged me to put the ships under sail.

The wet snow falling with a temperature of 34°
was very annoying; as it clung to each of the ropes
without actually melting, they became more than double
their original sizes, and only wanted the temperature
to fall below freezing point to cause great trouble in
working the sails.

It was now fairly dark at midnight, but fortunately
we met with few icebergs, except when within a distance of four miles of the land, and no floe-ice whatever.

On the 12th we experienced a southerly gale, with
very misty weather, and a rapidly falling barometer.
On standing towards the shore we made the land about
Barden Bay, and when under shelter of the hills I
steamed in to obtain an anchorage.

On entering we passed the dangerous rock, a-wash
at low-water, off Cape Powlett. It is apparently the
summit of a very extensive patch of rocky ground;
which is probably the terminal moraine of the glacier
which in former times existed in the neighbourhood.

On the northern side of the bay the level land
bordering the shore appeared to be well vegetated,
and on nearing the land we observed an inhabited
Eskimo encampment with seven natives and about a

dozen dogs. Finding no anchorage ground in less than forty-five fathoms, I ran into a bay on the south shore immediately west of the Tyndall Glacier. The side moraine near its end formed a steep ridge of rubble between a smooth pebbly beach in the bay and the glacier at the sea-level. In the north-east face we observed a large cave, whose sides displayed the

SMOOTH-TOPPED GLACIER IN BARDEN BAY.

richest tints of blue darkening to blackness as the depth of the cave receded to an unknown distance.

The extremely rugged and broken up surface and face of the Tyndall glacier, which projects far into the sea, is in remarkable contrast to the smooth surface and clean-cut perpendicular face of a smaller one near the mouth of the bay which projects only a short distance to seaward. We were extremely anxious to land, both to examine the very interesting glacier and to communi-

cate with the Arctic Highlanders, but the gale was
blowing so fiercely and the sea breaking so heavily
against the shore that it was dangerous to send a boat
away from the ship.

We looked forward to communicating with the
Eskimo early the following morning, and a number
of presents were prepared ; but during the night
the wind shifted round suddenly to the northward,
blowing directly into the bay. The low barometer,
thick snow-storm, dark night, and rocky shore compelled me to think more of the ships than the unfortunate Eskimo ; so expecting a strong gale from
the north, I steamed out to sea in order to obtain an
offing from the land.

We afterwards gladly learnt that Sir Allen Young
in the ' Pandora' had visited the same family only
a fortnight previously, and given them many valuable
presents.

Unsettled and misty weather prevented our communicating with the Cary Islands; the temperature
falling to 27° warning me to make our way south as
quickly as possible. The wind again coming from the
southward we crossed Baffin's Bay under sail, arriving
off Possession Bay on the south side of Lancaster
Sound at noon of the 16th. In crossing we met with
few icebergs and no floe-ice whatever. In misty
weather the numerous icebergs which are to be met
with close to the land between Cape York and Whale
Sound, would certainly warn ships of their proximity
to the shore.

Near Cape Atholl the temperature of the water
was 29°·5. This was unusually low, as we had found

it 31° and 30° farther north.   Half way across Baffin's
Bay, when abreast of Jones Sound, we met with a stream
of water fifty miles broad at a temperature of 34°,
which is evidently the extension northwards of the
warm Atlantic water.

I fully expected to find a strong current running
to the southward out of Lancaster Sound towards
Ponds Bay, but nothing of the kind was met with.

I accordingly decided to cross towards the Greenland shore in order to ensure rounding the north end of
the west-ice which, with the recent southerly gales, I
expected would be driven well to the northward.

Strong southerly winds continuing we were carried
towards Melville Bay, meeting with very few icebergs
and no drift ice.   The temperature of the water rose
to 35°, but fell again as we neared the Greenland
shore.   At noon of the 19th we were seventy miles
west of the Devil's Thumb.   A light northerly wind
then enabled us to make a direct course towards
Upernivik.

On the 20th and 21st southerly winds again obliged
me to put the ships under sail, our small supply of coal
rendering it prudent only to steam during a perfect
calm, and then for one ship to tow the other.

On the 22nd we met with the eastern edge of the
western pack, in latitude 71°·50 N., longitude 60°·18 W.
A temperature sounding obtained in its vicinity showed
that the temperature decreased gradually down to
29°·0 at a depth of twenty fathoms, it then gradually
increased to 30°·0 at the depth of a hundred fathoms.

As we neared the north entrance to the Waigat
Straits the temperature of the sea increased to 36°,

and off the Disco coast to 38°, that at a depth of forty-five fathoms being 32°·5.

On rounding the south-western point of Disco on the 25th we found the sea abounding in life : numerous finner whales, porpoises, and seals. Large flocks of eider ducks and dovekies in their winter plumage were feeding in this highly favoured locality.

On entering the well-known anchorage of Lievely we were warmly welcomed by our kind friends, Mr. and Mrs. Krärup Smith and Mr. and Mrs. Fencker, who informed us that the 'Pandora' had left for England only four days previously.

We remained two days at Disco, Mr. Smith kindly supplying us with a small quantity of coal. The weather felt to us extraordinarily mild, the temperature ranging from 40° to 48°. It appears that this harbour is never frozen over before the end of November, and is often open until January. Ships therefore need not fear when running for the port late in the season, or of making a passage to the southward if they keep in the warm stream near the Greenland shore.

Owing to the shortness and uncertainty of the cold season the settlement on the Whale Fish Islands has lately been abandoned. Thick ice certain to remain stationary affords a safer fishing-ground for the Eskimo than a warmer station with thin ice liable to be broken up.

At Disco the salmon fishing ends with the freezing of the shore lakes in October ; but cod can be procured all the winter.

Hans Heindrich and Frederick were landed at

Lievely, the few remaining dogs being given to them. These poor animals which had performed such good service during the travelling season had sickened much since we had experienced wet unsettled weather, and from their confinement on board during the passage south.

Hans was to remain at Disco until the following spring, when the ice would permit him to journey north and join his family at Proven.

Frederick in his excitement at returning home could scarcely find time to look after his own goods, but his numerous friends on board took care that he was not the loser ; with his many riches he has doubt-less long since found a wife.

On the 29th we arrived at Egedesminde, a well-protected anchorage at the south of Disco Bay.

The long and intricate passages between the nu-merous islets and rocks make it necessary for ships to have a pilot when entering and leaving the harbour.

Governor Bolbroe kindly supplied us with twenty tons of coal, but owing to a bad season he could only give us one haunch of venison : this was, however, suffi-cient for a meal for the former invalids, who by this time were, to all intents and purposes, well and strong. It was noticed that this venison possessed a musky flavour, especially the meat farthest from the bone.

Our visit to Egedesminde was rather opportune, as there were numerous cases of scurvy among the Eskimo and the few Europeans. I accordingly landed a large quantity of lime-juice and all the remaining private stock of sundries belonging to the officers, not the least acceptable present being a quantity of music, eau-de-cologne, and mittens, with which Mrs. Bolbroe, her children, and governess were supplied.

On the 2nd we bade adieu to our kind friends, and on the 4th recrossed the Arctic circle, after experiencing fifteen months' unnatural division of light and darkness.

Encountering a succession of strong contrary gales, very slow progress was made to the southward.

As the weather became warmer and damper many of the men were attacked by colds and rheumatism, after an almost total exemption from those ailments in the extremely cold but dry weather we had experienced in the far north.

Keeping near the Greenland coast only a few straggling icebergs were met with ; and floe-ice on only one occasion, when the wind had driven the ships over towards the west shore.

In Davis Strait the temperature of the water varied considerably, ranging between 33° and 39°, probably depending on our distance from the western ice.   The specific gravity in the cold streams denoted Polar water.

Vast numbers of little auks were observed migrating to the southward, in small flocks of about twenty to fifty in number, and many bottle-nose whales were seen.

On the 12th, during a very severe gale, in which the ships were hove-to under a close-reefed main topsail and storm staysail, the rudder-head of the ' Alert,' which had been sprung when the ship was in the ice, became hopelessly unserviceable, the lower part of the rudder remaining sound.

As the rudder pendants had necessarily been removed when the ship was amongst the ice, it was with no little difficulty that temporary ones were improvised; but by their means, and with careful attention to the trim of the sails, the ' Alert ' crossed the Atlantic.

On the 16th we fell in with the ' Pandora,' the only vessel met with during the voyage. The three ships kept company for two days, but on the night of the 19th we lost sight of each other during a strong gale.

On the 20th, in the middle of a very heavy storm, with the sea a mass of driving foam, the rudder pendants carried away; fortunately we were hove-to on the starboard tack. Before evening we succeeded in securing another pair, and during a lull in the wind bore up.

Expecting Captains Stephenson and Allen Young to be ahead, we made as much sail as possible; but it appeared afterwards that they also had been obliged to heave-to owing to the violence of the wind.

Not wishing to proceed up the English Channel under sail with a defective rudder, and the wind having driven us considerably to the northward, the ' Alert ' entered Valentia Harbour on the 27th of October; the ' Discovery ' arriving at Queenstown on the 29th. After shifting the rudder, the ' Alert ' proceeded to Queenstown, and the two ships having again joined company, entered Portsmouth Harbour on the 2nd of November; the ' Pandora ' arriving at Falmouth on the previous day.

I will not here dwell on the warm and hearty reception which the officers and men received from all classes of their countrymen, notwithstanding the somewhat natural disappointment that the North Pole had not been reached.

The Lords Commissioners of the Admiralty were pleased to express their warm approval of the conduct of all engaged in the Expedition, and we were honoured by receiving the following letter addressed to the First Lord of the Admiralty by direction of Her Most Gracious Majesty the Queen.

'BALMORAL: November 4, 1876.

'Dear Mr. Hunt,—

'I am commanded by the Queen to request that you will communicate to Captain Nares, and to the officers and men under his command, Her Majesty's hearty congratulations on their safe return.

'The Queen highly appreciates the valuable services which have been rendered by them in the late Arctic Expedition, and she fully sympathises in the hardships and sufferings they have endured, and laments the loss of life which has occurred.

'The Queen would be glad if her thanks could be duly conveyed to these gallant men for what they have accomplished.

'Yours very truly,

'HENRY F. PONSONBY.'

APPENDIX.

—⚬⚬⚬—

No. I.

ETHNOLOGY.[1]

By Henry W. Feilden, F.G.S., F.R.G.S., C.M.Z.S.

The Eskimo that inhabit the coasts of North Greenland between Cape York, the northern boundary of Melville Bay, and the Humboldt Glacier, are (with the exception perhaps of the natives of Ellesmere Land) the most northern inhabitants of our globe. These ἔσχατοι ἀνδρῶν were discovered by Captain Sir John Ross during his voyage to Baffin's Bay in 1818, and received from him the name of 'Arctic Highlanders,' an inappropriate designation for a people of purely littoral habits. The expedition of 1875–76 communicated with some of these people at Cape York on the voyage northwards ; but in July 1875 the village of Etah, on the north shore of Foulke Fiord, was found temporarily deserted. Etah is the most northern settlement of the Eskimo on the Greenland coast, and the one from where members of the tribe travel in their hunting expeditions as far north as the southern termination of the Humboldt Glacier, a little beyond lat. 79° N., where traces of ancient settlements were discovered by Dr. Kane in Dallas Bay. It has been assumed, somewhat too hastily, that the 'Arctic Highlanders' are a race completely isolated from any other human beings. From

---

[1] Extended from the 'Zoologist,' 1877, pp. 314–316.

information derived from one of the natives resident at Etah, the members of the ' Polaris ' Expedition [1]—who wintered 1872–73, in the vicinity of Port Foulke—ascertained that many Eskimo live in the neighbourhood of Cape Isabella, and along the coast of Ellesmere Land, their informant stating that it was called *Uming-muk Island*, from the number of musk-oxen that are found on it, and that he had frequently travelled round it himself.   Consequently the northern range of the natives of Ellesmere Land is in all probability equal to that of the Etah Eskimo.   There can be no doubt that there is casual, if not regular intercourse between the inhabitants of both sides of Smith Sound ; and one route, by which the migration of the Eskimo from North America to Greenland was effected, can be traced.   The narratives of Dr. Kane and Dr. Hayes, and more recently the official report of the ' Polaris ' Expedition, contain most interesting accounts of the habits and mode of life of the ' Arctic Highlanders ' ; and it is satisfactory to observe from the latest information that the number of this interesting community has in no way diminished during the last twenty years.

In 1875 we found at Cape Sabine, Ellesmere Land, the remains of several ancient Eskimo encampments, as well as an old sledge made of walrus bones, with cross-bars of narwhal horn, completely lichen-covered and of such antiquity that the bones were friable, and also fragments of a stone lamp ; but nearer to the shore were traces of a recent visit, consisting of a blackened fire-place, made of three stones placed against a rock, with the hairs of a white bear sticking to the grease-spots, a harpoon with iron tip, and the *excreta* of the dogs that had fed on the bear's hide.   Further north, on the shores of Buchanan Strait, we came upon deserted settlements containing the ruins of many *igloos* ; in one instance the ribs of a large cetacean had been used as the rafters of a hut ; bones of reindeer, musk-ox, bear, seal, and walrus were strewed around,

---

[1] Narr. ' Polaris,' North Polar Exp. (Washington, 1876), p. 477.

and we picked up many articles of human workmanship in bone, wood, and ivory. In Grinnell Land, still further north, we found that Norman Lockyer Island, in Franklin Pierce Bay, must at one time have been the home of numerous Eskimo. On August 11, 1875, I landed and walked along the northern shore of this island for some two miles; it was strewed with the bones of walrus, whilst skulls of this animal were lying about in hundreds, all broken more or less by human agency, in every instance the tusks having been extracted. Skulls of *Phoca barbata* and *Phoca hispida*, broken at the base in order to extract the brain, were numerous, and I came across large portions of the skeleton of a cetacean. Patches of green moss marked the sites of ancient dwellings, and circles of stones those of summer tents, whilst numerous stone *caches*, and cooking-places now overgrown with moss and lichen, but containing calcined bones, bore witness to the former presence of inhabitants. At Cape Harrison, on the western side of Franklin Pierce Bay, I observed two or three circles of stones placed on a terrace at a height of over 100 feet above present sea-level: this was the greatest elevation at which I observed remains of habitations on the shores of Smith Sound. At various other places in Grinnell Land, still further north, notably at Cape Hilgard, Cape Louis Napoleon, Cape Hayes, and Cape Frazer, we came across old traces of Eskimo. At Radmore Harbour, in lat. 80° 25′ N., we found the ruins of another large settlement, apparently as long deserted as the one on Norman Lockyer Island. After removing the green moss and overturning some of the stones that had once formed the walls of the *igloos*, several interesting ivory relics were discovered. On Bellot Island, at the entrance of Discovery Bay, lat. 81° 44′ N., were rings of lichen-covered stones that marked the sites of old encampments, fragments of bone and chips of drift-wood being strewn around. In the neighbourhood of Discovery Bay Dr. Moss, of H.M.S. ' Alert,' picked up the fragment of a human femur. A few miles south of Cape Beechey we found more circles of tent-stones; and near at hand a small heap of rock-crystals and flakes showed where the artificers in stone had been making arrow or harpoon heads. Close to Cape Beechey, and about six or seven miles from the eighty-second parallel of latitude, we came across the most northern traces of man that have yet been found; these consisted of the framework of a large wooden sledge, a stone lamp in good preservation, and a very perfect snow-scraper made out of a walrus tusk. Taking into consideration that where these relics were found is the narrowest part of Robeson Channel, at this point not more than thirteen miles across, and that a few miles to the south, on the opposite shore of Hall Land, the 'Polaris' Expedition found traces of summer encampments, I am inclined to believe that this must have been the spot selected for crossing over the channel; and owing probably to the difficult and dangerous nature of the ice to be encountered, the heavy sledge and *impedimenta* were left behind. On Offley Island, at the entrance of Petermann Fiord, Mr. Bryan [1] of the 'Polaris' found an old Eskimo settlement, consisting of the remains of several stone huts, whilst the ground around was strewed with the bleached bones of animals that had constituted the food of the inhabitants. Northwards from Cape Beechey no trace of man was discovered by any of our travelling parties, neither westward along the shores of Grinnell Land, nor eastward along the coasts of Greenland that border the Polar Sea. I feel satisfied that the men whose tracks we followed as far as lat. 82° N., never passed Cape Union. Even in July and August, animal life is too scarce along the shores of the Polar Sea to support a party of wandering Eskimo, whilst the idea of winter residence is beyond consideration. There is no essential reason why the Eskimo should have travelled around the northern shores of the Greenland continent in order to reach its eastern coast; the presence of the tribe seen by Sabine and Clavering on that side of Greenland may be accounted for by their having doubled Cape Farewell from the westward. It is well

---

[1] Narr. 'Polaris,' North Polar Exp., pp. 371–372.

known that formerly considerable numbers of Eskimo were living to the eastward of Cape Farewell, but year by year stragglers and small parties from these outside savages have re-entered the Danish colonies to the westward of the Cape, and have become absorbed amongst the civilised Greenlanders. This slow but steady return to the southward may account for the German Polar Expedition of 1869–70 not meeting with the Eskimo tribe seen by Sabine on the east coast. The result of our observations amounts to this, that along the shores of Smith Sound, Kennedy Channel, Hall Basin, and Robeson Channel, to a point three degrees north of the present extreme range of the Etah Eskimo, there are to be found not only traces of wanderings, but many proofs of former permanent habitation in places where, under present climatic conditions, it would be impossible for Eskimo to exist.

The abandonment by the Eskimo of these settlements in Grinnell Land and Greenland, as well as in the Parry Islands, is a subject of considerable interest. It points to a change in the physical conditions of an extensive area lying within the Arctic zone.

No. II.

MAMMALIA.[1]

By Henry W. Feilden, F.G.S., F.R.G.S., C.M.Z.S.

CARNIVORA.

1. Canis lupus (*Linn.*)—This animal was observed by the 'Polaris' Expedition in Hall Land on April 1, 1872.[2] Singularly enough, on the same day, 1876, several wolves made their appearance in the neighbourhood of the winter-quarters of the ' Alert.' They were evidently following a small herd of musk-oxen, whose tracks and traces were observed in the vicinity; and that they were able at times to secure these animals was shown by their dung being composed chiefly of musk-ox wool and splinters of bone. Several of our sportsmen started in pursuit of these wolves, but with one exception they did not allow anyone to approach them within three or four hundred yards. The following day, April 2, the wolves still continued in the neighbourhood of the ship, and at intervals their long, melancholy, but not unmusical wail reverberated from the hills. After this date we saw no more of these animals till May 25, when a single individual followed the sledge I was with for several days as we travelled along the coast. It was a most cunning beast, and eluded all our efforts to get a shot at it. Subsequently I procured a skull and part of the skeleton of one of these animals, which was picked up by a

---

[1] Extended from the 'Zoologist,' 1877, pp. 313-321, 353-361.

[2] Narr. ' Polaris,' North Polar Exp., p. 338.

sailor of the ship. This animal is infested by a species of *Tænia*.

2. VULPES LAGOPUS *(Linn.)*—The Arctic fox decreases in numbers as we proceed up Smith Sound. One was shot on the ice near Victoria Head, Grinnell Land, while prowling around the ship, and more than one specimen was obtained near the winter-quarters of the 'Discovery.' At Floeberg Beach, the winter-quarters of the 'Alert,' footprints of the fox were occasionally seen in the snow, but it was not till July 13, 1876, that I obtained a specimen in the flesh. On that occasion Lieutenant Parr and I were out on a hunting expedition, our tent being pitched at Dumbell Harbour, some miles north of Floeberg Beach, and from it we made daily incursions up the valleys leading to the uplands in hopes of meeting with big game. On the date above mentioned we had ascended to an altitude of 800 feet above the sea, and had emerged on a great plateau which stretched for several miles towards a range of mountains. All of a sudden we were startled by the sharp bark of a fox. A year had elapsed since we had heard such a sound. It seemed very close to us, and as the fog lifted we saw the animal standing on a little hill of piled-up rocks that rose like an islet from the plain. Separating, we approached the fox from opposite directions. Parr fired at it, when it dropped down and crawled below some large rocks; out rushed the female from its lair, and we secured her. The flora in the neighbourhood of this den was remarkably rich, the soil having been fertilised by the presence of the foxes. Several saxifrages, a *Stellaria*, a *Draba*, and two or three kinds of grasses were in bloom, and the yellow blossom of the *Potentilla* brightened the spot. As we rested there, many lemmings popped up from their holes, and undismayed by our presence, commenced feeding on the plants. We noticed that numerous dead lemmings were scattered around. In every case they had been killed in the same manner, the sharp canine teeth of the foxes had penetrated the brain. Presently we came upon two ermines killed in the same manner. These were joyful prizes, for up

to this time we had not obtained these animals in northern
Grinnell Land. Then to our surprise we discovered numerous
deposits of dead lemmings ; in one hidden nook under a rock
we pulled out a heap of over fifty. We disturbed numerous
‘ caches ’ of twenty and thirty, and the ground was honey-
combed with holes each of which contained several bodies of
these little animals, a small quantity of earth being placed over
them. In one hole we found the greater part of a hare hidden
away. The wings of young brent geese were also lying about ;
and as these birds were at that date only just hatching, it
showed that they must have been the results of successful
forays of prior seasons, and that consequently the foxes occupy
the same abodes from year to year. I had long wondered
how the Arctic fox existed during the winter. Professor
Newton had already suggested, in his ‘ Notes on the Zoology
of Spitsbergen,’[1] that it laid up a store of provisions, and I
was much pleased by thus being able to prove his theory
correct. Although I subsequently saw a second pair in the same
neighbourhood, yet the Arctic fox may be considered somewhat
rare in the northern part of Grinnell Land. The specimens
obtained did not differ in size from those killed further south.

3. MUSTELA ERMINEA (*Linn.*)—The ermine has followed
the lemming in its northern migrations to the shores of the
Polar Basin, and crossing Robeson Channel in pursuit of that
little rodent, it has invaded North Greenland, where Lieutenant Beaumont secured an example during his sledge journey in latitude 82° 15′ N. On the eastern shore of Greenland, where it was found by the Germans,[2] it doubtless
extends as far south as the range of the lemming. I obtained
specimens in Grinnell Land as far north as 82° 30′, and
several examples were shot near Discovery Bay. It is hunted
and killed by the Arctic fox. We noticed the tracks of this
little animal in the snow on the reappearance of sunlight, and
remarked that it is infested by a *Tænia.*

[1] ‘Proc. Zool. Soc.,’ 1864, p. 496.
[2] ‘Zweite Deutsch. Nordpolarf.’ II. p. 159.

4. URSUS MARITIMUS (*Linn.*)—There is little to tempt the Polar bear to leave the comparatively rich hunting-fields of the north-water of Baffin's Bay for the dreary shores of Smith Sound and northward. A single example was killed near Bessels' Bay by Joe the Eskimo[1] in 1872, and footmarks were observed by members of our expedition near Thank God Harbour and in the neighbourhood of Cape Hayes. At the present day I do not imagine the white bear ever enters the Polar Basin through Robeson Channel. The cranium of a very large example was found by Captain Markham on the northern shores of Grinnell Land in latitude 82° 30′ N., some distance from present high-water level. I think it is not improbable that this skull may have been washed out of the post-pliocene deposits which fill up the valleys of that region to an altitude of several hundred feet, and which contain the remains of seal, musk-ox, and other animals, with abundance of drift-wood, and the shells of most of the mollusca now inhabiting the adjacent sea. If I am right in this surmise, there is no saying from what distance or from what direction this cranium may have been brought on an ice-raft.

5. PHOCA HISPIDA (*Schreb.*)—The ringed seal was met with in most of the bays we entered during our passage up and down Smith Sound. It was the only species seen north of Cape Union, and which penetrates into the Polar Sea. Lieutenant Aldrich, during his autumn sledging in 1875, noticed a single example in a pool of water near Cape Joseph Henry, and a party which I accompanied in September 1875, secured one in Dumbell Harbour, some miles north of the winter-quarters of the 'Alert;' its stomach contained remains of crustaceans and annelids. In June of the following year I observed three or four of these animals on the ice of Dumbell Harbour. They had made holes in the bay ice that had formed in this protected inlet. The Polar pack was at this time of the year still firmly wedged against the shores of Grinnell Land, and so tightly packed in Robeson Channel

---

[1] Narr. 'Polaris,' North Polar Exp., p. 349.

that no seal could by any possibility have worked its way
into this inlet from outside. I am therefore quite satisfied
that *Phoca hispida* is resident throughout the year in the
localities mentioned. A female killed on August 23, 1876,
weighed sixty-five pounds.

6. PHOCA BARBATA (*Fab.*)—On several occasions while
proceeding up Smith Sound I observed this large seal. We
did not see it north of Robeson Channel. Individuals were
procured in Discovery Bay, lat. 81° 44′ N., and also at Thank
God Harbour, from whence it has been recorded by Dr.
Bessels. I found the skulls of this animal in the ancient
Eskimo settlements of Smith Sound. On August 31, 1876,
Hans, the Greenlander on board the 'Discovery,' shot one of
these seals in Dobbin Bay. I was informed that it weighed
510 pounds. On taking off its skin an Eskimo harpoon was
found buried in the blubber on its back ; the socket of the
dart was made of ivory, the blade being wrought iron. Hans
pronounced it to be a Greenland harpoon-head, and suggested
that the animal had been struck in the Danish settlements.
P. grœnlandica is recorded by Dr. Bessels[1] from Thank
God Harbour, but I did not observe it in Smith Sound or
northwards.

7. TRICHECUS ROSMARUS (*Linn.*)—Kane and Hayes describe the walrus as very abundant in the vicinity of Port
Foulke, and the Eskimo of Etah must capture a great
number of them, as many skulls and bones of this animal are
strewed about their settlement, which we found deserted in
July 1875. Curiously enough, we did not see one of these
animals in the vicinity of Port Foulke nor in Smith Sound,
until we reached Franklin Pierce Bay. There, in the vicinity
of Norman Lockyer Island, we saw several walruses, and
killed two or three. Their stomachs contained fragments of
Mya and *Saxicava*, and a considerable quantity of a green
oily matter. Near Cape Frazer I saw a single walrus, but as
far as my observation goes, it does not proceed further north

---

[1] 'Bulletin de la Société de Géographie,' 1875, p. 200.

than the meeting of the Baffin's Bay and Polar tides near the above-mentioned cape.

CETACEA.

8. BALÆNA MYSTICETUS (*Linn.*)—A portion of the rib of a Greenland whale was found by Lieutenant Egerton on the northern shores of Grinnell Land, in lat. 82° 33′ N. It was of great antiquity, but I am unprepared to advance any opinion as to how it got there. I am, however, quite satisfied on one point, and that is, no whale could inhabit at the present day the frozen sea to the north of Robeson Channel. To penetrate thither from the north-water of Baffin's Bay would be a hazardous task for this great animal, and in this opinion the experienced whaling quarter-masters who accompanied our Expedition coincided. We may dismiss from our minds the idea or hope that nearer to the Pole, and beyond the limits of present discovery, there may be haunts in the Polar Sea suitable for the right whale. I do not look for the speedy extinction of the Greenland whale ; but it is probable that in a few years the fishing will no longer prove profitable to the fine fleet of whalers that now sail from our northern ports, and I see no hope of Arctic discovery increasing our knowledge of the range of this animal.

9. MONODON MONOCEROS (*Linn.*)—During the month of August, while we were waiting in Payer Harbour, near Cape Sabine, we noticed several narwhals playing at the edge of the ice, but we saw no more of them after entering the pack of Smith Sound. The range of the narwhal in that direction is no doubt coincident with the summer extension of the north-water of Baffin's Bay. It is not included by Dr. Bessels among the animals of Hall Land. An ancient tusk of the narwhal was picked up by Lieutenant Parr on the shore of Grinnell Land, a little above the present sea-level, a few miles to the north of the winter quarters of the ' Alert.'

UNGULATA.

10. RANGIFER TARANDUS (*Linn.*)—The reindeer was not actually met with by our Expedition to the northward of Port Foulke, but its newly-shed horns were found in the Valley of the Twin Glacier, Buchanan Strait. I came across a skeleton recently picked by wolves in the neighbourhood of Radmore Harbour, lat. 80° 27′ N. At various points along the coast of Grinnell Land, further north, we came upon shed antlers, but these may have been of considerable antiquity, whilst Lieutenant Giffard found and brought to the ship a portion of an antler which he picked up in lat. 82° 45′ N. The horns of a reindeer were found at Thank God Harbour, by one of the 'Polaris' Expedition in June 1872.[1]

11. OVIBOS MOSCHATUS (*Zimm.*)—The fossil remains of *Ovibos* found in Siberia, North America, Germany, France and England have been determined by naturalists as identical with the species now found living in the northern regions of the American continent and the northern and eastern shores of Greenland, whilst most of the larger mammalia of the Pleistocene period, with which the musk-ox was associated, have passed away. The musk-ox, being truly an Arctic mammal, doubtless travelled northward as the glacial cold diminished; but in Europe and Asia it found its limit of withdrawal bounded by the mainlands of the Old World. No trace of it has been discovered in Spitsbergen or Franz Joseph Land; and the reasonable conclusion is that the great extent of sea which separates these groups of islands from the continents, formed an insuperable obstacle to its progress in that direction. Doubtless its remains are to be found in the New Siberian Islands, and there is no valid reason why it should not still inhabit Kellett Land. So far as we know, however, the musk-ox living on the Arctic shores of Asia had no inaccessible re-

---

[1] Narr. 'Polaris,' North Polar Exp., p. 378

treats analogous to the Parry Archipelago of America, and consequently when brought into collision with man must have quickly disappeared. Towards the close of the last Glacial period, when the Straits of Behring were doubtless as choked with ice as the passage now is between Banks' Land and Melville Island, there could have been no great obstacle to prevent the passage of the musk-ox from the Old World to the New; but whether its course of migration was from Asia to America, or contrariwise, there can be no question that on the latter continent it found a congenial home. Its remains have been discovered in greater or less quantities from Escholtz Bay on the west to the shores of Lancaster Sound, whilst the animal still inhabits the Barren-lands of the American continent. Even in this wilderness, sparsely inhabited by Eskimo, its southern range is slowly contracting, whilst, according to Richardson, the Mackenzie River is now its western limit. Melville Island and other lands to the north of the American continent have proved a safe asylum to the musk-ox, and there it will continue to propagate its species, undisturbed save by the casual appearance of Arctic voyagers. From the islands of the Parry group its range northwards across the eightieth parallel into Ellesmere and Grinnell Land, as high as the eighty-third parallel to the shores of the Polar Sea, is extremely natural; and Robeson Channel, which has presented no obstacle to the progress of the lemming and ermine, has also been crossed by the musk-ox, the 'Polaris' Expedition as well as ours finding it in Hall Land. After crossing the strait between the American islands and Greenland, the musk-ox appears to have followed the coasts both in a northerly and southerly direction, its range in Greenland to the southward being stopped by the great glaciers of Melville Bay. At one time it must have been abundant on the West Greenland coast as far south as the seventy-eighth parallel, for Dr. Kane found numerous remains in the vicinity of Rensselaer Bay, and Dr. Hayes found a skull in Chester Valley at the head of Foulke Fiord. During the single day we explored in the neighbourhood of that locality two skulls were found by members of our Expedition. The destruction of these animals would, I think, rapidly follow on the appearance of the Eskimo at Port Foulke; for I imagine few animals are less fitted to elude the wiles of the hunter. There can be no question that the musk-oxen found by the Germans on the east coast of Greenland are descendants of those that crossed Robeson Channel, rounded the north of the Greenland continent, and extended their range southward until they met with some physical obstruction that barred their further progress, as has also been the case on the western shore of Greenland. Dr. Robert Brown, in his ' Essay on the Physical Structure of Greenland,' published by the Geographical Society for the use of the recent Arctic Expedition, thus refers to this range of the musk-ox, lemming and ermine : ' These illustrations, though seemingly trivial in themselves, are yet of extreme zoo-geographical interest as tending to show that the Greenland land must end not far north of latitude 82° or 83°.' In the month of August, 1875, we met with abundant traces of the musk-ox in the valley of the Twin Glacier, leading inland from the shores of Buchanan Strait. I noticed where these animals had been sheltering themselves under the lee of big boulders, as sheep do on bleak hill-sides, and that the same spots were frequently occupied was shown by the holes tramped out by the animals, and the large quantities of their long soft wool which was scattered around. Musk-oxen were obtained in considerable numbers near to the winter-quarters of the ' Discovery,' over forty being shot ; but in the extreme north of Grinnell Land, nearer to the winter-quarters of the ' Alert,' they were much scarcer, only six having been obtained by the crew of that vessel, whilst at Thank God Harbour, where the ' Polaris ' Expedition obtained over a score, only one was seen and shot. The range of the musk-ox in Grinnell Land is confined to the coast-line and the valleys debouching thereon. It is an animal by no means fitted to travel through the deep soft snow which blocks up the heads of all these valleys. On one occasion, in Westward Ho ! Valley, in the month of May, Lieutenant Egerton and I came across fresh tracks of this animal in soft snow, through which it had sunk belly-deep, ploughing out a path, and leaving fragments of wool behind in its struggles. Its progression under such circumstances is similar to that of a snow-plough. We noticed that spots on hill-sides where the snow lay only a few inches deep had been selected for feeding grounds, the snow having been pushed away in furrows banked up at the end, as if the head and horns of the animal had been used for the task; a few blades of grass and roots of willow showed on what they had been feeding. The dung of the musk-ox, though usually dropped in pellets like sheep or deer, is very often undistinguishable from that of the genus *Bos*. No person, however, watching this animal in a state of nature, could fail to see how essentially ovine are its actions. When alarmed they gather together like a flock of sheep herded by a collie dog, and the way in which they pack closely together and follow blindly the vacillating leadership of the old ram is unquestionably sheep-like. When thoroughly frightened they take to the hills, ascending precipitous slopes, and scaling rocks with great agility. How the musk-ox obtains food during the long Arctic night is very extraordinary; but that it is a resident throughout the year cannot be doubted, as a month after the reappearance of sunlight, in the end of March, and at the very coldest season of the year, we found the fresh traces of these animals in the vicinity of our winter-quarters. I am quite sure that the number of musk-oxen in Grinnell Land is extremely limited, whilst the means of subsistence can only supply the wants of a fixed number; consequently, after an invasion such as ours, when every animal obtainable was slaughtered for food, it must take some years to restock the ground. The cause of the disagreeable odour which frequently taints the flesh of these animals has received no elucidation from my observations. It does not appear to be confined to either sex, or to any particular season of the year; for a young unweaned animal killed at its mother's side, and transferred within an hour

to the stew-pans, was rank and objectionable, whilst the flesh
of some adult animals of both sexes of which I have partaken,
was dark, tender and well-flavoured.   Richardson states that
the food of the musk-ox is at one season of the year grass,
at another lichen.   Only leaves and stems of willow, with
grasses, were in the stomachs I examined.   This animal is
infested with two species of worms, a *Tænia* and a *Filaria.*

GLIRES.

12.   MYODES TORQUATUS (*Pall.*)—The ringed lemming
was found in great abundance along the western shores of
Smith Sound, and was traced by our explorers to lat. 83° N.,
and to the extreme western point attained.   On the Greenland shore it was found by members of our Expedition at
Thank God Harbour, where it had previously been obtained
by Dr. Bessels,[1] and traces of it were noticed by our sledge
parties who travelled along the northern shores of Greenland.
There can be no doubt that the eastern migration of this
animal has been across Robeson Channel and around the north
coast of Greenland to Scoresby Sound on the east coast, from
which locality this animal was brought by Captain Scoresby
in 1822.   Apparently its southern range on the west coast of
Greenland is stopped by the great Humboldt Glacier.   This
lemming is a great wanderer ; we found it on the floes of
Robeson Channel at considerable distances from land, sometimes in a very exhausted state, but generally dead.   Its
habit of leaving the shore and wandering over the ice fully
accounts for the skeleton of one of this species being found on
a floe in lat. 81° 45′ N., sixty miles from Spitsbergen, by Sir
J. C. Ross during Parry's memorable attempt to reach the
North Pole in 1827.[2]   We are indebted to Dr. von Middendorff for an excellent account of the anatomy and external

---

[1] 'Bulletin de la Société de Géographie,' 1875, p. 296.
[2] 'Narr. Attempt to reach North Pole' (Parry), p. 190.

characters of this lemming.[1]   He was able to show that the
extraordinary development of the claws of the fore-feet which
is sometimes observed, is not a specific character, nor due to
age or sex, but he could not determine whether it was
seasonal, as specimens with such claws were known in both
winter and summer coats.   The series which I collected in
Grinnell Land enables me to determine this point.   The
strap-like development of the claws persists in these latitudes
during the greater part of the year, while the ground is
covered with snow, and is thus retained for some time after
the animal has put on the summer livery.   But by the end of
summer, when large areas are bared of snow, the claws are worn
down to an ordinary size and become pointed.   This seasonal
development is, in fact, analogous to what we find in some of
the northern *Tetraonidæ*.   The food of this lemming consists
of vegetable substances, especially the buds of *Saxifraga
oppositifolia*.   It makes nests of grass in the snow, which we
often found during summer as the snow thawed ; in most
cases large accumulations of the dung of these animals were
lying close to the nests.   I see no reason to suppose that this
animal hybernates, for on the return of light, with a temperature at minus 50° and a deep mantle of snow covering
the land, the lemming was to be seen on the surface of the
snow, close to its burrow, blinking at the first rays of the
sun ; and during the depths of winter there could be no
greater difficulty in procuring food than in February.   At
that season of the year I found the stomach of the lemming filled with green buds of saxifrage, which had been
gathered from under the snow.   Sometimes I came across
the lemming at some distance from the hole by which it
retreats to its galleries under the snow, and it was interesting to see the speed with which it could disappear,
throwing itself on its head, its fore-paws worked with great
rapidity, rotating outwards, and throwing up a cloud of
snow-dust some six inches high.   Later on in the year I

---

[1] 'Reise Sibir.,' II. Th. 2, pp. 87–99, pls. IV.–VII.

have seen a lemming baffle the attempts at capture of a long-tailed skua by the same tactics. The female brings forth from three to five at a birth in June and July, making a comfortable nest of grass for their reception.

13. LEPUS GLACIALIS (*Leach*).—The Polar hare was found, though in scanty numbers, along the shores of Grinnell Land, and its footprints were seen on the snow-clad ice of the Polar Sea by Captain Markham and Lieutenant Parr in lat. 83° 10′ N., a distance of about twenty miles north of the nearest land. In the autumn of 1875 three or four examples were shot in the neighbourhood of our winter-quarters, lat. 82° 27′ N., and as soon as a glimmer of light enabled us to make out their tracks in the snow we were off. in pursuit of them. On February 14, two weeks before the sun reappeared at midday, the temperature minus 56°, I started one from its burrow, a hole about four feet in length, scraped horizontally into a snowdrift. I have no doubt the same burrow is regularly occupied, as this one was discoloured by the feet of the animal, and a quantity of hair was sticking to the sides; all around the hare had been scratching up the snow and feeding on *Saxifraga oppositifolia*. Even where exposed by the wind, this hardy plant had delicate green buds showing on the brown withered surface of the last year's growth. The hare does not tear up this plant by the roots, but nibbles off the minute green shoots. On February 19, a hare was shot by Dr. Moss; it was a male, and weighed nine pounds and a half; and another was obtained on the 20th. On May 18, at Westward Ho! Valley, I shot two hares, one was a female and contained eight young ones. By the end of July the young were nearly as large as their parents, and were pure white, save the tips of the ears, which were mouse-grey, with a small streak of the same colour passing down from the apex of the head to the snout. The adults have the ears tipped with black. The number of young that we found in gravid females varied from seven to eight, which is much in excess of that produced in Great Britain by *Lepus variabilis*, from which naturalists have found difficulty in separating

the Arctic species.[1] Fabricius[2] records the fact of this animal
in Greenland having eight young ones. Near Lincoln Bay,
in lat. 82° 8′ N., a hare was shot on August 31, 1875, with a
very distorted skull, the nasal bones being twisted to the
right hand, the incisors of the upper jaw being deflected in
the same direction. In the lower jaw only the left incisor
was developed, and that · protruded in a nearly horizontal
direction. This specimen, though in good condition, was
small, and weighed only five pounds and a half; another,
killed the same day, nine pounds. They were both pure white,
with the tips of the ear black. We find, therefore, *Lepus
glacialis* inhabiting the most northern land yet visited, and
attaining its normal weight, eight to ten pounds, under
apparently very adverse circumstances. Still I must say it is
sparsely diffused, and we found that after killing a pair or
two out of each valley that afforded any vegetation the race
seemed to be extirpated in that district, and I imagine it will
take several years to restock the area over which we hunted
along the northern shore of Grinnell Land. Examples examined
by me contained many parasitical worms, *Filaria*, in the large
intestine.

[1] On the specific distinction of the Polar hare, cf. Peters; 2te.
Deutsch. Nordpolarf. II. pp. 164-7.

[2] 'Fauna Grœnlandica,' p. 25.

No. III.

ORNITHOLOGY.[1]

By Henry W. Feilden, F.G.S., F.R.G.S., C.M.Z.S.

The species of birds met with by the Arctic Expedition in Smith Sound and northward, between the seventy-eighth and eighty-third degrees of north latitude, are well known Polar forms, and the chief interest lies in the record of their great northern extension in the western hemisphere. The only other part of the globe lying within nearly the same parallels of latitude with which we are well acquainted is Spitsbergen; and though that group of islands has been frequently visited by naturalists, yet the number of species of birds, including stragglers, at present known to have occurred there is under thirty. Were I to include in this list species recorded by Dr. Bessels[2] from Thank God Harbour, not met with by me, the list of the avifauna of Smith Sound and Spitsbergen would be about numerically equal: thus according, as far as numbers are concerned, with the opinion published before the Expedition left England by Professor Newton[3] of Cambridge; and, except amongst those

[1] Condensed from 'The Ibis,' 1877, pp. 401–412.

[2] 'Bulletin de la Société de Géographie,' 1875, pp. 206–207. Twenty-three species are included by Dr. Bessels in this list from Hall Land. Of these, three species, *Tringa maritima*, *Xema Sabini*, and *Stercorarius parasiticus* (Baird), were not obtained by me. On the other hand four species, viz.: *Ægialitis hiaticula*, *Phalaropus fulicarius*, *Tringa canutus*, and a *Colymbus*, observed by me, are additional to Dr. Bessels' list, thus raising the aggregate of the species recorded from Smith Sound and northward, to twenty-seven.

[3] 'Arctic Manual,' p. 114, 1875.

sanguine persons who may still cling to a belief in the existence of an ' open Polar Sea,' I think it is impossible to doubt that, both specifically and numerically, bird-life must rapidly decrease with every degree of northern latitude after passing the eighty-second parallel. If, however, there be an extension of land to the northernmost part of our globe, I see no reason why a few species of birds should not resort there to breed ; and those most likely to proceed there are *Plectrophanes nivalis, Strepsilas interpres, Calidris arenaria, Tringa canutus,* and *Sterna macrura.* There would still be sufficient summer, if such a term may be used, for the period of incubation ; and from what I have seen of the transporting powers of the wind in drifting seeds over the frozen expanse of the Polar Sea, I cannot doubt that a scanty flora exists at the Pole itself, if there be any land there, and that the abundance of insect-life which exists as high as the eighty-third degree will be present at the ninetieth, sufficient to provide for a few knots, sanderlings, and turn-stones. The Arctic Sea at the most northern point reached abounds with Amphipoda, such as *Anonyx nugax,* which doubtless extend all through the Polar Basin ; and these crustaceans supply the Arctic tern with food in those parts where the continual presence of ice prevents fish coming to the surface ; for wherever there is land not cased in perennial ice, there must be tidal ice-cracks, which allow these minute animals to work their way up between the floes. The range of the brent-goose is probably coincident with the growth of *Saxifraga oppositifolia* ; and this plant also supplies subsistence to the knot, the turnstone, and the sanderling, before the long Arctic day has awakened the insect-life.

Dr. Horner, of the yacht ' Pandora,' kindly informed me that in July 1876 he saw an example of *Saxicola œnanthe* at Port Foulke, a far more northern range of this species than had previously been recorded.

I was much struck with the extreme shyness of all the birds we met with in the far north ; and until they had

settled down to nesting it was no easy matter to get within
gunshot range.

1. FALCO CANDICANS.—The Greenland falcon, though seen
on several occasions, was not procured by us in Smith Sound.
Mr. Hart noticed a pair of these birds nesting in the limestone cliffs near Cape Hayes, Grinnell Land (lat. 79° 42′ N.),
but was unable to secure a specimen. From this point to
our most northern extreme this falcon was not observed by
any member of the Expedition. On August 24, 1876, near
Cape Frazer (lat. 79° 44′ N.), when on our return southwards, a bird of this species flew round our vessels. The
following morning, when on shore between Cápe Hayes and
Cape Napoleon, I saw a magnificent example of *F. candicans*
seated on a rock; it permitted me to get within seventy
or eighty yards, but I failed in procuring it.

2. NYCTEA SCANDIACA.—The snowy owl is a common
spring and summer migrant to the northern part of Grinnell
Land. On October 2, 1875, I observed an individual of this
species seated on a hummock in the vicinity of our winter-
quarters (lat. 82° 27′ N.). On March 29, 1876, an example
was seen by Lieutenant Parr some three miles north of the
ship. On May 15, whilst travelling up a valley (lat. 82° 40′ N.)
in Grinnell Land, our party disturbed a snowy owl from the
ground. Subsequently this species was not unfrequently
observed; a pair seemed commonly to breed in each large
valley running down to the sea-shore. On June 24 we found
a snowy owl's nest containing seven eggs (lat. 82° 33′ N.);
the nest was a mere hollow scooped out of the earth, and
situated on the summit of an eminence which rose from the
centre of the valley. Several other nests were found in the
vicinity of our winter-quarters, at one time there were six or
seven fine young birds caged on board. In the vicinity of
Discovery Bay (lat. 81° 44′ N.) this owl bred abundantly.
During the month of August, while proceeding southwards,
it was no uncommon circumstance to see one or more of
these birds occupying a conspicuous post on the bold headlands we were passing under. By the end of the month all

had disappeared. The food of the snowy owl in Grinnell Land appears to consist entirely of the lemming (*Myodes torquatus*). Hundreds of their cast pellets, which I picked up and examined, consisted of the bones and fur of these little animals ; and the stomachs of all I opened contained the same.

3. PLECTROPHANES NIVALIS.—After passing the seventy-eighth degree of north latitude the snow-bunting is not met with in the same numbers as in the neighbourhood of the Danish settlements of West Greenland, but it is dispersed generally along the shores of Smith Sound and the Polar Basin. On August 28, 1875, at Shift-Rudder Bay (lat. 81° 52′ N.), I observed a flock of about eighty, and another, in which I counted over twenty birds, flying south. On September 14, Lieutenant Parr met with a solitary individual in lat. 82° 35′ N.; and the last one I observed that season flew past the ship on September 24.

Next spring I first heard this bird when travelling on May 13, 1876, in lat. 82° 35′ N.; the following day I observed one ; and after that day they were frequently met with. On May 27, Lieutenant Parr, on his journey from the north over the ice, saw a snow-bunting near to the eighty-third degree. I found a nest of this species on June 24 (lat. 82° 33′ N.), containing four eggs, within twenty feet of the nest of a snowy owl; it was neatly constructed of grasses, and lined with the owl's feathers. On another occasion I found a nest lined with the soft wool of the musk-ox.

4. CORVUS CORAX.—A pair of ravens were observed by Dr. Coppinger to be nesting in the cliffs of Cape Lupton during the month of July. While this officer was detained at Polaris Bay by the sickness of some of the sledge-crews, he noticed these birds visit his camp daily in search of offal. The raven was not observed by any of our Expedition along the shores of the Polar Basin ; so that I consider Cape Lupton (lat. 81° 44′ N.) the northernmost settlement of this species. August 29, 1876, at Dobbin Bay (lat. 79° 36′ N.), a female,

one of a pair, was shot by Dr. Moss, who enticed it within range by laying down a dead hare and concealing himself near at hand. South of Dobbin Bay I observed this species at several points in Smith Sound—namely, at Cape Hayes, Norman Lockyer Island, and Cape Sabine.

5. LAGOPUS RUPESTRIS.—The rock-ptarmigan was obtained by our sledging parties as far north as 82° 46′, two or three couples having been killed by me in the end of May on Feilden Peninsula. Lieutenant Aldrich found traces of ptarmigan on Cape Columbia (lat. 83° 6′ N.), the most northern land yet visited by man. On September 29, 1875, Captain Markham, in lat. 82° 40′ N., observed four of these birds; and the earliest date on which they were noticed in the spring of 1876 was on March 11.

6. STREPSILAS INTERPRES.—The turnstone is tolerably abundant in Smith Sound and the region north of it visited by the Expedition. It was observed as late as September 5, 1875, in lat. 82° 30′ N., and was first noticed on June 5, 1876, in the neighbourhood of the winter-quarters of H.M.S. 'Alert.' By August 12 the young broods were able to fly.

7. ÆGIALITIS HIATICULA.—Only a single example of the ringed-plover was observed in Smith Sound. It was obtained August 4, 1875, on the beach bordering the valley of the Twin-Glacier, in Buchanan Strait (lat. 78° 48′ N.) My attention was drawn to the bird by its note; and I then observed it threading its way among the stones and stranded blocks of ice near the water's edge. It was probably nesting in the neighbourhood, as it proved on examination to be a female, with the feathers worn off the underparts from incubation.

8. CALIDRIS ARENARIA (Plate I.)—I first observed the sanderling in Grinnell Land on June 5, 1876, flying in company with knots and turnstones; at this date it was feeding, like the other waders, on the buds of *Saxifraga oppositifolia*. This bird was by no means abundant along the coasts of Grinnell Land; but I observed several pairs in the aggregate, and found a nest of this species containing two eggs, in

EGGS OF CALIDRIS ARENARIA.

lat 82° 33′ N., on June 24, 1876. This nest, from which I killed the male bird, was placed on a gravel ridge at an altitude of several hundred feet above the sea ; and the eggs were deposited in a slight depression in the centre of a recumbent plant of willow, the lining of the nest consisting of a few withered leaves and some of the last year's catkins. August 8, 1876, along the shores of Robeson Channel, I saw several parties of young ones, three to four in number, following their parents, and led by the old birds, searching most diligently for insects. At this date they were in a very interesting stage of plumage, being just able to fly, but retaining some of the down on their feathers.

9. PHALAROPUS FULICARIUS.—I obtained an example of the grey phalarope, a female, near the ' Alert's ' winter-quarters (lat. 82° 27′ N.) on June 30, 1876 ; and during the month of July I observed a pair on a small fresh-water pond in lat. 82° 30′ N.; they were apparently breeding. The female of this species is larger and brighter-coloured than the male bird. Several other examples were observed in the neighbourhood of our winter-quarters by various members of the Expedition.

10. TRINGA CANUTUS.—I was not so fortunate as to obtain the eggs of the knot during our stay in the Polar regions, though it breeds in some numbers along the shores of Smith Sound and the north coast of Grinnell Land. It appears to be common throughout the Parry Islands during summer, as Sabine found it (in 1820) nesting in great numbers on Melville Island. I find it enumerated, in a list of birds preserved in the archives of the Admiralty, as procured by Dr. Anderson, of H.M.S. ' Enterprise,' at Cambridge Bay (lat. 69° 10′ N.) in July 1853. On July 28, 1875, Dr. Coppinger came across a party of six knots several miles inland from Port Foulke : these birds were feeding near a rill, and were very wild ; but he managed to secure a single specimen, a male in full breeding-plumage. August 25, 1875, I observed several of these birds near the water-edge

in Discovery Bay (lat. 81° 44′ N.) The rills and marshes
were by this time frozen, and the birds were feeding along
the shore on the small crustaceans so common in the Arctic
Sea; in pursuit of their food they ran breast-high into the
water. By this date they had lost their breeding-plumage.
On June 5, 1876, when camped near Knot Harbour, Grinnell
Land (lat. 82° 33′ N.), we noticed the first arrival of these
birds; a flock of fourteen or more were circling over a hill-
side, alighting on bare patches, and feeding eagerly on the
buds of *Saxifraga oppositifolia.* Subsequently we met with
this bird in considerable numbers; but they were always very
wild and most difficult of approach. The cry of the knot is
wild, and something like that of the curlew. Immediately
after arrival in June they began to mate, and at times I
noticed two or more males following a single female; at this
season they soar in the air, like the common snipe, and when
descending from a height beat their wings behind the back
with a rapid motion, which produces a loud whirring noise.
During the month of July my companions and I often
endeavoured to discover the nest of this bird; but none of us
were successful. However, on July 30, 1876, the day before
we broke out of our winter-quarters, where we had been
frozen-in eleven months, three of our seamen, walking by the
border of a small lake, not far from the ship, came upon an
old bird accompanied by three nestlings, which they brought
to me. The old bird proved to be a male; its stomach and
those of the young ones were filled with insects. The
following description of the newly-hatched birds was taken
down at the time:—Iris, black; tip of mandibles, dark
brown; bill, dark olive; toes, black; soles of feet, greenish
yellow; back of legs, the same; underpart of throat, satin-
white; back, beautifully mottled tortoise-shell. Dr. Coppinger informed me that this bird was not uncommon at
Thank God Harbour during July. In the first week of
August I saw family parties of knots at Shift-Rudder Bay
(lat. 81° 52′ N.); they were then in the grey autumn plumage. The knot bred in the vicinity of Discovery Bay; but

no eggs were found there, although the young were obtained in all stages of plumage.

11. STERNA MACRURA.—The Arctic tern is not uncommon in Smith Sound, and we found it breeding at several localities we visited on our way north. On August 11, 1875, on Norman Lockyer Island, I noticed several pairs, and picked up a bleached egg, probably an addled one of a former season. August 21, we found eight or ten pairs breeding on a small islet off the north end of Bellot Island (lat. 81° 44′ N.); the land at this date was covered with snow, and on the islet it lay about three inches deep. In one nest I found a newly-hatched tern; it seemed quite well and lively in its snow cradle. The parent birds had evidently thrown the snow out of the nest as it fell; for it was surrounded by a border of snow marked by the feet of the old birds, and raised at least two inches above the general level. The terns on this islet were rather shy, none coming within range until I touched the young one. There seemed to be abundance of fish in the pools between the floes, as the old birds were flying with them in their mandibles; the stomach of the female which I killed was empty, but that of the nestling contained remains of fish. On June 16, 1876, three Arctic terns appeared in the neighbourhood of the winter-quarters of the 'Alert.' By the end of June pairs of these birds were scattered at intervals along the coast; and a nest, scraped in the gravel and containing two eggs, was found June 27 about three miles north of our winter-quarters. During the first week in August we found a pair of young birds nearly ready to fly in lat. 81° 50′ N.

12. PAGOPHILA EBURNEA.—The ivory gull was not unfrequently observed in Smith Sound, but not beyond lat. 82° 20′ N. I found a pair nesting in a lofty and inaccessible cliff near Cape Hayes on August 16, 1875. On September 1 a single example flew around the 'Alert' when she lay moored to the ice in Lincoln Bay (lat. 82° 6′ N.) On August 2, 1876, I observed one of this species near Cape Union; on August 12 they were common in Discovery

Bay, and from there southward to the north-water of Baffin's Bay.

13. RISSA TRIDACTYLA.—I saw a few examples of the kittiwake flying over the open water in the vicinity of Port Foulke, July 28, 1875; but we did not observe it to the northward after entering the ice of Smith Sound; and in 1876 no specimen was seen as the Expedition returned south until the north-water of Baffin's Bay was reached.

14. LARUS GLAUCUS.—We did not find the glaucous gull breeding north of Cape Sabine; but stray individuals were observed as far north as lat. 82° 34′. September 1, 1875, was the latest date in the autumn on which I noticed this species; and it reappeared in the vicinity of our winter-quarters (lat. 82° 27′ N.) in the middle of June.

15. STERCORARIUS PARASITICUS.—Buffon's skua was the only one of the genus met with in Smith Sound. It arrived in the neighbourhood of our winter-quarters during the first week of June, and in considerable numbers. After that date it was to be seen during every hour of the day quartering the fells in search of lemmings. It lays its two eggs in a small hollow in the ground, and defends its nest with the utmost bravery. On several occasions I have struck the old birds with my gun-barrel while warding off their attacks as I plundered their nests. This species can generally be distinguished from its near ally, *S. crepidatus*, at every age, by the mottled colour of the tarsus and webs of the feet, which in *S. crepidatus* are usually black.

16. PROCELLARIA GLACIALIS.—The fulmar is common in the north-water of Baffin's Bay; and individuals followed our ships until we entered the pack off Cape Sabine. On June 26, 1876, Lieutenant Parr and I, when travelling on the coast of Grinnell Land (lat. 82° 30′ N.), observed one of these birds; and a few days later Lieutenant Egerton found one dead on the shore some two miles further to the northward. We did not observe this species again till our return to Baffin's Bay in September 1876.

17. URIA GRYLLE.—The black guillemot or dovekie was found breeding at various spots along the shores of Smith Sound and northward, notably at Washington Irving Island, Dobbin Bay, Cape Hayes, and Bessels Bay; it does not, I think, breed north of Cape Union. I saw two or three examples feeding in pools on the floe as far north as lat. 82° 33'; but they were evidently mere stragglers.

18. MERGULUS ALLE.—The north-water of Baffin's Bay is the summer home of countless numbers of little auks; they do not, however, penetrate in any numbers far up Smith Sound, the most northern point where I observed them being in Buchanan Strait (lat. 79°). I do not think that they breed to the north of Foulke Fiord; but the talus at the base of the cliffs which flank that inlet is occupied by myriads of them during the nesting-season. On July 28 we found the young just hatched; in that stage they are covered with black down. From the large amount of bones and feathers lying around the huts of the Eskimo village of Etah, it is evident that these birds contribute largely to the support of the Arctic Highlanders during summer.

19. ALCA BRUENNICHII.—I observed two looms in August as far north as Buchanan Strait (lat. 79°); but this bird was not seen again by me until our return southward in September 1876, after regaining navigable water south of Cape Sabine. The north-water of Baffin's Bay is evidently the limit of the northern range of the species in that direction; and I doubt if there are any breeding-haunts of this species north of Cape Alexander.

20. COLYMBUS ——.—On September 2, 1875, at Floeberg Beach (lat. 82° 27' N.), a diver, I think *C. septentrionalis*, alighted in a pool about a hundred yards from the ship. A boat was instantly lowered; but the noise made by pushing the boat through the young ice alarmed the bird, which rose and flew to another pool half a mile to the southward. I tried to make my way over the floe towards the bird; but the ice was unsafe, so I had to give up the pursuit. The numerous lakes and ponds in Grinnell Land abound with a

species of charr (*Salmo arcturus*, Günther), which doubtless might afford good living to birds of this family.

21. HARELDA GLACIALIS.—We observed a flock of long-tailed duck swimming in the pools of water between the floes on September 1, 1875, near Floeberg Beach (lat. 82° 27′ N.) On September 16 two were shot not far from the ship. During the summer of 1876 a few of these birds visited the northern shores of Grinnell Land, we found them in pairs on lakes and ponds, where they were evidently breeding. From the rapidity with which they dive they are very difficult to shoot, and when secured do not repay the outlay in powder and lead.

22. SOMATERIA MOLLISSIMA.—The eider-duck breeds abundantly in the neighbourhood of Port Foulke, but decreased in numbers as we advanced northwards. It became rare after passing Cape Frazer, the meeting-place of the Polar and Baffin's Bay tides, but was replaced to some extent by the next species. I did not obtain an eider north of Cape Union. Dr. Coppinger procured both eider and king-duck at Thank God Harbour (lat. 81° 38′ N.) in the month of July, 1876.

23. SOMATERIA SPECTABILIS.—I did not obtain the king-duck in Smith Sound during the autumn of 1875; but in the end of June 1876 several flocks of males and females, numbering from ten to twenty individuals, were seen near Floeberg Beach (lat. 82° 27′ N.) Most of these fell a prey to our gunners; but those that escaped settled down to breed along the coast, and several nests were found with fresh eggs in them from the 9th to the middle of July.

24. BERNICLA BRENTA.—During the first week of June, parties of brent-geese arrived in the vicinity of our winter-quarters (lat. 82° 27′ N.) For some days they continued flying up and down the coast-line, evidently looking out for places bare of snow to feed on. They were very wary, and kept well out of gun-shot range. On June 21 I found the first nest with eggs in lat. 82° 33′ N.; subsequently many were found. When the young are hatched, the parent birds and broods congregate on the lakes or in open water

spaces near the shore in large flocks; by the end of July the old birds were moulting and unable to fly, so that they were easily secured, and afforded most valuable change of diet to our sick.   The flesh of this bird is most excellent.

The gander remains in the vicinity of the nest while the goose is sitting, and accompanies the young brood.   In one instance where I killed a female as she left her nest, the gander came hissing at me.

No. IV.

ICHTHYOLOGY.[1]

By Albert Günther, M.A., Ph. D., M.D., F.R.S.

Ten species of fishes were collected between lat. 78° and 83° N., by the naturalists of the Arctic Expedition of 1875–76, and submitted to me for determination.

1. Cottus quadricornis (*L.*)—A young specimen, four inches long, was found dead by Mr. Egerton on the beach of Dumbell Harbour (lat. 82° 30′ N.) No other salt-water fish is known at present to have been found at a higher latitude. In this young specimen the nuchal tubercles are only indicated; but having compared it with a specimen obtained on the English coast, another from Lake Wettern, and with two from Sir J. Richardson's collection (the locality of which is not known, but which most probably were given to him by one of the previous Arctic explorers), I have no doubt as to their specific identity. Dr. Lütken has excluded this species from his list of Greenland fishes ('Arctic Manual,' p. 116).

2. Icelus hamatus (*Kröyer*).—Previously known from Spitsbergen and Greenland, it seems to be one of the most common fishes in the latitudes between 80° and 82°. Two specimens were obtained at Discovery Bay (81° 44′ N.), several at Franklin Pierce Bay (in fifteen fathoms), and seven at Cape Napoleon. All these specimens were caught in the month of August, and were ready for spawning.

3. Triglops pingelii (*Reinh.*)—No specimens of this fish were previously in the national collection. It appears to

---

[1] Abridged from 'Proc. Zool. Soc.,' 1877, pp. 293–295, 475–476.

be much scarcer than the preceding. Externally the ventral fin appears to be composed of three rays; but on dissection four long rays and one rudimentary one are found. Obtained at Franklin Pierce Bay, August 11, 1875.

4. CYCLOPTERUS SPINOSUS (*Müll.*)—Previously known from Iceland, Spitsbergen, and Greenland. Two specimens from Cape Napoleon, and four from Franklin Pierce Bay are all young, and interesting as showing the irregular manner in which the conical spines are developed. The largest of these young specimens is not quite two inches long; and the tubercles are much less numerous than in an adult specimen; it is rough, and covered with minute spines. In a specimen fifteen lines long, only traces of the tubercles are visible on the skin. A specimen twelve lines long is quite naked, whilst another of the same size has the tubercles as much developed as the largest, or even more so. The spines of the first dorsal fin are sometimes quite distinct, sometimes enveloped in loose skin.

CYCLOPTERUS SPINOSUS.

5. LIPARIS FABRICII (*Kröyer*).—Previously known from Spitsbergen, Greenland, Port Leopold. Is represented in the present collection by a specimen from Discovery Bay, and others from 'Franklin Pierce Bay.

6. GYMNELIS VIRIDIS (*Fabr.*)—One specimen obtained in lat. 81° 52′ N.; is only five inches long, and belongs to a highly-coloured variety, being brown with numerous white spots, and having four black ocelli on the dorsal fin. Another specimen was collected in Franklin Pierce Bay.

7. GADUS FABRICII (*Rich.*)—Widely distributed in the

Arctic regions of the western hemisphere. Two specimens obtained off Cape Hayes, Grinnell Land.

8. SALMO ARCTURUS (*sp. n.*)—The northernmost salmonoid known at present. This charr cannot be identified with any of the other races of this division of *Salmo*; it comes nearest to the charr of Killin (Inverness-shire), but differs from it in having a more slender body, rather smaller scales, shorter fins, and a less number of pyloric appendages.

Body rather elongate; head small, two-ninths or nearly one-fifth of the total length (without caudal), scarcely more than one-half of the distance between the snout and the vertical from the origin of the dorsal fin. The snout is, remarkably obtuse; the maxillary varies in length: in males of the same size it sometimes reaches scarcely to, sometimes a little behind, the hind margin of the orbit; in the female it is smaller and shorter. Teeth small; vomerine teeth limited to the anterior extremity of the bone; a band of villiform teeth along the middle of the hyoid bone. Præoperculum with a distinct lower limb; suboperculum about twice as long as deep; pectoral but little shorter than the head, exceeding in length one-half of the distance of its root from the ventral. Ventral terminating at a considerable distance from the vent. D. 13; the longest ray as long as the head (without snout). A. 12. Caudal moderately excised, its middle rays half the length of the outer ones. Scales minute. Branchiostegals 11.

Upper parts of a dull brownish green, passing on the sides into the silvery or reddish colour of the lower parts. Dorsal and caudal of the colour of the back; paired fins and anal yellowish. No dots or ocelli. Young with numerous parr-marks.

The number of pyloric appendages were found to vary; one male has 31, another 35, a third 44, and a female 42.

Several specimens were obtained in Victoria Lake (lat. 82° 34′ N.), and in freshwater lakes near Floeberg Beach (lat. 82° 28′ N.) Dr. E. Moss kindly communicated to me a coloured sketch of a specimen caught in North-Ravine Lake. Specimens twelve inches in length are full-grown; no larger ones were found. The ovaries and testicles in specimens caught in the month of August show the commencement of seasonal development.

9. SALMO ALIPES (*Rich.*)—Of this species two examples were obtained, about fifteen inches long; it is a well-marked species of charr, characterised by the deep radiating and concentric striation of the gill-covers. The typical specimens were obtained in Boothia Felix; so that this charr has an unusually wide range. Colour silvery, with scarcely any pinkish tinge. Cæc. pyl. 41. Obtained from a lake in the vicinity of Discovery Bay (lat. 81° 44′ N.)

10. SALMO NARESII (*n. sp.*)—The body much elongate, its greatest depth being one-fifth, or even one-sixth, of the total length, without caudal. The length of the head is one-fourth or two-ninths of the same length, and nearly one-half of the distance between the snout and the vertical from the origin of the dorsal fin. The snout is obtuse, the forehead flat; and the maxillary extends in the male to the vertical from the hind margin of the orbit, but in the female it is somewhat shorter. Teeth very small, those of the vomer limited to the anterior extremity of the bone, a band of villiform teeth along the middle of the hyoid. Præoperculum with the angle much rounded, and without a distinct lower limb; suboperculum more than twice as long as deep. The gill-cover shows scarcely a trace of the radiating and concentric striæ by which *Salmo nitidus* is characterised. Pectoral shorter than, or equal in length to, the head without snout; and at least one-half, or more than one-half, of the distance of its root from the ventral. Ventral fins terminating at a considerable distance from the vent. D. 13; the largest ray scarcely longer than the distance of the eye from the end of the operculum. A. 11. Caudal deeply excised, its middle rays not quite half as long as the outer ones. Scales minute. Branchiostegals 11.

Pyloric appendages 42. Vertebræ 65.

Upper parts light greenish olive, passing into deep reddish-pink on the sides. Lower part of a silvery colour. Sides with very small red spots. Dorsal and upper part of the caudal of the colour of the back. Paired fins and anal and lower part of caudal deep red, with yellowish-white margins.

Several specimens were obtained in a freshwater lake near to the winter-quarters of the 'Discovery,' in a depth of from ten to fifteen feet.

This is a small species, the largest example measuring ten inches, all the others, males and females, being only eight inches long. Yet the sexual organs were fully developed, and the ova ready for exclusion.

By associating the name of Sir George Nares with one of the novelties brought home by the Arctic Expedition, I pay only a small tribute of the esteem in which all zoologists hold the leader of the 'Challenger' and Arctic Expeditions.

No. V.

MOLLUSCA.[1]

By Edgar A. Smith, F.L.S., F.Z.S.,

Zoological Department, British Museum.

The chief interest attaching to the mollusca obtained during the Arctic Expedition arises from the collections being made at localities further north than any which had been previously investigated.

To save repetition, the exact position of the principal stations at which mollusca were dredged is here appended:—

> Dumbell Harbour, 82° 30′ N. lat.
> Discovery Bay, 81° 41′ N. lat.
> Cape Frazer, 79° 44′ N. lat.
> Dobbin Bay, Grinnell Land, 79° 40′ N. lat.
> Franklin Pierce Bay, 79° 25′ N. lat.

I. PTEROPODA.

Clione borealis, Pallas.

Hab. Abundant in Hartstene Bay (*Feilden*).

Captain Feilden informs me that this species was not observed in Smith Sound north of Cape Sabine.

Limacina arctica, Fabricius.

Hab. Abundant in Hartstene Bay (*Feilden*).

---

[1] Abridged from 'Ann. and Mag. Nat. Hist.,' 1877, pp. 131-146.

II. GASTROPODA.

Pleurotoma (Bela) violacea, Mighels and Adams.

Hab. Discovery Bay, 5 fathoms (*Feilden*).
Only one rather elongated specimen was obtained.

Fusus (Sipho) tortuosus? Reeve.

Hab. Shore of Hayes Sound, 79° N. lat. (*Feilden*);
Dobbin Bay 30, fms. (*Hart*).

Buccinum hydrophanum, Hancock.

Hab. Franklin Pierce Bay (*Feilden* and *Hart*); Dobbin
Bay, 30 fms. (*Hart*).

Buccinum Belcheri, var. Reeve.

Hab. Dobbin Bay, 30 fms. (*Hart*).
Shell ovately conical, very thin, purplish brown, with a
few paler streaks here and there; whorls 5½, very convex,
spirally distinctly ridged, the ridges being alternately longer, longitudinally rather coarsely striated by the lines of growth, and very obsoletely plicated; mouth irregularly ovate, large, occupying more than half the entire length of the shell, of the same colour as the exterior, terminating inferiorly in a short, slightly recurved canal; columella oblique, scarcely arcuated, smooth, shining, whitish towards the base; epidermis thin, olivaceous, and laminated slightly on the principal distinct incremental lines or raised lirulæ; operculum circularly ovate, with the nucleus rather central.

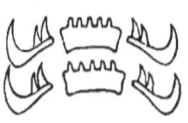

BUCCINUM BELCHERI.

Length 33 millims., diam. 17; aperture 19 millims. long
and 11 wide.

The dentition of the animal · of this species closely resembles that of *Buccinum grœnlandicum* and *Neptunea antiqua*, as represented by Troschel's figures in his work ' Das Gebiss der Schnecken,' vol. ii. pl. vi.

The above description was already prepared under the supposition that the specimen before me was distinct from *B. Belcheri*, when, through the kindness of Dr. Gwyn Jeffreys, I was enabled to compare it with the type of that species. It is less elongated, has a rather shorter spire; and the body-whorl is more ventricose. The columella also is less arcuate and more oblique, and the spiral ridges and lines of growth are more pronounced. The type does not display such regularity in the alternation of large and small transverse ridges as the variety. A specimen of this species from Finmark, in the collection of Mr. Jeffreys, very closely resembles the shell from Dobbin Bay.

Buccinum sericatum, Hancock.

Hab. Dobbin Bay, 30 fms. (*Hart*).

The radula of this species, which perhaps is only a variety of *B. Grœnlandicum*, is remarkable for the unequal dentition of the side plates, one of which is a trifle the narrower, and is furnished with only two fangs: they are subequal in length; but the inner one is slightly the stouter. The other lateral plate has three teeth, of which the outermost is longest, the median smallest, and at the base joins the inner fang. The median plate bears four small conical denticles.

RADULA OF BUC-
CINUM SERICATUM.

The only example of this species is a young shell. It agrees in all respects with Hancock's admirable description, except that the cilia of the epidermis are apparently closer together than in the type, in which they are said to be ' not much crowded,' whilst in the specimen before me there are about three in the space of a millimetre. The surface of the shell beneath the remarkable epidermis is very curiously wrinkly striated.   The operculum is roundish, greenish yellow on the inner side, and dirty yellow exteriorly; and the nucleus is rather less central than in *B. Belcheri.*

Trichotropis tenuis, sp. nov.

Shell very thin, light, semi-transparent, glossy white, globosely turbinate, widely and openly umbilicated, clothed with a dirty-yellowish epidermis, produced on the keels of the whorls into close-set, very short, bristle-like filaments, and rather coarsely obliquely striated, or rather lamellated,

TRICHOTROPIS TENUIS.

marking periods of growth; whorls six, the two apical ones smooth and rounded, the three following beautifully sculptured with raised oblique lines of growth and minute spiral striæ, keeled and angulated a trifle above the middle, convexly sloping above the keel and nearly straight beneath it; last whorl large, encircled with three faint keels, two near the middle and the third at the base, bordering the umbilicus; aperture subcircular, occupying about $\frac{6}{11}$ of the entire length of the shell, whitish within, streaked with irregular, curved, yellowish-olive stripes; the peristome is continuous, thin, with the epidermis produced beyond its extreme edges; columella white, arcuate, with a slight shallow channel at its base.

Greatest length 33 millims., diam. of last whorl above the aperture 18, greatest diam. 30; aperture 18½ long, nearly 17 wide.

Hab. Off Cape Louis Napoleon, Grinnell Land, 79° 38′ N. lat., in 25 fms. (*Feilden*).

Only a single specimen of this grand new *Trichotropis* was obtained. It is very different from any hitherto described, being remarkable for its circular aperture, conical spire, and extreme fragility. The entire surface under the epidermis is beautifully sculptured with oblique raised lines or lirulæ, and minutely striated in a spiral direction between them ; and the raised keels are also similarly striated.   The central keel of the last whorl is also visible on the upper ones, and is situated just above the suture.

In the 'Annals and Mag. Nat. Hist.' for August 1877, p. 136, I stated that the specimen upon which this species is founded had been seen by Dr. Jeffreys, who considered it an abnormal form of *T. bicarinata*.   Since then, in the September part of the same periodical, he has published this opinion, observing that in certain other species (*Littorina litorea* and *Fusus antiquus*) '*the same kind of distortion is observable.*'

I have again most closely scrutinised this shell, and still *I cannot trace the slightest irregularity of growth*, and therefore I confidently adhere to my opinion, shared by several conchologists, that this form is decidedly distinct from the well-known *bicarinata* ; and it only remains for me to point out its special characteristics, namely, the vast differences of form and epidermis, the open umbilicus, the slight prominence of the keels and the subcircular aperture.

Trichotropis borealis, Broderip and Sowerby.

Hab.   Discovery Bay, 5 fms. ; Dumbell Harbour (*Feilden*).

The specimens from the above localities agree precisely in shape and sculpture with that form of this species which was described by Hinds from shells found at Sitka, under the name of *T. inermis*.

Velutina (*Morvillia*) *zonata*, var. *grandis*.

Hab.   Franklin Pierce Bay (*Hart*).

The only specimen was taken out of the stomach of *Phoca barbata*, and is in very bad condition.   This variety is so very much larger than the ordinary size of the species that it almost appears that it must be distinct.   It measures 21 millims. in length, being about double that of Gould's figure. Hancock mentions one from the west coast of Davis Strait, which wâs about five-eighths of an inch (or 16 millims.) long.

Natica affinis, Gmelin.

Hab. Dobbin Bay, 30 fms., bottom stones and mud (*Hart*, August, 1876).

Only a single small specimen was obtained, which is remarkable for having the spire rather more elevated than usual.

Trochus (*Margarita*) *umbilicalis*, Broderip and Sowerby.

Hab. Franklin Pierce Bay, 15 fms.; Mushroom Point, 82° 29′ N. (*Feilden*).

This species is also reported by Jeffreys, 'Annals and Mag. Nat. Hist.' 1877, March, p. 237, from 'Discovery Bay, and fossil in Cane Valley,' from specimens collected by Captain Feilden during the expedition.

Trochus (*Margarita*) *glauca*, Möller.

Hab. With the preceding species at Franklin Pierce Bay (*Feilden*).

Trochus (*Margarita*) *helicinus*, Fabricius.

Hab. Franklin Pierce Bay (*Feilden*).

Trochus (*Margarita*), sp. jun.

Hab. Cape Frazer (*Feilden*).

This shell may be but a young specimen of *Margarita striata* of Broderip and Sowerby; but it differs from typical examples in the spire being comparatively small in proportion to the body-whorl, the base of which is almost destitute of revolving striæ; the umbilicus is larger and not bordered by a thickish ridge as is usually the case in this species.

Chiton (Tonicia) marmoreus, Fabricius.

Hab. Franklin Pierce Bay, 15 fms., temperature 29°·50 (*Hart* and *Feilden*).

Lepeta cæca, O. F. Müller.

Hab. Franklin Pierce Bay, 15 fms.; Cape Frazer, 30 fms.; and Richardson Bay, 70 fms. (*Feilden*).

The animal of this species (var. *concentrica*) has been briefly described by Middendorff, *l. c.* p. 186, and also by Dr. Jeffreys in the 'Ann. and Mag. Nat. Hist.' 1877, March, p. 231.

Bulla (Cylichna) alba, Brown.

Hab. Discovery Bay, 5 fms. (*Feilden*).

Bulla (Cylichna) striata, Brown.

Hab. Found with the preceding species (*Feilden*).

Onchidiopsis grœnlandica, Bergh.

Hab. Franklin Pierce Bay, 13–15 fms., stony bottom (*Hart*).

It is interesting to find this curious species, which was described by Bergh from South Greenland specimens, ranging so far north as the above locality.

Eolis salmonacea, Couthouy.

Hab. Discovery Bay (*Feilden*).

A single small specimen of this very pretty animal was found at the above spot. It is remarkable how easily the dorsal branchiæ fall off with the slightest touch.

III. CONCHIFERA.

Tellina (Macoma) tenera, Leach.

Hab. Discovery Bay, 5 fms. (*Feilden*).

Lyonsia arenosa, Möller.

Hab. Discovery Bay, 5 fms. (*Feilden*).

Cardium islandicum, Linn.

Hab. Dobbin Bay, 30 fms. (*Hart*).

Axinus Gouldii? Philippi.

Hab. Discovery Bay 5½ fms. (*Feilden*).

The shells associated with this species differ somewhat from the description given by Gould in having, besides ' the widened groove,' a lanceolate depression or posterior lunule which extends from the umbones down the dorsal slope. It is also very similar to *A. croulinensis*, Jeffreys.

Nucula inflata, Hancock.

Hab. Discovery Bay, 5½ fms. (*Feilden*).

Leda pernula, Müller.

Hab. Discovery Bay, 5½ fms. (*Feilden*).

Leda minuta, var., Fabricius.

Hab. Richardson Bay, 80° 2′ N. lat., 70 fms. (*Feilden*).

The specimens from the above locality have the transverse costæ rather finer than is usual.

Leda truncata, Brown.

Hab. Discovery Bay, 5 fms. (*Feilden*).

In a young example of this species the posterior beak is scarcely observable.

Astarte semisulcata, Leach.

Hab. Dumbell Harbour (*Feilden*); Discovery Bay, 5 fms. (*Feilden* and *Hart*).

The blackness of the epidermis in *A. lactea* is due, I think, to the specimens having been collected when dead ; for all the shells with this kind of dark epidermis are old and worn, and evidently have been untenanted by the living animal for some time.

Astarte striata, Leach.

Hab. Franklin Pierce Bay, 15 fms. (*Feilden* and *Hart*).

Astarte fabula, Reeve.

Hab. Dumbell Harbour and Discovery Bay (*Feilden*).

This species may be recognised by the peculiar ribbing near the umbones. In this region the ribs are more strongly developed than on the rest of the surface of the valve, and are not produced quite to the margins, so that in looking at the shell with the umbones towards the eye the dorsal areas appear comparatively smooth.

? *Astarte Warehami*, Hancock.

Hab. Franklin Pierce Bay, 13–15 fms., bottom stony (*Hart*); Richardson Bay, 80° 2′ N. lat., 70 fms. (*Feilden*).

I do not feel quite sure of the accuracy of the identification of the specimens before me. They differ slightly in form from Hancock's figure, being less elliptical by reason of the anterior end being less produced ; but with regard to the ribs and epidermis they agree exactly with the author's excellent description—the former being ' fine, close, regular,' and the latter pale greenish yellow. These shells, in shape, can certainly be matched with some specimens of *A. striata*, and do not appear to vary in any thing except the difference of colour of the epidermis, which in the latter species is brown or olive-brown. This species is considered the same as *A. fabula* by Jeffreys.

Mya truncata, Linn.

Hab. Discovery Bay, 5 and 25 fms. (*Hart* and *Feilden*) ; Dobbin Bay, 30 fms. (*Hart*).

All the specimens from these localities have the posterior marginal slopes directed inwards or towards the base of the shell, which peculiarity is characteristic of the variety *uddevalensis*. One shell is remarkable on account of the abruptness of the truncation and its narrowness, the width being only 6 millims. more than the length (30 millims.)

Saxicava arctica, Linn.

Hab. Discovery Bay, 5 fms. (*Feilden*); Franklin Pierce Bay (*Hart* and *Feilden*); Dobbin Bay, 30 fms. (*Hart*).

Some specimens from Franklin Pierce Bay are remarkable on account of their great solidity, the depth and distinctness of the muscular scars, and the purplish brown colour which stains both the inside and exterior of the valves.

Modiolaria lœvigata, Gray.

Hab. Franklin Pierce Bay, 15 fms. (*Feilden* and *Hart*).

This species is considered by some authors a variety of the British *M. discors*. There are, however, certain differences in form, colour, and sculpture which appear to me sufficient to distinguish the two species. The present is a larger species, transversely more elongate and proportionally narrower, the difference in width of the anterior and posterior ends being less marked. The striæ on the hinder area, in adult specimens, are distinct only towards the umbones, and gradually become obsolete towards the margin of the valves, which, on this account, are smooth and not denticulated within as in *discors*. The epidermis of *lœvigata* is brown on the greater portion of the shell, becoming pale olive or brownish green towards the umbones.

Pecten (Pseudamusium) grœnlandicus, Sowerby.

Hab. Off Cape Louis Napoleon, 25 fms.; Hayes Point, 35 fms. (*Feilden*); Discovery Bay, 5½ fms. (*Feilden* and *Hart*).

IV. BRACHIOPODA.

Rhynconella psittacea, Chemnitz.

Hab. 'Franklin Pierce Bay, 15 fms.; Cape Frazer, 80 fms.; Cape Napoleon, 25 fms.' (*Feilden*).

No. VI.

INSECTA AND ARACHNIDA.

By ROBERT McLACHLAN, F.R.S., F.L.S. &c.

WITH the consent of the Council of the Royal Society, all the *Arthropoda* (excepting the *Crustacea*) were placed in my hands for working out. These were principally collected by Captain H. W. Feilden, the Naturalist of the 'Alert;' but interesting forms also resulted from the researches of Mr. Hart, who occupied a similar position on board the 'Discovery.' A detailed Report on these collections was read by me at the meeting of the Linnæan Society on December 15, 1877. In that Report I made some justly merited eulogistic remarks on the entomological labours of the naturalists. The materials brought home from between the parallels of 78° and 83° N. latitude showed quite unexpected, and in some respects astonishing, results.

In all there are about 45 species of true *Insecta*, and 16 of *Arachnida*. Of the former 5 pertain to *Hymenoptera*, 1 to *Coleoptera*, 13 to *Lepidoptera*, 15 to *Diptera*, 1 to *Hemiptera*, 7 to *Mallophaga*, and 3 to *Collembola*. Of the *Arachnida* 6 are true spiders, and about 10 are mites.

In this Report I was assisted by Baron von Osten-Sacken, who examined the *Diptera*, by the Rev. O. Pickard Cambridge, who worked out the spiders, and by Mr. Andrew Murray, who attended to the mites.

I have no hesitation in saying that the most valuable of all the zoological collections are those belonging to the

entomological section, because these latter prove the existence of a comparatively rich insect fauna, and even of several
species of showy butterflies, in very high latitudes.

INSECTA.

HYMENOPTERA.

Bombus balteatus, Dahlbom.
  „   *polaris,* Curtis.
Ichneumon erythromelas, McLachlan, n. sp.
Cryptus arcticus, Schiödte?
Microgaster sp. ? (parasitic on *Dasychira* ; cocoons only).

The *Hymenoptera* comprise two species of humble-bees
(*Bombi*), and three parasitic forms that no doubt infest the
larvæ of *Lepidoptera.* The bees frequented the flowers of a
Pedicularis, and may perhaps be instrumental in effecting
the fertilisation of that plant.

COLEOPTERA.

Quedius fulgidus, Erichson.

The only species of *Coleoptera* is represented by one
example of the brachelytrous *Quedius fulgidus* from Discovery Bay, a very widely distributed insect, common in
Britain. The paucity of insects of this order is inexplicable.

LEPIDOPTERA.

Colias Hecla, Lef., var. *glacialis,* McLach.
Argynnis polaris, Boisd.
  „   *Chariclea,* Schneider (several forms).
Chrysophanus phlœas, L., var. *Feildeni,* McLach.
Lycœna Aquilo, Boisd.
Dasychira grœnlandica, Wocke.
Mamestra (?) *Feildeni,* McLach., n. sp.
Plusia parilis, Hübn.
Psycophora Sabini, Kirby.
Scoparia gelida, McLach., n. sp.
Penthina sp. ?
Mixodia sp. ?
    —— ? (Fam. *Tortricidœ,* but utterly worn).

The *Lepidoptera* form the most remarkable feature. Five of them (included in nearly 40 examples) are butterflies of genera such as one might expect to meet with on a summer-day's walk in England. One of these latter is a variety of *Colias Hecla*, a brightly coloured 'clouded yellow,' the typical form of which is a known boreal insect, but which neverthe-less would hardly have been expected from so far north. There are two species of *Argynnis* ('Fritillaries'): *A. polaris* (of which two examples were also found at 'Polaris' Bay by the naturalist of the American expedition, and were the first butterflies brought from extreme high latitudes), and *A. Chariclea*, the numerous examples of the latter running into endless varieties, so that it is almost impossible to say if all really pertain to this species. There are three examples of a pretty little *Chrysophanus* ('copper'), which appears to be a rather striking form (*Feildeni*) of our familiar *C. phlœas*. Also one example of *Lycœna Aquilo* (a 'blue'), a known Arctic insect, which is perhaps scarcely more than a form of *L. orbitulus* of the Alps of Europe. A peculiar smoky-looking *Bombyx* is *Dasychira grœnlandica*, having a large hairy larva not much unlike that of a tiger-moth, but with the hairs arranged in tufts on the back: this larva was found abundantly almost up to the highest point reached. There are two *Noctuœ*, one of which appears to be new. One species of *Geometridœ*, described by Curtis in the Insecta of Ross' voyage as *Psychophora Sabini*. A new species of *Scoparia*, and three species of *Tortricidœ*, the latter single examples not in very good condition. Captain Feilden assures me that, in the short summer, butterflies are on the wing any time during the twenty-four hours, supposing the sun's face be not obscured. One month in each year is the longest period in which they can appear in the perfect state, and six weeks is the period in each year in which phytophagous larvæ can feed; so it appears probable that more than one season is necessary, in most cases, for their full development, and this may partially account for the great variability often exhibited in Arctic insects.

DIPTERA.

Culex nigripes, Zett.
Chironomus polaris, Kirby (and about three other species).
Sciara sp. ?
Trichocera regelationis, L.
Tipula arctica, Curtis.
Tachina hirta, Curtis ? (and about two others).
Pyrellia cadaverina, L.
Anthomyia sp. ?
Scatophaga sp. ?

Among the *Diptera* there is nothing of any special importance. The most striking is a 'daddy-long-legs' (*Tipula arctica*), well known as an Arctic species. Of the others there are *Culicidæ* (gnats), *Trichocera* ('winter-gnat,' but appearing there after midsummer), *Chironomi* (plume gnats), and familiar-looking flies which appeared when offal was thrown away, or the carcase of an animal lay on the ground.

HEMIPTERA (ANOPLURA).

Hematopinus trichechi, Boheman.

The only so-called Hemipterous insect is a louse (*Hematopinus trichechi*) that infests the walrus; found in the axillæ and other parts where the skin is soft. This was originally described from Spitsbergen.

MALLOPHAGA.

Docophorus ceblebrachys, Nitzsch (and two others).
Nirmus cingulatus, Burm.
  ,,   *phæonotus*, Nitzsch.
Colpocephalum, sp. ?
Menopon gonophæum, Burm. var. ?

The *Mallophaga* (bird-lice) are rather numerous in individuals, some of them probably new species, others already familiar. These of course are carried hither and thither by their hosts.

COLLEMBOLA.

Isotoma Bessellsii, Packard ?
Podura hyperborea, Boheman ?
Lipura sp. ?

Of the *Collembola* two are familiar-looking species, often found on the surface of the snow (as in the Alps, &c.), and, from their habits of springing in short leaps, known as snow-fleas.

ARACHNIDA.

ARANEIDEA.

Tegenaria detestabilis, Cambridge, n. sp.
Erigone psycrophila, Thorell.
    „   *provocans*, Cambridge, n. sp.
    „   *vexatrix*, Cambridge, n. sp.
Lycosa glacialis, Thorell.
Tarantula exasperans, Cambridge, n. sp.

There appeared to be several new forms among the spiders, whereas others were already known.

ACARIDEA.

Bdella, two or three species.
Scirus, one species.
Hydrachna, probably two species.
Eylais, one species.
Oribata, probably two species.
Damæus, one species.
Dermaleichus, one species.

The *Acari* (or mites) present representatives of almost all the families, including the water-mites and the peculiar group parasitic upon birds.

It must be remembered that only about 80 species of insects have been observed in Greenland, although nearly a 100 years ago the fauna of the lower portion of that country was worked out by the Danish missionary Otto Fabricius. Iceland has over 300 species, Spitsbergen comparatively few,

and no butterfly is known from either. Thus we see that
Grinnell Land, ice-bound and ice-covered as it is for all but
a short period in each year, possesses an insect fauna that
cannot be styled otherwise than remarkable, and which in
butterflies is probably richer than Greenland.

The aspect of the fauna is decidedly what has been termed
' Scandinavian,' but I regard the representatives as the
remnants of a once more extensive Arctic fauna, which came
in, or was developed, after the close of the warm Miocene
period, and culminated before the glacial epoch ; and in this
am disposed to agree with the late Edward Forbes in a theory
advanced in 1846, in an attempt to account for the geological
relations of the fauna and flora of the British Isles, and
which has been accepted by many leading naturalists and
geologists.　According to this theory, the common origin of
the existing Alpine and Arctic flora and fauna is explained.
When the glacial period ceased, plants and animals began to
move northward ; some found a congenial home on the top of
high mountains, and established the existing Alpine flora and
fauna, whereas others reached the home of their ancestors in
the Arctic regions.　During the long period that has elapsed
since those times, scarcely any modification in Arctic and
Alpine forms has taken place in some cases ; in others, in
which the divergence is greater, evolution will account for it.

No. VII.

CRUSTACEA,

By Edward J. Miers, F.L.S., F.Z.S.

With Notes on the Copepoda, by the Rev. A. M. Norman, M.A.; and
on the Ostracoda, by George Brady, M.D., F.L.S.

The following account of the Crustacea is confined to the species collected between lat. 78° and 84° N.

The most northerly species collected is *Anonyx nugax*, one of the commonest and most abundantly distributed of the Arctic Amphipoda. Of this species several examples were collected by Commander Markham and Lieutenant Parr, at 83° 19′ N. lat., in May 1876, at a depth of 72 fathoms. The next most northerly species, the well-known *Hippolyte aculeata*, was found on the shore of Dumbell Harbour, in lat. 82 ° 30′ N.

The following are the principal stations at which Crustacea were collected by the naturalists on board the ' Alert' and ' Discovery.'

Floeberg Beach, the winter quarters of H.M.S. ' Alert,' in 82° 27′ N. lat.

Discovery Bay, winter quarters of the ' Discovery,' in 81° 41′ N. lat.

Cape Frazer, Grinnell Land, in 79° 44′ N. lat.

Dobbin Bay, Grinnell Land, in 79° 40′ N. lat.

Cape Louis Napoleon, in lat. 79° 38′ N.

Franklin Pierce Bay, in 79° 29′ N. lat

A small collection of Crustacea made by Dr. A. C. Horner, while on board the yacht ' Pandora,' which has been placed in my hands for examination, contains only two species collected north of lat. 78°, i.e. three specimens of *Atylus cari-*

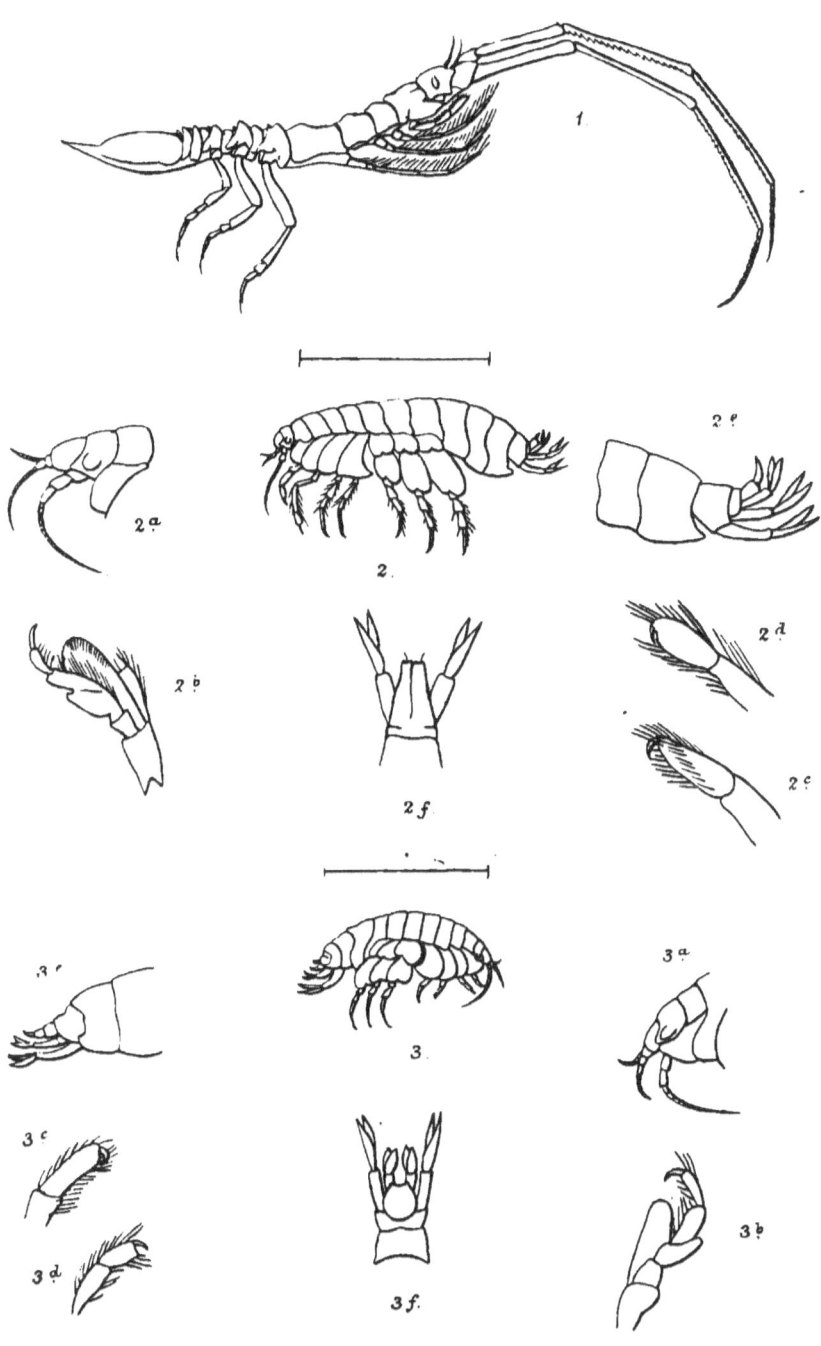

E Turck del.

London, Sampson Low. Marston & Co.

Mintern Bros imp.

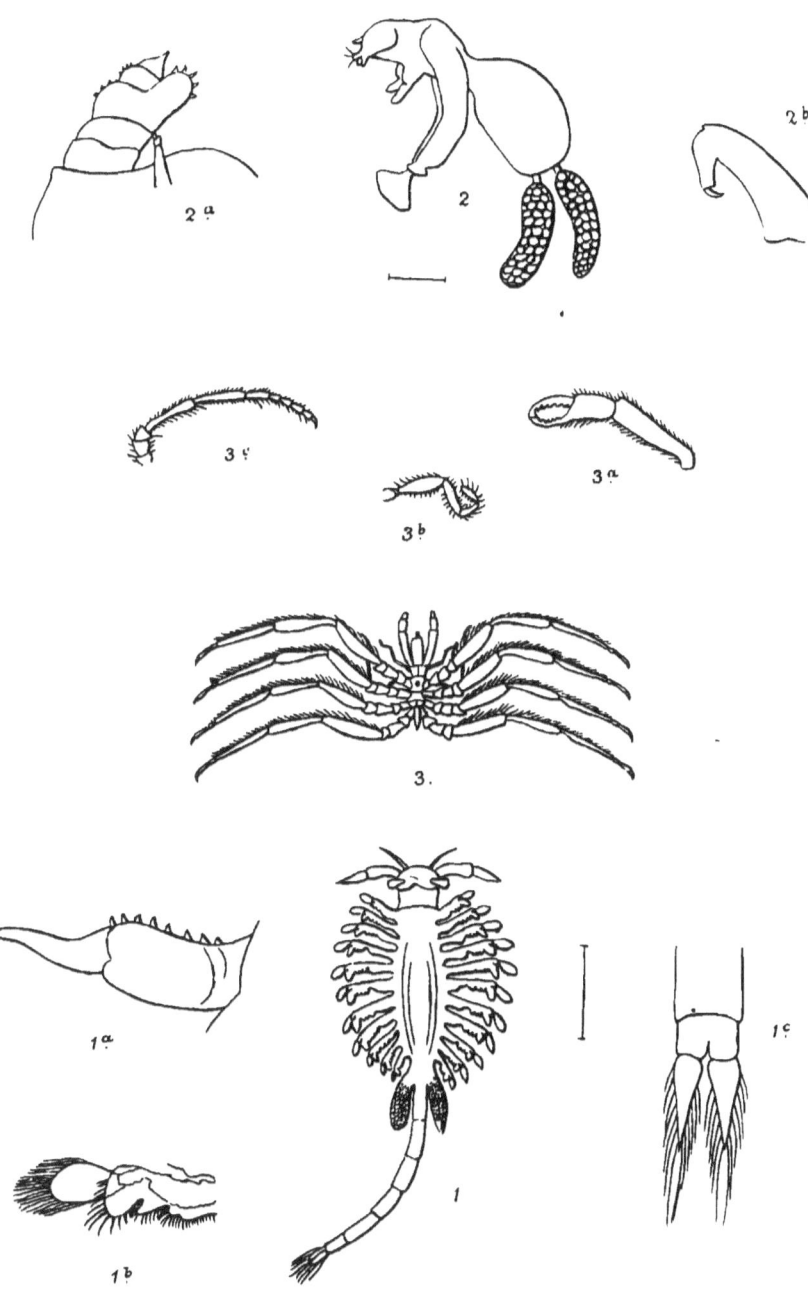

natus, and four very small specimens of an Amphipoda perhaps belonging to the genus *Pherusa.* Both these species were collected at a depth of 7 fathoms, on a clay bottom, in Pandora Harbour, Smith Sound, in lat. 78° 17′ N.

Since my Report was published,[1] to which I must refer for synonymical references, descriptive remarks, and notes on the geographical distribution of the species, a small collection has been sent me by Dr. Edward L. Moss, R. N., late surgeon of H.M.S. 'Alert,' containing a few *Amphipoda, Arcturus,* and *Nymphon,* and free-swimming *Copepoda.* The *Copepoda* were entrusted to the Rev. A. M. Norman for determination; the other species had all been obtained by Captain Feilden and Mr. Hart, the naturalists of the Expedition. To render the list of species complete, as regards the Crustacea inhabiting Smith Sound and the adjacent coasts, a few species, obtained by Dr. Hayes north of lat. 78°, and recorded by Stimpson ('P. Ac. N. Sci. Phil.' 1863), have been intercalated in the text and are placed within brackets.

DECAPODA.

CRANGONIDÆ.

Cheraphilus boreas, Phipps.

Discovery Bay, lat. 81° 44′ (both males and females), at depth of 25 fathoms; Cape Napoleon, one male example, at 25 fathoms; Franklin Pierce Bay, one female, at 15 fathoms: temperature of water 29°·50.

Stimpson records specimens collected by Dr. Hayes at Port Foulke and Littleton Island.

Sabinea septemcarinata, Sabine.

Discovery Bay, 25 fathoms, abundantly, both males and females; Cape Napoleon, 25 fathoms, three specimens, males.

Dobbin Bay, at a depth of 30 fathoms, one specimen, a female with ova.

'Ann. Mag. Nat. Hist.' **xx.** pp. 52–66, 96–110 (1877).

ALPHEIDÆ.

Hippolyte Gaimardii, Milne Edwards.

Franklin Pierce Bay, 13–15 fathoms, one female specimen.

Specimens were collected by Dr. Hayes at Port Foulke.

Hippolyte spinus, Sowerby.

Discovery Bay, 5 specimens, at 25 fathoms.

Hippolyte turgida, Kröyer.

Discovery Bay, 25 fathoms, one specimen.
Franklin Pierce Bay, one specimen, female with ova.
Cape Frazer, 20 fathoms, one female example.
Port Foulke (Dr. Hayes).

Hippolyte Phippsii? Kröyer.

Cape Frazer, 20 fathoms, one specimen.
Port Foulke (Dr. Hayes).

Hippolyte polaris, Sabine.

Discovery Bay, 25 fathoms, abundant; Cape Napoleon, five specimens; Franklin Pierce Bay, 15 fathoms, several specimens.
Dobbin Bay, 30 fathoms, one specimen.
Port Foulke and Littleton Island (Dr. Hayes).

Hippolyte borealis, Owen.

Discovery Bay, at 25 fathoms, several specimens; Cape Napoleon, at 25 fathoms, two specimens.
Franklin Pierce Bay, 13–15 fathoms, several specimens; Dobbin Bay, 30 fathoms, one specimen.
Littleton Island (Dr. Hayes).

Hippolyte grœnlandica, J. C. Fabricius.

Dumbell Harbour, lat. 82° 30′, one female specimen.
Franklin Pierce Bay, 13–15 fathoms, one male specimen.

STOMATOPODA.

MYSIDÆ.

Mysis oculata, O. Fabricius.

Cape Napoleon, 25 fathoms (temperature of water 29° 2′).

The single specimen collected is in a very much mutilated condition.

Brought by Dr. Hayes from Port Foulke.

ISOPODA.

Arcturus baffini, Sabine.

Cape Napoleon, at 25 fathoms, two specimens, male and female.

Dobbin Bay, 30 fathoms, one male and one female; Franklin Pierce Bay, 13–15 fathoms, four males and three females, and many young.

A single specimen was collected, with many of the variety I have designated *Feildeni*, by Dr. Moss, on the ice foot a mile north of H.M.S. ' Alert's ' winter-quarters.

Var. *Feildeni* (Miers), Pl. II. fig. 1.

This variety is distinguished by the absence of spines on the head and segments of the body.

Floeberg beach, 82° 27′ N. lat., very abundant, males, females, and young.

Gyge hippolytes, Kröyer.

Discovery Bay (on *Hippolyte polaris*), one male and one female specimen.

Dr. Hayes collected this species at Port Foulke.

Phryxus abdominalis, Kröyer.

Discovery Bay, male and female, on *Hippolyte polaris*; Cape Napoleon, male and female, on *H. polaris*.

Franklin Pierce Bay, 13–15 fathoms, five males and five females.

Munnopsis typica, Sars.

Cape Napoleon, two male specimens at a depth of 25 fathoms, temperature of the water 29°·2 ; at 50 fathoms' one male specimen.

Cape Frazer, 20 fathoms, one female specimen.

AMPHIPODA.

Anonyx nugax, Phipps.

Floeberg Beach, at 10 fathoms, male and females; fire-hole at lat. 82 24′ ; and at lat. 83° 19′ at 72 fathoms.

Winter-quarters of H.M.S. ' Discovery,' at 11 fathoms.

Brought from Gale Point by Dr. Hayes.

Anonyx gulosus, Kröyer. Pl. II. fig. 2.

Discovery Bay, 11 fathoms, three specimens.

I have referred these specimens with some doubt to the *Anonyx gulosus* of Kröyer, as the antero-lateral margin of the head is less broadly rounded, and the accessory flagellum is longer than that of *A. gulosus* according to Boeck's diagnosis. In the form of the first and second pairs of legs and of the terminal segment they agree well with the descriptions of *A. gulosus*, and particularly in the presence of a tooth on the inner margin of the dactyl, which is mentioned by Lilljeborg as characteristic of that species. From *A. pumilus* they differ in the shorter antennæ, and in the absence of a tooth on the posterior margin of the fifth post-abdominal segment.

Onesimus Edwardsii, Kröyer.   Pl. II. fig. 3.

Discovery Bay at 5½ fathoms, lat. 81° 44′, one specimen; Floeberg Beach, at 10 fathoms, males and females, abundantly.

Atylus carinatus, J. C. Fabricius.

Discovery Bay, at depths of 5½ and 25 fathoms, several specimens of both sexes were collected.

Acanthozone hystrix, Owen.

Discovery Bay, one specimen; Franklin Pierce Bay, five specimens.

Halirages fulvocinctus, Sars.

Discovery Bay, at 25 fathoms, one specimen; Floeberg Beach, one specimen.

Both of the specimens collected are in an imperfect condition: one is, I believe, an adult female; the other is a younger animal.

Specimens collected at Littleton Island by Dr. Hayes were described by the late Dr. Stimpson as new, under the name of *Pherusa tricuspis*.

Gammarus locusta, Linn.

Floeberg Beach, at depth of 10 fathoms, twenty-five specimens; crack between the floes in lat. 82° 24′, three specimens.

Port Foulke (Dr. Hayes).

Gammaracanthus loricatus, Sabine.

Floeberg Beach, at 10 fathoms, two males and two females.

Amathilla pinguis, Kröyer.

Crack between floes at lat. 82° 24'; one specimen, in imperfect condition.

Eusirus cuspidatus, Kröyer.

Franklin Pierce Bay, 13–15 fathoms, one female specimen.

Tritropis aculeata, Lepechin.

Discovery Bay, at 25 fathoms, one male, four females; Cape Napoleon, at 25 fathoms, three males, seven females; Floeberg Beach, at 10 fathoms, two males, five females; Franklin Pierce Bay, at 15 fathoms, many specimens.

Cape Frazer, 20 fathoms, three young females (?); Dobbin Bay, at 30 fathoms, one female.

[*Themisto libellula*, Mandt.

Cape Faraday, in the stomach of a seal (Dr. Hayes).]

Ægina spinosissima, Stimpson.

Cape Napoleon, 25 fathoms, temperature of water 29°·2, one small male specimen.

Dobbin Bay, 30 fathoms, one large male specimen.

ENTOMOSTRACA v. GNATHOPODA.

PHYLLOPODA.

BRANCHIPODIDÆ.

Branchipus (*Branchinecta*) *arcticus*, Verrill. Pl. III.
fig. 1.

Discovery Bay, in a small freshwater lake and in a stream under ice.

Several specimens were collected, including males and females, of a species of Phyllopoda, which I refer to the *B. arcticus* of Verrill.

These specimens differ slightly from the descriptions of *B. arcticus* and *grœnlandicus*, as will appear from my description.[1]   If distinct (which may be possible, although I think it more probable that the three forms are varieties of one and the same species), the species may be designated *B. Verrilli.*

COPEPODA PARASITICA.

LERNÆOPODIDÆ.

Lernæopoda arcturi, Miers, sp. n.   Pl. III. fig. 2.

This species, as will appear from the description, differs from its nearest ally, the *L. Edwardsii*, Olsson, in the somewhat shorter ovaries and abdomen, and the form of the claw of the first maxilliped.   The *L. Edwardsii* is known to me only from the description.

Floeberg Beach, parasitic on the gills of *Salmo arcturus* Gthr.

Lernæopoda elongata, Grant.

Port Foulke (Dr. Hayes).]

[*Hæmobaphes cyclopterina*, Fabricius.

Littleton Island ; attached to the gills of *Gymnetes viridis* (Dr Hayes).]

CIRRIPEDIA.

BALANIDÆ.

Balanus porcatus, Da Costa.

Cape Napoleon, from a depth of 50 fathoms, five speci-

---

[1] Op. cit.

mens; 25 fathoms, two specimens; Richardson Bay, 80° 2′ N. lat., 70 fathoms, one specimen.

Franklin Pierce Bay, 13–15 fathoms.

[*Balanus balanoides*, Linn.

Port Foulke (Dr Hayes).]

PYCNOGONIDA.

NYMPHONIDÆ.

? *Nymphon hirtum*, J. C. Fabricius.

Franklin Pierce Bay, eight specimens; Discovery Bay, one specimen; Floeberg Beach, at depth of 10 fathoms, two specimens. ·

Nymphon hirtum, var. *obtusidigitum* (Miers), Pl. III. fig. 3.

Among the specimens from Franklin Pierce Bay is a single example, which differs from the males of the foregoing variety only in the legs being cylindrical, not dilated and compressed, and in the form of the chelæ of the mandibles. These have the fingers arcuate, meeting only at the tips, which terminate in small knobs. The chelæ are slender, not globose, as in the form figured by Bell, in Belcher, ' Last of the Arctic Voyages,' p. 409, pl. xxxv. fig. 4, under the name of *N. robustum*, and that recently described by Heller as *N. hians* (' Sitz. der k.-k. Akad.; ' Wien., ' Naturw.' lxxi. p. 610, 1875), in which species the fingers although arcuate are represented as acute.

Nymphon Strömii (Kröyer).

Floeberg Beach, lat. 82° 27′, at depth of 10 fathoms, three specimens, and at lat. 81° 56′, one specimen; Cape Frazer, at a depth of 80 fathoms, bottom hard, one adult and three young specimens.

NOTES ON THE OCEANIC COPEPODA.

BY THE REV. A. M. NORMAN, M.A.

THE Copepodous Crustacea, though for the most part of very small size, and apparently insignificant, are nevertheless indirectly of no small consequence to mankind, inasmuch as they make up for their minuteness by their extraordinary productiveness and numbers, and constitute, in combination with the Mysidea and larval forms of higher Crustacea, a principal element in the food of the whale.

The oceanic species have not hitherto had that amount of attention paid to them which they undoubtedly deserve, yet Kröyer, Lubbock, Baird, and Buchholz have examined and described many forms which inhabit the Arctic seas.

Unfortunately the number of specimens brought home by the Arctic Expedition is very small, and, with the exception of a bottle of surface-gathering from Baffin's Bay, which contains an interesting series of some well-known forms, the species are represented only by one, or at the most two specimens, and these already mounted. In this condition it is almost impossible to determine accurately those minute details of structure in the mouth and other organs, which are absolutely essential to the correct definition of generic and specific characters. At the same time, the conditions under which the Copepoda were found, the extreme high latitude, and the extraordinary amount of cold which prevailed at the surface while these animals still remained living in the dead of winter beneath the mass of superincumbent ice, render them so interesting that I am unwilling to leave them wholly unnoticed, though the description which I shall be able to give must of necessity be extremely imperfect.

That the Copepodous Crustacea are able to exist under circumstances, with respect to cold, which are most extraordinary has long been known. Otho F. Müller froze individuals of *Cyclops quadricornis* in a glass vessel, and when fully frozen continued the cold for four and twenty hours. He then placed the vessel in a warm bath, and watched the effect. For four and twenty hours the Crustacea which had been frozen showed no signs of life; the next morning, however, to his surprise he found the greater part of them restored to life and swimming about as before congelation. It is a well-known fact also that the life of the eggs of Ostracoda and Cladocera can be maintained for many months, when ponds have been completely dried up in the summer months, or frozen to their very bottom in mid-winter.

In the extremely cold winter of 1859 and 1860 I instituted some experiments for the purpose of finding how far life could be maintained, under extraordinarily trying conditions, among the lower orders of the Crustacea. The water of the lake in Hardwicke Park, in the parish of Sedgefield, had in the month of October been let off so as to drain large mud-flats on the shelving sides, in order that the weeds, exposed by this means to the influence of the frost during the winter months, might be destroyed. The severest cold of which we have record ensued for five weeks. From the seventeenth day of December the mud-flats were continuously frozen into a solid block, and the frost on Christmas Eve reached five degrees below zero, Fahr. On the conclusion of the frost a portion of this mud was procured, and, yet further to test the vitality of the eggs embedded in it, the mud was thoroughly dried. On March 11 a small portion of the mud was placed in a glass jar of water and exposed to a genial temperature. A few days afterwards *Daphnia rotunda, Sida crystallina, Diaptomus castor*, and *Cyclops quadricornis*, together with some *Rotifera*, were swimming about merrily in the vessel.

It is no surprise therefore to us to meet with these minute Crustacea in mid-winter in the Arctic Sea, though the fact is of importance as bearing upon the supply of food existing during the winter months for the Greenland whales.

A towing-net gathering from Baffin's Bay, lat. 73° 33′ N., long. 76° 59′ W., made September 16, 1876, the water at the temperature of 34°·4, contains numerous specimens of *Metridina* (*Metridia*) *armata*, Boeck.[1] This species has been described by Professor Brady from the Irish coast under the name of *Paracalanus hibernicus*,[2] and I am indebted to him for the opportunity of comparing these Irish specimens (since synonymised by him with Boeck's genus) with those of the Arctic Sea. They agree in every respect except perhaps that the terminal spines of the swimming feet are longer in proportion to the joint from which they spring in the Arctic than they are in specimens from the warmer seas. With respect to size we find here, as in so many other instances among the .Invertebrata, an extraordinary development of the Arctic specimens, which are at least *six times* the size of those from the Irish coast, and measure five millimètres in length, exclusive of the antennæ. It is quite possible that this genus may prove to be synonymous with *Pleuromma* of Claus; but if that be so, the mature male of *Metridina armata* has not yet been observed, and the males which Professor Brady and myself have examined must be considered as immature, and not yet to have attained the full development of those limbs which specially characterise the male sex. Claus has named his genus '*Pleuromma*' to indicate the presence of an eye, which he describes and figures as situated ' penes maxillipedum posticorum basin.' It is not a little remarkable that, attached to the maxilliped of one of the specimens of *Metridina armata* procured by Dr. Moss, is a group of parasitic organisms, each of which is in the form of a little globular body supported on a pedicel of greater or less length. Sufficient cannot be made out of the organic structure of these parasites to determine the class of animals to which they should be referred. They are

---

[1] Boeck's genus is Metridia. I have slightly changed the termination to Metridina in order to avoid confusion with Metridium of Oken, of which our well-known sea-anemone (*Actinoloba dianthus*) is the type.

[2] 'Ann. Nat. Hist.,' S. IV. Vol. xii. p. 126, Pl. viii. fig. 1–3.

extremely small; but we find semiglobular bodies of larger size
figured in one of Kröyer's plates ('Voyages en Scandinavie,'
&c., Pl. xli. fig. 2, e, f), as attached in one case to the ventral,
and in the other to the dorsal, surface of *Calanus hyper-
boreus*. It may be that these are the more mature forms of
the parasites now observed on *Metridina armata*. Now, if
the young of such a parasite were attached to the base instead
of to the extremity of the maxilliped, it might very possibly
be mistaken for an organ of vision. I feel great hesitation in
even hinting at this possibility, knowing the extreme accuracy
of Claus' observations; but the mistake—if a mistake has
been made—is one which any observer might easily fall into,
more especially since organs, presumed to be supplemental
organs of sight, are not unknown among other orders of the
Crustacea (*Thysanopoda*), attached to the segments of the
body.

In this same gathering were large numbers of *Calani*,
the examination of which has cost me no small amount of
labour. I must take another opportunity of giving the
grounds on which the conclusions I have arrived at are based.
It will suffice now to state that I believe that the whole of
these specimens are referable to *Calanus Finmarchicus*,
Gunner, better known to British naturalists under the name
of *Cetochilus septentrionalis*, Goodsir, and that *Calanus
magnus, elegans* and *borealis* of Lubbock, and numerous
other so-called species, are merely states and conditions resulting from differences of the sex and age of our old friend.
The very great development in size of the Arctic examples
as compared with the British, which results in the young
immature forms of the former surpassing in size the fully
developed individuals of the latter, has tended much to
render the confusion greater.

A mounted specimen collected by Captain Feilden near
the same spot is referable to the same species which was also
procured by Dr. Moss in the summer months at the winter
quarters of the 'Alert,' lat. 82° 27′ N.

Two very interesting gatherings were made by Dr. Moss

from water drawn, in mid-winter, from under the ice-floes at the winter quarters of the 'Alert,' lat. 82° 27'. There are three species, unfortunately two of them represented only by a single specimen, which being mounted prevents the possibility of full examination; the first of these is a form closely resembling apparently our *Idya furcata* (Baird), but differs manifestly in the form of the last legs, which are ovate instead of produced and linear, as in the just-mentioned species; this new form may be named *Idya palæocrystica*.

The next species is remarkable on account of the numerous long setæ of the anterior antennæ, which are not longer than the cephalo-thorax, and also the very long setæ of the swimming feet; it is possibly a Dias, and may be called *Dias* (?) *Mossi*.

The last I doubtfully refer to the genus *Pseudocalanus* of Boeck, and it may be named *P. Feildeni*.

NOTES ON THE OSTRACODA.

By George Stewardson Brady, M.D., F.L.S.

1. Mud from ravine, Repulse Bay, Hall's Land; 150 feet elevation, lat. 82° 10′ N.

Cytheropteron montrosiense, Brady, Crosskey and Robertson.

2. Mud from Fiord Valley, lat. 82° 8′ N.; 200 feet elevation, from valves of shells.

Cypris curvata, nov. sp.

3. Mud-beds, Cave Ravine; 100 feet elevation. Lat. 82° 32′ N.

Cythere globulifera, Brady.

4. Franklin Pierce Bay, 13–15 fathoms, lat. 79° 25′ N.
   Cythere costata, Brady.
   Xestoleberis aurantia, Baird.
   Cytherura undata, Sars.
   Selerochilus contortus, Norman.

5. Off Victoria Head, Bache Island, 35 fathoms.

   Cythere leioderma, Norman.
      „   *tuberculata,* Sars.
   Cytheridea punctillata, Brady.
   Cytherura clathrata, Sars.
   Cytheropteron montrosiense, B., C. and R.

6. Hayes Point, 35 fathoms.

   Cythere Logani, Brady and Crosskey.

7. Cape Frazer, 50–80 fathoms.

   Cythere leioderma, Norman.
      „   *gibbosa,* B. and R.
      „   *concinna,* Jones.
      „   *globulifera,* Brady.
   Cytheridea punctillata, Brady.
      „   *sorbyana,* Jones.
   Cytherura concentrica, B., C. and R.
   Cytheropteron nodosum, var. Brady.
      „   *pyramidale,* Brady.
      „   *septentrionale,* nov. sp.
      „   *montrosiense,* B., C. and R.

8. Smith Sound, off Brevoort Island, 210 fathoms, lat. 78° 57′ N.
   Cythere costata, Brady.
   Cytherura similis, Sars.

9. Sounding.   6 fathoms.   Lat. 82° 27' N.

Cytheropteron montrosiense, B., C. and R.

10. Sand from Floeberg Beach.   Lat. 82° 29' N.

Cythere cribrosa, B., C. and R.

Respecting this list, all that it is needful here to observe is the general similarity of the fauna to that of the Post-tertiary glacial beds of Scotland, and also, of course, to that of the North British seas, *e.g.* Shetland and the Northern Hebrides. Two species appear to be undescribed, but all the rest are well known as glacial fossils. Considering the small amount of material obtained, the number of species—twenty-one—is large, and would seem to denote a very considerable development of minute crustacean life in the sea-bed of these remote regions.

	I.	II.	III.
Brachyura	3	—	—
Anomura .	1	—	—
Macrura .	11	6	9
Stomatopoda	—	1	1
Cumacea .	6	—	—
Isopoda .	7	2	4
Amphipoda	39	21	12
Phyllopoda	3	1	1
Ostracoda	34	—	21
Copepoda	2	1	5
Cirripedia	4	1	1
Pycnogonida	3	3	2
Total	113	36	56

The foregoing Table exhibits (I.) the number of species obtained during the 'Valorous' cruise on the west coast of Greenland and in Davis Strait; (II.) the number mentioned by Buchholz as occurring on the south and west coasts of Greenland; (III.) the number obtained by the British Arctic Expedition north of lat 78° N. in Smith Sound and on the coasts of Grinnell Land.

EXPLANATION OF THE PLATES.

PLATE II.

Fig. 1. *Arcturus baffini,* var. *Feildeni* ; natural size.

Fig. 2. *Anonyx gulosus?,* slightly enlarged: *a,* head and antennæ (lateral view); *b,* maxilliped; *c, d,* hands of first and second pairs of legs; *e,* end of postabdomen, showing the form of the third segment; *f,* terminal segment and last pair of uropoda; all much enlarged.

Fig. 3. *Onesimus Edwardsii,* slightly enlarged: *a,* head and antennæ (lateral view); *b,* maxilliped; *c, d,* hands of first and second pairs of legs; *e,* end of postabdomen, showing form of third segment (lateral view); *f,* terminal segment and last two pairs of uropoda ; all much enlarged.

PLATE III.

Fig. 1. *Branchipus (Branchinecta) arcticus,* greatly enlarged : *a,* one of the large prehensile antennæ ; *b,* one of the branchial feet; *c,* caudal appendages; all still further enlarged.

Fig. 2. *Lernæopoda arcturi,* greatly enlarged ; *a,* outer antennæ ; *b,* first maxilliped ; further enlarged.

Fig. 3. *Nymphon hirtum,* var. *obtusidigitum,* natural size : *a,* mandible ; *b, c,* one of the appendages of the first and second pairs ; enlarged.

No. VIII.

ANNELIDA.

By W. C. McIntosh, M.D., F.R.S.

Captain Feilden, one of the naturalists of the recent Arctic Expedition under Sir George Nares, placed in my hands a small collection of Annelids dredged between latitudes 79° and 82° 30′ N.

The majority of the species represented in this collection have a very wide range in northern waters, many being common to the British seas and the shores of the North Atlantic generally, and on the American side stretching from the Gulf of St. Lawrence northward to the Polar ice beyond Smith Sound. With two exceptions all the species occur in the seas of Spitsbergen, and one of them is Icelandic, while the second is a somewhat doubtful form.

In the account recently published by Dr. E. Marenzeller, of the annelids procured by the Austro-Hungarian North Polar Expedition under Lieutenants Weyprecht and Payer, 27 species are mentioned, of these no less than 18 do not occur in the following list; but no further weight should be put on this than is warranted by the fact that only a few of the abundant forms which possess a wide circumpolar range have been obtained in either case. Many of the 18, indeed, occur on the Canadian coast, and run northwards to Davis Strait; on the other hand, about half the species procured in the English Expedition do not appear in the Austro-Hungarian collection, made between latitudes 74° and 79° N.

POLYCHÆTA.

POLYNOIDÆ.

Nychia cirrosa, Pall.
Eunoa Œrstedii, Malmgren.
Eunoa nodosa, Sars.
Lagisca rarispina, Sars.
Harmathoë imbricata, L.
Antinoe Sarsii, Kbg.

PHYLLODOCIDÆ.

Phyllodoce grœnlandica, Œrsted.

SYLLIDÆ.

Autolytus longisetosus, Œrsted.

NEREIDÆ.

Nereis zonata, Malmgren.

LUMBRINEREIDÆ.

Lumbriconereis fragilis, O. F. Müller.

SCALIBREGMIDÆ.

Eumenia crassa, Œrsted.

HALELMINTHIDÆ.

Capitella capitata, Fabr.

AMPHICTENIDÆ.

Cistenides granulata, L.

AMPHARETIDÆ.

Amphicteis Sundevalli, Malmgren.

TEREBELLIDÆ.

Scione lobata, Malmgren.
Axionice flexuosa, Grube.
Thelepus circinnatus, Fabr.

SABELLIDÆ.

Sabella Spetsbergensis, Malmgren.
Euchone analis, Kröyer.
Chone infundibuliformis, Kröyer.

OLIGOCHÆTA.

LUMBRICIDÆ.

Clitellio arenarius, O. F. Müll.

GEPHYREA.

PRIAPULIDÆ.

Priapulus caudatus, Lmk.

CHÆTOGNATHA.

Sagitta bipunctata, Quoy and Gaimard.

I am indebted to Dr. E. L. Moss (late surgeon H.M.S. 'Alert'), who served with the Arctic Expedition, for the notice and determination of this *Sagitta*. He informs me that it was common in Melville Bay and Smith Sound. The most northern specimens were captured by him in Bessels' Bay, lat. 81° 7′ N. [This species has a very extensive range from the British shores northward, southward and westward.]

No. IX.

ECHINODERMATA.[1]

By Prof. P. Martin Duncan, M.B., Lond., F.R.S.,
Pres. Geol. Soc.

and

W. Percy Sladen, Esq., F.G.S., F.L.S., etc.

[The Echinodermata collected in Smith Sound and at the
winter-quarters of H.M.SS. ' Alert' and ' Discovery' were
obtained by the naturalists of the expedition, Capt. H. W.
Feilden, and Mr. Hart, under the superintendence of Capt.
Sir George Nares, R.N., F.R.S., under no small difficulty.
Apart from the trouble of dredging when the tangles froze on
coming out of the sea, the proceeding could not be frequently
attempted; yet the number of specimens collected was considerable. The collection, consisting of specimens admirably
cleaned and preserved in spirit, and of others equally well
taken care of in the dry state, was sent to the British
Museum. Dr. Günther confided it to me for description
and classification; and after I had determined the species, I
asked Mr. Percy Sladen, F.G.S., F.L.S., to examine the
forms independently and to join me in drawing up this report. Our results were nearly the same; but to my col-
league is due the new species of *Asteracanthion.* Dr.
Carpenter was good enough to examine and determine the
two species of *Comatula.* I am very glad to have this
opportunity of thanking Capt. Feilden for his assistance in

[1] Abridged from ' Ann. and Mag. Nat. Hist.' 1877, pp. 449–470.

giving information regarding the depth, temperatures, and localities relating to the specimens.

The collection is so interesting and the specimens are so variable, that we propose to describe it fully in a separate monograph.—P. MARTIN DUNCAN.]

Localities.—To avoid repetition, the following are the positions of the collecting-stations in Grinnell Land mentioned in this report :—

Floeberg Beach (the winter-quarters of H.M.S. ' Alert '), lat. 82° 27′ N., long. 61° 42′ W.

Discovery Bay (the winter-quarters of H.M.S. ' Discovery '), lat. 81° 41′ N., long. 64° 45′ W.

Richardson Bay, lat. 80° 5′ N.

Cape Frazer, lat. 79° 44′ N.

Hayes Point, lat. 79° 42′ N.

Dobbin Bay, lat. 79° 40′ N.

Cape Louis Napoleon, lat. 79° 38′ N.

Franklin Pierce Bay, lat. 79° 25′ N.

Although the present Report is chiefly confined to a description of the Echinoderms obtained north of lat. 78° N., it has been thought desirable and interesting to include the record of a dredging made by Capt. Feilden during the outward voyage, on July 2, 1875, in lat. 65° N. The station was 26 miles from the Greenland coast, and the depth 30 fathoms; bottom rocky, with rounded pebbles. The following Asteroids and Ophiurans were taken here :—*Asteracanthion polaris*, M. & T. ; *Solaster endeca* (Linn.), Forbes ; *Ophioglypha robusta* (Ayr.), Lym. ; *Ophioglypha Stuwitzii* (Lütk.), Lym. ; *Ophiopholis bellis* (Linck), Lym.

List of the Echinoderms collected during the Arctic Expedition of 1875–76.

HOLOTHUROIDEA.

Cucumaria frondosa (Gunn.), Forbes.

ECHINOIDEA.

Strongylocentrotus dröbachiensis (O. F. M.), A. Ag.

ASTEROIDEA.

Asteracanthion grœnlandicus, Stp.
—— *polaris*, M. & T.
—— *palæocrystallus*, nobis.
Stichaster albulus (Stimps.), Verrill.
Crossaster papposus (Linck), M. & T.
Solaster endeca (Linn.), Forbes.
—— *furcifer*, v. Düb. & Kor.
Pteraster militaris (O. F. M.), M. & T

OPHIUROIDEA.

Ophioglypha Sarsii (Lütk.), Lym.
—— *robusta* (Ayr.), Lym.
—— *Stuwitzii* (Lütk.), Lym.
Ophiocten sericeum (Forb.), Ljungm.
Ophiopholis bellis (Linck), Lym.
Amphiura Holbölli, Lütk.
Ophiacantha spinulosa, M. & T.
Astrophyton arcticum (Leach).

CRINOIDEA.

Antedon Eschrichtii (Müll.).
—— *celtica* (Barrett).

HOLOTHUROIDEA.

Cucumaria frondosa (Gunner.), Forbes.

Coll. Feilden : Baffin's Bay.

A *Cucumaria* with smooth tough body, of subpentagonal ovate form. Ambulacral suckers arranged in five longitudinal series, each being a double row, with the tube feet alternating. Suckers capable of entire retraction. Tentacles ten, pedunculate, frondose, all of equal size.

This Holothurian has a very extensive geographical distribution, being chronicled by Forbes, under the name of *C.*

fucicola, from Assistance Bay (Capt. Penny's voyage), and by Stimpson from Grand Manan in the Bay of Fundy. It is found also on the coast of Massachusetts, Gulf of Georgia (Salenka), San Francisco (Ayres), along the whole Scandinavian coast, Iceland, Færöe Islands, and in the English Channel.

C. frondosa attains great dimensions, the present individual (one specimen only was obtained) being but small; its length is 80 millims., and diameter about 50 millims.

ECHINOIDEA.

Strongylocentrotus dröbachiensis (Müller), A. Ag.

Coll. Feilden: Richardson Bay, 70 fms. (young); Franklin Pierce Bay, 15 fms., bottom-temperature 29°·5 F.; Cape Napoleon; Hayes Point, 35 fms., bottom-temperature 29°·5 F.

Coll. Hart: Discovery Bay, 15–20 fms., muddy bottom; Franklin Pierce Bay, 13–15 fms., stony.

Owing to the extensive range of this boreal echinoid, the variations to which it is subject are so great that there are perhaps few other species which include in their synonymy so large a number of modern determinations. Distant observers, depending upon the stability of 'local forms,' have founded numerous so-called new species, all of which have hitherto, however, proved untenable when due comparison has come to be made with a large series of specimens.

The northern varieties, known as *S. granulatus* (Say), Gould, and *S. chlorocentrotus*, Brandt, fail to present any characters of sufficient importance to warrant their separation from the *dröbachiensis* group, although when isolated and extreme examples are compared the differences at first sight appear very marked.

Similarly with the specimens collected by the recent Expedition, separate individuals placed by the side of a single *S. dröbachiensis* from a more southern habitat present superficially a striking divergence.

Of these Arctic forms the test is depressed, the spines of the abactinal surface so small (merely miliaries) and so widely spaced that the echinus has quite a naked appearance. The pores are arranged in arcs of 5–6. The primary tubercles are large, only one to each plate, and form prominent vertical rows. The scrobicular areas are wide and bounded by an irregular circlet of tubercles little larger than miliaries; and there are but few other tubercles in addition to these on the plates above the ambitus. Extending from the actinostome to the ambitus there is a moderate-sized secondary tubercle on each side of the primary.

All the specimens present the appearance of stunted growth.

The colour of the test is a varying shade of purplish brown, and that of the spines greenish grey.

On some examples the pedicellariæ are remarkably numerous, especially the large tridactyle form on the abactinal surface.

Good series of specimens were obtained at several stations, and in general facies present great constancy of character.

The largest individual (from Cape Napoleon) measures 43 millims. in diameter, 21 millims. in height, and has 20 primary interambulacral tubercles.

ASTEROIDEA.

Asteracanthion grönlandicus, Steenstrup.

Coll. Feilden: Discovery Bay, 25 fms.; Cape Frazer, 80 fms.; Hayes Point, 25 fms.; Franklin Pierce Bay, 15 fms.

Coll. Hart: Franklin Pierce Bay, 13–15 fms., stony.

This is a small starfish, with five moderately thick arms. Proportion of disk-radius to arm-radius 1 : 4·5 or 5. Ambulacral spines rather long and cylindrical, arranged (in very irregular alternation) two and one to each plate. The double spines radiate in opposite directions, the single ones standing vertical to the floor of the furrow. Except in young individuals, and near the tip of the arm, the double series are the most numerous, being generally borne by two or three plates in succession. After these follow two or three (according to age) longitudinal series of separate spines, not quite so long as the ambulacral spines, and tapering slightly at their tips. The middle series, when present, are smaller than the others, and placed midway upon the lateral imbricating pieces. At the base of each of the spines of these three series is a circlet of pedicellariæ. The ossicles and interspaces of the calcareous network on the abactinal surface of the rays present a very transversely elongate arrangement, in consequence of which the spinelets springing from the imbricating pieces assume the character (though irregularly) of a transverse position across the arm. The dorsal spinelets, which are much finer and shorter than the ventro-lateral series, are arranged in groups upon the ossicles, and in specimens preserved in spirit are more than half-covered by the thick corrugated skin which invests the body. The pedicellariæ are, as a rule, not very numerous upon the dorsal surface. The papulæ are single. Upon the disk the spinelets are more closely placed; and this, in spirit-examples, gives quite a distinct appearance to that portion of the animal, whilst in some specimens the disk-spinelets are rather longer than those which are found upon the rays.

Dr. Lütken is of opinion that this is the species cited by Forbes under the name of *Uraster violaceus*, from Assistance Bay (Capt. Penny's Expedition).[1] It seems probable to us, also, that the *Asterias violacea*, in Sabine's Report on Parry's voyage, is likewise *A. grönlandicus*, since the *Asterias rubens*, Fab. (non Linné), also there mentioned, is referable to *A. polaris*, M. & T.

Asteracanthion polaris, Müller and Troschel.

Some large specimens were taken on the Torske Bank, Greenland, on the outward journey; and several young

---

[1] 'Vidensk. Meddel. 1857, Overs. Grönl. Echin.' p. 29.

examples occurred in Capt. Feilden's dredging in lat. 65° N., 26 miles from the Greenland coast, at a depth of 30 fathoms.

Asteracanthion palæocrystallus, n. sp.

In general appearance this starfish bears a strong resemblance to a *Cribrella*, the rays, five in number, being round and tumid; they are long and taper considerably towards the point. The disk is small, its diameter being proportional to that of the rays as 1 : 5·5. Skin semitransparent, not corrugated, and investing thickly every appendage of the body. Ambulacral pores well spaced, forming two simple rows of sucker-feet, as in *Stichaster*. Each interambulacral plate bears two very slender spines, which form two regular rows, one radiating towards the furrow, the other to the margin. The spines upon the sides of the arms are much shorter than the ambulacral spines, and comparatively more robust, and are the same in size and character as the spinelets of the dorsal surface. The ossicles of the abactinal network are arranged more quadrilaterally than is usual in *Asteracanthion*; a regular median line passes down each ray, the others running parallel and transverse to this with more or less regularity. Only a single spinelet is given off at each decussation, with an additional one, frequently, on the imbricating ossicle; the spinelets are consequently widely spaced and assume (although somewhat irregularly) a fairly rectilineal arrangement. The spinelets are of the same shape and structure as in *Stichaster*; they are deeply grooved, and have 3–5 denticles proceeding from their truncate and slightly radiate apex. The ambulacral spines have the shafts also denticulate. The pedicellariæ ('croisés,' Perrier) are more numerous upon the dorsal surface than the spinelets, amongst which they are placed separately and at intervals apart. These pedicellariæ are large and closely resemble those of *Stichaster*, the fore part of the 'jaw' being very gibbous and truncate. The pedicellariæ together with the dorsal spinelets, which are but little longer, are covered with a thick investing membrane, which, in spirit preparations, gives quite a papillate appearance to the starfish.

Upon the disk the spines are somewhat more crowded than upon the rays; and the 'eye'-spines at the tip of the rays form a robust terminal fringe. The madreporiform plate is obscure; and of the large simple pedicellariæ there are but very few.

Although this species resembles *Stichaster* in so many respects, the arrangement of the dorsal ossicles is hardly such as would include it within that genus. *A. palæocrystallus* may fairly, however, be regarded as a connecting link between *Asteracanthion* and *Stichaster*.

From the character of the ambulacral spines, the absence of papulæ, and the obscurity of the madreporiform body, we are disposed to regard even the largest specimen we have as being not yet fully developed: it measures 30 millims. in its greatest diameter, and 5·5 millims. across the disk, and was collected by Capt. Feilden in Discovery Bay. Depth 25 fathoms, hard bottom. Another individual from Cape Frazer (80 fathoms) is only 10 millims. in greatest diameter, yet presents all the characters of the larger specimen.

Stichaster albulus (Stimps.), Verrill.

Coll. Feilden: Franklin Pierce Bay, 15 fathoms; Proven, 13 fathoms.

A little starfish with small disk and rounded or somewhat arched rays, the number of which is almost invariably six, three rays on one side being, as a rule, very much shorter than those on the other. Proportion of the diameter of the disk to that of the arms 1 : 5 · or rather more. The ambulacral furrows are wide, with suckers arranged in two simple rows. On each interambulacral plate are two 'ambulacral' spines radiating slightly to the right and left. Closely succeeding to those on the sides of the arms follow a series of three similar spines, but not always a series opposite to each interambulacral plate, owing to the imbricating pieces being more widely spaced. The dorsal ossicles present a regular rectangular arrangement; and the interspaces, which are very small and are occupied by a single papula, form, in consequence, regular longitudinal and transverse rectilineal series. From each intersection springs a small subquadrate group of from three to five short dorsal spines, amongst which are placed one or two pedicellariæ. Towards the sides the pedicellariæ are more numerous. The spine groups are regularly disposed in longitudinal and transverse lines, those of the middle row being more densely packed than the others, thereby forming a more or less distinct median line down each ray. The spinelets are of equal length, and, being closely set, give a smooth velvety appearance to the starfish. From the apices of the spinelets, which are broader than the bases, proceed three or four small denticles.

Only three specimens of this *Stichaster* were obtained in Franklin Pierce Bay, and were quite young individuals, the largest measuring 16 millims. in its largest diameter. A much finer example was dredged at Proven on the outward journey, in which the diameters of rays and disk were respectively 30 millims. and 6 millims.

Crossaster papposus (Linck), Müller and Troschel.[1]

Coll. Feilden: Discovery Bay, 25 fms., hard bottom; Cape Frazer, 80 fms.; Franklin Pierce Bay, 15 fms., bottom-temperature 29°·5 Fahr.

Coll. Hart: Franklin Pierce Bay, 13–15 fms.

---

[1] The genus *Solaster* of Forbes included the two starfishes known as *Asterias endeca*, Linn., and *A. papposa*, Fabr. (Linck). The morphological differences of these forms are such, however, as to necessitate their being regarded as representatives of two distinct genera. Confining, therefore, Forbes's *Solaster* to his own type (*S. endeca*), Müller and Troschel's genus *Crossaster* (synonym of *Solaster*, Forbes, published a year later) is naturally assigned to the *Asterias papposa* type, Gray's designation *Polyaster* having been appropriated by Ehrenberg (*Polyasterias*) at an earlier date. The propriety of the above limitation was suggested by Dr. Lütken so far back as 1857. (Cf. 'Vidensk. Meddelelser,' 1857, p. 35.

In the 'Oversigt over Grönlands Echinodermer,' [1] Dr. Lütken records that amongst the specimens of *C. papposus* which he had examined there occurred only one example of the ten-armed variety, those with twelve arms being the most common.

All the specimens of this collection are ten-armed, with the exception of one small and very young example having nine. Its greatest diameter is only 18 millims.

When compared with series of similar size from more temperate waters, the polar specimens are characterised by finer arms, fewer spine-clusters (bearing fewer but very much longer. spinelets), the spine-clusters more widely separated from one another, and the ventral spaces almost naked. These points are so striking in some individuals that at first sight one is tempted to consider that we have here a well-marked variety of this almost cosmopolitan starfish. Careful study, however, of the series leads us to the conclusion that no sound distinction can be drawn ; and we would offer as a suggestion explanatory of the divergence, that in these Arctic forms of *Crossaster* premature phases are more slowly passed through, and that development of detail takes place in a different ratio to the body-growth from that which obtains under more favourable conditions of life.

The largest specimen obtained measures 93 millims. in diameter.

Brandt founded a species, *Asterias affinis*, upon a single specimen obtained in Behring Straits, but which, from the short description given, appears only to have been similar to the specimens before us ; and, such being the case, the grounds are not sufficient to warrant the maintenance of his species. In all probability *A. alboverrucosa*, Brandt, is also identical.

A singular instance of the rapacity of this starfish may be here related. The disk of one of the large individuals from Discovery Bay being considerably distended, it was cut open; and the distention was found to result from the creature having gorged a young *Strongylocentrotus dröbachi-*

[1] 'Vidensk. Meddelelser' for 1857, p. 40.

ensis !, nothing but the clean calcareous plates of the test remaining. In the stomach of another (very much smaller) specimen was found the shell of *Trochus olivaceus*, Brown (kindly determined by Dr. Gwyn Jeffreys).

Solaster endeca (Linn.), Forbes.

One young specimen, 14 millims. in greatest diameter, was dredged by Capt. Feilden in lat. 65° N., 26 miles from the Greenland coast, at a depth of 30 fathoms.

Solaster furcifer, v. Düben and Koren.

Coll. Feilden : Cape Frazer, 80 fms.

A starfish of somewhat depressed form, having five broad flat arms. Proportion of disk-radius to length of arm 1 : 3. The calcareous network of the dorsal surface is very regular ; and the spine-clusters or paxillæ, which spring from the intersections, form longitudinal series which run parallel to the median line of the ray ; consequently only two or three of the middle series reach to the tip, although from fourteen to sixteen may be counted at the base of the arm. The paxillæ are very compact and have a stout rounded base, nearly twice as wide as high, bearing a crown of spinelets (about fifteen to twenty) in length about equal to the diameter of the base. The spinelets are, as a rule, flat ; and from the angles of the apex, which is as broad as or broader than the base, proceed two small denticles, giving the appearance to the spinelet of a two-pronged fork ; sometimes the spinelet is triangular, in which case there are three prongs. On the sides of the arms are two rows of large paxillæ or spine-clusters, the lower series being twice the breadth of the upper ones, and these themselves being much larger than the rest of the dorsal paxillæ just described. There are about twenty large marginal paxillæ from the arm-angle to the tip. Each interambulacral plate bears three equal-sized spines, running parallel to the furrow ; and exterior to these are three or four spines webbed together into a ' comb' and placed obliquely, or even in some cases at right angles, to the ambulacral series; whilst midway between the combs and the margin of the ray are three or four small spines (not sufficient to form a paxilla proper), which stand quite isolated and only extend about one third of the distance from the mouth to the tip of the ray. The madreporiform tubercle is excentral and situated at about one-third the distance from the centre to the margin of the disk. The mouth-plates are large and broad, the marginal spines interlocking with one another.

Only two specimens were obtained by Captain Feilden, the largest of which measures 65 millims. in its greatest diameter, and 21 millims. across the disk; the arms at the base are 13 millims. broad.

Pteraster militaris (O. F. M.), Müller and Troschel.

Coll. Hart : Dobbin Bay, 30 fms.

This starfish is readily distinguished from its congeners and the majority of other asteroids by the singular fin-like margin surrounding the arms, by the membranous skin which is spread over the upper surface, as well as by the series of webbed spines which stand, in transverse ranges like fans, by the side of the ambulacral furrow.

The form of the animal is pentagonal, the upper contour of the body high and arched, and the underside flat. Proportion of disk-radius to arm-radius 1 : 2. Each interambulacral plate is furnished with five or six long spines, which are connected together by a membrane into a webbed comb placed transversely to the ambulacral furrow. The outward spine of each comb is double the length of the others, and extends about half its length beyond the edge of the ray. These long spines are also united to one another by a connecting tissue, and thus form the fin-like fringe which surrounds the entire starfish. The ambulacral spines forming the fan-like comb are nearly equal in length, the middle ones being slightly longer.

The body-skeleton is composed of a calcareous network,

from each of the cross joinings of which proceeds a spine-fasciculus bearing three or four spinelets. The whole dorsal surface of the animal is covered and concealed by a membranous tissue supported above the body, like a tent-cloth, by the spinelets, to the tips of which it is attached. A hollow infradermal cavity is thus formed. Neither the anus nor the madreporiform tubercle has any special aperture in this investing membrane; there is, however, a single large-sized opening, surrounded by a margin of spines, situated nearly over the dorso-central axis. In and out of this aperture Dr. Stimpson has observed currents of water passing, as in the cloaca of a *Holothuria*, from which fact he was led to regard the functions of the cavity as subservient to respiration.[1] MM. Koren and Danielssen, however, have pointed out that this intermediate space between the double dorsal skin fulfils a further and more important purpose by becoming a chamber in which the development of the eggs and embryos takes place.[2]

Although our knowledge of marsupiation in Echinoderms has recently been largely augmented by the additional instances which Sir Wyville Thomson records as occurring in species from southern seas,[3] it is most interesting to find so special an adaptation for the purpose in this truly Arctic asteroid.

Two specimens only were obtained, being dredged by Mr. Hart in Dobbin Bay. They measure about 60 millims. in their greatest diameter.

OPHIUROIDEA.

Ophioglypha Sarsii (Lütken), Lyman.

Coll. Feilden: Floeberg Beach, 10 fms.; Discovery Bay, 25 fms.; Hayes Point.

An *Ophioglypha* with mouth-shields shield-shaped, longer

---

[1] Stimpson, 'Marine Invertebrata of Grand Manan,' p. 15, in Smithsonian Contributions, vol. vi.

[2] Koren and Danielssen, 'Fauna littoralis Norvegiæ,' Heft 2, p. 58.

[3] Wyville Thomson, 'Journ. Linn. Soc.' vol. xiii. p. 55.

than broad; length less than, or only equal to, their distance from the margin of the disk. Papillæ of the disk-incision about fifteen, and rather broad. Under arm-plates widely separate, of a very broad, short triangle-shape. Two tentacle-scales. No infrabrachial indentations. Spines rather long, equal in length to the side arm-plates.

This is the most northerly echinoderm brought home by the Expedition, a fine specimen with a disk-diameter of 26 millims. having been taken by Capt. Feilden at the winter-quarters of H.M.S. 'Alert,' in N. lat. 82° 27'. Other examples of this species were obtained at Discovery Bay, and among them one which is provided with remarkably long arm-spines, being in relative proportion fully twice the length of the spines generally occurring in *O. Sarsii*. In this individual the three spines of the sixth joint measure respectively 2·45 millims., 2·25 millims., 1·4 millim.; the under arm-plate being ·7 millim. long, the arm-joint 1 millim., and the disk-diameter 15 millims. The remaining features of the specimen agree too closely with the characters of *O. Sarsii* (Lütk.), Lym., to warrant its removal, in our opinion, from that species, even as a provisional variety.

In some cases great irregularity is exhibited in the mouth-papillæ, one abnormal example being particularly worthy of notice. In the *Ophioglyphæ* the innermost mouth-papilla generally stands immediately over the teeth, and might be easily mistaken for a tooth, being, in fact, affixed to the tooth-plate and not to the lateral plates. In *O. Sarsii*, as well as in other members of the genus, two additional papillæ are generally associated with it, one on either hand, and are in like manner borne by the ossicle upon which the teeth are placed.

In consequence of this arrangement it has long seemed probable to one of us that these subdental papillæ should be regarded as tooth-papillæ (of which they are in truth the homologues) rather than as mouth-papillæ, so-called, along with which they are commonly counted. One of the specimens taken in Discovery Bay throws considerable light upon this question.

In this individual the dental armature consists of four teeth regularly superposed, following upon which, and occupying the same breadth as a tooth, are three ossicles, which fit to one another wedgewise with sloping sides. Then come two which fit together and correspond in their shape with the irregularities of the upper and under tier, which latter consists of from three to five compact close-fitting papillæ; and these again are succeeded by three or four (in some rays five) moderately long, round-tipped, smaller papillæ, the whole forming a compact mass suggestive, in the highest degree, of ordinary tooth-papillæ, such as occur, for instance, in *Ophiothrix*; and yet in every detail, even to measurements, the specimen conforms to the diagnosis of *Ophioglypha Sarsii*. This individual has a disk-diameter of 22 millims.

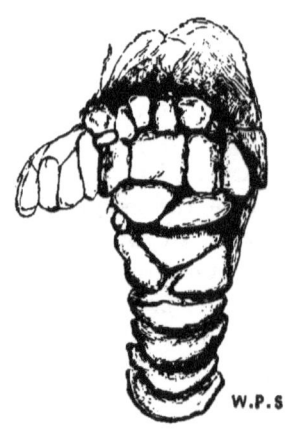

Abnormal development of the dental armature in *O. Sarsii.*

Bearing in mind the tendency towards vertical reduplication of the mouth-papillæ in some genera, this cannot fail to be regarded as suggestive of the manner in which primitive tooth-papillæ may have been developed ; nor is such an assumption by any means extravagant when the great irregularity of these parts amongst Arctic forms is taken into consideration.

Ophioglypha robusta (Ayres), Lyman.

Coll. Feilden : Discovery Bay, 25 fms., hard bottom ; Richardson Bay, 70 fms. ; Hayes Point, 35 fms., bottom temperature 29°·5, and also at 25 fms.; Franklin Pierce Bay, 15 fms., bottom-temperature 25°·5.

Coll. Hart: 'Winter-quarters,' Discovery Bay; Franklin Pierce Bay, 13–15 fms., bottom stony.

An *Ophioglypha* with arms very finely tapering, and disk with regularly arranged scales of nearly equal size. Mouth-shields ovate shield-shaped, length less than, or at most only equal to, their breadth; length much less than the distance from the margin of the disk. Papillæ of the disk-incision very short and stout, often grouped. Under arm-plates broadly heart-shaped; one tentacle-scale.

This species was obtained at various stations, as indicated in the list of localities; and though neither the abundance nor the size of the specimens was remarkable, several good series were collected. The characters which have been regarded as 'specific' are remarkably constant; and no essential difference can be traced between these Arctic forms and specimens taken from the coast of Maine, U. S., with which they have been compared, excepting that in the northern Ophiurans the arm-spines are longer and somewhat more delicate, and that the outer margin of the under arm-plates is more arched and the re-entering angle is far less developed, in certain specimens being even altogether untraceable. In some large examples the upper arm-plates are very markedly hexagonal.

Although this deviation is very constant, the foundation of 'a variety' on the strength of such characters alone is hardly justifiable.

The arm-spines are moderately stout and tapering, the upper one being flattened and much larger than the others.

In most of the specimens under present consideration, the under arm-plates are well separated from one another by the side plates and do not overlap, although in one individual from Discovery Bay the first ten impinge distinctly in consequence of their side arm-plates not meeting. This feature at the basal portion of the arm has been noted by Dr. Lütken as occurring in large specimens from Greenland, whilst he remarks at the same time that in none of the Danish examples examined by him do the under arm-plates touch.

The largest specimen was taken by Capt. Feilden in Franklin Pierce Bay, the diameter of the disk (dried) being 10 millims.

Ophioglypha Stuwitzii (Lütken), Lyman.

Two specimens were collected by Capt. Feilden in a dredging made in lat. 65° N., twenty-six miles from the Greenland coast, depth 30 fms.

Ophiocten sericeum (Forbes), Ljungman.

Coll. Feilden: Discovery Bay, 25 fms., hard bottom; Cape Frazer, 80 fms.; Hayes Point, 35 fms., bottom-temperature 29°·5.

Coll. Hart: Discovery Bay, 15–20 fms., muddy bottom, also at 11 fms.; Franklin Pierce Bay, 13–15 fms.

Disk very flat, with margin forming a sharp angle; covered with imbricating scales and a superficial squamo-granular layer, through which only portions of the radial shields and primary plates are visible. No disk-incisions, the disk forming a little arch over the base of the arms. A row of papillæ edges the genital slit, and passes over the arm along the disk-margin continuous with the series from the other side. The first three, or sometimes four, upper arm-plates at the base bear papillæ. Side arm plates meet below, but not above. One tentacle-scale. Three arm-spines, arranged along the outer edge of the side arm-plate, the two upper spines being much the largest.

The main variation which we have noted in the Arctic specimens of this species consists in the greater length of the arm-spines as compared with those of more southern examples. In a specimen 9·2 millims. in disk-diameter the length of the upper arm-spine of the sixth joint was 1·85 millim. (in one case 2·3 millims.!); in another, with a diameter of disk of 8·5 millims, the same spine was 1·8 millim. long, three arm-joints in this individual being exactly 2 millims. In addition to the above, variations occur in the contour of the mouth-shields, and in the larger examples considerable irregularity is also found in the number and position of the mouth-papillæ. Amongst this collection are several specimens having a very decidedly pentagonal form of disk.

In our opinion, none of the above variations can be regarded as of greater morphological significance than growth-phases, or at most individual variations only. The largest specimen obtained was 11 millims. in disk-diameter.

Ophiopholis bellis (Linck), Lyman.

Coll. Feilden : lat. 65° N., 26 miles from Greenland coast, 30 fms.

Amphiura Holbölli, Lütken.[1]

Coll. Feilden : Franklin Pierce Bay, 15 fms., bottom-temperature 29°·5 F.

An *Amphiura* with disk lobed ; radial shields long and narrow ; mouth-shields rounded ; side mouth-shields large, subtriangular, with the sides re-entering and angles rounded. Three pairs of mouth-papillæ, the middle ones placed higher than the others. Under arm-plates pentagonal. One tentacle-scale rounded ; arm-spines 3–4.

Only a single specimen of *Amphiura* was taken ; and this, although it differs slightly from the type form in the relative measurements of certain points of detail, we have little hesitation in assigning to Dr. Lütken's species, the variations, in our opinion, not being of greater importance than such as we should regard as dependent on locality and conditions of life.

The arms are less broad, and take their origin in a more

---

[1] So much confusion has arisen in consequence of uncertainty as to the identity of the original application of the appellation *O. Sundevalli*, that we prefer to retain Dr. Lütken's name, despite the example of certain recent writers to the contrary.

deeply re-entering curve of the disk-margin, the radial shields are narrower, and the breadth of upper arm-plates in proportion to their length is less than in the type forms, as the following measurements will indicate :—Diameter of disk 8 millims.; radial shield, length 1·3 millim., breadth ·35 millim.; sixth upper arm-plate, length ·6 millim., breadth ·9 millim.

The spines are hollow cylinders, stout, blunt, and but slightly tapering ; the upper spine on each side-plate tapers most. The first fifteen arm-joints bear four spines, the succeeding joints three only.

An interesting feature connected with this specimen is worthy of record, and is one which does not appear to have been noted by previous observers. The central spines are more or less flattened throughout their whole length; and at the tip compression has been carried to such a degree as to form a thin and somewhat expanded head—a peculiarity which is at once suggestive of a characteristic spine-appendage possessed by *A. filiformis*; and although in the specimen under notice this structural feature is by no means so fully developed as in that Ophiuran, it is still sufficiently marked to impress upon the mind the near relationship of the two species and the community of their descent—an hypothesis which is also further strengthened by the association of both the forms in more southern waters.

Ophiacantha spinulosa, Müller and Troschel.

Coll. Feilden: Discovery Bay, 25 fms., hard bottom ; Cape Frazer, 80 fms. ; Franklin Pierce Bay, 15 fms. Temperature 29°·5 Fahr.

Coll. Hart: Franklin Pierce Bay, 13–15 fms., bottom stony.

An *Ophiacantha* with disk covered with small round scales, each bearing a small short spinelet. Radial shields very obscure, sometimes quite covered. No disk-incision ; and the dorsal membrane is prolonged over the base of the rays. Mouth-shields twice as broad as long, irregular ovate. Side mouth-shields long, narrow, arched and meeting within. Under arm-plates heptagonal or subheptagonal, breadth equal to length. Dorsal arm-plates triangular. Side arm-plates meeting above and below. Spines 7–8, long, thin, and denticulate, placed on a keel.

A greater number of this Ophiuran have been brought home by the Expedition than of any other Echinoderm. The specimens range in size from those having a disk-diameter of 15 millims. to the young form of only 3 millims., and consequently furnish a most instructive series.

The variations dependent on growth are very considerable, so much so that isolated specimens taken from different stages in the series might easily be regarded as affording the types of distinct species.

Conclusive proof has been furnished by the material which we have had at our disposal that the *O. grönlandica*, M. and T., and the *O. arctica*, M. and T., are untenable species, as Dr. Lütken has already pointed out—and, further, that the characters which had hitherto been regarded as of specific value are not, as that eminent authority seems to infer, even variations such as can be regarded as dependent on distribution, but must be considered simply the phases incidental to age, together with ordinary individual variation.

Amongst the specimens procured by the naturalists of H.M.SS. ' Alert' and ' Discovery,' there are many presenting features developed in a manner which might be regarded as ' ultraspecific' when compared with the previously recognised modifications of this ' form.' In the present state of knowledge, however, it seems preferable to comprehend them under *O. spinulosa* of Müller and Troschel, rather than to burden further the nomenclature with novel designations.

The mouth-shields and the under arm-plates in this species are subject to very considerable changes and variation, both in contour and in their relative proportions of length to breadth. In large and adult specimens the number and arrangement of the mouth-papillæ is also irregular; and not only is there a frequent increase in number in the ordinal horizontal series, but there is also a great tendency toward reduplication of certain papillæ in the vertical axis of the Ophiuran. This seems to arise from the longitudinal cleavage of pre-existing papillæ.

In young individuals the spinelets of the disk are proportionally long, five or six times their own diameter, and present all the appearances of ordinary embryonic spines. During the process of growth, however, increase is made in thickness only, so that when maturity is attained, and the spinelets, along with the disk, are invested with the semi-transparent leathery membrane of the body, the appearance is more that of short stumpy prominences than of actual spines—a deception which at first sight gives a totally different character to the Ophiurans.

Astrophyton arcticum (Leach), *fide* Smith.

This Astrophyton was dredged off West Greenland by Mr. A. C. Horner, who accompanied Sir Allen Young in the 'Pandora,' at a depth of 600 fms. in Smith's Sound, lat. 78° 19′ N., long. 74° 30′ W. The present writers have not seen this specimen, and are indebted for the information to Mr. Edgar A. Smith, F.Z.S., of the British Museum, by whom it has been determined and referred to Leach's species. This is particularly interesting, as the original *Gorgonocephalus arcticus*, Leach, was obtained by Sir John Ross in Baffin's Bay, lat. 73° 37′ N., long. 77° 25′ W., at a depth of 800 fms. This was one of the earliest instances of a living organism being dredged from so great a depth.

CRINOIDEA.

Antedon Eschrichtii (Müller) and *Antedon celtica* (Barrett). Coll. Feilden: Discovery Bay, 25 fms., bottom hard.

The *Comatulæ* were handed over to Dr. Carpenter for determination; and he has kindly informed us of the occurrence of the above-named species.

Conclusions.

It is clearly manifest that extreme caution should be exercised in drawing conclusions as to the general character of a fauna, on the basis of such scanty material as it is possible for a single expedition to furnish ; and the authors feel that the great hesitation which they have in expressing definite opinion is fully warranted by the fact that considerable additions have recently been made to the Echinifauna of Northern-European waters, the details of which have not yet been published ; and these investigations may, in all probability, have the result of going far towards rendering present generalisations invalid.

Table showing the general Geographical Distribution of the various Species above mentioned ; together with an Indication of those obtained by the previous Arctic Explorers, Captains Parry and Penny.

Parry	Penny		Grinnell Land	Greenland	Arctic America	Iceland	Spitzbergen	Scandinavia	N. European.
	*	Cucumaria frondosa	. .	*	*	*	*	*	*
*	*	Strongylocentrotus dröbachiensis	*	*	*	*	*	*	*
?	*	Asteracanthion grönlandicus . .	*	*	*	. .	*	. .	*
*	. .	—— polaris	. .	*	*				
		—— palæocrystallus.	*						
		Stichaster albulus	*	*	*	*	*	. .	*
*	*	Crossaster papposus	*	*	*	*	. .	*	*
		Solaster endeca	. .	*	. .	*	. .	*	*
		—— furcifer	*	. .	. .	. .	. .	*	*
*	*	Pteraster militaris	*	*	*	. .	*	*	*
*	*	Ophioglypha Sarsii	*	*	*	*?	*	*	*
	*	—— robusta	*	*	*	*	*	*	*
	*	—— Stuwitzii	. .	*	*				
	*	Ophiocten sericeum	*	*	*	. .	*	. .	*
		Ophiopholis bellis	. .	*	*	*	*	*	*
?	?	Amphiura Holbölli	*	*	*?	. .	*	. .	*
*	*	Ophiacantha spinulosa	*	*	*	*	*	*	*
		Astrophyton arcticum [1] . . .	. .	*	*				
		Antedon Eschrichtii	*	*	*	. .	*?	. .	*
		—— celtica	*	?	. .	. .		. .	*

		The following were not obtained by this expedition :—
*	*	Ctenodiscus crispatus.
	*	Cucumaria Hyndmani = C. Korenii, Ltk.
	*	Chirodota brevis, Huxley, = Myriotrochus Rinkii, Stp.
	*	Ophiura glacialis, Forbes.

[1] This was dredged by Sir John Ross in 1818.

Of these twenty Greenland and Grinnell Land Echino-derms,

Fourteen are common to America and Europe ;

Three are known as American and *not* European ;

Two are known as European and *not* American ;

One now first recorded from Grinnell Land only.

Analysis similarly shows that fourteen out of the twenty are Grinnell-Landic.   And of these,

Eleven are common to America and Europe ;

Two are known as European and *not* American ;

One from Grinnell Land only.

Reasoning from present information, the writers are of opinion that the character of the Echinifauna under con-sideration is the effect of local modification acting upon a great polar distribution rather than of intercontinental emi-gration simply.

No. X.

POLÝZOA.

By George Busk, F.R.S.

The following list of the Polyzoa, collected on the late Arctic Expedition in Smith Sound and northwards by Captain H. W. Feilden, includes only about seventeen species. All except three have already been described, and are well known as high northern or Arctic forms. The three, which, so far as I am able to ascertain, appear to be new to science, are a species of *Flustra*, a minute species of *Eschara*, and a third supposed new species, belonging to the sub-order CTENOSTOMATA, represented unfortunately by such very scanty and imperfect specimens, that I only venture to propose it provisionally. And I may remark, with respect to some of the other forms, that the specimens are so covered with diatoms of numerous species as to be very difficult of examination. The collection is interesting, as perhaps giving the highest latitude, 82°. 27′ N., with which I am acquainted from which a Polyzoon has been procured.

Full descriptions and figures of the new forms will be pub-lished, if allowed, in the 'Proceedings of the Linnean Society.'

SUBORDER I. CHEILOSTOMATA. BK.

Fam. 1. *Cellulariadæ*. Bk.

Genus 1. *Scrupocellaria*. V. Ben.

1. *S. scabra*, V. B. (sp.)

Syn. *Cellarina scabra*, V. Ben. 'Bull. Brux.' tab. xv., p. 73, figs. 3–6.
　,,　*Cellularia scabra (forma typica)*, Smitt, 'Ofver S. Skand. Hafs Bryozoa,' 1867, pp. 283 and 314, tab. xvii. figs. 27–34.

Syn. *Cellularia scrupea*, Alder. 'Trans. Tynes Field Club,' vol. iii. fig. 148.
" *Scrupocellaria scrupea*, Bk. 'Quart. Journ. M. Sc.' iii. p. 254 (non aliter).
" *Scrupocellaria Delilii*, Alder, ib. N. Ser. iv. p. 107, pl. iv. figs. 4–8; P Bk. l. c. xii. p. 65, pl. xxii. figs. 1–3.
" *Scrupocellaria scabra*, Norman, 'On Rare British Polyzoa,' ' Q. J. M. S.' viii. p. 214; Hincks., ' Polyzoa from Iceland and Labrador,' ' Ann. N. Hist.' January 1877, p. 98.
" P *Crisia Delilii*, Andouin,·'Savign.' pl. xii. fig. 3.

Hab. Franklin Pierce Bay. 79° 29′ N. August 11, 1875, 13–15 fathoms. Stony bottom, H. W. F.; Sir Edward Belcher's ' Expedition !;' Hamilton Inlet, Labrador, Wallich; Godhavn Harbour, Disco, 5–20 fathoms, Norman; Sabine Island, German ' Polar Expedition ' (*teste* Hincks); Parry's Island, Spitsbergen, 61–50 fathoms, Smitt; Britain, Norman; Northumberland Coast, Alder; Coast of Belgium, V. Ben.

Genus 2. *Menipea*, Lamx.

1. *M. gracilis*, mihi.

Char. Zoœcia much elongated, subtubular downwards. Aperture oval, border slightly thickened; usually a single spine on the outer side above, and occasionally one on the inner; a broad arched gibbous entire operculum. Anterior avicularium small, and only (?) on the median zoœcium at a bifurcation. Median zoœcium not mucronate; five to nine cells in an internode. Polypide with twelve tentacles.

Syn. *Cellularia ternata* (*forma gracilis*), Smitt, l. c. 1867, pp. 283–310, pl. xvi. figs. 17–20, 23, 24 (*non* 21, 22), (excl. Synom.)

Hab. Franklin Pierce Bay, 79° 29′ N., 13–15 fathoms, H. W. F.; Spitsbergen, 200 fathoms, Smitt.

Fam. 2. BICELLARIADÆ, Bk.

Gen. 1. *Bugula*, Oken.

1. *B. murrayana*, Johnst. (sp.)

Syn. *Flustra murrayana*, Johnst.; Sars; Danielsen; Packard.
" *Flabellaria spiralis*, Gray.

Syn. *Bugula murrayana*, 'Brit. M. Cat.' p. 46, pl. lix., Smitt, l. c. 1867, pp. 201 and 348, tab. xviii. figs. 19–27.

" *Avicella multispina*, V. Ben.

Hab. Franklin Pierce Bay, 79° 29′ N., H. W. F.; Hunde or Hunes Islands, Davis Strait, Dr. Sutherland; Holsteinborg Harbour, Norman; Iceland, Wallich (*teste* Hincks.); Orkney, Lieutenant Thomas; Shetland, E. Forbes; Dublin Coast, W. McCalla.

2 *B.* (var. ?) *fruticosa*, Packard.

Syn. ? *Cellularia quadridentata*, Lovèn, MS. 1834 (*teste* Smitt).

" *Bugula murrayana* (*forma quadridentata*), Smitt, l. c. pp. 292 and 351, tab. xviii. figs. 25–27.

" *Menipea fruticosa*, Packard, 'List of Labrador Animals,' p. 9, pl. i. fig. 3.

" *Bugula murrayana* (var. *fruticosa*), Hincks, l. c. p. 98; Norman, 'Valorous Dredgings.'

Hab. Franklin Pierce Bay, 79° 29′ N., H.W.F.; Labrador, Packard.

Fam. 3. MEMBRANIPORIDÆ.

Gen. 1. *Membranipora*.

1. *M. unicornis*, Alder.

Syn. *M. unicornis*, Alder, 'Cat. Zooph. North. and Durham,' p. 56, pl. viii. fig. 6.

" *M. lineata* (*forma unicornis, ββ. stadium longius adultum*), Smitt, l. c. pp. 365–399, pl. xx. figs. 30, 31.

" ? *Reptoflustrella americana*, D'Orbigny.

Hab. Lat. 82° 27′ N., H. W. F.; Hamilton Inlet, Labrador, 15 fathoms, Wallich!; Spitsbergen, 6–50 fathoms, and boreal and Arctic seas generally, Smitt; Coasts of Northumberland and Durham, Alder.

Fam. 4. FLUSTRIDÆ.

Gen. 1. *Flustra*.

1. *Flustra serrulata*, n. sp.

Char. Zoarium constituted of narrow, ligulate, bifurcated branches slightly expanded at the ends; zoœcia ovoid or oblong, open in front except quite at the bottom, where there is a very narrow calcareous expansion; border of aperture finely serrated or beaded. Oœcia small, immersed.

Hab. Franklin Pierce Bay, 13 fathoms, H. W. F.

Fam. 5. ESCHARIDÆ.

Gen. 1. *Myriozoum*, Donati.

1. *M. coarctatum*, Sars (sp.)

Syn. *Cellepora coarctata*, Sars, ' Reise Löf. Finm.' p. 28.

,, *Leieschara (Leiescharia) coarctata*, id. ' N. Norsk Polyz.' p. 17.

,, *Myriozoum coarctatum* and *subgracile*, Hincks, l. c. p. 106; Smitt, l. c. pp. 18 and 119.

,, *Millepora truncata*, Fabricius, 'Faun. Grœnl.' p. 432; Packard, l. c. (*teste* Smitt).

,, ? *Myriozoum subgracile*, D'Orb., ' Pal. Franc.' p. 662.

,, *Millepora truncata*, (pars) Lamouroux ; Pallas.

Hab. (var. *subgracile*.) Franklin Pierce Bay, Smith Sound, 13–15 fathoms, H. W. F. ; Arctic Sea, Sir E. Belcher's ' Expedition ! ; ' South Labrador, Packard ; Newfoundland, D'Orb. ; Spitsbergen, 19–80 fathoms, Smitt ; Greenland, Möller and Torel, Holsteinborg Harbour, entrance of Baffin's Bay, 175 fathoms ; Norman, ' Valorous Dredgings ; ' Iceland, 100 fathoms, Wallich (*teste* Hincks).

(Var. *coarctatum*.) Iceland, 100 fathoms, Wallich ! ; Norway Ström, Sars, &c. ; Finmark, Lovèn, Sars.

Gen. 2. *Eschara*.

1. *E. elegantula*, D'Orb.

Syn. *E. elegantula*, D'Orb. (1851), ' Pal. Franc.' p. 102, Smitt, l. c. 1867, pp. 24 and 151, tab. xxvi. figs. 140-146, Norman, ' Valorous Dredgings.'

,, *E. saccata*, Bk. ' Ann. N. Hist.' Ser. 2, vol. xviii. p. 33, pl. i. fig. 1 ; Sars, l. c. 1862, p. 6.

Hab. Cape Napoleon, Cape Frazer, Franklin Pierce Bay, H. W. F. ; Norway and Finland, McAndrew ; Spitshergen, Greenland, Finmark, 30–60 fathoms, Torel, Lovèn, Sars ; Newfoundland, D'Orb. ; Hare Island, Waigat Straits, and Lat. 66° 59′ N., 55° 27′ W., 57 fathoms, Norman (' Valorous Dredgings ').

2. *E. perpusilla,* n. sp.

Char. Zoarium diminutive, constituted of irregularly forked branches rising from a short stem. Stem and lower part of branches cylindrical, flattened towards the ends. Zoœcia fusiform, elongate ; mouth looking directly upwards (horizontal); anterior lip tridentate, the median denticle wide and expanding, the lateral pointed, conical. Immediately in front of the median denticle an avicularium about half the length of the zoœcium, with a circular mandible which opens upwards and backwards.

Hab. Franklin Pierce Bay, Smith Sound; 13–15 fathoms, H. W. F.

3. *E. Sarsii,* Smitt. (sp.)

Syn. *Escharoides Sarsii,* Smitt, l. c. 1867, pp. 24 and 158, tab. xxvi. figs. 147–154.
„ *Eschara rosacea,* Sars, ' N. Norsk. Polyz.' p. 3 (non Busk).
„ *Cellepora cervicornis* (var.) Sars, ' Reise Löf. Finm.' p. 28.

Hab. Franklin Pierce Bay, Smith Sound, 13 fathoms, H. W. F. ; Spitsbergen, 20–60 fathoms, Smitt ; Greenland, Möller and Torel ; Finmark, 80–100 fathoms, Sars &c. ; Arctic Sea, Sir E. Belcher's ' Expedition ; ' in lat. 74° 0′ S., 172° 0′ E., 330 fathoms, Hooker, ' Voyage of the " Erebus " and " Terror." ' !

Gen. 3. *Hemeschara.*

1. *H. sincera,* Smitt. (sp.) (var. *inermis*).
Syn. *Discopora sincera* (*forma Hemeschara*), Smitt, l. c. 1867, pp. 28 and 177, tab. xxvii. figs. 178–180.
„ *Lepralia* (*Discopora*) *sincera,* Hincks, l. c. p. 102.

Hab. Franklin Pierce Bay, Smith Sound, 13 fathoms (on *Cellepora cervicornis*), H. W. F. ; Spitsbergen, 19–61 fathoms, Smitt ; Finmark, Lovèn ; Arctic Sea ? 100 fathoms,

Wallich !; Iceland, Wallich (*teste* Hincks); Hare Island, Waigat Strait, entrance of Baffin's Bay, 175 'fathoms, Norman.

Gen. 4. *Lepralia*, Johnst. (pars).

1. *L. Landsborovii* ? Johnst.

Syn. *L. Landsborovii*, Johnst. (pars); ? ' Brit. M. Cat.' p. 66, pl. lxxxvi. fig.
  ,,   1. *Escarella Landsborovii* (*forma typica*), Smitt, l. c. 1867, pp. 12 and 94, tab. xxiv. figs. 60–62 (non cetera).

Hab. Cape Frazer, 80 fathoms, H. W. F. (on worm tube); Spitsbergen, Smith; Greenland, Copenhagen Museum (*teste* Smitt).

Fam. 6. CELLEPORIDÆ.

Gen. 1. *Cellepora*, Fabr.

1. *C. cervicornis*, mihi (? Couch).

Syn. *Cellepora cervicornis*, Bk. 'Ann. N. Hist.' Ser. 2, vol. xviii. p. 32, pl. i. fig. 1.
  ,,   *Cellepora pumicosa*, Sars, 'Reise Löf. Finm. ;' Danielssen (*teste* Smitt).
  ,,   *Celleporaria incrassata*, Smitt, l. c. 1867, pp. 33 and 198, tab. xviii. figs. 212-216; D'Orb. (pars) (non Lamarck).
  ,,   *Celleporaria surcularis*, Packard (*teste* Smitt).
  ,,   ? *Cellepora coronopus*, S. Wood, 'Cray Polyzoa,' p. 57, pl. ix. figs. 1-3.
  ,,   ,,   *incrassata*, Hincks, l. c. p. 105.

Hab. Cape Napoleon, Cape Frazer, H. W. F.; Norway and Finmark, McAndrew, Lovèn, &c.; Spitsbergen and Greenland (very abundant), 16–160 fathoms (clay and stone), Smith; Newfoundland, D'Orb.; Crag (fossil), S. Wood; in lat. 66° 59' N. lon. 55° 27' W. 57 fathoms Norman.

SUBORDER II. CYCLOSTOMATA.

Fam. 1. DIASTOPORIDÆ (Bk. ' Brit. N. Cat.' Part iii. p. 27).

Gen. 1. *Mesenteripora*. Blainv.

1. *M. meandrina* ? S. Wood (sp.)

Syn. *Diastopera meandrina*, S. Wood, 'Ann. Nat. Hist.' xiii. p. 14.
  ,,   *Mesenteripora meandrina*, Bk. 'Crag Polyzoa,' p. 109, pl. xvii.
  ,,   fig. 2; xviii. fig. 4; xx. fig. 2, Smitt, l. c. 1866, pp. 398 and 432.

Syn. ? „ *Eudesiana*, M. Edw., 'Sur les Crisiés,' &c. pl. xiv. fig. 1.
„ ? „ *compressa*, D'Orb. 1. c. p. 756.
„ ? *Ditaxia compressa*, Hagenou, 'Bryoz. Maastr.' p. 50, pl. iv. fig. 10.

Hab. Franklin Pierce Bay, August 10, 1875; 15 fathoms, H. W. F.; Greenland, 16–40 fathoms, Torel; ? Coralline Crag (fossil), S. Wood.

Gen. 2. *Tubulipora.*

1. *T. ventricosa*, Bk.

Syn. *Tubulipora ventricosa*, Bk. 'Q. Journ. M. Sc.' iii. p. 256, pl. ii. figs. 3-4; 'Brit. M. Cat.' part iii. p. 26; pl. xxxii. fig. 4 (same figure).
„ „ (subgenus *Proboscina*) *incrassata* (var. and *forma erecta*), Smitt. l. c. 1866, p. 402, tab. v. fig. 4.

Hab. Franklin Pierce Bay, August 11, 1875, 13–1 fathoms, H. W. F.; Greenland (on Fucus), Dr. Sutherland.

SUBORDER III. CTENOSTOMATA.

Fam. 1. VESICULARIADÆ.

Gen. 1. *Farella*, Ehrenberg.

1. *F. arctica*, n. sp. ?

Char. Zoœcia in opposite pairs at very distant intervals, Zoœcia, largest 0· 06 × 0·013.

Hab. Franklin Pierce Bay, August 11, 1875. H. W. F. The Ctenostomata are represented by this single species parasitic upon *Bugula fruticosa*. The specimens, however, are so few, and so much injured and overgrown by diatoms, that it is with considerable difficulty that I have been able to make out even the scanty diagnosis given above, which must be regarded as provisional. The zoœcia are very large, reaching apparently an extreme length of 0·12–13 inch by 0.06 inch in diameter. The Polypides have about twelve tentacles and no gizzard, so far as appears in the bad state of the specimens.

No. XI.

HYDROZOA.

By George J. Allman, M.D., LL.D., F.R.S., etc.

The elegant little medusa here described was taken in the towing-net by Captain Feilden in lat. 81° 44′ N.   It is re-

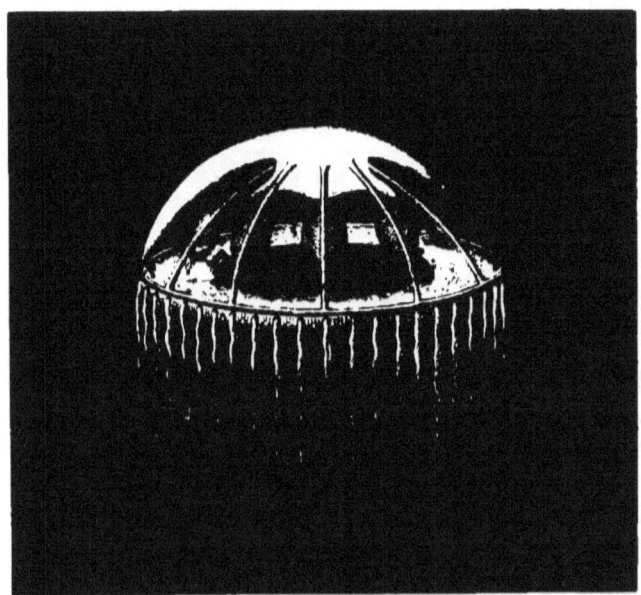

Fig. 1.   Lateral view; magnified.

PTYCHOGASTRIA POLARIS.

markable among hydroid medusæ by its lobed umbrella-margin, which thus presents a character belonging to the discophorous rather than to the hydroid medusæ, while the folds, with their thickened, convoluted, and gland-like margin, which run longitudinally along the inner surface of the

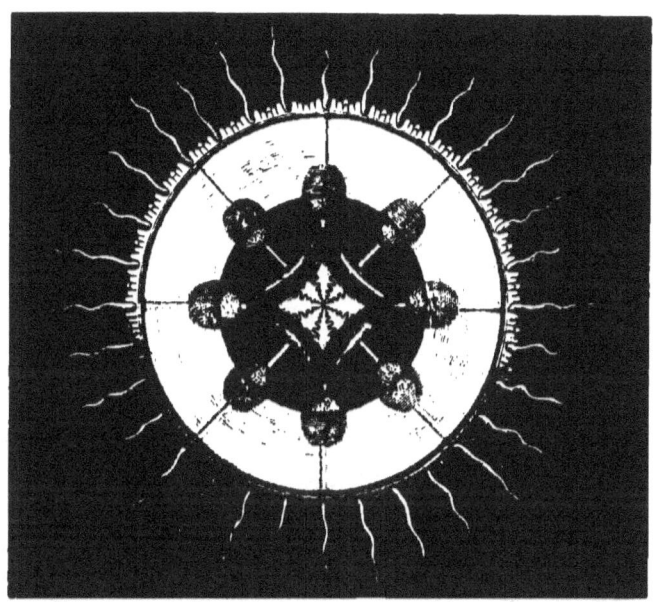

Fig. 2. Equatorial projection, magnified. This view is from below through the widely open mouth, and shows the convoluted edges of the eight longitudinal gastric folds.

Fig. 3. Natural size.

manubrium, constitute a very exceptional and striking character.

The marginal lobes of the umbrella are in the form of short truncated cones, each carrying several papilliform and probably extensile processes, and separated from its neighbour by a deep notch. The condition of the specimen, whose transparency was lost by its preservation in alcohol, rendered it impossible to determine anything regarding lithocysts, while my unwillingness to destroy a unique specimen has rendered the determination of some other points of structure not so complete as I could have wished. Each tentacle corresponds to one of the notches which separate the marginal lobes. The tentacles are manifestly very extensile, but are easily detached, and had mostly fallen from the specimen. They have the cavity divided into chambers by close septa, and show a very distinct longitudinal fibrillation of their walls. The velum is wide and strong. The eight radiating canals with their large oval reproductive sacs are very distinct, but the circular canal, in consequence of the opaque condition of the specimen, was but faintly indicated.

The specimen appears to be a male.

There can be little doubt that *Ptychogastria polaris* is the planoblast of some hydroid trophosome as yet unknown.

PTYCHOGASTRIA.

Gen. Char. Umbella hemispherical, with lobed margin and filiform tentacles; lithocysts?; velum broad; manubrium short and wide, carrying a wide mouth with quadrangular lip; inner walls of manubrium thrown into eight longitudinal folds, along whose free edge runs a thick convoluted gland-like chord; radiating canals, eight; reproductive sacs oval, large, developed near the middle point of each radiating canal.

Ptychogastria polaris.

Umbella about half an inch in diameter; marginal tentacles numerous (32 ?)

Captured in Discovery Bay. Captain Feilden.

No. XII.

SPONGIDA.[1]

By H. J. CARTER, F.R.S., ETC.

THE collection of Sponges brought from Smith Sound by the Arctic Expedition of 1875-6 consists of five species, one of which, viz. the following, has hitherto not been described.

No. 1. *Semisuberites arctica*, n. sp.

General form funnel-shaped, hollow, with a long round stem, diminishing in size to the point of attachment; mouth subcircular, margin thick, round, undulating. Colour light grey. Surface reticulate, even. Pores external, microscopic; vents internal, large, plentifully and uniformly scattered over the inner surface of the funnel. Internal structure loose, light, composed of acuate spicules united together by sarcode into bundles which, crossing each other, produce the usual areolated tissue of sponge. Spicules of one kind only, viz. skeleton, but of two forms, viz.—1, acuate, slightly curved towards the large end, smooth, and gradually diminishing towards the smaller one, which is rather abruptly pointed; average largest size $\frac{1}{48}$th by $\frac{1}{3000}$th inch in its greatest diameters: 2, the same, but with a slight subterminal inflation. Size of largest specimen about 3 inches long by $1\frac{3}{4}$ inch across the brim of the funnel.

Hab. Marine, Arctic regions. Growing singly or in plurality on hard objects.

Loc. Smith Sound, Cape Napoleon, in 50 fathoms.

Obs. There is much interest attaching to this sponge in

---

[1] Abridged from 'Ann. and Mag. Nat. Hist.' 1877, pp. 38-42.

many ways. First it is almost identical in elementary structure with *Halichondria sanguinea*, Johnston ('Brit. Spong.' 1842, p. 133), originally described, with a figure of its spicule, by Dr. Grant in 1826, under the name of *Spongia sanguinea* ('Edinb. Phil. Journ.' pl. cxxi., fig. 9), which, together with his *Sp. papillaris*, are the two commonest sponges on this coast (Budleigh-Salterton, Devon), where they can be found at all tides in great abundance a little below high-water mark. Secondly, Dr. Bowerbank, from the orange colour and cork-like tissue of *Halichondria sanguinea*, the tendency of its spicules to a pin-like form, and the fact that, in one instance, he found the identical form of flesh-spicule which characterises *Vioa Johnstonii*, Sdt., and (as I hope soon to show) several other sponges of this kind ('Brit. Spong.,' vol. i. pl. iii. fig. 72, p. 239), points out that both *Semisuberites arctica* and *Halichondria sanguinea* belong to the family Suberitida, of which I also hope soon to give a full account with all hitherto described species in its different groups. Thirdly, a similar specimen of the same sponge, but much larger, from Spitsbergen, was presented to the British Museum by the Rev. A. E. Eaton in 1873.

No. 2. *Halichondria panicea*, Johnston.

With larger spicules than those of the common British species, and histodermal coat like that of the deep-sea (Atlantic) form.

Nos. 3, 4, and 5. *Sycon raphanus*, Sdt., *Ute glabra*, Sdt., and *Leucosolenia coriacea*, Bk. These three are calcareous sponges.

In the mounted sand taken from the jar which contained *Semisuberites arctica* are also present the remains of many other sponges, viz. the perfected flesh-spicule of *Melonanchora elliptica* ('Ann.' 1874, vol. xiv. p. 212, pl. xiii. fig. 9), the larger spicule of *Corticium abyssi* (ib. 1873, vol. xii. p. 18, pl. i. figs. 3–5), also large bihamates (*fibulæ*), probably of an *Esperia*, and many other spicules whose forms, although different, do not characterise any sponge in particular.

No. XIII.

RHIZOPODA RETICULARIA.

FORAMINIFERA.

By Henry B. Brady, F.R.S., F.L.S.

About fifty samples of material were preserved, to be examined for Microzoa and Microphyta. These were for the most part soundings in depths of from 10 to 260 fathoms, dust from ice-hummocks, or mud from beds of glacial deposit of greater or less age. The Rhizopod-fauna of the mud-beds requires no separate treatment, as it is practically identical with that of the present sea-bottom of the same latitudes.

Many of the soundings were exceedingly small in quantity, and after the washing required to rid them of impalpable inorganic matter left scarcely any residue, but of the entire number about forty furnished sufficient specimens to give a general, if not an exhaustive, idea of their constituent organisms. In some cases the close proximity of several soundings, and their similar depth, permitted the treatment of two or three together, or at least the incorporation of the results in one list, and in a few instances the quantity of material was not sufficient to show adequately the nature of the sea-bottom; but after condensation as described, and the omission of those furnishing defective data, there remained sufficient basis for the construction of a distribution-table comprising twenty-four localities. The table represents fairly the salient features of the Foraminifera-fauna of an area lying between the entrance of Smith Sound in lat. 73° N. or thereabouts and the most northerly point attained by the

Expedition, namely lat. 83° 19′ N. This, considering the few opportunities for sounding, and the difficulties under which material was obtained, may be regarded as very satisfactory— the more so because whatever facts are derived from specimens procured between the latitudes named are distinct accessions to our knowledge, no previous observations of the same sort having extended even to the southern limit. It is not proposed in this place to do more than give a list of species, and to make a few remarks on the general aspect of the fauna; technical details are better suited for publication elsewhere.

Our knowledge of Arctic Rhizopoda is chiefly derived from the researches of Professors W. K. Parker and T. Rupert Jones, and of the Rev. A. M. Norman. The memoir of Messrs. Parker and Jones in the 'Philosophical Transactions' for 1865 forms the text-book of the subject. It comprises the results of the examination of the soundings taken by Sir E. Parry in Baffin's Bay, between latitudes 74° 45′, and 76° 30′ N., of those by Dr. Sutherland off the Hunde Islands, Davis Straits, in lat. 68° 50′ N., and of dredgings made by Mr. MacAndrew off the coast of Norway between lat. 65° and 71° N. Mr. Norman's investigations are founded upon the dredgings brought home by Dr. J. Gwyn Jeffreys from the cruise of the 'Valorous,' and a summary of them forms one section of the Report published in the 'Proceedings of the Royal Society' for 1876. In the same Report Dr. Carpenter also adds a few general observations on some of the larger forms of Foraminifera. Six of the dredgings brought home in the 'Valorous' were from within the Arctic Circle, the most northerly being about lat. 70° N.

Thus it will be seen that the area embraced by the soundings which form the subject of the present notice stretches nearly seven degrees further north than any hitherto examined—in point of fact, it covers about half the distance between the highest latitude of Sir E. Parry's series and the actual North Pole. The following is the list of the Foraminifera which have been obtained :—

Cornuspira foliacea, Phil.
*   ,,   *involvens*, Reuss.
* *Triloculina tricarinata*, D'Orb.
* *Quinqueloculina seminulum*, Linné.
    ,,   *subrotunda*, Montag.
Lituola fusiformis, Will.
    ,,   *scorpiurus*, Montfort.
    ,,   *canariensis*, D'Orb.
    ,,   *glomerata*, nov.
Hyperammina elongata, nov. gen. et sp.
Lagena globosa, Montag.
    ,,   *lævis*, Montag.
*   ,,   *marginata*, Montag.
    ,,   *apiculata*, Reuss.
    ,,   *sulcata*, W. and J.
    ,,   *striata*, D'Orb.
*   ,,   *caudata*, D'Orb.
    ,,   *striatopunctata*, P. and J.
    ,,   *melo*, D'Orb.
    ,,   *squamosa*, Montag.
Glandulina lævigata, D'Orb.
Dentalina communis, D'Orb.
    ,,   *pauperata*, D'Orb.
Cristellaria rotulata, Lamk.
Polymorphina lactea, W. and J.
    ,,   *compressa*, D'Orb.
    ,,   *problema;* D'Orb.
    ,,   *acuminata*, D'Orb.
    ,,   *rotundata*, Bornem.
* *Spirillina vivipara*, Ehrb.
* *Globigerina bulloides*, D'Orb.
    ,,   *inflata*, D'Orb.
Uvigerina pygmæa, D'Orb. (var.)
* *Cassidulina lævigata*, D'Orb.
*   ,,   *crassa*, D'Orb.
* *Bulimina ovata*, D'Orb.
* *Bulimina elegantissima*, D'Orb.

Virgulina Schreibersii, Czjzek.
Bolivina punctata, D'Orb.
Textularia biformis, P. and J.
Verneuilina polystropha, Reuss.
Discorbina obtusa, D'Orb.
* *Truncatulina lobatula,* W. and J.
* *Pulvinulina Karsteni,* Reuss.
    „   *Micheliniana,* D'Orb.
* *Patellina corrugata,* Will.
* *Nonionina scapha,* F. and M.
    „   *umbilicatula,* Montag.
    „   *depressula,* W. and J.
    „   *stelligera,* D'Orb.
Polystomella arctica, P. and J.
    „   *striatopunctata,* F. and M.

The list comprises fifty-two species, and a few doubtful specimens remain which may increase the number by one or two. Messrs. Parker and Jones, in their list of Arctic forms give a total of seventy-five, but of these twenty are recorded from the Norwegian coast only, leaving fifty-five for Baffin's Bay south of Smith Sound and Davis Straits. There is fair ground, therefore, for supposing that the number of species of Foraminifera does not suffer any considerable diminution northwards from the Arctic Circle. The species, fifteen in number, marked with an asterisk, in the foregoing table, are those which were found in the sounding made in lat. 83° 19′ N. at a depth of 71 fathoms, and are, except a few Radiolaria, the unique representatives of the fauna of the sea-bottom at the highest latitude yet attained by explorers. The greatest variety of forms from any single Arctic locality is furnished by mud from 80 fathoms off Cape Frazer, which gives a list of thirty-two species. As already stated, it is not to be supposed that material so limited in quantity has furnished anything like complete details of the fauna; it may nevertheless be of interest to compare the list above enumerated with the columns referring to Baffin's Bay and Davis Straits in Messrs. Parker and Jones's table. It will then be seen that thirty-six of the species are common to both areas, and that the remainders contain many nearly related forms, which further opportunity may probably show to have a distribution extending more or less northwards or southwards, as the case may be.

Two new, or rather undescribed, species have been mentioned; of these detailed descriptions will appear elsewhere. One of them, *Lituola glomerata*, is of minute size, not much exceeding $\frac{1}{100}$ of an inch in diameter, and spiral or nautiloid in mode of growth. It has a thin, arenaceous, non-labyrinthic test, nearly spherical in contour, the longer diameter being often in the direction of the axis, and consists of a few long, narrow, slightly ventricose segments. It can scarcely be said to be new, for it occurs in more than one of the 'Challenger' dredgings, but it has not hitherto been described or named.

The other, for which the generic term *Hyperammina* (ὕπερος, a pestle, and ἄμμος, sand) has been adopted, is one of the arenaceous types probably first recognized in the 'Porcupine' dredgings from the North Atlantic in 1869, but since found in many parts of the world. Its form is that of a club, or still more nearly that of a pestle, and it consists of a straight sandy tube with one end rounded and closed, gradually tapering towards the other extremity, which forms the aperture. The Arctic examples are small, none being more than a tenth of an inch in length, but under favourable conditions specimens are met with many times as large.

The effects of climate, direct or indirect, are noticeable in the modification of form assumed by some of the species, which occur over considerable range of latitude. The Arctic specimens of such species are often dwarfed and usually more compactly built than those obtained in more southern areas.

Note.—Whilst working out the Foraminifera of the various samples of material from the sea-bottom, any Polycystina that were found were carefully preserved. They were only noticed in seven of the soundings, and the specimens were for the most part few in number, and presented no great variety of form. An exception, however, must be made in the case of the most northerly sounding (lat. 83° 19′ N.), which, taking into account the very small quantity of material, yielded a considerable series.

The species of Radiolaria have not been determined, but the following is a list of the more prominent genera represented:—*Dictyopodium, Haliomma, Tetrapyle, Heliodiscus, Actinomma, Spongodiscus, Spongotrochus, Spongaster, Trematodiscus,* and *Euchitonia.*—H. B. B.

No. XIV.

BOTANY.

By Sir Joseph D. Hooker, C.B., K.C.S.I.,

President Royal Society.

With Lists of Flowering Plants, by Professor D. Oliver; Musci, by W. Mitten; Fungi, by Rev. W. J. Berkeley; Algæ and Diatomaceæ, by Professor George Dickie.

THE very excellent collections of flowering plants and ferns brought by Captain Feilden and Mr. Hart from lat. 80°–83° North, along the shores of Kennedy Channel, Hall Basin, and Robeson Channel, and particularly from the N.E. part of Grinnell Land, have been examined and named by Professor Oliver, by comparison with the Arctic collections at Kew. They prove that the vegetation of this meridian of the Polar area is entirely Greenlandic, showing no further relationship than does Greenland itself to the floras of the American Polar islands to the west of it and of Spitsbergen to the east of it. In other words, it possesses Greenland plants that are wanting in either or in both of these localities, and wants plants that either or both of these regions possess, but which are absent in Greenland.

In my essay on the 'Outlines of the Distribution of Arctic Plants,'[1] I have shown that the Greenland flora was in origin essentially a European one; but owing to causes which I have there attempted to explain, it has lost some of its European characteristics, and acquired others, of which some few

[1] 'Trans. Linn. Soc.,' xxiii. 251.

are derived from America and others are peculiar to itself; and that under this latter point of view it should be regarded as a subdivision of the European flora, and when discussing questions of Arctic distribution be called Greenlandic.

No fewer than sixty-nine identifiable flowering plants and ferns, and about six more, in too imperfect a condition to be named accurately, have been brought by the Polar Expedition from the latitudes mentioned above (besides nearly as many more from the Greenland coast south of it); a considerably larger number (ten) than have rewarded the researches of the various explorers of Melville Island (containing about sixty), situated 5° further south, and in a much milder climate; and only twenty-three less than are found in Spitsbergen (containing about ninety [1]), which lies wholly to the south of lat. 80°, is a much larger area, is washed on its west coast by the comparatively warm Gulf Stream, and has been explored by trained botanists.

The elements of the Flora may be thus expressed :—

1. Spitsbergen species 49
2. Melville Island 41
3. Greenland species not found either in Spitsbergen or Melville Island 12
4. Species not found in Greenland, Spitzbergen, or Melville Island 2

I. The species not found in Spitsbergen are :—

Vesicaria arctica . .	Greenland and E. Arctic America.
Cheiranthus pygmæus .	Do. ,, ,,
Arenaria grœnlandica .	Do. and Mts. of E. U. States.
Saxifraga tricuspidata .	Melville Island and Arctic America generally.
Epilobium latifolium .	Do. and Northern Regions generally.

---

[1] 'Malmgren in Ofvers af K. Vel. Akad. Forh.' 1862, pp. 229–268; translated in Seemann's 'Journal of Botany,' 1864, pp. 130 and 162. A few additions have subsequently been made.

Antennaria alpina	Melville Island and Northern Regions generally.
Erigeron compositus	Arctic and Alpine N. America.
Vaccinium uliginosum	N. Temp. and Arctic Regions.
Pedicularis lapponica	N. Temp. and Arctic Regions.
„ *capitata*	Arctic America, only to 72° N.
Androsace septentrionalis	N. Temp. and Arctic Regions generally, but not beyond 72° N.
Salix arctica	Arctic America and Greenland.
Luzula campestris, var. *congesta*	Temp. and Arctic Regions generally.
Carex rigida	Do. „ „ „
„ *holostoma* [?] (*alpina*)	Arctic Europe and E. America.
„ *stans* (*aquatilis*)	N. Temp. and Arctic Regions generally.
Deschampsia cæspitosa	E. Greenland and Arctic and Temp. Regions.
Colpodium latifolium	Arctic Regions generally.
Woodsia ilvensis	N. Temp. and Arctic Regions generally.

Of these the first three are peculiar to Greenland except the *Arenaria*, which is also found in the mountains of the Eastern United States.

II. The species not found in Melville Island are :—

Braya alpina	Spitsbergen and all Arctic Regions.
Vesicaria arctica	Greenland and E. Arctic America.
Cardamine pratensis	Spitsbergen and N. Temp. and Arctic Regions.
Cheiranthus pygmœus	Greenland and E. Arctic America.
Draba hirta	Spitsbergen and Arctic and N. Alpine Regions.

Draba rupestris .	. Spitsbergen and Arctic and N. Alpine Regions.
„ *alpina* .	. Do. „ „
Silene acaulis .	. Do. „ „
Arenaria grœnlandica .	Greenland and E. U. States Mountains.
Stellaria humifusa	. Spitsbergen and all Arctic Regions.
Erigeron alpinus .	. Do. „ „
„ *compositus*	. Confined to Arctic and Alpine N. America.
Vaccinium uliginosum .	N. Temp. and Arctic Regions.
Cassiope tetragona .	Do. „ „
Pedicularis capitata	. Not in Greenland, but in Arctic America and Asia.
„ *lapponica* .	N. Temp. and Arctic Regions.
Androsace septentrion-alis . . .	. Not in Greenland, but in the N. Temp. and Arctic Regions generally.
Luzula campestris var. .	N. Temp. and Arctic Regions.
Carex nardina .	. Spitsbergen „ „
„ *rigida* .	. N. Temp. „ „
„ *holostoma* [?]	. Temp. Arctic Regions.
Glyceria maritima var. .	Spitsbergen and Arctic Regions.
Equisetum variegatum .	Do. „ various Arctic and Temp. Regions.
„ *arvense*	. Spitsbergen and N. Temp. and Arctic Regions.
Lycopodium Selago .	Do. „ „
Woodsia ilvensis .	. N. Temp. „ „
„ *hyperborea*	. Spitsbergen and Arctic Europe and E. America.
Cystopteris fragilis .	Do. „ „

III. The Greenland species found neither in Spitsbergen nor Melville Island are : —

Vesicaria arctica . .	East Arctic America.
Cheiranthus pygmœus .	Do. ,,
Arenaria grœnlandica .	Mountains of E. U. States.
Erigeron compositus .	East Arctic America and Rocky Mountains.
Vaccinium uliginosum .	N. Temp. and Arctic Regions.
Pedicularis lapponica .	Do. ,, ,,
Luzula campestris var. *congesta.* . .	Do. ,, ,,
Carex rigida . . .	Do. ,, ,,
,, *holostoma* [?] .	Do. ,, ,,
Woodsia ilvensis . .	Do. ,, ,,

IV. The species of plants found in lat 80°–83°, but which do not occur in Spitsbergen, Melville Island, or Greenland, are *Androsace septentrionalis*, an Arctic plant and native also of the cold Alpine regions of the New and Old World, but which finds its northern limit elsewhere in 72° on the south shores of the Polar islands opposite the American coast; and *Pedicularis capitata*, a beautiful plant confined to Arctic Asia and America, but not hitherto found north of Port Kennedy in lat. 72°. The recurrence and the abundance of these two plants in the extreme latitudes visited by the Expedition are very singular facts. To these plants might also be added the *Deschampsia cœspitosa*, which, though so common a plant of the Temperate Zone and the Arctic Regions generally, is found nowhere either in Temperate or Arctic Greenland, except on its east coast; a peculiarity which it shares with *Ranunculus glacialis*, *Saxifraga Hirculus*, *S. hieracifolia*, and others, all of which are either unknown in W. Greenland or are very rare there.

Of seventy-three high Arctic plants—namely, such as reach the north coast of the Spitsbergen Group (lat. 80° to 80° 40′)—Malmgren cites thirteen as not found elsewhere in those islands; and of these he remarks that they establish a relationship with the Polar island flora, while the rest of the polar Spitsbergen flora is essentially Greenlandic and European. Of these thirteen the following only were found by our Polar Expedition in the lat. 80° to 83° :—

> *Carex nardina.*
> *Poa abbreviata.*
> *Festuca ovina* var. *brevifolia.*

The Arctic plants common in Spitsbergen and Melville Island, and which hence might have been expected to occur in lat. 80° to 83°, but do not, are—

> G. *Ranunculus auricomus.*
> G.   „   *pygmæus.*
> *Parrya arctica.*
> G. *Draba androsacea.*
> *Potentilla frigida.*
> G. *Saxifraga stellaris.*
> ——— *Hirculus* (East Greenland only).
> G. *Chrysosplenium alternifolium.*
> *Nardosmia frigida.*
> G. *Campanula uniflora.*
> *Salix polaris.*
> G. *Dupontia Fisheri.*

Of these the seven with a G prefixed are also Greenlandic, and hence their absence from the higher latitudes visited by the Polar Expedition may be attributed to cold or other climatic causes; and the other five not being Greenlandic (except one found only in E. Greenland), their occurrence was not to be expected in the regions under consideration.

Of Melville Island plants found neither in lat. 80° to 83°, nor in Spitsbergen, are :—

> *Caltha palustris.**
> *Astragalus alpinus.**
> *Oxytropis uralensis.**
> *Sieversia Rossii.*
> *Senecio palustris.**
> *Pleuropogon Sabinii.*

It is noteworthy that not one of these is a Greenland plant, though all those marked with an asterisk inhabit Arctic Regions in Europe. The absence of all *Leguminosæ* in Spitsbergen and in Greenland (except two temperate species in the south of that peninsula) is a most singular fact. The collection has been searched in vain for any specimen of the remarkable and beautiful little grass *Pleuropogon Sabinii*, the sole representative of the only genus peculiar to the Arctic regions, and which has been found nowhere but in Melville Island and its immediate neighbourhood. It still holds its place as the rarest and most inaccessible of known flowering plants.

The proportion of Monocotyledons to Dicotyledons in lat. 80° to 83° is 20 to 49 = 1 : 2·45, which is nearly that of Arctic Europe flowering plants as given in my essay, namely, 1 : 2·3 ; while that of the plants of all Greenland is 1 : 2·1.

The proportion of genera to species is 42 : 69 = 1 : 1·7, that for Arctic Europe being 1 : 2·3, and for all Greenland 1 : 2·0. This diminution of genera in proportion to species with the dwindling flora is quite normal.

It remains to add that the flora of 80° to 83° proves that vegetation may be expected up to the Pole in this longitude —though probably not in all, the contrast between the vegetation of lat. 80° to 83° in Grinnell Island and Franz Josef's Land, in the same latitude, being most striking in respect of number and variety of plants. Here there is a sward covering a deep layer of vegetable matter exhibiting a brilliant assemblage of gay-coloured flowers, the resort of butterflies and bees ; in Franz Josef's Land vegetation exists only in rare and isolated patches. Such dissimilarities were not anticipated in islands occupying so very small an area as the Polar N. of 80°, and on the supposed extreme limits of vegetation.

The northward extension of the Greenlandic flora so near the Pole, and the retention of its characteristics as distinguished from the Spitsbergen and Polar Island floras, indicate that the distribution of plants in the Arctic regions has been meridional, and that the subsequent spread of the species in latitude has, for some unknown reason, been restricted, and has not been sufficient to obliterate the evidence of this prior direction of migration.

The comparative richness of the flora from 80° to 83°, taken especially in connection with that of Smith Sound, in lat. 78° to 80°, which contains many Subarctic plants, indicates some peculiarity of climate or other condition in this longitude that favours the northern spread of vegetation in this more than in any other Arctic longitude. Thus in Smith Sound there have been gathered :—

> *Alchemilla vulgaris.*
> *Pyrola grandiflora.*
> *Bartsia alpina.*
> *Armeria vulgaris.*
> *Tofieldia palustris.*
> *Hierochloe borealis*, and
> *Lycopodium annotinum.*

None of them high Arctic plants in other longitudes, though all of them except the *Hierochloe* are natives of Greenland.

These facts seem to indicate that vegetation may be more abundant in the interior of Greenland than is supposed, and that the glacier-bound coast-ranges of that country may protect a comparatively fertile interior. And to this view the altitudinal distribution of vegetation in Grinnell Land lends support : there, where the land is only hilly, flowering plants ascend on unsnowed slopes that dip down to the sea from 1,000 feet elevation ; showing that it is to the presence of lofty mountains on the Greenland coast, and not to its latitude, that its ice-bound shores are due. Thus, too, the abundance of animal life met with between 80° and 83° may be accounted for. Barely sufficient pasture is found along the shores of Grinnell Land during winter for the support of musk-oxen, and from what we know of the vegetation of the Polar Islands to the westward, they are not likely to provide pasturage for large animals, at that season : so that we are almost driven to conclude that Grinnell Land, as well as

Greenland, now known to be an island (partly by the coast surveys of the Polar Expedition, and more demonstrably from the results deduced by Professor Haughton from the tidal observations), are, instead of ice-capped, merely ice-girt lands.

The cryptogamic flora of the regions visited produced little novelty except amongst the lichens. These have been submitted to Professor Theodore Fries of Upsala for determination, who sends the following interesting statement regarding them:—

'The lichens brought home by the Expedition were gathered chiefly in Grinnell Land, in the vicinity of the winter-quarters of the two vessels. It is easy to understand how great an interest this collection must have for every botanist, considering that, with the exception of nine species, which Payer indicates as having been found in the northern part of Franz Josef's Land, not a single lichen is as yet known from any more northern region than the Seven Islands, situated south of 81° N. lat.

'On this account I submitted the material entrusted to me to the most minute examination. Not only the more developed specimens have passed a microscopical examination, but every morsel has been examined with a powerful lens, and every little fragment of a lichen thus found has afterwards been examined under the microscope. The result of this rather troublesome but very interesting examination has been, that the number of lichens represented in this collection from north of lat. 81° is about ninety species. Three of these at least are new to science, whilst several are not known before from the Arctic regions, but only from localities much further to the south.

'On reviewing the collections as a whole, the eye is immediately struck with the paucity of more developed erect-growing and leaflike species, as well as the contracted shape of those which were found. This is the more remarkable, as it might naturally be expected that such lichens would, during the long winter season, constitute the principal or only food of the musk-oxen that exist in those regions. It is strange that the reindeer moss (*Cladonia rangiferina*), so common in other Arctic regions, appears to be absent from Grinnell Land.

'The nature of the lichen flora between the parallels of 81° and 83° North by no means indicates that the northern boundary of the lichen flora has been reached. On the contrary, many circumstances combine to show that, if there be land at the North Pole, lichens will be found there. The majority of the lower lichens brought from Grinnell Land appear to be as well developed as those found in regions farther south; and even from a height of 1,200 feet Captain Feilden has brought home several normally and well-developed species. The most luxuriant specimen of the leaflike genus *Gyrophora* which is brought home by the Expedition is, strange to say, from lat. 83° 6′ N.

'The remaining, and considerably smaller, part of the collections was obtained partly at more southern stations in Smith Sound, partly during short visits to some of the Danish colonies in Greenland. The former (about forty species) undoubtedly give welcome assistance to our knowledge of the lichen flora of Arctic America; naturally these are of a subordinate interest, as gathered in localities previously subjected to the careful search of lichenologists: however, my examination of this material is too little advanced to permit me to report on them in detail.'

LIST OF FLOWERING PLANTS,

FROM ELLESMERE LAND AND GRINNELL LAND.

BY PROFESSOR D. OLIVER, F.R.S.

Ranunculus nivalis, L.; and
    ,,   ,,   var. *floribus minoribus, pilis calycinis pallidioribus.*
Papaver alpinum, L. (*P. nudicaule*, auct.)

Cochlearia officinalis, L. (*C. fenestrata*, Br.)
Braya alpina, Sternb.
Vesicaria arctica, Rich.
Cardamine pratensis, L. (leafy specimen only).
„   *bellidifolia*, L.
Cheiranthus pygmœus, Adams. (*Hesperis pygmœa*, Hk.,
     H. minima, T. and G.)
Draba hirta, L.
„   *rupestris*, R. Br.
„   *alpina*, L.
Silene acaulis, L.
Lychnis apetala, L.
     „   „   var. (*L. triflora*, Br.)
Arenaria grœnlandica, Spr.? (Leaves only.)
     „   *verna*, L. (incl. *A. rubella*, Br.)
Cerastium alpinum, L.; and
     „   „   *forma: foliis ellipticis, confertis,*
     crassiusculis, glabrescentibus.
Stellaria longipes, Goldie.
Potentilla nivea, L.; and
     „   „   var. (*P. pulchella*, Br.)
     „   „   var. (*P. Vahliana*, &c.)
Dryas octopetala, L. (*D. integrifolia*, V.)
Saxifraga oppositifolia, L.
     „   *flagellaris*, W. '
Saxifraga tricuspidata, Retz.
     „   *cæspitosa*, L.
     „   *nivalis*, L.
     „   „   *forma monstrosa, floribus proliferis.*
     Shift-rudder Bay (F.)
     „   *cernua*, L.
Epilobium latifolium, L.
? *Arnica montana*, L. (*A. angustifolia*, V.)   A leafy frag-
     ment only, from winter-quarters of ' Discovery.'   (H.)
Erigeron alpinus, L.
     „   *compositus*, Pursh.
Taraxacum Dens-leonis, Desf. var

[*Vaccinium uliginosum*, L. (Hayes Sound, F.)]
[*Cassiope tetragona*, L.   („   F. and H.)]
Pedicularis capitata, Adams.
    „   *sudetica*, L. (*P. Langsdorffii*, Fisch.)
    „   *lapponica*, L.
Androsace septentrionalis, L.
Salix arctica, Pallas (varieties).
Salix, barren fragments, not identified (Shift-rudder Bay, F.)
    „   „   (Joseph Henry Peninsula, F.)
Polygonum viviparum, L.
Oxyria reniformis, Hk.
Luzula campestris, Sm. var. conjecta.
    „   „   var. (L. hyperborea, Br.)
Juncus biglumis, L.
Eriophorum polystachyon, L.
    „   *capitatum*, Host.
Carex nardina, Fries.
    „   *rigida*, Good. var.
    „   *rigida*, Good. (Hayes Sound, F. and H.)
Carex trifida? Good. abnormalis forma? an C. holostoma?
    Drej. (Hayes Sound, F.)
    „ .   *rigida*, Good. var.? (Shift-rudder Bay, F.)
    „   *stans?* Drej. (Ptarmigan Hill, Hayes Sound, H.)
    „   *fuliginosa*, S and H.
    „   „   var.? (Dobbin's Bay, H.)
Deschampsia cæspitosa, P. de B.
Colpodium latifolium, Br.
Phippsia algida, Br.
Trisetum subspicatum, P. de B.
[*Hierochloe alpina*, L. (Hayes Sound, F.)]
Alopecurus alpinus, L.
Poa abbreviata, Br.
    „   *cenisea*, All.
Festuca ovina, L. var. *brevifolia*.
Glyceria angustata, Br.
[*Poa cæsia*, Sm. var. (Twin Glacier, Hayes Sound, H.)]

MOSSES AND JUNGERMANNIÆ.

By W. Mitten, A.L.S.

A SMALL collection of Mosses and Jungermanniæ, made by the naturalists attached to the late Polar Expedition, was placed in my hands for examination. A portion of this collection was made at some of the North Greenland ports, where the ships touched on their way north; but this enumeration is confined to the specimens brought back from Smith Sound, and the shores of the Polar Basin, or in other words, from an area lying between the seventy-eighth and eighty-third parallels of north latitude. Captain Feilden's collection consists of twenty-two species of mosses.

Distichium inclinatum, Sw.—Floeberg Beach, lat. 82° 27′ N.; with young fruit. This moss is seldom wanting in collections made in the Arctic regions, and although, in an exceptional case, it is found on the sea shore in North Britain, near Dundee, it is throughout Europe and North America a Subalpine and Alpine species. In North Africa it is found on the Abyssinian mountains, and in Thibet it ascends to the elevation of 18,700 feet on the top of Herà La; but it has not been recorded from any localities south of the equator. In this respect it differs from its congener, *D. capillaceum*, also commonly found amongst Arctic mosses, and which ascends to equal elevation in India, and to 14,000 feet on the Andes. But it is also found in mountains of much less elevation than that which would appear to be required by *D. inclinatum*; and it is probably generally distributed, for it occurs on the Cameroons mountain in equatorial Africa, and is found in New Zealand.

Dicranoweisia crispula, Hedw.—Payer Harbour, lat. 78° 42′ N.; a tall state not in fruit. Like the *Distichium*, this moss perfects its fruit in Arctic regions; completely fruited specimens were gathered by Parry in Spitzbergen, and others in Davis Straits by Mr. Taylor. In Europe and

North America this species is entirely Subalpine and Alpine, and it does not appear to pass southward beyond the northern temperate zone. A nearly resembling species is found on the Andes, and two others on the Himalaya; in Antarctic regions it is represented by a species so similar that it was at first considered in the ' Flora Antarctica' to be the same. All the species are very similar, and the South American were placed in the section *Isocarpus*, of the genus *Dicranum*. In M. Schimper's first edition of the ' Synopsis of European Mosses ' the group of species, of which *D. crispula* is the largest, formed his section *Euweisia*, of the genus *Weisia*; but in the second edition of the same work they are removed from the genus *Weisia*, and now bear the generic name here used for the species, although still considered by him to belong to the family *Weisieæ*.

Rhacomitrium lanuginosum. Dill.—Payer Harbour, lat. 78° 42′ N.; barren. The specimen is but moderately hoary, and as usual in Arctic specimens quite barren; although a moss which abounds in Subalpine and Alpine situations, it is widely dispersed in the plains of Europe, occurring even on tiled buildings but little above the sea level. Antarctic specimens are usually more hoary, and have received various names, on the presumption of their being distinct; Chilian specimens were described by De Notaris as *R. senile*, Antarctic; by C. Muller as *R. geronticum*.

Pottia Heimii, Hedw.—Floeberg Beach; with ripe capsules. These specimens show this species in a form very different from those so common on the coasts of Britain, for the leaves are oblong and obtuse, and it is only here and there that a trace is observable of the serrulation usually so evident; the lower leaves are very short and very widely ovate, with the nerve vanishing below the apex, and the rather thick apiculus of the operculum does not exceed in length half the diameter of the mouth of the capsule. Specimens gathered in Beechey Island by Doctor Lyall do not differ from the usual European states, except that, as in the case of those from Floeberg Beach, the foliage is more distinctly bordered with the paler cells.

In Britain this species is exclusively maritime, but it is found in inland stations on the continent of Europe as well as in British North America ; and it, or some other species so closely resembling it as to have been mistaken for it, has been brought from Fuegia, but, like many other species belonging to the family of Tortuloid mosses, it is not recorded from the United States.

Tortula (Barbula) icmadophila, Schimper.—Floeberg Beach ; a few small barren stems amongst *Distichium inclinatum* ; Mushroom Point, in the same condition amongst *Zygotrichia leucostoma*. This species has not before been seen amongst Arctic mosses, but fine specimens with fruit were in some sets of Drummond's Musci Americani, No. 139, as *T. fallax*, from banks of rivers near the Rocky Mountains. In Europe, so far as known, it is Subalpine or Alpine.

T. (Zygotrichia) leucostoma, Brown.—Mushroom Point, lat. 82° 29′ 12″ N. ; July 1876 ; with perfected capsules. Originally described by Brown in the Appendix to Parry's first voyage as a *Barbula*, it was considered by Bridsl the type of a new genus on account of the peristomial teeth being connected below by trabeculæ ; and he thought Hooker and Greville, who say, in the ' Edinburgh Journal of Science,' under the name of *Tortula leucostoma*, that the lower half of the peristome is united into a tube, were wrong, and seems himself surprised that Brown should have overlooked the important distinction. The species is entirely Arctic, and belongs to the same group of species as the common European *Tortula subulata*, a group which may be said to have the foliage and habit of *Pottia* with the capsules and peristome of *Syntrichia*.

T. (Syntrichia) ruralis, Linn.—Mushroom Point ; a fragment adhering to a piece of Peltigera. Common amongst Arctic mosses, but always sterile. Widely spread in temperate Europe from the sea to Subalpine regions. Inhabits British North America ; but appears to be rare in the United States, and has not been traced farther southwards.

Didymodon rubellus, Roth. — Floeberg Beach, with

Bryum Brownii; very small and barren. A very variable moss in size. Small states have the point of the leaf nearly entire ; but there is always some trace of the teeth, which are so evident in the larger forms. The presence of these teeth with rusty foliage, and the habit of the whole moss, seem to indicate a close affinity with several Andean species ; and the Austral *Tortula serrulata*, Hook. et Grev., in which the peristome is more decidedly that of *Tortula*. *D. rubellus* is in Europe from the sea to the highest mountains a common moss, and it is found also in North Africa and Northern India as well as in British North America, but is said to be rare in the United States. A very similar species is found in central America, and another in New Zealand, but it cannot be said to be distinctly traced south of the Equator.

Encalypta rhabdocarpa, Schw.—Floeberg Beach ; with young fruit. Mushroom Point; adhering to a fragment of *Peltigera*, with capsule past maturity ; July, 1876. A boreal Subalpine and Alpine species, which in America does not reach the United States.

Voitia hyperborea, Grev. et Arn.—Floeberg Beach ; in fine condition, with fruit in several stages. In one of the specimens of this elegant moss the stems are a portion of a tuft more than two inches in height. A single abnormal capsule is present among the specimens ; it has the point produced into an erect beak, which is about three times longer than the diameter of the capsule : the calyptra had been removed.

Splachnum Wormskioldii, Hornem.—Hayes Sound, Floeberg Beach, and Mushroom Point ; all fertile. An elegant Arctic species which in Europe reaches the Scandinavian mountains.

Tetraplodon urceolatus, B. and S.—Mushroom Point, and Port Foulke. This species is not known to grow further south than the Alps, and although found in British North America, it does not occur in the United States. Its congener, *T. mnioides*, which grows also in the same Arctic and Alpine regions, but which also is able to maintain itself at considerably less altitudes, and has been gathered in Patagonia, would thus seem to be, like *Distichium capillaceum*, enabled, by its capacity to exist and mature its fructification in comparatively lower and warmer situations, to attain a much more extensive distribution.

Bartramia (Philonotis) fontana, Lin.—Floeberg Beach; a very small state, barren, growing with *Voitia hyperborea*. Everywhere distributed in northern and temperate Europe and North America, but although found in North Africa it does not seem to pass south of the equator.

Bryum pendulum, Hornsch.—Dumbell Harbour, lat. 82° 30′ N., with unripe fruit. Frequent amongst Arctic mosses and widely distributed throughout temperate Europe, it probably continues through the Andes and reaches Antarctic regions, being a species able to grow as well on the sea shore as upon the loftier mountains.

B. Brownii, Br. et Schimp.—Floeberg Beach; originally described by Brown as *Pohlia bryoides* from Melville Island, it has since been found on the Dovrefield Mountains.

B. calophyllum, Brown.—Floeberg Beach, and Payer Harbour; barren. Long supposed to be an Arctic species; it has in recent times been found to occur on the western shores of Britain, and in some few localities on the European continent.

Timmia austriaca, Hedw.—Floeberg Beach and Payer Harbour; barren.

Myurella apiculata, Hueb.—Floeberg Beach, with *Pogonatum alpinum*; and a fragment on *Peltigera* from Mushroom Point; all barren.

Orthothecium chryseum, Schwaegr.—Floeberg Beach with *Voitia hyperborea*; barren. In Europe an Alpine moss found in the Scandinavian mountains and Carinthian Alps.

Stercodon plicatilis, Mitt.—Mushroom Point; adhering to a fragment of *Peltigera*; barren. Described first in the ' Linnæan Society's Journal,' v. viii., from specimens gathered in Davis Straits and the Rocky Mountains: the distribution of the species seems not yet ascertained.

Camptothecium nitens, Schreb.—Floeberg Beach; barren. More plentiful in Arctic America and Northern Europe than in the more temperate regions: it is found in the plains and ascends the Alps.

Pogonatum alpinum, L.—Floeberg Beach; barren.

Mr. Hart's collection consists of twenty-six Mosses and one Jungermannia.

Distichium inclinatum, Sw.—Winter-quarters, H.M.S. ' Discovery,' lat. 81° 44′ N.

Rhacomitrium lanuginosum, Linn.—Hayes' Sound, lat. 78° 52′ N.

Tortula (Zygotrichia) leucostoma, Brown.—St. Patrick's Bay, lat. 81° 46′ N.; with *Orthothecium chryseum*.

Orthotrichum speciosum, Nees. — Winter - quarters, H.M.S. ' Discovery '; barren.

Voitia hyperborea, Grev. et Arn.—Musk Ox Bay, lat. 81° 40′ N.

Tetraplodon mnioides, L.—With the preceding, very small and short, but perfectly fruiting.

T. urceolatus, B. et S.—Musk Ox Bay.

Splachnum Wormskioldii, Hornem.—Winter-quarters, H.M.S. ' Discovery,' and Hayes Sound.

S. vasculosum, L.—Musk Ox Bay; very small and short, but fertile.

Aulucomnion turgidum, Wahl.—Hayes' Sound; barren.

Leptobryum pyriforme, Linn.—Hayes' Sound; with fruit.

Bryum (Webera) longicollum, Sw.—Hayes' Sound; with old capsules.

B. (W.) crudum, Dicks.—Hayes' Sound; barren.

B. arcticum, Brown.—Musk Ox Bay.

B. Brownii, B. et S.—Same locality.

B. æneum, Blytt.—Winter-quarters H.M.S. ' Discovery.' This species very closely resembles small states of *B. pallens*.

B. calophyllum, Brown.—Winter-quarters, H.M.S. ' Discovery.'

Timmia austriaca, Hedw.—Winter-quarters, H.M.S. 'Discovery'; barren.

Orthothecium chryseum, Schw.—St. Patrick's Bay, Hayes' Sound; all short stems and barren.

O. rubellum, Mitt.—Musk Ox Bay; growing with *Tetraplodon urceolatus*; barren.

Stercodon plicatilis, Mitt.—Winter-quarters, H.M.S. 'Discovery'; barren.

Amblystegiun uncinatum, Hedw. — Winter-quarters, H.M.S. 'Discovery.'

A. lycopodioides, Schw.—Winter-quarters, H.M.S. 'Discovery;' barren and small.

. *A. (Acroceratium) trifarium*, Wet. et M.—Hayes' Sound; barren.

A (A.) sarmentosum, Wahl.—Hayes' Sound; a very small short state; barren.

Brachythecium cirrhosum, Schw. — Winter-quarters H.M.S. 'Discovery;' in very small quantity; barren.

Blepharozia trichophylla, Linn.—Hayes' Sound; barren.

ENUMERATION OF THE FUNGI

COLLECTED DURING THE ARCTIC EXPEDITION OF 1875 AND 1876.

BY THE REV. M. J. BERKELEY, M.A., F.L.S.

THE collection consists of twenty-six species, of which I have been able with tolerable certainty to determine all but two; at least I have indicated the closest affinities in one or two which were difficult cases from the condition of the specimens, if there is some doubt as to the exact species to which they are referred. Of the twenty-six species seventeen are widely distributed, and seven hitherto undescribed, besides the two which I have been unable to determine. Of the new species two at least are very interesting, *Agaricus Feildeni* and *Urnula Hartii*. The former belongs to a group very little understood, and I have, therefore, to regret that the specimens were so roughly dried that some of the characters are more or less obscure; the latter is a new form of the curious genus *Urnula*, Fr., and so exactly like the figure in ' Flora Danica,' referred by Fries as a variety to *Peziza ciborium*, that it is very probable that the Danish may be identical with the Arctic plant. The occurrence of *Chæto-mium glabrum* on the walls of the cabins of the 'Alert' in such abundance is very curious. In this country it is widely diffused not only on papered walls, but on bare stone, basket-work, &c., and it is remarkable that the sporidia are notably smaller in the Arctic specimens. *Agaricus Feildeni*, which occurred several times, is probably esculent, as is certainly the case with *Russula integra*. I ought, perhaps, to apologise for describing *A. sphærosporus* and *A. Bello-tianus* from single specimens, but the characters are such as to separate them from all allied species which have been previously described.

There are two observations which it is but justice to add to the above notes. It is absolutely necessary to take into consideration the extreme difficulty under which collectors labour in Polar regions. The room on board is necessarily very limited, and the damp atmosphere of the cabins peculiarly unfavourable to drying plants, added to which the numerous matters constantly in hand make it impossible to change the drying papers frequently enough to insure the absorption of all the moisture, without which specimens never turn out in good condition.

It was, moreover, impossible to give any information as to the edible qualities of any species which occurred, as the number of individuals was extremely small and sometimes confined to a single specimen. The wonder is that, under the circumstances, so much was done in a department which presents peculiar difficulties.

1. *Agaricus* (*Omphalia*) *umbilicatus*, Schœff. t. 207, Fr. Hym. Eur. p. 155. On peaty soil. Mount Prospect, Discovery Bay; lat. 81° 41′ N.; H. C. Hart. Spores minute, slightly kidney-shaped.

2. *A.* (*Omphalia*) *umbelliferus*, L. On peat. The yellow form. Proven with *Peltigera*, Disco, July 1875. Proven, July 1875, Discovery Bay; H. C. Hart. Upernivik, July 22, 1875; H. W. Feilden. Pileus tomentose. Stem thickest below, tomentose about two lines high. The specimens are small, but mostly well developed. In those from Discovery Bay the gills are so thickened as to be almost subglobose. The species is very common in mountainous countries, and is sometimes extremely beautiful.

3. *A.* (*Omphalia*) *sphærosporus*, B. Pileo membranaceo, profunde umbilicato; lamellis latis distantibus, decurrentibus; sporis globosis pedicellatis. On moss. Upernivik; H. C. Hart. About one inch across.

4. *A.* (*Clitopilus*) *undatus*. Fr. Hym. Eur. p. 199. Ic. tab. 96, fig. 4. Cape Sabine, August 1, 1875; H. W. Feilden.

5. *A.* (*Naucoria*) *Bellotianus*, B. Nov. sp. Bellot Island, August 14, 1876; H. W. Feilden.

6. *A.* (*Tubaria*) *furfuraceus*, P. Syn. p. 454; Fr. Hym. Eur., p. 272. Westward Ho! Valley; lat. 82° 40′ N.; H. W. Feilden. Mount Prospect, 81° 41′ N.; H. C. Hart.

7. *A.* (*Tubaria*) *pellucidus*, Bull. Tab. 550, fig. 2; Fr. Hym. Eur., p. 273. Hayes' Sound; lat. 79° N., August 4, 1875; H. C. Hart.

8. *A.* (*Stropharia*) *Feildeni*, B. Nova sp. Bellot Island, lat. 81° 41′ N.; August 1876; H. W. Feilden, Mount Prospect, Discovery Harbour, July 4, 1876; H. C. Hart.

9. *Hygrophorus virgineus*. Fr. Hym. Eur., p. 413. Small specimens, September 29, 1875; lat. 82° 27′; H. W. Feilden.

10. *H. miniatus*. Fr. Hym. Eur. p. 418. Hayes' Sound, August 4, 1875; H. C. Hart.

11. *Russula integra.* Fr. Hym. Eur. p. 450. Bellot Island; lat. 81° 41′ N., August 13, 1876; H. W. Feilden.

12. *Cantharellus mucigenus.* Fr. Hym. Eur. p. 460. On moss from Discovery Bay; H. C. Hart.

13. *Merulius aurantiacus.* Fr. Hym. Eur. p. 591; Kl. in Berk., Eng. Fl. v., p. 128; Discovery Bay, 81° 41′ N; H. C. Hart.

14. *Lycoperdon cretaceum,* B. Nov. sp.; Bellot Island, August 14, 1876; H. W. Feilden.

15. *L. atropurpureum.* Vitt. Monog. Lyc. p. 42, tab. ii. fig. 6; Discovery Bay, Mount Prospect; H. C. Hart; Bellot Island, August 18, 1876, and Hayes' Sound, August 4, 1875; H. W. Feilden.

16. *Trichobasis Pyrolæ,* B. Out. p. 332; Uredo Pyrolæ, Grev. H. Ed., p. 440; Proven, on leaves of Pyrola.

17. *Stilbum arcticum,* B. Nov. sp. on the stem of *Agaricus sphærosporus,* B.; Upernivik; H. C. Hart.

18. *Peziza stercorea.* P. Obs. 2, p. 89: Fr. Syst. Myc. ii. p. 87; Cooke, Micr. fig. 147; Discovery Bay on dung of musk-ox; H. C. Hart.

19. *Ascobolus furfuraceus.* P. Obs. 1. t. 4, f. 3–6. On dung of musk-ox with preceding.

20. *Urnula Hartii,* B. Nov. sp. Upernivik; H. C. Hart. Grinnell Land; lat. 82° 29′ N.; July 1876; H. W. Feilden.

21. *Chætomium glabrum,* B. and Br. Ann. Nat. Hist., May 1873, p. 349, tab. x., fig. 15. On damp surface in cabin of H.M.S. 'Alert' at Floeberg Beach; lat. 82° 27′ N.

22. *Venturia myrtilli,* Cooke. Journ. of Bot., August 1866, tab. 50, fig. 4. On semiputrid leaves, Discovery Bay; H. C. Hart.

23. *Sphærella lineolata,* De Not. Sphæria lineolata Desm. Pl. Crypt, No. 1263; Cooke, l.c. tab. 51, fig. 31. On grass with the last.

24. *Dothidea bullulata,* B. Nov. sp. On leaves, Disco; H. C. Hart. Some species of *Mucor* appears to have occurred with *Chætomium glabrum.*

ALGÆ AND DIATOMACEÆ.

By G. Dickie, M.A., M.D., F.L.S.

During the Arctic Expedition of 1875–76 but few species of the higher orders of marine algæ were collected beyond 78° N. lat.; the following are all that have come under my notice among the collections made by Captain Feilden and Mr. Hart :—

> *Desmarestia aculeata*, Lamour.
> *Laminaria longicruris*, De la Pyl.
>   ,,   *caperata*,   ,,
> *Dictyosiphon fœniculaceus*, Grev.
> *Chordaria flagelliformis*, Ag.[1]
> *Ectocarpus siliculosus*, Lyngb.
> *Chætopteris plumosa*,   ,,

These all belong to the olive-coloured series, and, with the exception of the two species of Laminaria, are well known European forms.

Dr. Moss and Captain Feilden sent to me fragments of stems of Laminaria from the mud of a raised beach or 'shell flat' 200 feet above the present level of the sea at Floeberg Beach, N. lat. 82° 27', W. long. 61° 22', also from mud-beds in Cane Valley, Grinnell Land, N. lat. 82° 33'. The fragments seem to belong to both species of Laminaria above mentioned, and Captain Feilden states that they retained the peculiar marine smell as strongly as in recent specimens. The beds from which the specimens were taken are exposed, by the action of a stream, to a depth of not less than thirty feet in thickness: along with them were found shells of *Mya truncata*, *Astarte borealis*, &c.

I could not find any trace of marine algæ belonging to the red series.

---

[1] The specimens very dwarf and fragmentary, nevertheless I think they must be referred to this species.

The most complete list of the marine algæ of Spitsbergen known to me is one given by Professor J. G. Agardh, comprehending seventeen olive and twenty of the red—therefore comparatively rich when contrasted with those above enumerated: all the species are also included in the Spitsbergen list with one exception, viz. Dictyosiphon.

The marine species of the green series found by the naturalists of the Expedition are—

> *Ulva latissima*, L., very fragmentary.
> *Enteromorpha clathrata*, Grev.
> *Chaetomorpha Melagonium*, Web. and Mohr.

These have very wide distribution in European and other seas.

There are also representatives of several genera found in fresh water, namely :—

> *Prasiola Sauteri*, Menegh.
> *Zygogonium Agardhii*, Rabh.
> *Closterium lunula*, Müller.
> *Zonotrichia*, species.
> *Nostoc commune*, Vaucher.
>   „   *aureum*, Ktz.
> *Hormosiphon arcticum*, Berk.
> *Hormospora*, species.
> *Chroococcus*, species.
> *Gloeocapsa Magma*, Ktr.
> *Oscillaria tenuis*, Ag.
> *Hypheothrix coriacea*, Ktz.
>   „   *obscura*, n. sp.
> *Chthonoblastus*, sp.
> *Tolypothrix*, sp.

The most abundant of these appears to be *Nostoc commune*, which occurs in Spitsbergen, and is widely diffused in Europe, as indeed also are the other genera.

Gloecapsa I have previously seen as found at Disco ; the specimens sent to me by Dr. Moss were found at 82° 27′ N.

It thus appears that certain well-known European genera have their representatives in the cold marshes of lands beyond 80° N.

The *Diatomaceæ* are also, on the whole, well represented in the collections made by Captain Feilden, Dr. Moss, and Mr. Hart.

I have observed the following genera, and it may be sufficient to record here merely the number of species of each genus, a complete list of names being preserved for full report elsewhere.

LIST OF DIATOMS, BEYOND LAT. 78° N.

Name of Genus	No. of Species	Name of Genus	No. of Species
Achnanthes . . .	2	*Navicula* . . .	13
Achnanthidium . .	2	*Nitzschia* . . .	3
Amphiprora . .	2	*Orthosira* . .	1
Amphora . .	4	*Pleurosigma* . .	2
Biddulphia . .	1	*Podosira* . .	1
Chaetoceros . .	2	*Podosphœnia* . .	1
Cocconeis . .	4	*Raphoncis* . .	1
Coscinodiscus . .	4	*Rhabdonema* . .	2
Cymbella . .	1	*Rhoicosphenia* . .	1
Denticula . .	1	*Surirella* . .	3
Diatoma . .	1	*Stauroneis* . .	3
Eunotia . .	2	*Synedra* . .	4
Fragilaria . .	2	*Thalassiosira* . .	1
Grammatophora .	2	*Triceratium* . .	1
Melosira . .	1	*Tryblionella* . .	1
Meridion . .	1		

Making in all thirty-one genera and seventy species so far as I have observed; most of them are marine, those of fresh-water being fewer.

P. T. Cleve, in a communication to the Swedish Academy of Sciences, March 12, 1873, states that the whole number found in the Arctic Sea is 181; but he considers seventeen of these as of doubtful occurrence in that region. In the same paper he specifies those found at Spitsbergen, which seems, as in the case of the higher algæ already alluded to, to be richer in species than the parts of the Arctic Sea visited by the late Expedition.

The presence and abundance of these minute organisms, with their exquisitely sculptured silicious investments, is a point of much interest in relation to the existence of animal life.   It has been long known that they abound in the alimentary canal of certain radiata and bivalve mollusca, and where they are abundant, which seems to be the rule, this implies the possible presence of certain animal forms which find abundant *pabulum* in the organic contents of the Diatoms; these lower are preyed upon by those of higher type, and we thus have a very notable and interesting chain of dependence and an illustration of the proverbial ' power of the littles.'

It is, therefore, not surprising to find that at least sixteen species of bivalve mollusca were collected beyond 80° N. by the naturalists of the Expedition.

[The botanical collections treated of in the preceding pages were mainly, though not entirely, made in Grinnell Land between the latitudes of 81° 40′ N., and 83° 6′ N.   The vicinity of Discovery Bay, and as far north as lat. 81° 50′, was carefully botanised by Mr. Hart, and from that latitude to the eighty-third parallel the collections were made by the writer.   Though the period for collecting phanerogamic plants was confined to a month or six weeks in the summer of 1876, yet it is probable that few flowering plants escaped observation, and that the collections brought back give an accurate and adequate idea of the phanerogamic flora of Grinnell Land.   The number of species of lichens obtained is astonishing, yet this result may fairly be considered only as a contribution to the lichenology of Grinnell Land, and not by any means an exhaustive collection; the same remark applies to the collections of fungi, confervæ, and diatomaceæ.—H. W. FEILDEN.]

No. XV.

GEOLOGY.

ON THE GEOLOGICAL STRUCTURE OF THE COASTS OF GRINNELL LAND AND HALL BASIN,

VISITED BY THE BRITISH ARCTIC EXPEDITION OF 1875–6.

By C. E. De Rance, F.G.S., Assoc. Inst. C.E.,

of the Geological Survey of England and Wales

AND

H. W. Feilden, F.G.S., F.R.G.S., C.M.Z.S.,

Naturalist to the Expedition.

The collection of rocks and fossils, more than 2,000 in number, made during the expedition in the lands lying between the parallels of 78° and 83° 6′ North, enable the following sequence of formations to be established for these far Arctic Lands :—

GRINNELL LAND, &c.	N. AMERICA EQUIVALENTS.
Glacio-marine beds.	Glacio-marine beds.
Miocene shales and clays with thirty feet coal seam.	
Carboniferous limestone.	Carboniferous limestone.
Dana Bay beds.	Devonian.
Upper Silurians.	
Lower Silurians.	Quebec (Llandeilo) group.
Cape Rawson beds.	Huronian ?
Fundamental gneiss, &c.	Laurentian ?

PALÆOZOIC ROCKS.—The ancient fundamental gneiss and crystalline rocks, that have been described by so many observers as fringing the coasts of Greenland, and underlying the synclinal of palæozoic rocks of the Parry Archipelago, continue northwards, and form the shores of Smith Sound on either side, occupying the entire coast of Ellesmere Land from Cape Isabella to Cape Sabine, rising to a height of 2,000 feet.

At Port Foulke the syenitic and gneissic rocks are overlaid by sandstone and conglomerate, the former largely rippled, and probably of Miocene age, overlaid by sheets of basalt, which have altered in some cases into porcellanite.

Cape Rawson Beds.—A vast series of azoic rocks, newer than the fundamental gneiss, and probably unconformable to it, but older than the fossiliferous Silurians, occupy the country between Scoresby Bay and Cape Creswell, in lat. 82° 40′ N., and probably represent in time the Huronian of North America, but formed possibly in a different basin, as they are not present in the Arctic Archipelago.

At Cape Rawson the strata are thrown into a series of sharp anticlinal folds, which range W.S.W., are abruptly terminated by sea-cliffs, as at Black Cape, Cape Union, and other prominent headlands, and exhibit fine sections of jet-black slates, in strong contrast to the frozen sea beneath and the snow-clad slopes above.

Associated with the slates are beds of impure limestones frequently traversed with veins of quartz and chert; the slates are sometimes exceedingly well cleaved, the planes of cleavage being generally inclined at high angles, and more rarely horizontal, their strike being N.N.E. to S.S.W. The true dip of the slates is almost invariably at very high angles.

These beds give place further north to a vast series of quartzites and grits, which commence in latitude 82° 33′: they rise in Westward Ho! Valley to ridges 3,000 feet in height. An anticlinal axis passes through this valley and carries down these strata beneath the carboniferous limestones of Feilden Peninsula.

Silurian Limestones.—Mural cliffs of limestone, with conglomerate at the base, rise to a height of more than 1000 feet on the east coast of Bache Island. These beds at the south end of Bache Island, as viewed from Buchanan Strait, appear to rest on syenitic and granitoid rocks, and dip gently to the N.N.W. as far as Victoria Head, where a landing was effected and some fossils obtained : the mural cliffs, forming the northern shore of the island, consist of this formation, and correspond in direction to the strike of the strata.

The limestones of Norman Lockyer Island, lat. 79° 52′ N., at the mouth of Franklin Pierce Bay, dip at a high angle to the north. The south side of the island is a steep bluff rising to 600 feet, glaciated at the top, in a north and south direction. To the north is a low shelving shore ; and between the island and the mainland there is a fault bringing in the basement conglomerate beds of Bache Island. It is well seen at Cape Prescott, in Allman and Dobbin Bays, Cape Louis Napoleon, and Hayes Point, as are the limestones, by which it is overlaid.

A north-east anticlinal passing through Cape Hilgard probably brings in older Silúrian rocks, as some of the fossils from this locality have been determined by Mr. Etheridge to be *Lower Silurian* forms : *Maclurea magna, Receptaculites occidentalis, R. arctica,* Eth. Several of these types appear to have been previously brought from the Parry Archipelago, where there is probably an unbroken sequence from the Lower Silurian, through the Upper Silurian into the Devonian, without any physical break.

The Cape Hilgard conglomerate appears to correspond in time and position to the red sandstone and coarse grit underlying the Silurian limestones of North Somerset, which are described as like those found between Wolstenholme and Whale Sounds, West Greenland. Whether the Lower Silurian horizon is that portion of the section lying between the limestones and the conglomerate or grit bed, has not been clearly made out either in Grinnell Land or in the Arctic Archipelago ; but this view is strongly supported by the fact that

the basement beds in both areas indicate a period of denudation, shallow water, or at all events erosion of coast-lines,
that no older fossiliferous beds are known, and that the
conglomerate or grit bed rests directly on the fundamental
rock. Silurian limestones continued to Cape Norton Shaw :
both in this locality and at Cape Barrow they contain a
numerous assemblage of fossils, described in a very exhaustive
report by Mr. Etheridge.[1] Amongst them may be mentioned
*Favosites alveolaris, F. gothlandica, Favistella reticulata,
Halysites catenulatus*, var. *feildeni*, Eth., *Pentamerus
coppingeri*, Eth.

On the northern side of Scoresby Bay the extension of
the limestone ceases, and the more ancient Cape Rawson beds
rise to day. Whether the line of junction is a fault, or a
natural boundary, is doubtful ; of whatever character it may
be, it is certain that it traverses Kennedy Channel, and
reappears on the opposite coast in Hall Land, where its
situation is determined within narrow limits, trending from
Polaris Bay to Newman Bay. These beds outcrop on the
north side of Thank God Harbour, and there is an exposure
of Silurian limestones at Cape Tyson and Offley Island to
the south : from this point southwards to the great Humboldt
glacier, the Silurians form the rock of the country, by way
of Petermann Fiord, Bessels Bay, Franklin and Crozier
Islands, and Capes Constitution and Andrew Jackson.

Dana Bay Beds.—Green slates associated with meta-
morphosed rocks belonging to the Cape Rawson beds are seen
on the slope below the carboniferous limestone on the neck
of Feilden Peninsula, but the boundary is doubtful, and may
be faulted.

On the south side of the valley in Dana Bay, at the head
of Porter Bay, the carboniferous limestone is repeated by a
strike fault, and the base is not seen.

A small exposure of fossiliferous beds was observed in a
torrent course, the fossils are referred by Mr. Etheridge to
the Devonian era ; but as the nature of the underlying rocks

' Journal Geological Soc.,' London, 1878.

could not be determined, it is doubtful whether these rocks represent the 'Ursa stage' of Heer, and whether they form the base of the carboniferous limestone. Should it be eventually proved by future researches that the 'Ursa stage' is absent, it would appear probable that these beds were only deposited further south.

The rocks lying above the Silurian limestone of the Arctic Archipelago occur in a synclinal trough or hollow, ranging W.S.W. and E.N.E. from Banks Land through the Parry Islands. At Byam Martin Island, M'Clintock describes two sandstones, the one red, finely stratified, associated with purple slate, resembling the red sandstone of North Somerset, Cape Bunny, and that found between Wolstenholme and Whale Sounds, W. Greenland; and another, fine-grained, greyish-yellow coloured, resembling the coal-bearing sandstone of Cape Hamilton, Bank's Land (Baring Island). It contains numerous casts of a brachiopod, allied, according to Dr. Haughton, to *Terebratula* (*Atrypa*), *primipilaris*, Von Buch (and to *A. fallax* of the carboniferous rocks of Ireland), found abundantly at Gerolstein in the Eifel, now known as *Rhynchonella primipilaris*. Associated with these later sandstones are coal-seams striking E.N.E. to Bathurst Island. The coals have a lignaceous texture, consisting of thin layers of brown coal and jetty-black glossy coal, with a wooden ring under the hammer.

The identity of genera and of some species of the flora of the pre-carboniferous limestone 'Ursa stage' with those of the rocks of Europe, lying immediately above the limestone, point to the equable and identical climate prevailing over very large areas of the earth's surface, and to the local and temporary character of the deep sea conditions expressed by the formation of the mountain limestone, in the midst of a long continental episode, marked by the first rich land flora, in the earth's history, which can be traced both in the old world and in the new, from 47° to 74° and 76° north lat., and which was as fully developed beyond the Arctic Circle, as in Central Europe: the leaves of the evergreen tree *Lepidodendra*, and the large fronds of *Cardiopteris frondosa*, being as well grown in the Arctic as those from the Vosges and the south of Iceland.

Carboniferous Limestone.—Rocks of this age occur in Feilden and Parry Peninsulas, on the north coast of Grinnell Land, and extend as far west as Clements Markham Inlet, attaining a height of more than 2,000 feet at Mount Julia, and probably to still greater height in the United States Range, which corresponds in direction with the strike of the beds, and probably continues in a south-westerly direction, across the whole of the tract lying between the limestones of this age in the synclinal of the Parry Archipelago.   Amongst the fossils of Feilden Peninsula may be mentioned *Productus mesolobus, P. costatus, Spirifer ovalis, S. duplicata, Zaphrentis* like *Cylindrica.*   It is worthy of note that, had the strike of the above limestones changed in direction northwards, it would probably have been noticed by the sledge parties that examined the coast east and west of this tract, and that, assuming the same strike continues over the Polar area, a prolongation of the trend of these limestones would pass through Spitsbergen, where this formation has been recognized, and contains some identical species.

In the Carboniferous Limestones occur a group of cephalopoda, encrinites and corals, that, judging by their analogues in the secondary rocks, would indicate a warm climate ; and unless the corals, which all belong to the Palæozoic types of the Rugosa and Tabulata corals, had marvellous powers of adaptation to different climates, they prove a more equable climate in the world than exists at the present time, and when taken with the fact that the plants of the ' Ursa stage ' of the Arctic regions lived before the deposition of the mountain limestone in that area, and doubtless in other areas, and reappeared in the coal measures overlying those limestones in Europe and North America, the supposition that an equable warm moist climate overspread a large surface of the globe during the whole of the carboniferous era becomes something stronger than even a working hypothesis.

The Arctic area and North Eastern America are marked by an absence of Permian rocks; and it is worthy of note that the strata of this age, occurring in Kansas, consist of conglomerates, shales with fossils allied to those of the coal measures, and beds of gypsum resting conformably on the carboniferous, indicating shallow water, proximity of land, and lacustrine or inland sea conditions. Our limited knowledge of the Arctic regions renders it doubtful whether the absence of the Permian in the northern area indicates that, after the deposition of the carboniferous limestone, the sea bottom was upheaved, and formed continental land until the Liassic era, or whether the coal measures, Permian and Triassic strata, were deposited or afterwards denuded, before the deposition of the lias resting on the carboniferous limestone of Eglinton Isle. That the former sequence occurred is supported by the absence of the Triassic strata in the Parry Archipelago.

In America, the carboniferous rocks experienced a period of physical disturbance, throwing them into folds and plications, happening in pre-triassic times as in England, the trias lying on the upturned and denuded edges of the American carboniferous.

There would appear to be little doubt that the dip observable in the carboniferous limestone of the Parry Archipelago was obtained before the deposition of the lias, which occurs directly upon it at various levels; and it would appear to be more probable that the trias was never deposited over this area, than that it had been formed and denuded away in the era intervening between plication of the carboniferous and the subsidence of the land beneath the liassic sea.

TERTIARY ROCKS. *Miocene.*—Resting unconformably on the azoic schists of Water-course Bay, on the west side of Smith Sound, in the vicinity of Discovery Harbour, where the 'Discovery' wintered 1874–6, occurs a bed of coal from twenty-five to thirty feet in thickness, overlaid by fine-grained black shale and sandstone from which plant remains were collected by Feilden, these shales closely resembling those of Cape Staratschin, in the ice fiord of Spitsbergen.

The strata are laid bare in a deep gully excavated by the stream flowing across them, and are seen to dip towards the east at ten degrees. Overlying the tertiary deposits occur beds of fine mud and glacial drift, with well-preserved shells of mollusca of species now living in the neighbouring seas, such as *Saxicava* and *Astarte*, which beds rise to a height of no less than 1,000 feet above the sea-level, proving a submergence of the lignite and plant-bearing beds to that amount, and a subsequent re-elevation.

Beds with plant-bearing shales may possibly occur in other parts of Grinnell Land not visited by the Expedition, and those of Discovery Bay were not recognized until a period which only permitted a few visits to that interesting locality. However, a collection was made of thirty species, of which eighteen are known to be common to the *Miocene* deposits of the Arctic Zone, seventeen of them occurring in Spitsbergen, and eight in Greenland ; the flora of the Grinnell Land Miocene, therefore, more closely approximating to that of Spitsbergen, lying 3° to 4° of latitude further south, than to that of Greenland, situated 11° further south. Six species are common to Europe, four to America (Alaska), two to Asia.

The muddy shore of a sea or river is indicated by *Equisetum arcticum*, Hr., of Grinnell Land and King Bay, Spitsbergen, and, presuming it had a similar habitat, its nearest ally to *Equisetum limosum*, Lin. Conifers in both these districts hold the first place, four families with the species occurring in Grinnell Land. *Torellia rigida*, Hr., must have been very abundant ; it was previously only known, in a fragmentary condition, from Cape Staratschin in Spitsbergen. It is allied to the genus *Phœnicopsis* of the oolitic Brown Jura, which forms a link between the *Cordaites* of the carboniferous and the *Torellia* of the Arctic Tertiary.

Taxodium distichum miocenum is most abundant, and well-preserved male flowers, resembling those of Spitsbergen, occur, while the genus is now confined to Mexico and the south of the United States.

The discovery of two twigs of the Norway spruce (*Pinus abies*) with leaves, in Grinnell Land, is of great interest, as some meagre traces of it had previously been received from Spitsbergen, and the species doubtless extended, in the previous period, as far as the Pole, if at that epoch land extended so far. The home of this tree was evidently in the north, and in Miocene times it doubtless had not travelled as far south as Europe, its first appearance being in the Norfolk Forest-bed, and the interglacial lignites of Switzerland. Though now a principal constituent of our forests, its extreme northern limit is in Scandinavia, in latitude $69\frac{1}{2}°$ N., and from thence spreads over twenty-five degrees of latitude, though confined in Miocene times to the Arctic Zone ; while *Taxodium distichum*, now confined to so small an area, in Miocene times overspread the northern hemisphere from central Italy to 82° N.

The Monocotyledons, *Phragmites œningensis*, Br., and *Carex noursoakensis*, Hr., of Grinnell Land, Greenland, and Spitsbergen, indicate damp localities with beds and sedges, the former of a large size with narrow leaves and a mid-rib.

Six families of Dicotyledons occur, the more abundant species being *Populus arctica*, Hr., which range through the whole Arctic Zone. The presence of large specimens of bark from Grinnell Land of *Betula prisca* prove that trees of the birch attained a considerable size. Leaves and fruit of *Betula brongniarti*, Ett., could also be identified, the species agreeing with the specimens from Spitsbergen.

The Grinnell Land lignite indicates a thick peat moss, with probably a small lake, with water lilies on the surface of the water, and reeds on the edges, and birches and poplars, and taxodias, on the banks, with pines, firs, spruce elms, and hazel bushes on the neighbouring hills. Further research of these remarkable beds would doubtless afford a rich harvest of vegetable remains, and possibly those of a vertebrate fauna, as well as of the insects that probably tenanted the forest ; but at present the elytron of a beetle (*Carabites feildenianus*, Hr.) attests their former presence.

If lands formerly extended to the Pole, they were probably covered with these Arctic forests. The climatic differences indicated by the flora of the north and west part of Spitsbergen (King's Bay and Ice Fiord) to that of Disco Island and Finmark are still more apparent in comparing the latter with that of Grinnell Land, which indicates the same conditions as Spitsbergen, which, though colder than Disco, was evidently not Arctic, as the water lily proves fresh water, water that must have remained open for the greater part of the year, and the *Taxodium distichum* cannot be now got to grow unartificially in Christiania, and is only maintained in northern Germany by cultivation.

Existing representative Arctic plants are wanting in the Grinnell Land Miocenes, but most of the genera occurring in them still exist within the Arctic Zone, but all of them have their present limit, at least, from twelve to fifteen degrees further south, only *Equisetum*, *Carex*, and *Populus* extending beyond 70° N. : of the remainder, *Pinus abies* ceases at 69° 30′ ; *Phragmites communis* at 69° 45′ in Finmark ; *Corylus avellana* in 67° 56′ ; *Ulmus montana* in 66° 59′, and cultivated to nearly 70° in Norway.

The writers are indebted to Professor Oswald Heer of Zurich for the following determination of the fossil remains from the Miocene shales of Grinnell Land :—

PLANTÆ.

Equisetum arcticum, Hr.
    „   *cœtatum*, Hr.
Torellia rigida, Hr.
    „   *major*, Hr.
    „   *bifida*, Hr.
    „   *mossiana*, Hr.
Thuites ehrenswardi, Hr. ?
Taxodium distichum miocenum.
Pinus feildeniana, Hr.
    „   *polaris*, Hr.

Pinus abies, Linn.
   „   *dicksoniana,* Hr.
   „   *hayesiana,* Hr.
Phragmites halliana, Hr.
      „   *œningensis,* Al. Br.
Castinites articus, Hr.
Carex nourgsoakensis, Hr.
Tridium grœnlandicum, Hr.?
Populus arctica, Hr.
Populus faddacki, Hr.
Salix sp.
Betula prisca, Ett.
   „   *brongniarti,* Ett.
Corylus macquarrii, Forbes.
   „   *insignis,* Hr.
Ulmus borealis, Hr.
Viburnum nordenskiöldi, Hr.
Nymphœa arctica, Hr.
Filia malmgreni, Hr.
Phyllites fagopyrinus, Hr.

INSECTA.

Carabites feildenianus, Hr.

Mr. R. J. Moss, F.C.S., has recently examined a specimen of the coal from the winter-quarters of the 'Discovery,' deposited in the Museum of Science and Art, Dublin, and found it to possess the lustre and fracture of good bituminous coal, to cake when heated, and to have 61 per cent. of coherent coke. It contains :—

Carbon	75·49
Hydrogen	5·60
Oxygen and nitrogen.	9·89
Sulphur	0·52
Ash	6·49
Water	2·01
	100·00

Excluding water, sulphur, and ash, its compositions are :—

Carbon . . . . . . 82·97
Hydrogen. . . . . . 6·16
Oxygen and nitrogen. . . . 10 87
                              ———
                              100.00

Its ash contains 7·58 per cent. of potash, a quantity un-usually large ; and Mr. Moss compares the chemical composi-tion of the coal to the thick era of the carboniferous of the Bay of Fundy, Nova Scotia, and to a lignite of Miocene age in the Island of Sardinia, containing 82·26 of carbon.[1]

The specific gravity of the Grinnell Land coal is 1·3, corresponding to those from Disco, though it differs in con-taining so much larger an amount of carbon.

From the large number of analyses made by Mr. A. Marvine of the U. S. Survey of the Territories of the Lignites of the Western States,[2] it appears they resemble the Grinnell Land coal in their compact character, black colour and shining lustre, resembling that of bituminous coals ; the ash is low, seldom reaching 6 per cent., while the sulphur is generally less than 2 per cent. Volatile products evolved below a dull red heat usually vary from 25 to 37 per cent., while fixed carbon lies between 45 and 60 per cent., indi-cating qualities above those of ordinary European brown coals or lignite, but containing less carbon than the true bituminous coal of Grinnell Land.

The extensive tracts of Cretaceous and Tertiary rocks ranging from the Gulf of Mexico to Vancouver Island, and occupying so large an area in the centre of North America, have been shown to consist of an unbroken sequence, without any physical break, but contain a succession of distinct floras, the details and relative age of which have been so ably worked

[1] On the chemical composition of the coal discovered by the Arctic Expedition of 1875-6.—'Scientific Proc. of the Royal Dublin Soc.,' 1877.

[2] 'Report of the U. S. Geol. and Geog. Survey of the Territories,' Washington, 1874. p. 112.

out in the magnificent volumes published by the U. S. Geological Survey of the Territories, containing the researches of Professors Leo Lesquereux, Meek, Mudge, Drs. Hayden and Newberry, and others.

The flora of the base of the Cretaceous of America, the Dakota group, has much in common with the Greenland Upper Cretaceous Flora, some of the twenty-eight species determined by Prof. Heer being identical. The vast extent and homogeneousness of the formation in America point to a marine deposit, formed during a period of subsidence, followed by a long stationary era, experiencing a land climate—dry, and proportionally cold.

The marine forms, which occur in the Dakota group, and which have so large a development in the overlying beds, are absent in the Greenland beds, and the Lower Cretaceous flora appears to be unrepresented in North America, pointing to a long and unbroken continental epoch in the Arctic Circle, ranging through the entire Cretaceous and Tertiary eras. In the overlying American Eocenes occur types of plants, occurring in the European Miocenes, and still living, proving the truth of Professor Lesquereux's postulate that the plant types appear in America a stage in advance of their advent in Europe. These plants point to a far higher mean temperature than those of the Dakota group, to a dense atmosphere of vapour, and a luxuriance of ferns and palms. The subtropical flora of the Eocene Tertiary lignitic group is absent in the Arctic lands, though a certain amount of mingling of temperate forms occurs; these, however, come in great force in the overlying Lower Miocene beds, many of the species being common to the Greenland and Mackenzie rocks of that age, and some of them reappearing in the plant-bearing shales of Grinnell Land; the successive Miocene deposits pointing to a gradual lowering of the mean temperature.

The American origin of the Miocene flora of Europe, as Dr. Newberry points out, is strongly supported by the occurrence of the plant *Onoclea sensibilis* (*Felicites hebridicus* of Forbes), discovered long ago by the Duke of Argyll in the leaf-beds of Mull in the American tertiaries ; and he suggests that the temperate flora, which drove the warmer Eocene flora to the south and east of Europe, travelled by way of Greenland, Iceland, and the Hebrides.

In Miocene times the climate of Greenland and Alaska was that of New York and St. Louis, while, in the succeeding glacial era, the climate now existing in Greenland came down to the latitude of New York, a cold temperate climate prevailed in Mexico, into which the advancing cold forced the herds of mammals which covered the plains of North America, where they were nearly all exterminated.

Glaciation.—During the thaw produced by the short episode of warmth that represents in the Arctic regions the summer of other lands, sub-aerial denudation of the surface of the cliffs takes place on a gigantic scale, vast masses of rock fall from the cliffs, and form a talus concealing their base, like the ' screes ' of the English Lake District.

On the close of the transient summer the rocks are saturated with moisture, cleaved slate cliffs and the loose material forming the ' screes ' being alike charged with water to their utmost capacity ; without any warning or gradual approach winter conditions appear, and the face of nature is changed in a few hours ; moisture and running water are converted into ice, which in process of expansion exercise a destructive force on the rocks which is hardly comparable with the sub-aerial denudation going on in more temperate climes ; and on the first appearance of thaw, masses of rock, separating along lines of weakness formed by planes of jointing and bedding, are detached from the cliff, and falling on the snow-covered ' screes ' slide down to the ice-foot beneath, the impetus being often sufficient to carry them on to the floe, where they remain until they are carried seaward on the general break-up of the ice.

The ice-foot is built up not so much by the act of freezing of the sea-water in contact with the coast, as by the accumulation of the autumn snow-fall, which drifting to the beach is met by the sea-water at a temperature below the freezing point of fresh-water and instantaneously is converted into ice, and forms a solid wall from the bottom of the sea upwards and increasing in height as the snow falls.

When the ' season floe,' or young ice, is first formed there is little difference in the level of the floe and that of the ice-foot, but as the latter is constantly increasing in height, while the former is daily oscillating with movement of the tides, a junction of the two never takes place ; for the height of the surface of the ice-foot above the level of high-water is mainly dependent on the amount of snow-fall, while its depth below that level is dependent upon the slope of the sea-bottom and the vertical range of the tides.

Like the beaches of more temperate regions, the ice-foot is absent on exposed and projecting headlands, and it is best developed in the sweeping curves and deeper bays of the coast-line. Its typical aspect in Smith Sound is a flat terrace 50 to 100 yards in breadth, stretching from the base of the ' scree ' to the sea-margin, its width, varying with the slope of the sea-bottom, decreasing in direct proportion to the increase of the land slope.

When the solar rays exert their force, the snow forming the upper layer of the ice-foot lying nearest to the ' scree ' is first melted, owing to the dark surface of the talus absorbing heat, and a deep trench is formed, which becomes filled with water, received from the cliffs above, and derived from the melting of the snow below ; these united streams soon cut deep channels in the ice, and make their way to the sea through transverse gullies, often exposing the rock beneath, which at low-water become dry, but filled with sea-water on the return of the tide, which rushing through the apertures with great violence, sweeps right and left, occupies the ditch at the face of the talus, and reassorts its materials. These fall to the bottom, and form the old sea margins, which, through the gradual rise of the land, form a characteristic series of successive terraces at various elevations up to 200 or 300 feet, especially in sheltered bays and inlets, and occasionally in positions where wave-action was impossible.

These terraces were doubtless formerly much more continuous than at present, later denudation having destroyed portions of them; but the numerous fragments that remain, preserved by a protective snow mantle, are sufficient to show that they were formed by the processes now in progress of operation.

The mud and sand-beds formed during the earlier stage of upheaval are carried down by summer torrents, and discharged into fiords and arms of the sea; the heated and turbid waters melting the floes lying around the delta, and causing it to discharge its freight of stones and gravel into the mud-beds beneath, into which also fall the shells of the mollusca inhabiting the coast. These mud-beds on the upheaval of the country are covered by stream-action with unfossiliferous gravels, which, together with the mud-beds, often form a thickness in the valleys of 200 or 300 feet.

The sequence of formation is constantly repeated as the rise of the land gradually goes on; the turbid matter in the summer torrent is precipitated, the delta increases in thickness, until the bay is silted up by a bar across it in great measure thrown up by the irresistible pressure of the Polar pack exerted on the floebergs, which buries them deep in the soft material, and thrusts it up into a bar; and the bay becomes a lake. Upheaval continuing, the waters seek an outlet; a passage through the barrier is cut, the waters of the lake are lowered, and expanses of mud, strewed with *Mya truncata*, *Saxicava rugosa*, *Astarte borealis*, are exposed. This surface during ten months of the year is frozen as hard as any rock, but during the thaw episode is exposed to extensive denudation, and its materials carried down to lower levels.

The molluscan fauna, found in the glacio-marine deposits of Grinnell Land and North Greenland at various levels up to 1,000 feet above the present sea-level, is practically identical with that now living in the neighbouring sea, and the species *Pecten grœnlandicus*, *Mya truncata*, and *Saxicava rugosa* are alike most abundant in the modern seas, and in the older mud-beds; and it is especially worthy of note, as indicating the comparatively modern elevation of this coast-line, that stems of two species of *Laminaria*, which grow in considerable abundance in the Polar sea, occur in the mud-beds at elevations of 200 feet, still retaining their peculiar sea-shore odour.

Coniferous wood, still retaining its buoyancy, occurs at elevations of several hundred feet, of a precisely similar character to that now being stranded on the existing coast-line. No evidence was discovered in the mud-beds of Grinnell Land to encourage the idea that any of these trees had grown *in situ*, or that during the period occupied by the elevation of this tract of country a thousand feet, it had experienced an interglacial period during which such trees might have flourished.

Sea-ice moved up and down by tidal action, or driven on shore by gales, was found to be a very potent agent in the glaciation of rocks and pebbles; the work was seen in progress along the shores of the Polar Basin,[1] 'at the south end of a small island in Blackcliff Bay, lat. 82° 30' N., the bottoms of the hummocks, some eight to fifteen feet thick, were studded with hard limestone pebbles, which when extracted from the ice were found to be rounded and scratched on the exposed surface only.'

On shelving shores, as the tide recedes, the hummocks, sliding over the subjacent material down to a position of rest, make a well-marked and peculiar sound, resulting from the grating of included pebbles, with the rocky floor beneath, or in some cases on other pebbles included in drift overlying the rock.

The rock surface at considerable elevations, between gaps in the lines of old terrace, is often found to be glaciated; and there can be little doubt that this glaciation was produced by shore-ice, during ebbing of the tide, when the land stood lower than at present; and the condition of the terrace precludes the idea of glacier action. 　　　　　　 :

The absence of an ice-cap in Grinnell Land, and the paucity of the glaciers in that region, are worthy of note, none descending to the sea-level north of 81°; while on the same

[1] Feilden's MSS. Journal.

parallel on the opposite coast of Hall Basin, on the Greenland coast, the country is ice-clad to the water's edge.

Petermann Fiord is described by Dr. Coppinger as bounded by vertical cliffs, of fossiliferous (Silurian) limestone rock, 1,100 feet in height, surmounted by an ice-cap, which flows steadily over the cliffs, from which it hangs in gigantic masses, which from time to time fall in a series of avalanches, carrying with them rocks torn from the face of the cliff, and precipitate them on the floe beneath.

The surface of the floe is traversed by deep wave-like furrows, thirty feet in depth, moving obliquely across it, and exceedingly difficult to traverse, especially where lateral glaciers come in, and break the continuity of the ridges, and separate them by wide fissures and gaps. The ice brought down by these lateral gaps affects but little the volume of the immense glacier flowing down from the eastern country, which appears to have formerly filled the entire valley.

The continuity of the molluscan fauna to the Grinnell Land mud-beds with those now living on the coast, already referred to, points to a uniformity of climatal conditions prevailing, through a period marked by considerable physical change, in the relative proportions of sea and land in the North Polar area, changes which appear to have alike uninfluenced the molluscan fauna of the seas and the mammalian fauna of the land ; the mud-beds having afforded bones of the lemming (*Myodes torquatus*), the ringed seal (*Phoca hispida*), the reindeer, and the musk-ox (*Ovibos moschatus*).

The greater precipitation of snow on the east coast of the basin, and consequent greater size of the effluent glaciers, and more extensive work of glaciation affected, appear to have long gone on, and to have been formerly more important than now ; but the conditions do not ever appear to have been so rigorous as to preclude the existence of animals, and the somewhat local character of the more extensive glaciation is worthy of note, as throwing some light on the origin ' of areas of no glaciation,' in portions of the British Isles, and as helping to explain the occurrence of a fauna in glacial deposits, thought by some to indicate an interglacial episode in the last British Glacial era.

We will not enter into the question whether the area, embraced by the conditions which caused the glaciation of Britain, included the Arctic area, nor as to the causes, geographical, astronomical, or physical, that led to it ; but we think it worthy of note that no records of former glacial episodes have yet been discovered in the Polar lands, which were tenanted by the molluscs of the Silurian, Carboniferous, Liassic, and Oolitic seas, and its land covered with the rich vegetation of the ' Ursa stage,' and of the Cretacean and Miocene eras.

The fauna and flora of the Arctic Palæozoic and older Secondary rocks point to a uniformity of conditions of temperature, climate does not appear to have existed, in the ordinary sense of the word, as temperature of the air affected by local geographical conditions; the striking uniformity of condition appears to have been unbroken up to the close of the Secondary Epoch.

No. XVI.

REPORT ON PETERMANN GLACIER.

By RICHARD W. COPPINGER, M.D.,

Staff Surgeon Royal Navy.

THE party under the command of Lieutenant Fulford, to which I was attached, started from Thank God Harbour on May 22, 1876, and on the second journey rounded Cape Tyson and entered the fiord. On leaving Cape Tyson and Offley Island, which were considered to mark the north-east side of the mouth of the fiord, we saw some miles before us an abrupt, precipitous wall of ice, extending in an irregularly wavy but unbroken line from shore to shore. When we had got about ten miles S.S.E. of Offley Island, the young floe on which we had been travelling terminated, and was connected through the intervention of a hummock hedge with an old glassy-hummocked floe, over which we proceeded until we reached the margin of the heavy ice above mentioned.

There at eleven and a half miles S.S.E. of Offley Island, and about 1,000 yards from the high precipitous cliffs which form the north-east shore of the fiord, we made our second camp. The old floe on which we camped was rigidly connected with the heavy ice ; in some places the precipitous and cleanly-fractured face of the latter meeting the old floe at a sharp right angle. On examining the surface of the heavy ice, we found it to be totally different in character from that of a floe. It was of glassy smoothness, and so slippery

and uneven that walking (in the ordinary sense of the word)
was impossible, and to get along at all it was frequently
necessary to resort to crawling. The surface was thickly
studded with circular pits, about six inches deep, and from one
to eighteen inches in diameter, usually containing a little snow
and some dark powder. In general configuration the surface
of this ice was arranged for the most part in undulating ridges,
extending obliquely down the fiord in a northerly and southerly
direction ; but as a rule interrupted by wide fissures and
faults, so that few of the ridges were directly continuous for
a greater length than two miles. The height from crest to
furrow was usually about thirty feet, and the slope so steep
and slippery that in many places it was quite impracticable
to cross the ridges except by cutting steps, or some such con-
trivance. The furrows, as a rule, had a certain amount of
snow-bed, and so far as they went afforded good travelling ;
but where the ice was devoid of snow, not even a dog could
obtain foothold. It is not to be understood from the above
that the ice-surface was everywhere disposed in these great
ridges and furrows : for there were many patches from five to
six acres in extent of bare ice exhibiting an irregularly undulating surface from thirty to thirty-five feet above the water-
level, and intersected by narrow fissures.

Having explored all the ice within a day's journey of this
camp, and found that by keeping for three-quarters of a mile
to the old floe, which sent a tongue under the north-east
cliffs, and taking to a furrow of the glacier ice for another
three-quarters of a mile we could advance our position, we
packed up and proceeded.

Our third camp, reached on the 25th of May, was
thirteen miles from Offley Island and two hundred yards
from the north-east line of cliffs. Here Lieutenant Fulford
obtained ' sights ' for latitude. From four miles to the
northward of this position, these cliffs presented a vertical
face about 1,100 feet high, composed of alternating bands
of light-grey and dark slate-coloured fossiliferous limestone
rock, and from abreast our third camp, were surmounted by

an ice-cap, whose blue, jagged edge lying flush with the face of the cliffs we estimated at a thickness of forty feet. The cliffs of the south-west shore of the fiord presented a similar ice-cap, but of greater extent, as it began about ten miles to the southward of Cape Lucie Marie, i.e. on the south side of the first glacier, and was continuous to the southward as far as the cliffs were seen to extend.

From both sides the ice seemed to be flowing steadily over the cliffs, as evidenced by frequent avalanches in which great masses of the ice-cap projecting over the precipices became detached, and carrying with them in their descent masses of rock torn from the face of the cliffs, came thundering down to the floe, marking their flight by dense clouds of snow, and accompanied by a long series of echoes, creating a most grand and imposing spectacle. Some idea of the force with which these avalanches came down may be gathered from the fact that large stones were projected on to the floe to a distance of eighty yards from the foot of the perpendicular walls of rock.

At this third camp, the furthest position to which with our disabled sledge and unsuitable equipments we could move our baggage, we spent three days devoted to walking excursions. The greatest distance up the fiord to which we could proceed was six miles from camp, and to attain this distance we had to run some risks of falling through hidden crevasses, and slipping from high ice slopes into water-chasms ; so that we had to content ourselves with making our furthest look-out point on the summit of an ice-pinnacle eighteen and a half miles from Offley Island.

About one mile from us was the nearest glacier of the north-east shore, two miles beyond it a second, and half a mile further on a third. We had found, as we approached these glaciers, that the main ice of the fiord became more and more fissured, and that the faults in the continuity of the ridges and the furrows were more frequent and embarrassing ; but from the eminence now attained it seemed that these glaciers were the nuclei of disruptions of the main ice, and hence the progressively increasing difficulties of travelling.

Carrying the eye along the north-east line of cliffs, we saw the land terminate abruptly about twenty miles off in a prominent bluff, and from this point to a quarter of the way across the head of the fiord no land was to be seen, but the same extraordinary undulating sea of ice which, from the main ridges lying in a north and south direction, would seem to be flowing into the fiord in an east to west direction. The fact of our distinctly seeing those ridges at so great a distance was perhaps due to the gradual shoaling of the water up the fiord, and the consequent rise in the elevation of the ice.

To the south-east a background of land about thirty miles distant was clearly seen extending behind, and as it were overlapping the apparent termination of the south-west line of cliffs. The latter cliffs presented to the eye an appearance almost precisely similar to that of the north-east cliffs, and they seemed to correspond as if originally parts of the same land. Both were of about equal height, were equally precipitous, presented the same arrangement of strata, the same description of ice-cap; and both were grooved by glaciers, there being four on the south-west side and three on the north-east side of the fiord.

When about a mile from the nearest glacier we came to a wide fissure, about thirty yards broad, which seemed to extend nearly across the fiord, and whose precipitous glassy walls, fifty feet high from brink to water, we had no means of descending. The bottom of this fissure was composed of treacherous-looking, slushy ice, with a lane of dark water two feet wide along the middle; so that had we succeeded in getting down we should probably have been unable to cross. About this same locality were several narrow fissures, some of which, from the very slippery nature of the ice, it was difficult to avoid falling into. One of these, in a tolerably level part of the ice, we found by measurement to be two feet wide above, and twenty-three feet deep, from brink to a probable false bottom of loose snow, on which the light weight of our measuring line rested.

The ice seemed to be incessantly cracking. Wherever we

stood we heard about every half minute a noise varying between the sharp crack of a whip and the report of a gun-cap, resulting, as we soon discovered, from the formation of thread-like cracks, many yards in length, which formed a kind of network over the surface of the ice.

The behaviour of the water in the wide fissures was very puzzling. It seemed to rise and fall to a certain extent through the ice, but not enough to account for the whole tidal movement; and we were therefore inclined to believe that the glacier ice was only aground at certain periods of the tide, and that it consequently behaved in some respects like a floe, and in others like grounded ice. Not being provided with a sounding line, no estimate of the depth of any part of the fiord was made. However, to solve the question as to the existence of a vertical tidal movement in the ice, Lieutenant Fulford took a series of sextant angles between the summit of the cliff adjoining our camp and a marked spot on the ice, and observing at different periods of the tide, came to the conclusion that there was a certain amount of vertical motion.

Having failed to get up the fiord by the north-east side to a greater distance than eighteen and a half miles from Offley Island, Lieutenant Fulford decided on moving round by the edge of the glacier ice to the opposite or south-west side, and on trying there to discover a more practicable route than we had hitherto encountered. In the latter attempt, however, we were disappointed, for after travelling along the floe under the south-west cliffs to a distance of thirteen miles from Cape Lucie Marie, we found the glacier ice jammed right against the face of the cliffs, and not affording anywhere a practicable route for our sledge. Between the young floe and the glacier ice was a well-marked tidal crack, which extended for three-fourths of the way across the fiord, that is, as far as the young floe and the glacier ice met without the intervention of an old floe.

On the 3rd of June we commenced our return journey, and stopping for one day at Offley Island, had opportunities of collecting specimens of Silurian fossils, and of observing the glacial planings and scorings which this island exhibits to a remarkable degree. These scorings run uniformly from the summit of the island, at its north-east extremity to the beach at the south-west end, grooving successive layers of grey and black limestone. These layers of rock lie horizontally; both are fossiliferous, the grey abounding in fossil, corals, and molluscs, the black containing corals, but to a less extent. The north-east extremity presents an abrupt precipitous face, 513 feet high, showing the same arrangement of stratified rock as on the glaciated slope, and closely corresponding with the appearance presented by the opposite face of Cape Tyson, one mile distant. Subsequent observations at Cape Tyson showed that in geological formation it closely corresponded with Offley Island.

It is manifest from the above that the results of the Expedition have not been as decisive as could be wished, yet I think enough has been done to justify us in concluding that the Petermann Fiord is the outlet of a huge glacier stream flowing probably from the eastward, to which the glaciers flowing through the north-east and south-west cliffs are insignificant tributaries, not adding materially to the main volume of ice.

In several particulars this glacier presented features deviating considerably from the general rule, which, although already touched on in this Report, it may be as well to summarise as follows :—1. The absence of onward sliding motion, probably due to the immobility of the floe in the mouth of the fiord, the low gradient of the glacier, and the prolonged cold season. 2. Its partial subjection to tidal influence for more than a mile above the snout. 3. The absence of detached bergs below the snout. 4. The diminutive height of the terminal cliff, ranging from sixteen to thirty feet above the sea-level. 5. The presence of water in the fissures two miles above the snout, when the mean altitude was forty feet. 6. The low gradient of the glacier.

No. XVII.

GAME LIST.

LIST OF ANIMALS PROCURED IN SMITH SOUND AND NORTHWARDS BY THE CREW OF H.M. SHIP 'ALERT,' BETWEEN JULY 28, 1875, AND SEPTEMBER 8, 1876.

Species	On Passage North from Hartstene Bay to Winter-Quarters, Lat. 82° 27′ N.	Winter-Quarters including sledge parties	On Passage South from Floeberg Beach to Hayes Sound	Total
Fox (*Vulpes lagopus*) . . .	—	3	1	4
Seal (*Phoca hispida*) . . .	1	1	6	8
Walrus (*Trichecus rosmarus*) . .	2	—	—	2
Hare (*Lepus glacialis*) . . .	8	20	35	63
Musk-ox (*Ovibos moschatus*) . .	12	6	—	18
Ptarmigan (*Lagopus rupestris*) .	7	17	10	34
Eider-duck (*Somateria spectabilis* and *mollissima*)	58	16	25	99
Long-tailed duck (*Harelda glacialis*)	—	9	1	10
Brent goose (*Bernicla brenta*) . .	—	75	132	207
Dovekie (*Uria grylle*) . . .	7	2	4	13

LIST OF ANIMALS PROCURED IN SMITH SOUND BY THE CREW OF H.M.
SHIP 'DISCOVERY,' BETWEEN JULY 28, 1875, AND SEPTEMBER 8, 1876.

Species	On Passage North from Hartstene Bay to Discovery Bay	In vicinity of Winter-Quarters	At Polaris Bay	On Passage South from Discovery Bay to Hayes Sound	Total
Fox (*Vulpes lagopus*) . . .	—	4	—	—	4
Seal (*Phoca barbata*) . . .	1	4	3	1	9
Seal (*Phoca hispida*) . . .	1	5	9	1	16
Hare (*Lepus glacialis*) . . .	9	139	5	—	153
Reindeer (*Cervus tarandus*) . .	1	—	—	—	1
Musk-ox (*Ovibos moschatus*) . .	—	44	1	—	45
Ptarmigan (*Lagopus rupestris*) .	1	13	4	—	18
Eider duck (*Somateria spectabilis* and *mollissima*)	4	9	6	—	19
Long-tailed duck (*Harelda glacialis*)	—	6	—	—	6
Brent goose (*Bernicla brenta*). .	—	56	26	—	82
Dovekie (*Uria grylle*) . . .	1	—	8	—	9

The temperature of air is recorded in degrees of Fahr
recorded wind and weather lasted. In the column he
measure for a 'strong breeze;' force 7 indicating a

Date	THERMOMETER			
	Maximum	Minimum	Mean	
August 1875–76	+ 44·0°	+ 24·5°	+ 31·913°	
September 1875	+ 36·5	+ 0·2	+ 15·603	
October ,,	+ 21·2	− 32·2	− 4·987	
November ,,	+ 23·0	− 45·7	− 16·847	
December ,,	+ 35·0	− 46·5	− 22·115	
January 1876	+ 8·5	− 59·2	− 32·916	
February ,,	+ 2·0	− 66·5	− 37·975	
March ,,	− 8·0	− 73·75	− 39·768	
April ,,	+ 15·0	− 46·5	− 17·963	
May ,,	+ 32·5	− 14·9	+ 11·212	
June ,,	+ 44·0	+ 18·2	+ 32·455	
July ,,	+ 50·0	+ 29·0	+ 38·356	
366 days . .	+ 50·0	− 73·75	− 3·473	
Proportion . .	—	—	—	

Date	THERMOMETER			
	Maximum	Minimum	Mean	
August 1875–76	+ 41·0°	+ 26·0°	+ 32·72°	
September 1875	+ 43·0	+ 2·4	+ 18·52	
October ,,	+ 21·5	− 39·0	− 9·79	
November ,,	+ 19·0	− 46·0	− 18·41	
December ,,	+ 26·0	− 54·0	− 24·54	
January 1876	− 13·0	− 63·0	− 40·64	
February ,,	+ 2·0	− 62·0	− 35·00	
March ,,	− 8·0	− 70·8	− 37·05	
April ,,	+ 13·0	− 42·5	− 17·27	
May ,,	+ 33·6	− 20·5	+ 10·04	
June ,,	+ 41·0	+ 16·5	+ 32·50	
July ,,	+ 46·3	+ 29·6	+ 37·21	
366 days . .	+ 46·0	− 70·8	− 4·232	
Proportion . .	—	—	—	

RACT.

)f weather ' are the relative number of hours in each month during which the of hours the force of the wind reached to or exceeded force 6, the nautical with detached clouds.

'Alert,' 1875-76.

			HOURS OF WIND					Aver-age hourly force			HOURS OF WEATHER			
N.E.	E.	S.E.	S.	S.W.	W.	N.W.	N.		Strong Wind	b.c.	Over-cast	Fog	Snow or Rain	Mer-cury frozen
94	60	42	104	104	37	17	20	1·4	25	476	268	49	74	—
8	6	30	21	192	39	227	29	2·2	111	218	502	36	173	—
8	10	36	16	46	84	144	46	0·8	—	346	398	136	178	—
1	1	36	27	66	61	183	44	1·0	10	566	154	25	29	35
—	—	24	34	65	35	211	75	0·9	2	586	158	54	140	46
11	3	12	75	63	28	175	54	1·3	45	697	47	7	58	286
6	10	6	24	51	17	198	56	1·25	52	543	153	14	67	398
17	22	50	26	59	22	237	48	1·1	20	644	100	37	46	285
27	3	40	13	10	11	191	128	0·8	—	450	270	—	61	10
8	12	—	28	22	108	172	94	1·0	12	304	440	—	180	—
12	14	22	2	140	38	204	80	1·7	122	410	310	22	168	—
10	34	54	74	74	28	128	136	1·2	17	424	320	34	118	—
02	175	352	444	892	508	2,087	810	1·2	616	5,664	3,120	414	1,292	1,060
·02	0·02	0·04	0·05	0·10	0·06	0·24	0·09	—	0·07	0·65	0·35	0·05	0·16	0·12

'Discovery,' 1875-76.

			HOURS OF WIND					Maxi-mum force			HOURS OF WEATHER			
N.E.	E.	S.E.	S.	S.W.	W.	N.W.	N.		Strong Wind	b.c.	Over-cast	Fog	Snow or Rain	Mer-cury frozen
17	24	53	117	77	10	8	32	8	34	521	223	29	28	—
40	16	20	80	100	16	52	76	7	16	308	412	80	120	—
40	8	—	4	20	4	44	20	4	—	504	240	—	144	—
16	20	29	1	1	13	64	112	3	—	624	96	4	68	32
44	32	4	—	8	8	12	32	8	12	596	148	16	92	194
28	—	20	8	—	8	24	72	2	—	608	136	—	92	472
86	13	12	9	21	14	56	34	10	23	509	187	—	66	352
44	—	28	20	16	4	20	40	8	4	612	132	—	72	280
20	16	8	8	16	8	8	16	3	—	600	120	—	90	4
24	16	20	44	8	4	—	76	8	12	628	116	—	44	—
60	12	68	100	44	—	4	16	8	56	544	176	--	48	—
4	12	40	100	40	12	12	4	6	10	476	268	16	80	—
23	169	302	491	351	101	304	530	—	167	6,530	2,254	145	944	1,334
·05	0·02	0·03	0·06	0·04	0·01	0·04	0·06	—	0·02	0·74	0·26	0·01	0·11	0·15

No. XIX.

ABSTRACT OF RESULTS OBTAINED FROM THE TIDAL OBSERVATIONS

MADE ON BOARD H.M. SHIPS 'DISCOVERY' AND 'ALERT' IN 1875-6.

BY THE REV. SAMUEL HAUGHTON, M.D., D.C.L., F.R.S.

Fellow of Trinity College, Dublin.

THE tidal observations made during the recent Arctic Expedition were of great value, and confirm the opinion, formed on other grounds, that Greenland is an island.

During seven months (twenty-eight days each) on board the 'Discovery' at Bellot Harbour, lat. 81° 45', long. 65° W., hourly observations were made, broken by interpolations in six days only.

On board the 'Alert,' near Cape Sheridan, lat. 82° 25', long. 61° 30' W., the difficulties of observation were greater, owing to the more exposed position of the ship; notwithstanding which, two months of hourly observations (with interpolations in fifteen days) were secured; and these hourly observations were supplemented by valuable determinations of the times of high and low water, and by four hourly observations made at other times.

The expedition, proceeding northwards up Smith Sound,

met the tide coming from the north, at or near Cape Frazer, lat. 79° 40′, and left behind the tides of Baffin's Bay.

The new tidal wave, observed on board both ships, is *specifically* distinct from the Baffin's Bay tide, and from the tide that enters the Arctic Ocean through Behring's Straits ; and it is, without question, a tide that has passed from the Atlantic Ocean, round Greenland, northwards, and then westwards.

The 'Discovery,' being situated nearer to the head of the tide (Cape Frazer) than the 'Alert,' had experience of a much larger tide, and it is in every way fortunate that her officers succeeded in making so complete a series of observations.[1]

The following is a summary of the principal results.

I. 'Discovery.'   Bellot Harbour.

The apparent Lunitidal interval (full and change of moon) ranges from $11^h\ 00^m$ to $12^h\ 00^m$, and has a mean value

$$i_m = 11^h\ 34^m\ 8$$

corrected for the moon's motion in the interval from the passage of the meridian of Greenwich.

In the discussion of the tide, which is being prepared for publication in the 'Transactions of the Royal Society,' the Semidiurnal Tide is separated from the Diurnal Tide, and its constants carefully determined.   Contrary to what is found in the Baffin's Bay tide, the Diurnal Tide is very small, so that much the largest part of the apparent tide is composed of the Semidiurnal Tide, and in this respect it closely resembles the tides of the British coasts, which are an eastern Atlantic tide.

This is well shown in the following table, which gives the *apparent* maximum Spring range, and minimum Neap range of the tide at Bellot Harbour ; contrasted with the

---

[1] I believe that the credit of these observations is mainly due to Lieutenant Archer, who was aided by Dr. Coppinger as a volunteer.

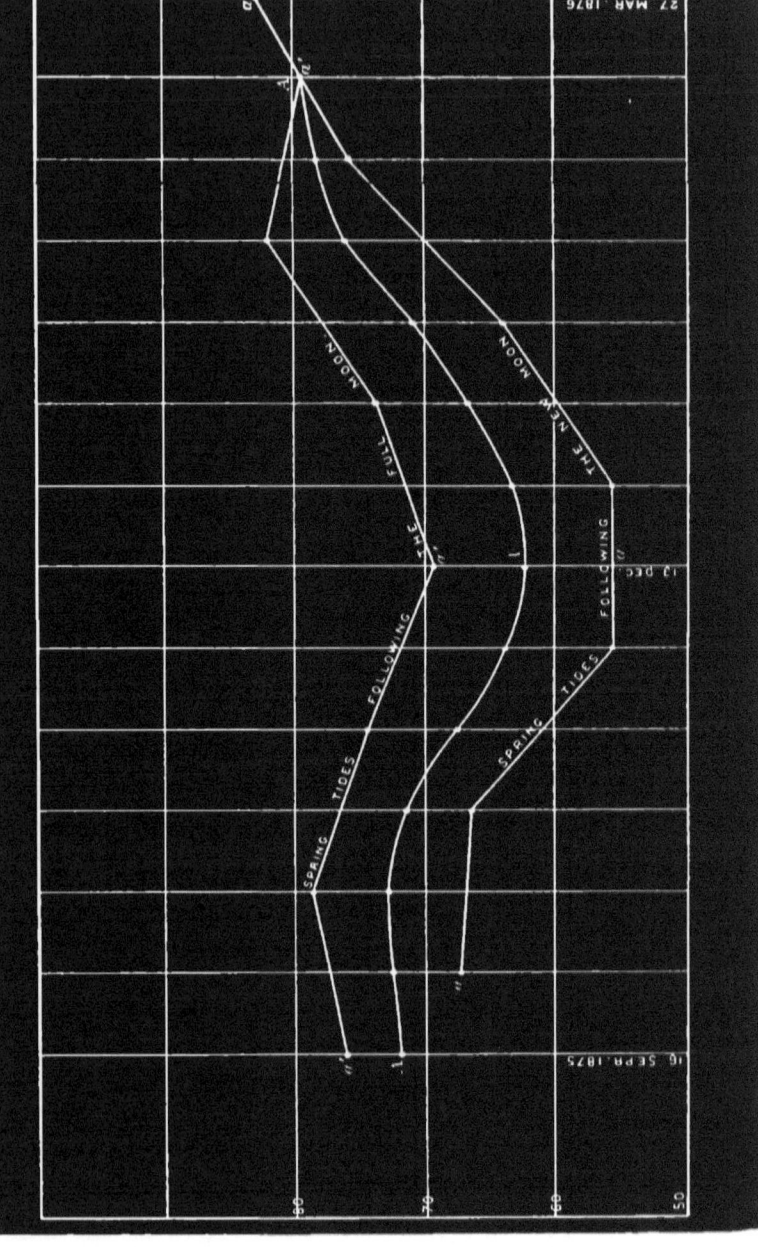

Semidiurnal Tide at Port Bellot (1875–6), showing the Lunar Parallactic Tide, and the Lunisolar Fortnightly Tide, at Springs and Neaps.

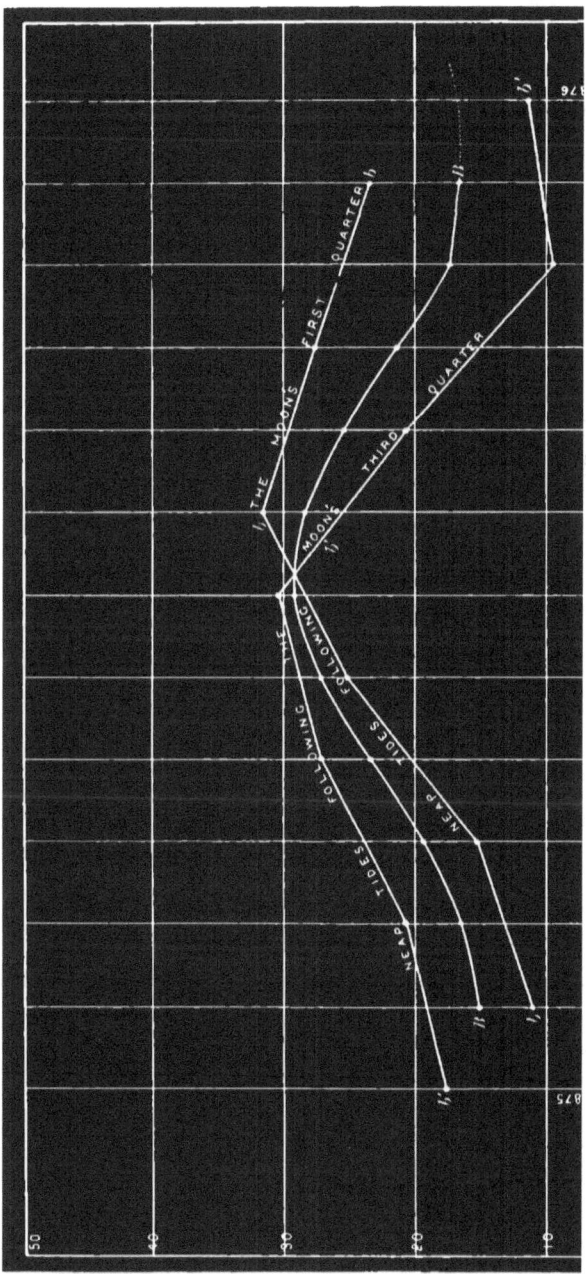

Semidiurnal maximum Spring range and minimum Neap range.

Date	APPARENT RANGE		SEMIDIURNAL RANGE	
	Springs	Neaps	Springs	Neaps
1875	Inches	Inches	Inches	Inches
September 16	78·0	—	76·0	—
„ 23	—	26·0	—	17·8
„ 30	73·0	—	67·6	—
October 8	—	15·5	—	11·0
„ 15	79·0	—	· 78·4	—
„ 22	—	31·5	—	20·8
„ 28	66·0	—	66·6	—
November 6	—	20·0	—	15·2
„ 14	79·5	—	74·6	—
„ 20	—	34·0	—	27·3
„ 28	65·0	—	55·6	—
December 6	—	32·0	– –	25·5
„ 13	73·0	—	69·4	–
„ 21	—	34·5	—	30·2
„ 29	66·0	—	55·8	—
1876				
January 5	—	41·0	—	31·8
„ 13	77·0	—	74·0	—
„ 20	—	25·5	—	20·7
„ 28	71·5	·	64·0	—
February 5	—	33·0	—	27·9
„ 11	83·0	—	80·2	—
„ 18	—	21·5	—	9·6
„ 27	78·5	—	76·8	—
March 4	—	27·5	—	23·5
„ 12	84·0	—	79·6	—
„ 19	—	20·0	—	11·6
„ 27	—	—	83·0	—

In the accompanying diagram, I have plotted the fourth and fifth columns of the preceding table, as follows :—

a a is the range of Spring tides following the new moon.

a′ a′ is the range of Spring tides following the full moon.

A A is the mean of the two foregoing curves.

b b is the range of Neap tides following the moon's first quarter.

b′ b′ is the range of Neap tides following the moon's third quarter.

B B is the mean of the two foregoing curves.

The space between $a\,a$ and $a'\,a'$ represents the Lunar Parallactic Tide deduced from Spring tides, and the space between $b\,b$ and $b'\,b'$ represents the Lunar Parallactic Tide deduced from Neap tides.

The range of the Lunar Parallactic Tide deduced from each is sixteen inches.

The curves A A and B B show the semiannual variation of the Lunisolar fortnightly tide cleared of lunar parallax.

II. 'ALERT.'   CAPE SHERIDAN.

The apparent Lunitidal interval (full and change of moon) observed on board the ' Alert ' was—

$$22^{\text{h}}\ 37^{\text{m}}.$$

The following table shows the relation which the apparent Spring and Neap tides bear to the calculated Semidiurnal Spring and Neap tides, and shows, as before, that the chief tide is the Semidiurnal :—

Maximum Spring and Minimum Neap Tides.—Range in Inches.

Date	Apparent	Semidiurnal
1875	Inches	Inches
September 30	30·0	30·0
October 14	28·5	32·8
„ 22	12·5	9·0
December 14	⌐ 36·5	31·0
„ 21	17·5	13·6
„ 29	29·5	25·0

INDEX.

THE END.

LONDON : PRINTED BY
SPOTTISWOODE AND CO., NEW-STREET SQUARE
AND PARLIAMENT STREET

A Catalogue of American and Foreign Books Published or Imported by MESSRS. SAMPSON LOW & CO. *can be had on application.*

Crown Buildings, 188, *Fleet Street, London,*
April, 1878.

A List of Books

PUBLISHED BY

SAMPSON LOW, MARSTON, SEARLE, & RIVINGTON.

———◆———

ALPHABETICAL LIST.

A CLASSIFIED *Educational Catalogue of Works* published in Great Britain. Demy 8vo, cloth extra. Second Edition, revised and corrected to Christmas, 1877, 5s.

Abney (Captain W. de W., R.E., F.R.S.) Thebes, *and its Five* Greater Temples. Forty large Permanent Photographs, with descriptive letter-press. Super-royal 4to, cloth extra, 63s.

Adventures of Captain Mago. A Phœnician's Explorations 1000 years B.C. By LEON CAHUN. Numerous Illustrations. Crown 8vo, cloth extra, gilt, 7s. 6d.

Adventures of a Young Naturalist. By LUCIEN BIART, with 117 beautiful Illustrations on Wood. Edited and adapted by PARKER GILLMORE. Post 8vo, cloth extra, gilt edges, New Edition, 7s. 6d.

Adventures in New Guinea. The Narrative of the Captivity of a French Sailor for Nine Years among the Savages in the Interior. Small post 8vo, with Illustrations and Map, cloth, gilt, 6s.

Africa, and the Brussels Geographical Conference. Translated from the French of EMILE BANNING, by R. H. MAJOR, F.S.A. With Map, crown 8vo, 7s. 6d.

Alcott (Louisa M.) Aunt Jo's Scrap-Bag. Square 16mo, 2s. 6d. (Rose Library, 1s.)

——— *Cupid and Chow-Chow.* Small post 8vo, 3s. 6d.

——— *Little Men: Life at Plumfield with Jo's Boys.* Small post 8vo, cloth, gilt edges, 2s. 6d. (Rose Library, 1s.)

——— *Little Women.* 2 vols., 2s. 6d. each. (Rose Library, 2 vols., 1s. each.)

——— *Old-Fashioned Girl.* Best Edition, small post 8vo, cloth extra, gilt edges, 2s. 6d. (Rose Library, 2s.)

A

Alcott (Louisa M.) Work and Beginning Again. A Story of
Experience. 1 vol., small post 8vo, cloth extra, 6s. Several Illustrations. (Rose Library, 2 vols., 1s. each.)

—— *Shawl Straps.* Small post 8vo, cloth extra, gilt, 3s. 6d.

—— *Eight Cousins; or, the Aunt Hill.* Small post 8vo,
with Illustrations, 3s. 6d.

—— *The Rose in Bloom.* Small post 8vo, cloth extra, 3s. 6d.

—— *Silver Pitchers.* Small post 8vo, cloth extra, 3s. 6d.

—— *Under the Lilacs.* In monthly parts, price 6d.

"Miss Alcott's stories are thoroughly healthy, full of racy fun and humour . . .
exceedingly entertaining . . . . We can recommend the 'Eight Cousins '"—
Athenæum.

Alpine Ascents and Adventures; or, Rock and Snow Sketches.
By H. Schütz Wilson, of the Alpine Club. With Illustrations by
Whymper and Marcus Stone. Crown 8vo, cloth extra, 10s. 6d.

Andersen (Hans Christian) Fairy Tales. With Illustrations in
Colours by E. V. B. Royal 4to, cloth, 25s.

Andrews (Dr.) Latin-English Lexicon. 14th Edition. Royal
8vo, 1670 pp., cloth extra, price 18s.

Anecdotes of the Queen and Royal Family. Collected and
Edited by J. G. Hodgins, with Illustrations. New Edition, 5s.

Animals Painted by Themselves. Adapted from the French of
Balzac, Georges Sands, &c., with 200 Illustrations by Grandville.
8vo, cloth extra, gilt, 10s. 6d.

Art of Reading Aloud (The) in Pulpit, Lecture Room, or Private
Reunions, with a perfect system of Economy of Lung Power on just
principles for acquiring ease in Delivery, and a thorough command of
the Voice. By G. Vandenhoff, M.A. Crown 8vo, cloth extra, 6s.

Atmosphere (The). See Flammarion.

BANNING (M. Emile). See "Africa and the Brussels
Geographical Conference." Crown 8vo, cloth, 8s. 6d.

Barton Experiment (The). By the Author of "Helen's
Babies." 1s.

THE BAYARD SERIES,

Edited by the late J. Hain Friswell.

Comprising Pleasure Books of Literature produced in the Choicest Style as
Companionable Volumes at Home and Abroad.

"We can hardly imagine better books for boys to read or for men to ponder
over."—*Times.*

*Price 2s. 6d. each Volume, complete in itself, flexible cloth extra, gilt edges,
with silk Headbands and Registers.*

The Story of the Chevalier Bayard. By M. De Berville.

De Joinville's St. Louis, King of France.

The Essays of Abraham Cowley, including all his Prose Works.

Abdallah; or the Four Leaves. By Edouard Laboullaye.

Table-Talk and Opinions of Napoleon Buonaparte.

The Bayard Series, continued :—
Vathek : An Oriental Romance. By WILLIAM BECKFORD.
The King and the Commons. A Selection of Cavalier and
Puritan Songs. Edited by Prof. MORLEY.
*Words of Wellington: Maxims and Opinions of the ·Great
Duke.*
Dr. Johnson's Rasselas, Prince of Abyssinia. With Notes.
Hazlitt's Round Table. With Biographical Introduction.
The Religio Medici, Hydriotaphia, and the Letter to a Friend.
By Sir THOMAS BROWNE, Knt.
Ballad Poetry of the Affections. By ROBERT BUCHANAN.
Coleridge's Christabel, and other Imaginative Poems. With
Preface by ALGERNON C. SWINBURNE.
Lord Chesterfield's Letters, Sentences, and Maxims. With
Introduction by the Editor, and Essay on Chesterfield by M. DE STE.-
BEUVE, of the French Academy.
Essays in Mosaic. By THOS. BALLANTYNE.
My Uncle Toby; his Story and his Friends. Edited by
P. FITZGERALD.
*Reflections; or, Moral Sentences and Maxims of the Duke de
la Rochefoucauld.*
*Socrates: Memoirs for English Readers from Xenophon's Memo-
rabilia.* By EDW. LEVIEN.
Prince Albert's Golden Precepts.
A *suitable Case containing* 12 *Volumes, price* 31s. 6d. ; *or the Case separately,
price* 3s. 6d.

Beauty and the Beast. An Old Tale retold, with Pictures by
B. V. B. Demy 4to, cloth extra, novel binding. 10 Illustrations
in Colours (in same style as those in the First Edition of " Story
without an End "). 12s. 6d.
Bees and Beekeeping. By the Times' Beemaster. Illustrated,
crown 8vo, new Edition with additions, 2s. 6d.
Beumer's German Copybooks. In six gradations at 4d. each.
Biart (Lucien). See " Adventures of a Young Naturalist."
——— *See* " My Rambles in the New World."
Bickersteth's Hymnal Companion to Book of Common Prayer.
List *of the Original Editions, containing* 403 *Hymns, always
kept in Print.*

				s.	d.
1A	Small type Edition, medium 32mo, cloth limp .		. . .	0	6
1B	ditto	ditto	roan limp, red edges .	1	0
1C	ditto	ditto	morocco limp, gilt edges	2	0
2	Second size Type, super-royal 32mo, cloth limp .		. .	1	0
2A	ditto	ditto	roan limp, red edges .	2	0
2B	ditto	ditto	morocco limp, gilt edges	3	0

Bickersteth's Hymnal Companion (Original Editions), continued:

3	Large type Edition, crown 8vo, cloth, red edges .		.	2 6
3A	ditto	ditto roan limp, red edges	.	3 6
3B	ditto	ditto morocco limp, gilt edges .		5 6
4	ditto	with Introduction and Notes, cloth, red edges		3 6
4A	ditto	ditto roan limp, red edges		4 6
4B	ditto	ditto morocco, red edges.		6 6
5	Crown 8vo, with accompanying Tunes to every Hymn		.	3 0
5A	ditto with Chants		.	4 0
5B	ditto Chants only		.	1 6
5C	Large Edition for the Organ, with Tunes and Chants		.	7 6
5D	ditto Chants only .		.	3 6
6	Long Primer, cloth limp . . .		.	1 6
6A	ditto roan limp, red edges . .		.	2 6
6B	ditto morocco limp, gilt edges .		.	4 6
	Penny Edition, paper wrapper . .		.	0 1
	Ditto bound in cloth . .		.	0 2
	Ditto with Common Prayer .		.	0 9
	Ditto ditto roan .		.	1 6
	Ditto ditto morocco .		.	2 6
	The Church Mission Hymn-Book . .		*per* 100	8 4

Revised and Enlarged Edition, containing 550 Hymns—

7A	Medium 32mo, cloth limp . . .		.	0 8
7B	ditto roan . . .		.	1 2
7C	ditto morocco or calf . .		.	2 6
8A	Super-royal 32mo, cloth limp . .		.	1 0
8B	ditto red edges . .		.	1 2
8C	ditto roan . . .		.	2 2
8D	ditto morocco or calf . .		.	3 6
9A	Crown 8vo, cloth, red edges . .		.	3 0
9B	ditto roan . . .		.	4 0
9C	ditto morocco or calf . .		.	6 0
10A	Crown 8vo, with Introduction and Notes, red edges .		.	4 0
10B	ditto roan . . .		.	5 0
10C	ditto morocco . .		.	7 6
11A	Penny Edition in Wrapper . .		.	0 1
11B	ditto cloth . .		.	0 2
11C	With Prayer Book, cloth . .		.	0 9
11D	ditto roan . .		.	1 6
11E	ditto morocco . .		.	2 6
12A	Crown 8vo, with Tunes, cloth, plain edges .		.	4 0
12B	ditto ditto persian, red edges .		.	6 6
12C	ditto ditto limp morocco, gilt edges .		.	7 6

Bickersteth's Hymnal Companion (Revised Editions), continued :

13A	Small 4to, for Organ	.	.	.	.	.	.	8	6
13B	ditto ditto limp russia	.	.	.	.	.	21		o
	Chant Book Supplement (Music)	.	.	.	.	1			6
	Ditto 4to, for Organ	.	.	.	.	3			6
14A	Tonic Sol-fa Edition	.	.	.	.	.	.	3	6
14B	ditto treble and alto only	.	.	.	.	1			o
5B	Chants only	.	.	.	.	.	.	1	6
5D	ditto 4to, for Organ	.	.	.	.	.	3		6
	The Church Mission Hymn-Book	.	.	.	*per* 100	8			4

☞ *Nos. 7, 8, and 11 can be had in various styles of binding forming one volume with the Prayer-Book.*

*** *The Revised Editions are entirely distinct from, and cannot be used with, the original editions.*

The Church Mission Hymn-Book has been recently issued : it contains 154 Hymns for Special Mission and Schoolroom Services, selected from the Hymnal Companion. Price 8s. 4d. per 100, or 1½d. each.

The Hymnal Companion. Strongly bound with a Sunday-School Liturgy, in two sizes, price 4d. and 8d.

Bickersteth (Rev. E. H., M.A.) The Reef and other Parables. 1 vol., square 8vo, with numerous very beautiful Engravings, 7s. 6d.

——— *The Master's Home-Call; or, Brief Memorials of* Alice Frances Bickersteth. 20th Thousand. 32mo, cloth gilt, 1s.
" They recall in a touching manner a character of which the religious beauty has a warmth and grace almost too tender to be definite."—*The Guardian.*

——— *The Shadow of the Rock.* A Selection of Religious Poetry. 18mo, cloth extra, 2s. 6d.

——— *The Clergyman in his Home.* Small post 8vo, 1s.

——— *The Shadowed Home and the Light Beyond.* 7th Edition, crown 8vo, cloth extra, 5s.

Bida. The Authorized Version of the Four Gospels, with the whole of the magnificent Etchings on Steel, after drawings by M. BIDA, in 4 vols., appropriately bound in cloth extra, price 3l. 3s. each. Also the four volumes in two, bound in the best morocco, by Suttaby, extra gilt edges, 18l. 18s., half-morocco, 12l. 12s.
" Bida's Illustrations of the Gospels of St. Matthew and St. John have already received here and elsewhere a full recognition of their great merits."—*Times.*

Bidwell (C. T.) The Balearic Islands. Illustrations and a Map. Crown 8vo, cloth, 10s. 6d.

——— *The Cost of Living Abroad.* Crown 8vo, 6s.

Black (Wm.) Three Feathers. Small post 8vo, cloth extra, 6s.

——— *Lady Silverdale's Sweetheart, and other Stories.* 1 vol., small post 8vo, 6s.

——— *Kilmeny: a Novel.* Small post 8vo, cloth, 6s.

Black (Wm.) In Silk Attire. 3rd Edition, small post 8vo, 6s.
" A work which deserves a hearty welcome for its skill and power in delineation of character."—*Saturday Review.*

——— *A Daughter of Heth.* 11th Edition, small post 8vo, 6s.
' If humour, sweetness, and pathos, and a story told with simplicity and vigour, ought to insure success, 'A Daughter of Heth' is of the kind to deserve it."—*Saturday Review.*

Blackmore (R. D.) Lorna Doone. 10th Edition, cr. 8vo, 6s.
"The reader at times holds his breath, so graphically yet so simply does John Ridd tell his tale."—*Saturday Review.*

——— *Alice Lorraine.* 1 vol., small post 8vo, 6th Edition, 6s.

——— *Clara Vaughan.* Revised Edition, 6s.

——— *Cradock Nowell.* New Edition, 6s.

——— *Cripps the Carrier.* 3rd Edition, small post 8vo, 6s.

——— *Georgics of Virgil.* Small 4to, 4s. 6d.

Blossoms from the King's Garden : Sermons for Children. By the Rev. CLAUDE BOSANQUET. Small post 8vo, cloth extra, 6s.

Blue Banner (The); or, The Adventures of a Mussulman, a Christian, and a Pagan, in the time of the Crusades and Mongol Conquest. By LEON CAHUN. Translated from the French by W. COLLETT SANDARS. With Seventy-six Wood Engravings. 1 vol., square imperial 16mo, cloth extra, 7s. 6d.

Book of the Play. By DUTTON COOK. 2 vols., crown 8vo, 24s.

Bradford (Wm.) The Arctic Regions. Illustrated with Photographs, taken on an Art Expedition to Greenland. With Descriptive Narrative by the Artist. In One Volume, royal broadside, 25 inches by 20, beautifully bound in morocco extra, price Twenty-Five Guineas.

Brave Men in Action. By S. J. MACKENNA. Crown 8vo, 480 pp., cloth, 7s. 6d.

Breck (Samuel). See " Recollections."

Brett (E.) Notes on Yachts. Fcp. 8vo, 6s.

Broke (Admiral Sir B. V. P., Bt., K.C.B.) Biography of. 1l.

Browning (Mrs. E. B.) The Rhyme of the Duchess May. Demy 4to, Illustrated with Eight Photographs, after Drawings by CHARLOTTE M. B. MORRELL. 21s.

Bryant (W. C., assisted by S. H. Gay) A Popular History of the United States. About 4 vols., to be profusely Illustrated with Engravings on Steel and Wood, after Designs by the best Artists. Vol. I., super-royal 8vo, cloth extra, gilt, 42s., is ready.

Burton (Captain R. F.) Two Trips to Gorilla Land and the Cataracts of the Congo. By Captain R. F. BURTON. 2 vols, demy 8vo, with numerous Illustrations and Map, cloth extra, 28s.

Butler (W. F.) The Great Lone Land; an Account of the Red River Expedition, 1869-70, and Subsequent Travels and Adventures in the Manitoba Country, and a Winter Journey across the Saskatchewan Valley to the Rocky Mountains. With Illustrations and Map. Fifth and Cheaper Edition, crown 8vo, cloth extra, 7s. 6d.

Butler (W. F.) The Wild North Land; the Story of a Winter Journey with Dogs across Northern North America. Demy 8vo, cloth, with numerous Woodcuts and a Map, 4th Edition, 18*s.* Cr. 8vo, 7*s.* 6*d.*

—— *Akim-foo : the History of a Failure.* Demy 8vo, cloth, 2nd Edition, 16*s.* Also, in crown 8vo, 7*s.* 6*d.*

By Celia's Arbour. New Novel by the Authors of " Ready-Money Mortiboy," " This Son of Vulcan," &c. 3 vols., 31*s.* 6*d.*

By Land and Ocean; or, The Journal and Letters of a Tour round the World by a Young Girl, who went *alone* to Victoria, New Zealand, Sydney, Singapore, China, Japan, and across the Continent of America home. By F. L. RAINS. Crown 8vo, cloth, 7*s.* 6*d.*

CADOGAN (Lady A.) Illustrated Games of Patience. Twenty-four Diagrams in Colours, with Descriptive Text. Foolscap 4to, cloth extra, gilt edges, 3rd Edition, 12*s.* 6*d.*

Cahun (Leon) Adventures of Captain Mago. See " Adventures."

—— *Blue Banner,* which see.

Carbon Process (A Manual of). See LIESEGANG.

Ceramic Art. See JACQUEMART.

Changed Cross (The), and other Religious Poems. 16mo, 2*s.* 6*d.*

Child of the Cavern (The) ; or, Strange Doings Underground. By JULES VERNE. Translated by W. H. G. KINGSTON, Author of "Snow Shoes and Canoes," "Peter the Whaler," "The Three Midshipmen," &c., &c., &c. Numerous Illustrations. Square crown 8vo, cloth extra, gilt edges, 7*s.* 6*d.*

Child's Play, with 16 Coloured Drawings by E. V. B. Printed on thick paper, with tints, 7*s.* 6*d.*

—— *New.* By E. V. B. Similar to the above. *See* New.

Choice Editions of Choice Books. 2*s.* 6*d.* each, Illustrated by C. W. COPE, R.A., T. CRESWICK, R.A., E. DUNCAN, BIRKET FOSTER, J. C. HORSLEY, A.R.A., G. HICKS, R. REDGRAVE, R.A., C. STONEHOUSE, F. TAYLER, G. THOMAS, H. J. TOWNSHEND, E. H. WEHNERT, HARRISON WEIR, &c.

Bloomfield's Farmer's Boy.	Milton's L'Allegro.
Campbell's Pleasures of Hope.	Poetry of Nature. Harrison Weir.
Coleridge's Ancient Mariner.	Rogers' (Sam.) Pleasures of Memory.
Goldsmith's Deserted Village.	Shakespeare's Songs and Sonnets.
Goldsmith's Vicar of Wakefield.	Tennyson's May Queen.
Gray's Elegy in a Churchyard.	Elizabethan Poets.
Keat's Eve of St. Agnes.	Wordsworth's Pastoral Poems.

" Such works are a glorious beatification for a poet."—*Athenæum.*

Christian Activity. By ELEANOR C. PRICE. Cloth extra, 6*s.*

Christmas Story-teller (The). A Medley for the Season of Turkey and Mince Pie ; Pantomime and Plum-pudding ; Smiles, Tears, and Frolics ; Charades, Ghosts, and Christmas Trees. By Old Hands and New Ones. Crown 8vo, cloth extra, gilt edges, Fifty-two Illustrations, 10*s.* 6*d.*

Collins (Mortimer): His Letters and Friendships, with some Account of his Life. By FRANCES COLLINS. 2 vols., crown 8vo, with a Portrait, 2nd Edition, 21*s.*

Cook (D.) Young Mr. Nightingale. A Novel. 3 vols., 31*s.* 6*d.*

———— *The Banns of Marriage.* 2 vols., crown 8vo, 21*s.*

———— *Book of the Play.* 2 vols., crown 8vo, 24*s.*

———— *Doubleday's Children.* 3 vols., crown 8vo, 31*s.* 6*d.*

Coope (Col. W. Jesser) A Prisoner of War in Russia. By Col. W. JESSER COOPE, Imperial Ottoman Gendarmerie. Crown 8vo, cloth extra, 10*s.* 6*d.*

"Simply enthralling in interest. He is absolutely incapable of gush. . . . We hope this excellent, pithy book may be widely read."—*Vanity Fair.*
"Colonel Coope writes bluntly and straightforwardly, in a curt, soldierly fashion, that is eminently effective. . . . His words have an air of truth and soberness about them that is irresistibly persuasive. . . . It should be, we think, emphatically *the* book of the war."—*London.*

Craik (Mrs.) The Adventures of a Brownie. By the Author of "John Halifax, Gentleman." With numerous Illustrations by Miss PATERSON. Square cloth, extra gilt edges, 5*s.*

Cripps the Carrier. 3rd Edition, 6*s.* *See* BLACKMORE.

Cruise of H.M.S. "Challenger" (The). By W. J. J. SPRY, R.N. With Route Map and many Illustrations. 6th Edition, demy 8vo, cloth, 18*s.* Cheap Edition, crown 8vo, small type, some of the Illustrations, 7*s.* 6*d.*

"The book before us supplies the information in a manner that leaves little to be desired. 'The Cruise of H.M.S. *Challenger*' is an exceedingly well-written, entertaining, and instructive book."—*United Service Gazette.*
"Agreeably written, full of information, and copiously illustrated." — *Broad Arrow.*

Cumming (Miss C. F. G.) From the Hebrides to the Himalayas; Eighteen Months' Wanderings in Western Isles and Eastern Highlands. By Miss CONSTANCE F. GORDON CUMMING, with very numerous Full-page and other Woodcut Illustrations, from the Author's own Drawings. 2 vols., medium 8vo, cloth extra, 42*s.*

*D*ANA *(R. H.) Two Years before the Mast and Twenty-Four* years After. Revised Edition with Notes, 12mo, 6*s.*

Dana (Jas. D.) Corals and Coral Islands. Numerous Illustrations, Charts, &c. New and Cheaper Edition, with numerous important Additions and Corrections. Crown 8vo, cloth extra, 8*s.* 6*d.*

Daughter (A) of Heth. By W. BLACK. Crown 8vo, 6*s.*

Day of My Life (A) ; or, Every Day Experiences at Eton. By an ETON BOY. 16mo, cloth extra, 2*s.* 6*d.* 6th Thousand.

Dick Sands, the Boy Captain. By JULES VERNE. With
nearly 100 Illustrations, cloth extra, gilt edges, 10s. 6d.

Discoveries of Prince Henry the Navigator, and their Results ;
being the Narrative of the Discovery by Sea, within One Century, of
more than Half the World. By RICHARD HENRY MAJOR, F.S.A.
Demy 8vo, with several Woodcuts, 4 Maps, and a Portrait of Prince
Henry in Colours. Cloth extra, 15s.

Dodge (Mrs. M.) Hans Brinker; or, the Silver Skates. An
entirely New Edition, with 59 Full-page and other Woodcuts.
Square crown 8vo, cloth extra, 7s. 6d. ; Text only, paper, 1s.

—— *Theophilus and Others.* 1 vol., small post 8vo, cloth
extra, gilt, 3s. 6d.

Doré's Spain. *See* "Spain."

Dougall's (J. D.) Shooting; its Appliances, Practice, and
Purpose. With Illustrations, cloth extra, 10s. 6d. *See* "Shooting."

EARLY History of the Colony of Victoria (The), from its
Discovery to its Establishment as a Self-Governing Province of the
British Empire. By FRANCIS P. LABILLIERE, Fellow of the Royal
Colonial Institute, &c. 2 vols., crown 8vo, 21s.

Echoes of the Heart. *See* MOODY.

English Catalogue of Books (The). Published during 1863 to
1871 inclusive, comprising also important American Publications.
This Volume, occupying over 450 Pages, shows the Titles of
32,000 New Books and New Editions issued during Nine Years, with
the Size, Price, and Publisher's Name, the Lists of Learned Societies,
Printing Clubs, and other Literary Associations, and the Books
issued by them; as also the Publisher's Series and Collections—
altogether forming an indispensable adjunct to the Bookseller's
Establishment, as well as to every Learned and Literary Club and
Association. 30s., half-bound.

** The previous Volume, 1835 to 1862, of which very few
remain on sale, price 2l. 5s. ; as also the Index Volume, 1837 to
1857, price 1l. 6s.

—— *Supplements,* 1863, 1864, 1865, 3s. 6d. each; 1866,
1867, to 1877, 5s. each.

Eight Cousins. *See* ALCOTT.

English Writers, Chapters for Self-Improvement in English
Literature. By the Author of "The Gentle Life," 6s.

—— *Matrons and their Professions;* with some Considerations
as to its Various Branches, its National Value, and the Education it
requires. By M. L. F., Writer of "My Life, and what shall I do
with it." Crown 8vo, cloth extra, 7s. 6d.

English Painters of the Georgian Era. Hogarth to Turner.
Biographical Notices. Illustrated with 48 permanent Photographs,
after the most celebrated Works. Demy 4to, cloth extra, 18s.

Erckmann-Chatrian.   Forest House and Catherine's Lovers.
Crown 8vo, 3s. 6d.
——— *The Brothers Rantzau: a Story of the Vosges.* 2 vols.,
crown 8vo, cloth, 21s.   New Edition, 1 vol., profusely Illustrated,
cloth extra, 5s.

Eton.   See "Day of my Life," and "Out of School."

Evans (C.) Over the Hills and Far Away. By C. EVANS.
One Volume, crown 8vo, cloth extra, 10s. 6d.
——— *A Strange Friendship.*   Crown 8vo, cloth, 5s.

*F*AITH *Gartney's Girlhood.* By the Author of "The
Gayworthy's."   Fcap. with Coloured Frontispiece, 3s. 6d.

Familiar Letters on some Mysteries of Nature. See PHIPSON.

Fern Paradise (The): A Plea for the Culture of Ferns. By F. G.
HEATH.   New Edition, entirely Rewritten, Illustrated with eighteen
full-page and numerous other Woodcuts, and four permanent Photographs, large post 8vo, handsomely bound in cloth, 12s. 6d.

Fern World (The).   By F. G. HEATH.   Illustrated by Twelve
Coloured Plates, giving complete Figures (Sixty-four in all) of every
Species of British Fern, specially printed from Nature ; by several full-
page Engravings and a permanent Photograph.   Large post 8vo.,
cloth, gilt edges, 400 pp., 4th Edition, 12s. 6d.

Few (A) Hints on Proving Wills.   Enlarged Edition, 1s.

Five Weeks in Greece.   By J. F. YOUNG.   Crown 8vo, 10s. 6d.

Flammarion (C.) The Atmosphere.   Translated from the
French of CAMILLE FLAMMARION.   Edited by JAMES GLAISHER,
F.R.S., Superintendent of the Magnetical and Meteorological Depart-
ment of the Royal Observatory at Greenwich.   With 10 Chromo-
Lithographs and 81 Woodcuts.   Royal 8vo, cloth extra, 30s.

Flooding of the Sahara (The).   An Account of the project for
opening direct communication with 38,000,000 people.   With a description of North-West Africa and Soudan.   By DONALD MACKENZIE.
8vo, cloth extra, with Illustrations, 10s. 6d.

Footsteps of the Master. See STOWE (Mrs. BEECHER).

Forrest (John) Explorations in Australia.   Being Mr. JOHN
FORREST's Personal Account of his Journeys.   1 vol., demy 8vo,
cloth, with several Illustrations and 3 Maps, 16s.

Forrest's (R. W.) Gleanings from the Pastures of Tekoa.
Sermons by the Rev. R. W. FORREST, D.D., Vicar of St. Jude's,
South Kensington.   Small post 8vo, 260 pp., 6s.

Franc (Maude Jeane).   The following form one Series, small
post 8vo, in uniform cloth bindings :—
——— *Emily's Choice.*   5s.

Frank (Maude Jeane) Hall's Vineyard. 4s.

—— *John's Wife ; a Story of Life in South Australia.* 4s.

——-- *Marian ; or, the Light of Some One's Home.* 5s.

—— *Silken Cords and Iron Fetters.* 4s.

—— *Vermont Vale.* 5s.

—— *Minnie's Mission.* 4s.

——— *Little Mercy.* 5s.

French Heiress (A) in her own Chateau. Crown 8vo, 12s. 6d.

Funny Foreigners and Eccentric Englishmen. 16 coloured comic Illustrations for Children. Demy 4to, in picture wrappper.

GAMES of Patience. See CADOGAN.

Garvagh (Lord) The Pilgrim of Scandinavia. By LORD GARVAGH, B.A., Christ Church, Oxford, and Member of the Alpine Club. 8vo, cloth extra, with Illustrations, 10s. 6d.

Gayworthys (The) : a Story of New England Life. Small post 8vo, 3s. 6d.

Gentle Life (Queen Edition). 2 vols. in 1, small 4to, 10s. 6d.

THE GENTLE LIFE SERIES.

Price 6s. each ; or in calf extra, price 10s. 6d.

The Gentle Life. Essays in aid of the Formation of Character of Gentlemen and Gentlewomen. 21st Edition.

" Deserves to be printed in letters of gold, and circulated in every house."—*Chambers' Journal.*

About in the World. Essays by the Author of "The Gentle Life."

" It is not easy to open it at any page without finding some handy idea."—*Morning Post.*

Like unto Christ. A New Translation of Thomas à Kempis' " De Imitatione Christi." With a Vignette from an Original Drawing by Sir THOMAS LAWRENCE. 2nd Edition.

" Could not be presented in a more exquisite form, for a more sightly volume was never seen."—*Illustrated London News.*

Familiar Words. An Index Verborum, or Quotation Handbook. Affording an immediate Reference to Phrases and Sentences that have become embedded in the English language. 3rd and enlarged Edition.

"The most extensive dictionary of quotation we have met with."—*Notes and Queries.*

Essays by Montaigne. Edited, Compared, Revised, and Annotated by the Author of "The Gentle Life." With Vignette Portrait. 2nd Edition.

" We should be glad if any words of ours could help to bespeak a large circulation for this handsome attractive book."—*Illustrated Times.*

The Gentle Life Series, continued:—

The Countess of Pembroke's Arcadia. Written by Sir PHILIP
SIDNEY. Edited with Notes by Author of "The Gentle Life." 7s. 6d.
"All the best things in the Arcadia are retained intact in Mr. Friswell's edition."
—Examiner.

The Gentle Life. 2nd Series, 8th Edition.
"There is not a single thought in the volume that does not contribute in some
measure to the formation of a true gentleman."—*Daily News.*

Varia: Readings from Rare Books. Reprinted, by permission,
from the *Saturday Review, Spectator,* &c.
"The books discussed in this volume are no less valuable than they are rare, and
the compiler is entitled to the gratitude of the public."—*Observer.*

The Silent Hour: Essays, Original and Selected. By the
Author of "The Gentle Life." 3rd Edition.
"All who possess 'The Gentle Life' should own this volume."—*Standard.*

Half-Length Portraits. Short Studies of Notable Persons.
By J. HAIN FRISWELL. Small post 8vo, cloth extra, 6s.

Essays on English Writers, for the Self-improvement of
Students in English Literature.
"To all (both men and women) who have neglected to read and study their native
literature we would certainly suggest the volume before us as a fitting introduction."
—Examiner.

Other People's Windows. By J. HAIN FRISWELL. 3rd Edition.
"The chapters are so lively in themselves, so mingled with shrewd views of
human nature, so full of illustrative anecdotes, that the reader cannot fail to be
amused."—*Morning Post.*

A Man's Thoughts. By J. HAIN FRISWELL.

German Primer. Being an Introduction to First Steps in
German. By M. T. PREU. 2s. 6d.

Getting On in the World; or, Hints on Success in Life. By
W. MATHEWS, LL.D. Small post 8vo, cloth, 2s. 6d.; gilt edges, 3s. 6d.

Gleams through the Mists; Literary and Domestic. By C.
BICKERSTETH WHEELER, Author of "John Lang Bickersteth,"
&c. 1 vol., post 8vo, cloth extra, 3s. 6d.

Gouffé. The Royal Cookery Book. By JULES GOUFFÉ; translated and adapted for English use by ALPHONSE GOUFFÉ, Head
Pastrycook to Her Majesty the Queen. Illustrated with large plates
printed in colours. 161 Woodcuts, 8vo, cloth extra, gilt edges, 2l. 2s.

——— Domestic Edition, half-bound, 10s. 6d.
"By far the ablest and most complete work on cookery that has ever been submitted to the gastronomical world."—*Pall Mall Gazette.*

——— *The Book of Preserves; or, Receipts for Preparing and*
Preserving Meat, Fish salt and smoked, Terrines, Gelatines, Vege-
tables, Fruit, Confitures, Syrups, Liqueurs de Famille, Petits Fours,
Bonbons, &c., &c. 1 vol., royal 8vo, containing upwards of 500
Receipts and 34 Illustrations, 10s. 6d.

Gouffé. Royal Book of Pastry and Confectionery. By JULES
GOUFFÉ, Chef-de-Cuisine of the Paris Jockey Club. Royal 8vo, Illus-

trated with 10 Chromo-lithographs and 137 Woodcuts, from Drawings by E. MONJAT.   Cloth extra, gilt edges, 35*s.*

Gouraud (Mdlle.) Four Gold Pieces.   Numerous Illustrations. Small post 8vo, cloth, 2*s.* 6*d.*   *See also* Rose Library.

Gower (Lord Ronald) Handbook to the Art Galleries, Public and Private, of Belgium and Holland.   18mo, cloth, 5*s.*

—————— *The Castle Howard Portraits.* 2 vols., folio, cl. extra, 6*l.* 6*s.*

Greek Grammar.   *See* WALLER.

Guizot's History of France.   Translated by ROBERT BLACK. Super-royal 8vo, very numerous Full-page and other Illustrations.   In 5 vols., cloth extra, gilt, each 24*s.*
    "It supplies a want which has long been felt, and ought to be in the hands of all students of history."—*Times.*
    "'Three-fourths of M. Guizot's great work are now completed, and the 'History of France,' which was so nobly planned, has been hitherto no less admirably executed."—*From long Review of Vol. III. in the Times.*
    "M. Guizot's main merit is this, that, in a style at once clear and vigorous, he sketches the essential and most characteristic features of the times and personages described, and seizes upon every salient point which can best illustrate and bring out to view what is most significant and instructive in the spirit of the age described."—*Evening Standard,* Sept. 23, 1874.

—————— *History of England.*   In 3 vols. of about 500 pp. each, containing 60 to 70 Full-page and other Illustrations, cloth extra, gilt, 24*s.* each.
    "For luxury of typography, plainness of print, and beauty of illustration, these volumes, of which but one has as yet appeared in English, will hold their own against any production of an age so luxurious as our own in everything, typography not excepted."—*Times.*

Guillemin.   *See* "World of Comets."

Guyon (Mde.) Life.   By UPHAM.   6th Edition, crown 8vo, 6*s.*

Guyot (A.) Physical Geography.   By ARNOLD GUYOT, Author of "Earth and Man."   In 1 volume, large 4to, 128 pp., numerous coloured Diagrams, Maps, and Woodcuts, price 10*s.* 6*d.*

HABITATIONS of Man in all Ages.   *See* LE-DUC.

Handbook to the Charities of London.   *See* LOW'S.

————————— *Principal Schools of England.*   *See* Practical.

Half-Length Portraits.   Short Studies of Notable Persons. By J. HAIN FRISWELL.   Small post 8vo, cloth extra, 6*s.*

Hall (S. P.) Sketches from an Artist's Portfolio.   *See* Sketches.

Hall (W. W.) How to Live Long; or, 1408 *Health Maxims,* Physical, Mental, and Moral.   By W. W. HALL, A.M., M.D. Small post 8vo, cloth, 2*s.*   Second Edition.
    "We can cordially commend it to all who wish to possess the *mens sana in corpore sano.*"—*Standard.*

Hans Brinker; or, the Silver Skates.   *See* DODGE.

Harcus (W. J. P.).   *See* "South Australia."

Healy (*M.*) *A Summer's Romance.* Crown 8vo, cloth, 10s. 6d.
—————— *The Home Theatre.* Small post 8vo, 3s. 6d.
Heath (*F. G.*). *See* "Fern World," and "Fern Paradise."
Heber's (*Bishop*) *Illustrated Edition of Hymns.* With upwards
    of 100 beautiful Engravings. Small 4to, handsomely bound, 7s. 6d.
    Morocco, 18s. 6d. and 21s.
Hector Servadac. See VERNE. The heroes of this story were
    carried away through space on the Comet "Gallia," and their ad-
    ventures are recorded with all Jules Verne's characteristic spirit. With
    nearly 100 Illustrations, cloth extra, gilt edges, 10s. 6d.
Henderson (*A.*) *Latin Proverbs and Quotations;* with Transla-
    tions and Parallel Passages, and a copious English Index. By ALFRED
    HENDERSON. Fcap. 4to, 530 pp., 10s. 6d.
History and Handbook of Photography. Translated from the
    French of GASTON TISSANDIER. Edited by J. THOMSON. Imperial
    16mo, over 300 pages, 70 Woodcuts, and Specimens of Prints by the
    best Permanent Processes, cloth extra, 6s. Second Edition, with an
    Appendix by the late Mr. HENRY FOX TALBOT, giving an account of
    his researches.
History of a Crime (*The*) *; Deposition of an Eye-witness.* By
    VICTOR HUGO. First and Second Days, 2 vols., crown 8vo, 21s.;
    also Third and Fourth Days. 2 vols., 21s.
        This work, which is a history of the "The coup d'état," was written
    at Brussels in December, 1851, January and February, 1852. M. Hugo
    was president of the Council of Resistance. He has here stated all that
    he did with his friends and everything he saw, day by day and hour by
    hour. The work is as dramatic as a romance, and as startling as the
    reality it relates, and that reality has the interest and grandeur of one
    of the most considerable events of the nineteenth century, which has
    had such an enormous influence over France and the whole of Europe.
—————— *England. See* GUIZOT.
—————— *France. See* GUIZOT.
—————— *Merchant Shipping. See* LINDSAY.
—————— *United States. See* BRYANT.
—————— *Ireland.* By STANDISH O'GRADY. Vol. I. ready, 7s. 6d.
Hitherto. By the Author of "The Gayworthys." New Edition,
    cloth extra, 3s. 6d. Also, in Rose Library, 2 vols., 2s.
Hofmann (*Carl*) *A Practical Treatise on the Manufacture of*
    Paper in all its Branches. Illustrated by 110 Wood Engravings, and 5
    large Folding Plates. In 1 vol., 4to, cloth; about 400 pp., 3l. 13s. 6d.
How to Build a House. See LE-DUC.
How to Live Long. See HALL.
Hugo (*Victor*) *"Ninety-Three."* Illustrated. Crown 8vo, 6s.
—————— *Toilers of the Sea.* Crown 8vo. Illustrated, 6s.; fancy
    boards, 2s.; cloth, 2s. 6d.; On large paper with all the original
    Illustrations, 10s. 6d.

Hugo (Victor) See "History of a Crime."

Hunting, Shooting, and Fishing; A Sporting Miscellany. Illustrated. Crown 8vo, cloth extra, 7s. 6d.

Hymnal Companion to Book of Common Prayer. See BICKERSTETH.

ILLUSTRATIONS of China and its People. By J. THOMSON, F.R.G.S. Being 200 permanent Photographs from the Author's Negatives, with Letterpress Descriptions of the Places and People represented. Four Volumes imperial 4to, each 3l. 3s.

In my Indian Garden. By PHIL. ROBINSON. With a Preface by EDWIN ARNOLD, M.A., C.S.I., &c. Crown 8vo, limp cloth, 3s. 6d.

Is that All? By a well-known American Author. Small post 8vo, cloth extra, 3s. 6d.

JACQUEMART (A.) History of the Ceramic Art: Descriptive and Analytical Study of the Potteries of all Times and of all Nations. By ALBERT JACQUEMART. 200 Woodcuts by H. Catenacci and J. Jacquemart. 12 Steel-plate Engravings, and 1000 Marks and Monograms. Translated by Mrs. BURY PALLISER. In 1 vol., super-royal 8vo, of about 700 pp., cloth extra, gilt edges, 28s.
"This is one of those few gift-books which, while they can certainly lie on a table and look beautiful, can also be read through with real pleasure and profit."—*Times.*

KENNEDY'S (Capt. W. R.) Sporting Adventures in the Pacific. With Illustrations, demy 8vo, 18s.

—— *(Capt. A. W. M. Clark). See* "To the Arctic Regions."

Khedive's Egypt (The); or, The old House of Bondage under New Masters. By EDWIN DE LEON, Ex-Agent and Consul-General in Egypt. In 1 vol., demy 8vo, cloth extra, Third Edition, 18s.

Kingston (W. H. G.). See "Snow-Shoes."

—— *Child of the Cavern.*

—— *Two Supercargoes.*

—— *With Axe and Rifle.*

Koldewey (Capt.) The Second North German Polar Expedition in the Year 1869-70, of the Ships "Germania" and "Honsa," under command of Captain Koldewey. Edited and condensed by H. W. BATES, Esq. Numerous Woodcuts, Maps, and Chromo-lithographs. Royal 8vo, cloth extra, 1l. 15s.

LADY Silverdale's Sweetheart. 6s. *See* BLACK.

Land of Bolivar (The); or, War, Peace, and Adventure in the Republic of Venezuela. By JAMES MUDIE SPENCE, F.R.G.S., F.Z.S. 2 vols., demy 8vo, cloth extra, with numerous Woodcuts and Maps, 31s. 6d. Second Edition.

Landseer Gallery (The). Containing thirty-six Autotype Reproductions of Engravings from the most important early works of Sir EDWIN LANDSEER. With a Memoir of the Artist's Life, and Descriptions of the Plates. Imperial 4to, handsomely bound in cloth, gilt edges, 2*l.* 2*s.*

Leared (A.) Morocco and the Moors. Being an Account of Travels, with a Description of the Country and its People. By ARTHUR LEARED, M.D. With Illustrations, 8vo, cloth extra, 18*s.*

Le-Duc (V.) How to build a House. By VIOLLET-LE-DUC, Author of "The Dictionary of Architecture," &c. Numerous Illustrations, Plans, &c. Medium 8vo, cloth, gilt, 12*s.*

———— *Annals of a Fortress.* Numerous Illustrations and Diagrams. Demy 8vo, cloth extra, 15*s.*

———— *The Habitations of Man in all Ages.* By E. VIOLLET-LE-DUC. Illustrated by 103 Woodcuts. Translated by BENJAMIN BUCKNALL, Architect. 8vo, cloth extra, 16*s.*

———— *Lectures on Architecture.* By VIOLLET-LE-DUC. Translated from the French by BENJAMIN BUCKNALL, Architect. In 2 vols., royal 8vo, 3*l.* 3*s.* Also in Parts, 10*s.* 6*d.* each.

———— *Mont Blanc: a Treatise on its Geodesical and Geo-*logical Constitution—its Transformations, and the Old and Modern state of its Glaciers. By EUGENE VIOLLET-LE-DUC. With 120 Illustrations. Translated by B. BUCKNALL. 1 vol., demy 8vo, 14*s.*

———— *On Restoration;* with a Notice of his Works by CHARLES WETHERED. Crown 8vo, with a Portrait on Steel of VIOLLET-LE-DUC, cloth extra, 2*s.* 6*d.*

Lenten Meditations. In Two Series, each complete in itself. By the Rev. CLAUDE BOSANQUET, Author of "Blossoms from the King's Garden." 16mo, cloth, First Series, 1*s.* 6*d.* ; Second Series, 2*s.*

Liesegang (Dr. Paul E.) A Manual of the Carbon Process of Photography, and its use in Making Enlargements, &c. Translated from the Sixth German Edition by R. B. MARSTON. Demy 8vo, half-bound, with Illustrations, 4*s.*

Life and Letters of the Honourable Charles Sumner (The). 2 vols., royal 8vo, cloth. The Letters give full description of London Society—Lawyers—Judges—Visits to Lords Fitzwilliam, Leicester, Wharncliffe, Brougham—Association with Sydney Smith, Hallam, Macaulay, Dean Milman, Rogers, and Talfourd ; also, a full Journal which Sumner kept in Paris. Second Edition, 36*s.*

Lindsay (W. S.) History of Merchant Shipping and Ancient Commerce. Over 150 Illustrations, Maps and Charts. In 4 vols., demy 8vo, cloth extra. Vols. 1 and 2, 21*s.* ; vols. 3 and 4, 24*s.* each.

Lion Jack: a Story of Perilous Adventures amongst Wild Men and Beasts. Showing how Menageries are made. By P. T. BARNUM. With Illustrations. Crown 8vo, cloth extra, price 6*s.*

Little King; or, the Taming of a Young Russian Count. By
S. BLANDY. Translated from the French. 64 Illustrations. Crown
8vo, cloth extra, gilt, 7s. 6d.

Little Mercy; or, For Better for Worse. By MAUDE JEANNE
FRANC, Author of "Marian," "Vermont Vale," &c., &c. Small
post 8vo, cloth extra, 4s.

Locker (A.) The Village Surgeon. A Fragment of Auto-
biography. By ARTHUR LOCKER. Crown 8vo, cloth, 3s. 6d.

Long (Col. C. Chaillé) Central Africa. Naked Truths of
Naked People : an Account of Expeditions to Lake Victoria Nyanza
and the Mabraka Niam-Niam. Demy 8vo, numerous Illustrations, 18s.

Lost Sir Massingberd. New Edition, 16mo, boards, coloured
wrapper, 2s.

Low's German Series—
1. **The Illustrated German Primer.** Being the easiest introduction
   to the study of German for all beginners. 1s.
2. **The Children's own German Book.** A Selection of Amusing
   and Instructive Stories in Prose. Edited by Dr. A. L. MEISSNER,
   Professor of Modern Languages in the Queen's University in
   Ireland. Small post 8vo, cloth, 1s. 6d.
3. **The First German Reader, for Children from Ten to
   Fourteen.** Edited by Dr. A. L. MEISSNER. Small post 8vo,
   cloth, 1s. 6d.
4. **The Second German Reader.** Edited by Dr. A. L. MEISSNER,
   Small post 8vo, cloth, 1s. 6d.
   Buchheim's Deutsche Prosa. Two Volumes, sold separately :—
5. **Schiller's Prosa.** Containing Selections from the Prose Works
   of Schiller, with Notes for English Students. By Dr. BUCHHEIM,
   Professor of the German Language and Literature, King's
   College, London. Small post 8vo, 2s. 6d.
6. **Goethe's Prosa.** Containing Selections from the Prose Works of
   Goethe, with Notes for English Students. By Dr. BUCHHEIM.
   Small post 8vo, 3s. 6d.

Low's Standard Library of Travel and Adventure. Crown 8vo,
bound uniformly in cloth extra, price 7s. 6d.
1. **The Great Lone Land.** By W. F. BUTLER, C.B.
2. **The Wild North Land.** By W. F. BUTLER, C.B.
3. **How I found Livingstone.** By H. M. STANLEY.
4. **The Threshold of the Unknown Region.** By C. R. MARK-
   HAM. (4th Edition, with Additional Chapters, 10s. 6d.)
5. **A Whaling Cruise to Baffin's Bay and the Gulf of Boothia.**
   By A. H. MARKHAM.
6. **Campaigning on the Oxus.** By J. A. MACGAHAN.
7. **Akim-foo: the History of a Failure.** By MAJOR W. F.
   BUTLER, C.B.
8. **Ocean to Ocean.** By the Rev. GEORGE M. GRANT. With
   Illustrations.
9. **Cruise of the Challenger.** By W. J. J. SPRY, R.N.

Low's Standard Novels.   Crown 8vo, 6s. each, cloth extra.

Three Feathers. By WILLIAM BLACK.

A Daughter of Heth. 13th Edition.   By W. BLACK.   With
   Frontispiece by F. WALKER, A.R.A.

Kilmeny. A Novel. By W. BLACK.

In Silk Attire. By W. BLACK.

Lady Silverdale's Sweetheart. By W. BLACK.

Alice Lorraine. By R. D. BLACKMORE.

Lorna Doone. By R. D. BLACKMORE.   8th Edition.

Cradock Nowell. By R. D. BLACKMORE.

Clara Vaughan. By R. D. BLACKMORE.

Cripps the Carrier. By R. D. BLACKMORE.

Innocent. By Mrs. OLIPHANT.   Eight Illustrations.

Work. A Story of Experience. By LOUISA M. ALCOTT.   Illustrations. *See also* Rose Library.

Mistress Judith. A Cambridgeshire Story. By C. C. FRAZER-
   TYTLER.

Never Again. By Dr. MAYO, Author of "Kaloolah."

Ninety-Three. By VICTOR HUGO.   Numerous Illustrations.

My Wife and I. By Mrs. BEECHER STOWE.

Low's Handbook to the Charities of London for 1877.   Edited
   and revised to July, 1877, by C. MACKESON, F.S.S., Editor of
   "A Guide to the Churches of London and its Suburbs," &c.   1s.

*M*ACGAHAN *(J. A.) Campaigning on the Oxus, and the*
   Fall of Khiva. With Map and numerous Illustrations, 4th Edition,
   small post 8vo, cloth extra, 7s. 6d.

———— *Under the Northern Lights; or, the Cruise of the*
   "Pandora" to Peel's Straits, in Search of Sir John Franklin's Papers.
   With Illustrations by Mr. DE WYLDE, who accompanied the Expedi-
   tion. Demy 8vo, cloth extra, 18s.

Macgregor (John) "Rob Roy" on the Baltic.   3rd Edition,
   small post 8vo, 2s. 6d.

———— *A Thousand Miles in the "Rob Roy" Canoe.*   11th
   Edition, small post 8vo, 2s. 6d.

———— *Description of the "Rob Roy" Canoe,* with Plans, &c., 1s.

———— *The Voyage Alone in the Yawl "Rob Roy."*   2nd Edition,
   small post 8vo, 5s.

Mackenzie (D). The Flooding of the Sahara.   An Account of
   the Project for opening direct communication with 38,000,000 people.
   With a Description of North-West Africa and Soudan. By DONALD
   MACKENZIE. 8vo, cloth extra, with Illustrations, 10s. 6d.

Markham (A. H.) The Cruise of the "Rosario."   By A. H.
   MARKHAM, R.N. 8vo, cloth extra, with Map and Illustrations.

———— *A Whaling Cruise to Baffin's Bay and the Gulf of*
   Boothia. With an Account of the Rescue by his Ship, of the Sur-

vivors of the Crew of the "Polaris;" and a Description of Modern Whale Fishing. 3rd and Cheaper Edition, crown 8vo, 2 Maps and several Illustrations, cloth extra, 7*s.* 6*d.*

Markham (C. R.) The Threshold of the Unknown Region. Crown 8vo, with Four Maps, 4th Edition, with Additional Chapters, giving the History of our present Expedition, as far as known, and an Account of the Cruise of the "Pandora." Cloth extra, 10*s.* 6*d.*

Maury (Commander) Physical Geography of the Sea, and its Meteorology. Being a Reconstruction and Enlargement of his former Work, with Charts and Diagrams. New Edition, crown 8vo, 6*s.*

Men of Mark : a Gallery of Contemporary Portraits of the most Eminent Men of the Day taken from Life, especially for this publication, price 1*s.* 6*d.* monthly. Vols. I. and II. handsomely bound, cloth, gilt edges, 25*s.* each.

Mercy Philbrick's Choice. Small post 8vo, 3*s.* 6*d.*
"The story is of a high character, and the play of feeling is very subtilely and cleverly wrought out."—*British Quarterly Review.*

Michael Strogoff. 10*s.* 6*d.* See VERNE.

Mistress Judith. A Cambridgeshire Story. By C. C. FRASER-TYTLER, Author of "Jasmine Leigh." A New and Cheaper Edition in 1 vol., small post 8vo, cloth extra, 6*s.*

Mohr (E.) To the Victoria Falls of the Zambesi. By EDWARD MOHR. Translated by N. D'ANVERS. Numerous Full-page and other Woodcut Illustrations, four Chromo-lithographs, and Map. Demy 8vo, cloth extra, 24*s.*

Mongolia, Travels in. See PREJAVALSKY.

Montaigne's Essays. See Gentle Life Series.

Mont Blanc. See LE-DUC.

Moody (Emma) Echoes of the Heart. A Collection of upwards of 200 Sacred Poems. 16mo, cloth, gilt edges, price 3*s.* 6*d.*

Morocco, Adventures in. See ROHLFS.

—— *and the Moors.* See LEARED.

My Brother Jack ; or, The Story of Whatd'yecallem. Written by Himself. From the French of ALPHONSE DAUDET. Illustrated by P. PHILIPPOTEAUX. Square imperial 16mo, cloth extra, 7*s.* 6*d.*
" He would answer to Hi ! or to any loud cry,
To What-you-may-call-'em, or What was his name ;
But especially Thingamy-jig."—*Hunting of the Snark.*

My Rambles in the New World. By LUCIEN BIART, Author of " The Adventures of a Young Naturalist." Translated by MARY DE HAUTEVILLE. Crown 8vo, cloth extra. Numerous Full-page Illustrations, 7*s.* 6*d.*

*N*APOLEON I., *Recollections of.* By Mrs. ABELL. 3rd Edition. Revised, with additional matter by her daughter Mrs. CHARLES JOHNSTONE. Demy 8vo, with Steel Portrait and Woodcuts, cloth extra, gilt edges, 10*s.* 6*d.*

Napoleon III. in Exile. The Posthumous Works and Un-published Autographs. Collected and arranged by COUNT DE LA CHAPELLE. 8vo, cloth extra, 14s.

Nares (Sir G. S., K.C.B.) Narrative of a Voyage to the Polar Sea during 1875-76, in H.M.'s Ships "Alert" and "Discovery." By Captain Sir G. S. NARES, R.N., K.C.B., F.R.S. Published by per-mission of the Lords Commissioners of the Admiralty. With Notes on the Natural History, edited by H. W. FEILDEN, F.G.S., C.M.Z.S., F.R.G.S., Naturalist to the Expedition. Two Volumes, demy 8vo, with numerous Woodcut Illustrations and Photographs from Negatives taken by Members of the Expedition, Maps, &c.

New Child's Play (A). Sixteen Drawings by E. V. B. Re-produced by the Heliotype process. 4to, cloth extra, 10s. 6d. Also coloured edition, in fac-simile, from the original drawings.

New Ireland. By A. M. SULLIVAN, M.P. for Louth. 2 vols., demy 8vo, cloth extra, 30s. One of the main objects which the Author has had in view in writing this work has been to lay before England and the world a true and faithful history of Ireland, in a series of descriptive sketches of the numerous eventful episodes in Ireland's career during the last quarter of a century. Fifth edition.

New Novels.

Through my Spectacles. By "PROAVIA." 3 vols., 31s. 6d.
A Young Wife's Story. By HARRIETTE BOWRA. 3 vols., 31s. 6d.
Jaspar Deane. By JOHN SAUNDERS. 1 vol., cr. 8vo, cl., 10s. 6d.
Doubleday's Children. By DUTTON COOK. 3 vols., 31s. 6d.
The Wreck of the Grosvenor. 3 vols., 31s. 6d. Second Edition.
　　"We recommend all who can relish a good sea story to read 'The Wreck of the Grosvenor.'"—*Morning Post.*
　　"We do not hesitate to pronounce the book a fascinating one. . . . It is ad-mirably written, in a clear and fluent style, which never permits the reader's attention to flag for a moment, and it abounds in descriptive passages, full of force and colour."—*Spectator.*
Five Chimney Farm. By MARY A. M. HOPPUS. 3 vols., 31s. 6d.
Like Dian's Kiss. By RITA, Author of "Vivienne," &c. 3 vols., 31s. 6d.
By Celia's Arbour. By the Authors of "Ready-Money Mortiboy," and "This Son of Vulcan." 3 vols., 31s. 6d.
Proud Maisie. 3 vols., crown 8vo, cloth, 31s. 6d.
In a Minor Key. 2 vols., small post 8vo, 15s.
Sir Gilbert Leigh. By W. L. REES. 2 vols., 21s.
　　"There is a wealth of fact, a power of descriptive writing, and an earnestness in all he says which raises Mr. Rees' book far above the level of the ordinary novel."—*Pall Mall Gazette.*
As Silver is Tried. By M. E. KERMODE. 3 vols., 31s. 6d.
A French Heiress. By the Author of "One Only," &c. With Illustrations, 12s. 6d.

New Testament. The Authorized English Version; with various readings from the most celebrated Manuscripts, including the

Sinaitic, the Vatican, and the Alexandrian MSS., in English. With Notes by the Editor, Dr. TISCHENDORF. Revised and carefully collected for the Thousandth Volume of Baron Tauchnitz's Collection. Cloth flexible, gilt edges, 2*s.* 6*d.* ; cheaper style, 2*s.* ; or sewed, 1*s.* 6*d.*

Noble Words and Noble Deeds. Translated from the French of E. MULLER, by DORA LEIGH. Containing many Full-page Illustrations by PHILIPPOTEAUX. Square imperial 16mo, cloth extra, 7*s.* 6*d.*
" This is a book which will delight the young. . . . We cannot imagine a nicer present than this book for children."—*Standard.*
" Is certain to become a favourite with young people."—*Court Journal.*

Notes and Sketches of an Architect taken during a Journey in the North-West of Europe. Translated from the French of FELIX NARJOUX. 214 Full-page and other Illustrations. Demy 8vo, cloth extra, 16*s.*
"His book is vivacious and sometimes brilliant. It is admirably printed and illustrated."—*British Quarterly Review.*

Notes on Fish and Fishing. By the Rev. J. J. MANLEY, M.A. With Illustrations, crown 8vo, cloth extra, leatherette binding, 10*s.* 6*d.*
" We commend the work."—*Field.*
" He has a page for every day in the year, or nearly so, and there is not a dull one amongst them."—*Notes and Queries.*
" A pleasant and attractive volume."—*Graphic.*
" Brightly and pleasantly written."—*John Bull.*

Nothing to Wear, and Two Millions. By W. A. BUTLER. 1*s.*

Nursery Playmates (Prince of.) 217 Coloured pictures for Children by eminent Artists. Folio.

OCEAN to Ocean: Sandford Fleming's Expedition through Canada in 1872. By the Rev. GEORGE M. GRANT. With Illustrations. Revised and enlarged Edition, crown 8vo, cloth, 7*s.* 6*d.*

Old English Homes. See THOMPSON.

Old-Fashioned Girl. See ALCOTT.

Old Masters. Da Vinci, Bartolomeo, Michael Angelo, Romagna, Carlo Dolci, &c., &c. Reproduced in Photography from the Celebrated Engravings by Longhi, Anderloni, Garavaglia, Toschi, and Raimondi, in the Collection of Prints and Drawings in the British Museum, with Biographical Notices, by STEPHEN THOMPSON. Imperial folio, cloth extra, 3*l.* 13*s.* 6*d.*

Oleographs. (Catalogues and price lists on application.)

Oliphant (Mrs.) Innocent. A Tale of Modern Life. By Mrs. OLIPHANT, Author of "The Chronicles of Carlingford," &c., &c. With Eight Full-page Illustrations, small post 8vo, cloth extra, 6*s.*

On Horseback through Asia Minor. By Capt. FRED BURNABY, Royal Horse Guards, Author of "A Ride to Khiva." 2 vols., demy 8vo, with three Maps and Portrait of Author, cloth extra, 38*s.* This work describes a ride of over 2000 miles through the heart of Asia Minor, and gives an account of five months with Turks, Circassians, Christians, and Devil-worshippers. 6th Edition.

On Restoration. See LE-DUC.

On Trek in the Transvaal; or, Over Berg and Veldt in South
 Africa. By Mrs. HARRIET A. ROCHE. Crown 8vo, cloth, 10s. 6d.

Our Little Ones in Heaven. Edited by the Rev. H. ROBBINS.
 With Frontispiece after Sir JOSHUA REYNOLDS. Fcap., cloth extra,
 New Edition—the 3rd, with Illustrations, 5s.

Out of School at Eton. Being a collection of Poetry and Prose
 Writings. By SOME PRESENT ETONIANS. Foolscap 8vo, cloth 3s. 6d.

*P*AINTERS *of All Schools.* By LOUIS VIARDOT, and other
 Writers. 500 pp., super-royal 8vo, 20 Full-page and 70 smaller
 Engravings, cloth extra, 25s. A New Edition is being issued in Half-
 crown parts, with fifty additional portraits, cloth, gilt edges, 31s. 6d.
   "A handsome volume, full of information and sound criticism."—*Times.*
   "Almost an encyclopædia of painting. . . . . It may be recommended as a handy
 and elegant guide to beginners in the study of the history of art."—*Saturday Review.*

Palliser (Mrs.) A History of Lace, from the Earliest Period.
 A New and Revised Edition, with additional cuts and text, upwards
 of 100 Illustrations and coloured Designs. 1 vol. 8vo, 1l. 1s.
   "One of the most readable books of the season; permanently valuable, always interesting, often amusing, and not inferior in all the essentials of a gift book."—*Times.*

—————— *Historic Devices, Badges, and War Cries.* 8vo, 1l. 1s.

—————— *The China Collector's Pocket Companion.* With upwards
 of 1000 Illustrations of Marks and Monograms. 2nd Edition, with
 Additions. Small post 8vo, limp cloth, 5s.
   "We scarcely need add that a more trustworthy and convenient handbook does
 not exist, and that others besides ourselves will feel grateful to Mrs. Palliser for the
 care and skill she has bestowed upon it."—*Academy.*

Petites Leçons de Conversation et de Grammaire: Oral and
 Conversational Method; being Little Lessons introducing the most
 Useful Topics of Daily Conversation, the French Verbs (Regular and
 Irregular) upon an entirely new principle, Anecdotes and Correspond-
 ence, &c. By F. JULIEN, French Master at King Edward the
 Sixth's Grammar School, Birmingham. Crown 8vo, cloth, 3s. 6d.

Phelps (Miss) Gates Ajar. 32mo, 6d.

—————— *Men, Women, and Ghosts.* 12mo, sewed, 1s. 6d.; cl., 2s.

—————— *Hedged In.* 12mo, sewed, 1s. 6d.; cloth, 2s.

—————— *Silent Partner.* 5s.

—————— *Trotty's Wedding Tour.* Small post 8vo, 3s. 6d.

—————— *What to Wear.* Fcap. 8vo, fancy boards, 1s.

Phillips (L.) Dictionary of Biographical Reference. 8vo,
 1l. 11s. 6d.

Phipson (Dr. T. L.) Familiar Letters on some Mysteries of
 Nature and Discoveries in Science. Crown 8vo, cloth extra, 7s. 6d.

Photography (History and Handbook of). See TISSANDIER.

Picture Gallery of British Art (The). 38 Permanent Photographs after the most celebrated English Painters. With Descriptive Letterpress. Vols. 1 to 5, cloth extra, 18s. each. Vol. 6 for 1877, commencing New Series, demy folio, 31s. 6d. Monthly Parts, 1s. 6d.

Pike (N.) Sub-Tropical Rambles in the Land of the Aphanapteryx. In 1 vol., demy 8vo, 18s. Profusely Illustrated from the Author's own Sketches. Also with Maps and Meteorological Charts.

Plutarch's Lives. An Entirely New and Library Edition. Edited by A. H. CLOUGH, Esq. 5 vols., 8vo, 2l. 10s.; half-morocco, gilt top, 3l. Also in 1 vol., royal 8vo, 800 pp., cloth extra, 18s.; half-bound, 21s.

—— *Morals.* Uniform with Clough's Edition of "Lives of Plutarch." Edited by Professor GOODWIN. 5 vols., 8vo, 3l. 3s.

Poe (E. A.) The Works of. 4 vols., 2l. 2s.

Poems of the Inner Life. A New Edition, Revised, with many additional Poems, inserted by permission of the Authors. Small post 8vo, cloth, 5s.

Polar Expeditions. See KOLDEWEY, MARKHAM, MACGAHAN, and NARES.

Practical (A) Handbook to the Principal Schools of England. By C. E. PASCOE. Showing the cost of living at the Great Schools, Scholarships, &c., &c. New Edition corrected to 1878, crown 8vo, cloth extra, 3s. 6d.
"This is an exceedingly useful work, and one that was much wanted."—*Examiner.*

Prejevalsky (N. M.) Travels in Mongolia. By N. M. PREJEVALSKY, Lieutenant-Colonel, Russian Staff. Translated by E. DELMAR MORGAN, F.R.G.S., and Annotated by Colonel YULE, C.B. 2 vols., demy 8vo, cloth extra, numerous Illustrations and Maps, 2l. 2s.

Price (Sir Rose, Bart.). See "Two Americas."

Prince Ritto; or, The Four-leaved Shamrock. By FANNY W. CURREY. With 10 Full-page Facsimile Reproductions of Original Drawings by HELEN O'HARA. Demy 4to, cloth extra, gilt, 10s. 6d.

Prisoner of War in Russia. See COOPE.

Publishers' Circular (The), and General Record of British and Foreign Literature. Published on the 1st and 15th of every Month.

*R*ALSTON *(W. R. S.) Early Russian History.* Four Lectures delivered at Oxford by W. R. S. RALSTON, M.A. Crown 8vo, cloth extra, 5s.

Read (S.) Leaves from a Sketch Book. Pencillings of Travel at Home and Abroad. By SAMUEL READ. Royal 4to, containing about 130 Engravings on Wood, cloth extra, 25s.
"We do not think that the season is likely to yield a more artistic, suggestive, and beautiful gift-book than this."—*Nonconformist.*

Recollections of Samuel Breck, the American Pepys. With Passages from his Note-Books (1771—1862). Crown 8vo, cloth, 10s. 6d.
  "The book is admirable."—*Standard.*

Retzsch (M.) Outlines to Burger's Ballads. 15 Etchings by MORITZ RETZSCH. With Text, Explanations, and Notes. Oblong 4to, cloth extra, 10s. 6d.

—— *Outlines to Goethe's Faust.* Etchings by MORITZ RETZSCH. 26 Etchings. Oblong 4to, cloth extra, 10s. 6d.

—— *Outlines to Schiller's "Fight with the Dragon," and* "Fridolin." 26 Etchings by MORITZ RETZSCH. Oblong 4to, cloth extra, 10s. 6d.

—— *Outlines to Schiller's "Lay of the Bell."* Comprising 42 Etchings engraved by MORITZ RETZSCH. With Lord Lytton's Translation. New Edition. Oblong 4to, cloth extra, 10s. 6d.

Reynard the Fox. The Prose Translation by the late THOMAS ROSCOE. With about 100 exquisite Illustrations on Wood, after designs by A. J. ELWES. Imperial 16mo, cloth extra, 7s. 6d.

Robinson (Phil.). See " In my Indian Garden."

Roche (Mrs. H.). See " On Trek in the Transvaal."

Rochefoucauld's Reflections. Bayard Series, 2s. 6d.

Rogers (S.) Pleasures of Memory. See " Choice Editions of Choice Books." 2s. 6d.

Rohlfs (Dr. G.) Adventures in Morocco, and Journeys through the Oases of Draa and Tafilet. By Dr. G. ROHLFS. Demy 8vo, Map, and Portrait of the Author, 12s.

Rose in Bloom. See ALCOTT.

Rose Library (The). Popular Literature of all countries. Each volume, 1s. ; cloth, 2s. 6d. Many of the Volumes are Illustrated—
  1. **Sea-Gull Rock.** By JULES SANDEAU. Illustrated.
  2. **Little Women.** By LOUISA M. ALCOTT.
  3. **Little Women Wedded.** Forming a Sequel to "Little Women."
  4. **The House on Wheels.** By MADAME DE STOLZ. Illustrated.
  5. **Little Men.** By LOUISA M. ALCOTT. Dble. vol., 2s. ; cloth, 3s. 6d.
  6. **The Old-Fashioned Girl.** By LOUISA M. ALCOTT. Double vol., 2s. ; cloth, 3s. 6d.
  7. **The Mistress of the Manse.** By J. G. HOLLAND.
  8. **Timothy Titcomb's Letters to Young People, Single and Married.**
  9. **Undine, and the Two Captains.** By Baron DE LA MOTTE FOUQUÉ. A New Translation by F. E. BUNNETT. Illustrated.
  10. **Draxy Miller's Dowry, and the Elder's Wife.** By SAXE HOLM.
  11. **The Four Gold Pieces.** By Madame GOURAUD. Numerous Illustrations.
  12. **Work.** A Story of Experience. First Portion. By LOUISA M. ALCOTT.

Rose Library (*The*), *continued :—*

13. **Beginning Again.** Being a Continuation of "Work." By LOUISA M. ALCOTT.
14. **Picciola; or, the Prison Flower.** By X. B. SAINTINE. Numerous Graphic Illustrations.
15. **Robert's Holidays.** Illustrated.
16. **The Two Children of St. Domingo.** Numerous Illustrations.
17. **Aunt Jo's Scrap Bag.**
18. **Stowe (Mrs. H. B.) The Pearl of Orr's Island.**
19. —— **The Minister's Wooing.**
20. —— **Betty's Bright Idea.**
21. —— **The Ghost in the Mill.**
22. —— **Captain Kidd's Money.**
23. —— **We and our Neighbours.** Double vol., 2*s*.
24. —— **My Wife and I.** Double vol., 2*s*. ; cloth, gilt, 3*s*. 6*d*.
25. **Hans Brinker ; or, the Silver Skates.**
26. **Lowell's My Study Window.**
27. **Holmes (O. W.) The Guardian Angel.**
28. **Warner (C. D.) My Summer in a Garden.**
29. **Hitherto.** By the Author of "The Gayworthys." 2 vols., 1*s*. each.
30. **Helen's Babies.** By their Latest Victim.
31. **The Barton Experiment.** By the Author of "Helen's Babies."
32. **Dred.** By Mrs. BEECHER STOWE. Double vol., 2*s*. Cloth, gilt, 3*s*. 6*d*.

Russell (*W. H., LL.D.*) *The Tour of the Prince of Wales in* India, and his Visits to the Courts of Greece, Egypt, Spain, and Portugal. By W. H. RUSSELL, LL.D., who accompanied the Prince throughout his journey ; fully Illustrated by SYDNEY P. HALL, M.A., the Prince's Private Artist, with his Royal Highness's special permission to use the Sketches made during the Tour. Super-royal 8vo, cloth extra, gilt edges, 52*s*. 6*d*. ; Large Paper Edition, 84*s*.

"The Prince's visit to India was a great political event, and this imposing volume is a not unworthy memorial of it. A most entertaining and instructive book."—*Times*.

SCHWEINFURTH (*Dr. G.*) *The Heart of Africa; or,* Three Years' Travels and Adventures in the Unexplored Regions of the Centre of Africa. By Dr. GEORGE SCHWEINFURTH. Translated by ELLEN E. FREWER. 2 vols., 8vo, with 130 Woodcuts from Drawings made by the Author, and 2 Maps, 2nd Edition, 42*s*.

—— *Artes Africanæ.* Illustrations and Description of Productions of the Natural Arts of Central African Tribes. With 26 Lithographed Plates, imperial 4to, boards, 28*s*.

Sea-Gull Rock. By JULES SANDEAU, of the French Academy. Translated by ROBERT BLACK, M.A. With 79 very beautiful Woodcuts. Royal 16mo, cloth extra, gilt edges, 7*s*. 6*d*. Cheaper Edition, cloth gilt, 2*s*. 6*d*. *See also* Rose Library.

"It deserves to please the new nation of boys to whom it is presented."—*Times*.

Seonee: Sporting in the Satpura Range of Central India, and in
the Valley of the Nerbudda. By R. A. STERNDALE, F.R.G.S. 8vo,
with numerous Illustrations, 21*s*.

"This is in every respect a volume worthy of praise."—*Spectator.*

Shakespeare from an American Point of View; including an
Inquiry as to his Religious Faith and his Knowledge of Law; with
the Baconian Theory considered. By G. WILKES. Demy 8vo, 16*s*.

—— *(The Boudoir).* Edited by HENRY CUNDELL.
Carefully bracketted for reading aloud; freed from all objectionable
matter, and altogether free from notes. Price 2*s*. 6*d*. each volume,
cloth extra, gilt edges. Contents :—Vol I., Cymbeline—Merchant of
Venice. Each play separately, paper cover, 1*s*. Vol. II., As You
Like It—King Lear—Much Ado about Nothing. Vol. III., Romeo
and Juliet—Twelfth Night—King John. The latter six plays separately, paper cover, 9*d*.

Shooting: its Appliances, Practice, and Purpose. By JAMES
DALZIEL DOUGALL, F.S.A., F.Z.A. Author of "Scottish Field
Sports," &c. Crown 8vo, cloth extra, 10*s*. 6*d*.

"The book is admirable in every way. . . . . We wish it every success."—*Globe.*
"A very complete treatise. . . . . Likely to take high rank as an authority on
shooting."—*Daily News.*

Silent Hour (The). *See* Gentle Life Series.

Silver Pitchers. *See* ALCOTT.

Six Hundred Robinson Crusoes; or, The Voyage of the Golden
Fleece. A true Story for old and young. By GILBERT MORTIMER.
Illustrated. Post 8vo, cloth extra, 5*s*.

Sketches from an Artist's Portfolio. By SYDNEY P. HALL.
About 60 Fac-similes of his Sketches during Travels in various parts of
Europe. Folio, cloth extra, 3*l*. 3*s*.

"A portfolio which any one might be glad to call their own."—*Times.*

Sketches of Life and Scenery in Australia. By a Twenty-five
Years' Resident. 1 vol., demy 8vo, cloth extra, 14*s*.

Sleepy Sketches; or, How we Live, and How we Do Not Live.
From Bombay. 1 vol., small post 8vo, cloth, 6*s*.

"Well-written and amusing sketches of Indian society."—*Morning Post.*

Smith (G.) Assyrian Explorations and Discoveries. By the late
GEORGE SMITH. Illustrated by Photographs and Woodcuts. Demy
8vo, 6th Edition, 18*s*.

Smith (G.) The Chaldean Account of Genesis. Containing the
Description of the Creation, the Fall of Man, the Deluge, the Tower
of Babel, the Times of the Patriarchs, and Nimrod; Babylonian
Fables, and Legends of the Gods; from the Cuneiform Inscriptions.
By the late G. SMITH, of the Departmennt of Oriental Antiquities,
British Museum. With many Illustrations. Demy 8vo, cloth extra,
5th Edition, 16*s*.

Snow-Shoes and Canoes ; or, the Adventures of a Fur-Hunter in the Hudson's Bay Territory. By W. H. G. KINGSTON. 2nd Edition. With numerous Illustrations. Square crown 8vo, cloth extra, gilt, 7*s.* 6*d.*

South Australia: its History, Resources, and Productions. Edited by W. HARCUS, J.P., with 66 full-page Woodcut Illustrations from Photographs taken in the Colony, and 2 Maps. Demy 8vo, 21*s.*

Spain. Illustrated by GUSTAVE DORÉ. Text by the BARON CH. D'AVILLIER. Containing over 240 Wood Engravings by DORÉ, half of them being Full-page size. Imperial 4to, elaborately bound in cloth, extra gilt edges, 3*l.* 3*s.*

Stanley (H. M.) How I Found Livingstone. Crown 8vo, cloth extra, 7*s.* 6*d.* ; large Paper Edition, 10*s.* 6*d.*

—— *" My Kalulu," Prince, King, and Slave.* A Story from Central Africa. Crown 8vo, about 430 pp., with numerous graphic Illustrations, after Original Designs by the Author. Cloth, 7*s.* 6*d.*

—— *Coomassie + and Magdala.* A Story of Two British Campaigns in Africa. Demy 8vo, with Maps and Illustrations, 16*s.*

——– *Through the Dark Continent,* which see.

St. Nicholas for 1878. The First Number of the New Series commenced November 1st, 1877, and contains a New Story by LOUISA M. ALCOTT, entitled "Under the Lilacs." 1*s.* Monthly.

Stolz (Madame) The House on Wheels. Small post 8vo, 2*s.* 6*d.* *See also* Rose Library.

Story without an End. From the German of Carové, by the late Mrs. SARAH T. AUSTIN. Crown 4to, with 15 Exquisite Drawings by E. V. B., printed in Colours in Fac-simile of the original Water Colours ; and numerous other Illustrations. New Edition, 7*s.* 6*d.*

—— square 4to, with Illustrations by HARVEY. 2*s.* 6*d.*

Stowe (Mrs. Beecher) Dred. Cheap Edition, boards, 2*s.* Cloth, gilt edges, 3*s.* 6*d.*

——– *Footsteps of the Master.* With Illustrations and red borders. Small post 8vo, cloth extra, 6*s.*

—— *Geography,* with 60 Illustrations. Square cloth, 4*s.* 6*d.*

—— *Little Foxes.* Cheap Edition, 1*s.* ; Library Edition, 4*s.* 6*d.*

—— *Betty's Bright Idea.*

——– *My Wife and I; or, Harry Henderson's History.* Small post 8vo, cloth extra, 6*s.* *

—— *Minister's Wooing,* 5*s.*; Copyright Series, 1*s.* 6*d.*; cl., 2*s.* *

——– *Old Town Folk.* 6*s.* : Cheap Edition, 2*s.* 6*d.*

—— *Old Town Fireside Stories.* Cloth extra, 3*s.* 6*d.*

* *See also* Rose Library.

Stowe (Mrs. Beecher) We and our Neighbours. 1 vol., small
post 8vo, 6s. Sequel to "My Wife and I."*
——— *Pink and White Tyranny.* Small post 8vo, 3s. 6d.;
Cheap Edition, 1s. 6d. and 2s.
——— *Queer Little People.* 1s.; cloth, 2s.
——— *Chimney Corner.* 1s.; cloth, 1s. 6d.
——— *The Pearl of Orr's Island.* Crown 8vo, 5s.*
——— *Little Pussey Willow.* Fcap., 2s.
——— *Woman in Sacred History.* Illustrated with 15 Chromo-
lithographs and about 200 pages of Letterpress. Demy 4to, cloth
extra, gilt edges, 25s.
Street Life in London. By J. THOMSON, F.R.G.S., and ADOLPHE
SMITH. One volume, 4to, containing 40 Permanent Photographs of
Scenes of London Street Life, with Descriptive Letterpress, 25s.
Studies from Nature. 24 Photographs, with Descriptive Letter-
press. By STEVEN THOMPSON. Imperial 4to, 35s.
Sub-Tropical Rambles. See PIKE (N).   •
Sullivan (A.M., M.P.). See "New Ireland."
Summer Holiday in Scandinavia (A). By E. L. L. ARNOLD.
Crown 8vo, cloth extra, 10s. 6d.
Sumner (Hon. Charles). See Life and Letters.

TAUCHNITZ'S English Editions of German Authors.
Each volume, cloth flexible, 2s.; or sewed, 1s. 6d. (Catalogues post
free on application.)
Tauchnitz (B.) German and English Dictionary. Paper, 1s.
cloth, 1s. 6d.; roan, 2s.
——— *French and English.* Paper, 1s. 6d.; cloth, 2s; roan,
2s. 6d.
——— *Italian and English.* Paper, 1s. 6d.; cloth, 2s.;
roan, 2s. 6d.
——— *Spanish and English.* Paper, 1s. 6d.; cloth, 2s.; roan,
2s. 6d.
——— *New Testament.* Cloth, 2s.; gilt, 2s. 6d.
The Telephone. An Account of the Phenomena of Electricity,
Magnetism, and Sound, as Involved in its Action; with Directions for
Making a Speaking Telephone. By Prof. A. E. DOLBEAR, Author of
"The Art of Projecting," &c. Second Edition, with an Appendix De-
scriptive of Prof. BELL's Present Instrument. 130 pp., with 19 Illus-
trations, 1s. Contents: Electricity—Magnets—The Galvanic Battery—
Thermo-Electricity—Magneto-Electricity—Magnetic Induction—Mag-
neto-Electric Machines—Secondary Currents—What is Electricity?—

* *See also* Rose Library.

—Theories—Velocity—Sound—Constitution of a single sound-wave—
Pitch—Limits of Audibility—Effects of sound upon other bodies—
Sympathetic Vibrations—Resonance—Timbre—Tone Composition—
Form of a compound sound-wave—Correlation—Magnetic Sounds—
Helmholtz' Electric Interruptor—Reiss' Telephone—Gray's Telephones
—Bell's Telephone—The Author's Telephone—How to make a Tele-
phone—Appendix.

"The book is illustrated with numerous figures; it describes several forms of
the Telephone, and is, besides, a clear and masterly compendium of a large part of
science."—*Morning Post.*

Tennyson's May Queen. Choicely Illustrated from designs by
the Hon. Mrs. BOYLE. Crown 8vo (*See* Choice Series), 2s. 6d.

Textbook (A) of Harmony. For the Use. of Schools and
Students. By the late CHARLES EDWARD HORSLEY. Revised for
the Press by WESTLEY RICHARDS and W. H. CALCOTT. Small post
8vo, cloth extra, 3s. 6d.

The Banns of Marriage. By DUTTON COOK, Author of
" Hobson's Choice," " A Book of the Play," "Doubleday's Children,"
&c. 2 vols., crown 8vo, 21s.

Thebes, and its Five Greater Temples. See ABNEY.

Thomson (J.) The Straits of Malacca, Indo-China, and China ;
or, Ten Years' Travels, Adventures, and Residence Abroad. By J.
THOMSON, F.R.G.S., Author of " Illustrations of China and its
People." Upwards of 60 Woodcuts, from the Author's own Photographs and Sketches. Demy 8vo, cloth extra, 21s.

Thompson (Stephen) Old English Homes : a Summer's Sketch-
Book. By STEPHEN THOMPSON. 25 very fine Permanent Photographs by the Author. Demy 4to, cloth extra, gilt edges, 2l. 2s.

Thorne (E.) The Queen of the Colonies ; or, Queensland as I
saw it. 1 vol., with Map, 6s.

Through the Dark Continent : The Sources of the Nile ; Around
the Great Lakes, and down the Congo. By HENRY M. STANLEY.
2 vols., demy 8vo, containing about 100 Full-page and other Illustrations and 8 Maps, 42s.

" One of the greatest geographical discoveries of the age."—*Spectator.*
" Mr. Stanley has penetrated the very heart of the mystery. . . . He has opened
up a perfectly virgin region, never before, so far as known, visited by a white
man."—*Times.*

To the Arctic Regions and Back in Six Weeks. By Captain
A. W. M. CLARK KENNEDY (late of the Coldstream Guards). With
Illustrations and Maps. 8vo, cloth, 15s.

Tour of the Prince of Wales in India. See RUSSELL.

Trollope (A.) Harry Heathcote of Gangoil. A Story of Bush
Life in Australia. With Graphic Illustrations. Small post, cloth, 5s.

Turkistan. Notes of a Journey in the Russian Provinces of
Central Asia and the Khanates of Bokhara and Kokand. By EUGENE
SCHUYLER, Secretary to the American Legation, St. Petersburg.
Numerous Illustrations. 2 vols, 8vo, cloth extra, 5th Edition, 2l. 2s.

Two Americas ; being an Account of Sport and Travel, with
Notes on Men and Manners in North and South America. By Sir
ROSE PRICE, Bart. 1 vol., demy 8vo, with Illustrations, cloth
extra, 2nd Edition, 18*s*.
> "We have seldom come across a book which has given us so much pleasure."—
> *Land and Water.*

Two Supercargoes (The) ; or, Adventures in Savage Africa.
By W. H. G. KINGSTON.   Square imperial 16mo, cloth extra, 7*s*. 6*d*.
Numerous Full-page Illustrations.

VANDENHOFF (George, M.A.).   See "Art of Reading
Aloud."
—— *Clerical Assistant.*   Fcap., 3*s*. 6*d*.
—— *Ladies' Reader (The).*   Fcap., 5*s*.
Verne's (Jules) Works.   Translated from the French, with
from 50 to 100 Illustrations.   Each cloth extra, gilt edges—

Large post 8vo, price 10*s*. 6*d*. *each*—

1. **Fur Country.**
2. **Twenty Thousand Leagues under the Sea.**
3. **From the Earth to the Moon, and a Trip round It.**
4. **Michael Strogoff, the Courier of the Czar.**
5. **Hector Servadac.**
6. **Dick Sands, the Boy Captain.**

Imperial 16*mo, price* 7*s*. 6*d*. *each*—

1. **Five Weeks in a Balloon.**
2. **Adventures of Three Englishmen and Three Russians in South Africa.**
3. **Around the World in Eighty Days.**
4. **A Floating City, and the Blockade Runners.**
5. **Dr. Ox's Experiment, Master Zacharius, A Drama in the Air, A Winter amid the Ice, &c.**
6. **The Survivors of the "Chancellor."**
7. **Dropped from the Clouds.** }
8. **Abandoned.**   } **The Mysterious Island.** 3 vols.,
9. **Secret of the Island.**   }   22*s*. 6*d*.
10. **The Child of the Cavern.**

The following Cheaper Editions are issued with a few of the
Illustrations, in paper wrapper, price 1*s*.; *cloth gilt,* 2*s*. *each.*

1. **Adventures of Three Englishmen and Three Russians in South Africa.**
2. **Five Weeks in a Balloon.**
3. **A Floating City.**
4. **The Blockade Runners.**

Verne's (Jules) Works (Cheap Editions), continued:

5. **From the Earth to the Moon.**
6. **Around the Moon.**
7. **Twenty Thousand Leagues under the Sea.** Vol. I.
8. —— Vol. II. The two parts in one, cloth, gilt, 3s. 6d.
9. **Around the World in Eighty Days.**
10. **Dr. Ox's Experiment, and Master Zacharius.**
11. **Martin Paz, the Indian Patriot.**
12. **A Winter amid the Ice.**
13. **The Fur Country.** Vol. I.
14. —— Vol. II. Both parts in one, cloth gilt, 3s. 6d.

Viardot (Louis). See "Painters of all Schools."

WALLER (Rev. C. H.) The Names on the Gates of Pearl, and other Studies. By the Rev. C. H. WALLER, M.A. Crown 8vo, cloth extra, 6s.

—— *A Grammar and Analytical Vocabulary of the Words in* the Greek Testament. Compiled from Brüder's Concordance. For the use of Divinity Students and Greek Testament Classes. By the Rev. C. H. WALLER, M.A., late Scholar of University College, Oxford. Tutor of the London College of Divinity, St. John's Hall, Highbury. Part I., The Grammar. Small post 8vo, cloth, 2s. 6d. Part II. The Vocabulary.

—— *Adoption and the Covenant.* Some Thoughts on Confirmation. Super-royal 16mo, cloth limp, 2s. 6d.

Warburton's (Col. Egerton) Journey across Australia. An Account of the Exploring Expedition sent out under the command of Colonel E. Warburton. With Illustrations and a Map. Edited by H. W. BATES, Esq., F.R.G.S. Demy 8vo, cloth, 16s.

Warner (C. D.) My Summer in a Garden. Boards, 1s. 6d.; cloth, 2s. (Low's Copyright Series.)

—— *Back-log Studies.* Boards, 1s. 6d.; cloth, 2s.

—— *Mummies and Moslems.* 8vo, cloth, 12s.

Westropp (H. M.) A Manual of Precious Stones and Antique Gems. By HODDER M. WESTROPP, Author of "The Traveller's Art Companion," "Pre-Historic Phases," &c. Numerous Illustrations. Small post 8vo, cloth extra, 6s.

Whitney (Mrs. A. D. T.) The Gayworthys. Cloth, 3s. 6d.

—— *Faith Gartney.* Small post 8vo, 3s. 6d. Cheaper Editions, 1s. 6d. and 2s.

—— *Real Folks.* 12mo, crown, 3s. 6d.

—— *Hitherto.* Small post 8vo, 3s. 6d. and 2s. 6d.

Whitney (Mrs. A. D. T.) Sights and Insights. 3 vols., crown 8vo, 31s. 6d.

—— *Summer in Leslie Goldthwaite's Life.* Cloth, 3s. 6d.

—— *The Other Girls.* Small post 8vo, cloth extra, 3s. 6d.

—— *We Girls.* Small post 8vo, 3s. 6d.; Cheap Edition, 1s. 6d. and 2s.

Wikoff (H.) The Four Civilizations of the World. An Historical Retrospect. Crown 8vo, cloth, 12s.

Wills, A Few Hints on Proving, without Professional Assistance. By a PROBATE COURT OFFICIAL. 5th Edition, revised with Forms of Wills, Residuary Accounts, &c. Fcap. 8vo, cloth limp, 1s.

Wilson (H. Schültz). See "Alpine Ascents and Adventures."

With Axe and Rifle. By W. H. G. KINGSTON. With numerous Illustrations, square crown 8vo, cloth, extra gilt, 7s. 6d.

*Woolsey (C. D., LL.D.) Introduction to the Study of Inter-*national Law; designed as an Aid in Teaching and in Historical Studies. Reprinted from the last American Edition, and at a much lower price. Crown 8vo, cloth extra, 8s. 6d.

Words of Wellington: Maxims and Opinions, Sentences and Reflections of the Great Duke, gathered from his Despatches, Letters, and Speeches (Bayard Series). 2s. 6d.

World of Comets. By A. GUILLEMIN, Author of "The Heavens." Translated and edited by JAMES GLAISHER, F.R.S. 1 vol., super-royal 8vo, with numerous Woodcut Illustrations, and 3 Chromo-lithographs, cloth extra, 31s. 6d.

"The mass of information collected in the volume is immense, an the treatment of the subject is so purely popular, that none need be deterred from a perusal of it."—*British Quarterly Review.*

XENOPHON'S Anabasis; or, Expedition of Cyrus. A Literal Translation, chiefly from the Text of Dintorff, by GEORGE B. WHEELER. Books I to III. Crown 8vo, boards, 2s.

—— *Books I. to VII.* Boards, 3s. 6d.

YOUNG (J. F.) Five Weeks in Greece. Crown 8vo, 10s. 6d.

London:

SAMPSON LOW, MARSTON, SEARLE, & RIVINGTON,

CROWN BUILDINGS, 188, FLEET STREET.